The IMF, World Bank and Policy Reform

Globalization is presenting the World Bank and the IMF with new challenges by imposing a rethinking of the nature of development and a reassessment of the appropriateness of current development policies. The International Financial Institutions (IFIs) have responded by redefining their international roles, their priorities and their forms of intervention.

In particular, they have made the achievement of poverty reduction and other Millennium Development Goals their overriding objective. In addition, they have redefined their role as that of providing support for locally owned pro-poor reform programmes.

This book examines the extent to which the new emphasis on poverty reduction and local ownership has been accompanied by true changes in the IFIs' assistance to developing countries. The book also evaluates the respective roles of internal and external forces, such as the commitment to 'neo-liberalism' and the influence of the United States, in shaping the IFIs' policy agenda.

This impressive collection uses an interdisciplinary approach to present a leading-edge analysis of topical and controversial issues which are critical for the effectiveness of financial assistance to developing countries, and examines the ensuing policy implications and required actions. *The IMF, World Bank and Policy Reform* will be essential reading for students, academics and practitioners of development economics, development studies and political economy.

Alberto Paloni is Senior Lecturer in Economics and Director of the Centre for Development Studies at the University of Glasgow, UK.

Maurizio Zanardi is Assistant Professor of Economics and member of CentER at Tilburg University, the Netherlands.

Routledge Studies in Development Economics

The IMF, World Bank and Policy Reform

**Edited by
Alberto Paloni and
Maurizio Zanardi**

Routledge
Taylor & Francis Group

LONDON AND NEW YORK

First published 2006
by Routledge
2 Park Square, Milton Park, Abingdon, Oxon OX14 4RN

Simultaneously published in the USA and Canada
by Routledge
270 Madison Ave, New York, NY 10016

Transferred to Digital Printing 2006

Routledge is an imprint of the Taylor & Francis Group, an informa business

Typeset in Times New Roman by
Newgen Imaging Systems (P) Ltd, Chennai, India
Printed and bound in Great Britain by
Biddles Ltd, King's Lynn

British Library Cataloguing in Publication Data
A catalogue record for this book is available from the British Library

Library of Congress Cataloging in Publication Data
A catalog record for this book has been requested

ISBN 10: 0–415–35399–8
ISBN 13: 978–0–415–35399–1

Contents

Figures

Tables

Contributors

Graham Bird is Professor of Economics at the University of Surrey (UK) and Director of the Surrey Centre for International Economic Studies.

John Cameron is Reader in Economics at the University of East Anglia (UK).

Gordon Crawford is a Senior Lecturer in Development Studies at the University of Leeds (UK).

Hamed El-Said is Senior Lecturer in the Business School of the Manchester Metropolitan University (UK).

Brigitte Granville is Professor of International Economics and Economic Policy at the Queen Mary, University of London (UK).

Jane Harrigan is Reader in Economics at SOAS, University of London (UK).

Tony Killick is Senior Research Associate of the Overseas Development Institute in London (UK).

Dennis Leech is Reader in Economics at the University of Warwick (UK).

Robert Leech is a Graduate Student in the School of Psychology at Birkbeck College, University of London (UK).

Sushanta Mallick is Lecturer in Economics at Loughborough University (UK).

Oliver Morrissey is Professor of Development Economics at the University of Nottingham (UK).

Paul Mosley is Professor of Economics at the University of Sheffield (UK).

Farhad Noorbakhsh is Professor of Economics at the University of Glasgow (UK).

Shadan Noorbakhsh is a recent Graduate in Economics from the University of Glasgow (UK).

Alberto Paloni is Senior Lecturer in Economics and Director of the Centre for Development Studies at the University of Glasgow (UK).

Dane Rowlands is Associate Professor and Associate Director at the Norman Paterson School of International Affairs at Carleton University (Canada).

Kunal Sen is Reader in Economics at the University of East Anglia (UK).

Mehdi S. Shafaeddin is Senior Economist and Head of the Macroeconomics and Development Policies Branch, Globalization and Development Strategy Division of UNCTAD (Geneva, Switzerland).

Arjan Verschoor is Lecturer in Economics at the University of East Anglia (UK).

Chengang Wang is Research Associate in Economics at the University of Manchester (UK).

John Weeks is Professor of Development Economics and Director of the Centre for Development Policy and Research at SOAS, University of London (UK).

Maurizio Zanardi is Assistant Professor of Economics and member of CentER at Tilburg University (the Netherlands).

Foreword

Robert Chambers famously observed – one imagines with a sigh of frustration – that natural scientists are trained to act, but that social scientists are trained to criticize. There's a 'merely' implied here, which does not refer to the natural scientists. The argument is that we social scientists – and that includes the authors of this book, though not necessarily all its readers – criticize but do not act. We are, allegedly, adept at deconstructing narratives, expert in speaking truth to power (though mainly from the safety of papers in academic journals), and world class in offering policy-makers so many options that they find themselves unable to move forward. Most of the jokes about economists capture exactly this idea: the African President who insisted that all his economic advisers be one-handed, to stop them saying 'on the one hand…on the other hand'; or the economist on a desert island with a can of beans but no can-opener, whose suggestion was 'let us assume we have a can opener'.

There are two kinds of answer one might make to such a critique of social science, and this book illustrates both. The first is that criticism – or dispassionate analysis as we might prefer to call it – is an essential foundation for better policy. The second is that social scientists are actually pretty good at policy. Take these in turn, and relate both to the core question tackled in the book – the reform of international institutions which should and could help reduce poverty in the world, and could and should do better.

On the first question, we need to know not just whether or to what extent the World Bank and the IMF contribute to poverty reduction, but why their record is as it is. That job is about explanation – and explanation needs theory. As the social psychologist Kurt Lewin observed, 'there's nothing so practical as a good theory'. We learn here that the record is patchy, but we also learn why: the ideology of the institutions, the power structures which run them, the geo-politics of aid allocation, the technical weaknesses of programme design – and also, if we are to be fair, the severity of the underlying problems and the diversity of country situations. These are important findings, and they stem from the careful application of theory, whether discourse analysis to unpack the politics of policy making in the Bretton Woods Institutions, or more technically the implications of asymmetric access to information for the use of conditionality in aid relationships.

Of course, all this would be interesting but essentially useless if it did not lead to practical policy. The acid test of applied research is that it should redirect energy and lead to change. Here, the book also scores well. We are shown how to integrate poverty concerns into macro-economic planning, told about the importance of safety nets in managing adjustment programmes, and reminded, repeatedly, about the importance of gradual approaches, of learning-by-doing, and of the need for international institutions to be responsive to varying conditions in developing countries.

The power of these conclusions lies partly in their aggregate impact: we have here the elements of a story-line on international development as a whole, what Roe calls a 'narrative'. There should be no doubt about the impact of such narratives: think of the power of narratives about structural adjustment, the Washington Consensus, or what Joe Stiglitz has termed the post-Washington Consensus. Narratives simplify, of course. But they also help policy-makers handle complexity and find solutions. In the title of Diane Stone's book about think-tanks, they 'capture the political imagination'.

The world certainly needs inspiring narratives, if the Millennium Development Goals and the wider ambitions of the UN's Millennium Declaration are to be reached. The widespread adoption of the MDGs signals political commitment. So does the investment in initiatives like the Africa Commission. The challenge we face as researchers and policy analysts is to stand ready in support, with theory, with explanation, and with practical proposals.

My own take is inspired by the kind of discussion found in the pages of this book. With due acknowledgement to the risk of over-generalization and the importance of path dependency, I call it the 'meta-narrative'. There are three ways in which a new meta-narrative might develop current conventional wisdom.

First, the MDGs provide a powerful and politically attractive frame within which to approach international development, but they are incomplete. In addition to the MDGs, the Millennium Declaration includes a statement of values and a commitment to peace, security and the rule of law. The additional material widens and internationalizes the frame. It also provides the basis for saying that there is more to poverty than lack of income: equity and social justice also matter, for intrinsic as well as instrumental reasons.

Second, there is evidence that the story about how to get to poverty reduction, equity and social justice is more nuanced than the current donor narrative suggests. As the papers in the book illustrate, a crude characterization of the current approach is to encourage internal and external liberalisation, and simultaneously to invest in health and education, so that people are able to take advantage of new economic opportunities. Stiglitz has not been the only one to worry that supply side constraints and high levels of vulnerability make this strategy both difficult and risky. The recent British Government White Paper on trade and investment, published in 2004, illustrates a new approach in one of its key themes: 'same destination, different speeds'.

Third, there are issues about how well the current approach guides international support to the development process. The approach involves channelling more aid to well-governed countries with good policies – using the MDGs as an objective, Poverty Reduction Strategies as both a guide to policy and an indicator of ownership, better public expenditure as the main instrument, and budget support as the main vehicle for aid. This approach faces especially big problems in dealing with failed states and poorly performing countries. There are also more general issues about what 'partnership' might mean in international development, especially in terms of the accountability of developed countries for their policies on trade, aid, finance and security. A new development cooperation regime will require close cooperation between ministries and international institutions dealing with finance, foreign affairs and security, as well as development aid, and will need a mechanism which holds rich countries to account.

And how is this going to happen? What about the ideology, the power structures, the geo-politics and other themes emphasized in the book? One answer is to say that if the political will is in place, which it seems to be, then the institutional changes will follow – for example, to voting structures in the World Bank and the IMF. That may be too easy an answer. My own approach has been to tackle the problem head-on as a research issue in its own right, using ideas from collective action theory to try and understand why people cooperate and what incentives might decrease the probability of defection. For example, Elinor Ostrom teaches that the risk of defection lessens when the cost of doing so rises. Does this suggest that donors committed to harmonization or UN reform should find ways to sanction the non-cooperators?

That is the kind of question the book inspires. It illustrates a final point, that the problems we are dealing with cannot be resolved by one discipline alone. Collective action theory draws on the insights of economists, sociologists, political scientists, psychologists – and, of course, biologists. Development studies are necessarily and proudly multi-disciplinary.

The book you are about to read draws on the multi-disciplinary tradition of development studies. Its combination of applied theory and practical policy is also characteristic in our field. All this makes it especially appropriate that the papers were presented at the 2003 conference, held at the University of Strathclyde, of the Development Studies Association of the UK and Ireland.

Simon Maxwell
Director of the Overseas Development Institute
and
President of the Development Studies Association
of the UK and Ireland

The IMF, World Bank and policy reform

Introduction and overview

Alberto Paloni and Maurizio Zanardi

This book is a collection of papers prepared for the Development Studies Association (DSA) annual conference held in Glasgow (UK) in September 2003. The theme of the conference was 'Globalization and Development'. The choice of this topic needs little explanation, as the process of globalization is transforming the world and presenting new challenges for all donors, international organizations, developing as well as industrialized countries. We are assisting in a major rethinking of the nature of development and of development policy, which is remodelling the relationships between the different parties. Within the context of the conference, the editors of this book organized a set of parallel sessions on the 'IMF, World Bank and policy reform'. These institutions have shown throughout their history an extraordinary capacity for change. Whether they can rise to the new challenges and their intervention strategies can stimulate economic growth and help reduce poverty on a significant scale are fundamental questions that deserve careful debate. The papers collected in this volume were prepared for these parallel sessions. The issues that they raise are as topical today as they were at the conference.

In the face of the increasing importance of private sources of finance, it goes often unnoticed that the loans from the International Financial Institutions (IFIs) have in fact been the fastest growing source of debt for developing countries over the last twenty years. Recognizing this, one might convincingly argue that an association of academics and practitioners sharing expertise and concerns in the area of development studies should always be reflecting about the role of the IMF and the World Bank and about the effects of their assistance on developing countries. However, these parallel sessions at the DSA conference were not an instance of such routine evaluations. The reason is that we are currently assisting in a radical redefinition by both the IMF and the World Bank of their international roles, their priorities, and their forms of intervention.

Without unduly downplaying the significance of the new agendas on health and education, environmental protection and institutional building – to mention just a few – there can be little doubt that the most important change in both institutions is their commitment to poverty reduction (and to the achievement of all the other Millennium Development Goals) as their overriding objective. Moreover, there is now consensus – shared by the IMF and the World Bank – that operationally, effective poverty reduction is only possible if the poor countries themselves take this as their objective and implement appropriate policies. Both institutions have accordingly redefined their role as that of providing financial assistance and technical expertise to support locally owned pro-poor reform programmes. If truly meant and put into practice, the new emphases on poverty reduction and reform ownership represent a dramatic transformation compared with the years of structural adjustment.

With the exception of a few years in the 1970s under McNamara's presidency, when the World Bank took poverty reduction as its priority and became concerned with income distribution and basic needs, poverty reduction per se had never been high on the Bank's agenda. Attention to distributional and poverty issues had often been seen as a useless diversion of resources from the central objective of economic growth, which was regarded as the only mechanism through which poverty could be reduced. This trickle down doctrine also characterized the Bank's insistence on structural adjustment, with its focus on stabilization, privatization and liberalization. Despite a greater appreciation of the trade-offs between poverty reduction and growth in the 1990s, it was only in 1999, with the launch of the Enhanced-Highly Indebted Poor Countries (HIPC) initiative and the Poverty Reduction Strategy process, that poverty reduction became once again a priority for the Bank.

The journey towards preoccupation with poverty reduction by the IMF is even more remarkable, since the Fund has a long history of orthodox policies and has never been a development agency. While after the oil crisis in 1973 low-income countries had become its main customers, the debt crisis in 1982 saw the Fund restarting to lend to emerging countries. Moreover, particularly after the financial crises in East Asia towards the end of the 1990s, there was significant pressure on the IMF to disengage from low-income countries and cease its lending activities to them. The Fund responded by joining the World Bank in launching the Enhanced-HIPC and by designing a new facility directed to poor countries, namely, the Poverty Reduction and Growth Facility (PRGF), which replaced the Enhanced Structural Adjustment Facility (ESAF). Outspokenly and unambiguously, the then Managing Director of the IMF, Michel Camdessus, declared that the IMF was 'the best friend of the poor'.

During the life of the two institutions, changes to their views about conditionality have also been radical. The principle of conditionality is central to the relationship between the IFIs and recipient countries, that is, recipient countries should commit to an agreed set of policies (conditions) if they are to receive funding from the IFIs. The World Bank has always imposed some conditionality, though under project-based lending this had a more macroeconomic focus. In contrast, the principle of conditionality was formally included in the IMF's Articles of Agreement only in 1969. Even then IMF conditionality remained relatively loose, though it started to intensify with the introduction of the Extended Fund Facility in 1974. The World Bank extended its conditionality when it shifted from project-based to policy-based lending with its Structural Adjustment Lending, which included detailed microeconomic conditionality. The debt crisis marked a profound change in the use of conditionality by IFIs, as both the IMF and, especially, the World Bank attached more and more conditions to their programmes.

During the 1980s and most of the 1990s conditionality exploded both in detail and scope, as the IFIs extended their conditions from traditional areas of expertise to new ones. Conditionality came to affect macroeconomic stabilization, structural reforms of the trade and financial sectors, privatization, governance (the expansion of conditions in this area is particularly relevant), the environment, gender issues and the labour market. Moreover, the conditionality of the two institutions has converged as a result of their decision to pursue similar aims, namely, economic growth and poverty reduction in their member countries. Often, developing countries had no option but to accept such conditionality in order to obtain access to new funding. Such financial incentives have remained at least as strong with the HIPC initiative for debt relief.

Despite the increase in the use of conditionality (but, according to some critics, because of such an increase), there is overwhelming evidence that conditionality has not accomplished the role that was intended, proving to be unable to persuade reluctant governments to undertake the recommended policy reforms. This has led to calls from all quarters for the IFIs to pay far greater attention to local ownership of the reform process, a call which the IFIs claim to have acceded to. Both institutions have committed to a drastic streamlining of conditionality by focusing only on those reforms that are crucial for programme success.

The question arises as to whether the new priority on poverty reduction and the associated emphasis on borrower ownership represent an authentic redefinition of the institutions' roles or whether such changes are merely a cosmetic exercise. Are the institutions 'masters of reinvention' (an expression which, turning upside down its usual meaning, is given here a positive connotation as it is meant to reflect the institutions' capacity to learn from experience and adapt to changing environments) or 'masters of illusion'?

In their own way, all the chapters in this book provide some elements for an answer to this question. They attempt to evaluate the significance of the changes in the institutions' direction, raise concerns over some of their limitations, highlight some of the obstacles to greater effectiveness of the institutions' intervention and point to important areas for future research. They do so from different perspectives: some are theoretical, others are methodological or empirical contributions and, while all are written by economists, they make use of insights from other disciplines, particularly public policy and political science. Remaining true to the tradition in the area of development studies, where theory is married to practice, all chapters also have important policy implications. The chapters are grouped around three main themes, which are essential for the understanding of the redefinition of the institutions' roles, namely, 'Geopolitics and ideology', 'Poverty reduction strategies' and 'Borrower ownership and the reform of conditionality'.

1 Geopolitics and ideology

An assessment of the true extent of the institutional and policy changes within the IMF and the World Bank cannot ignore the special role of the USA in shaping the IFIs' policy agenda. It has been argued, for example, that the important changes in policy within the IFIs have always largely reflected the shifting priorities of the US foreign policy. The USA has at its disposal a number of mechanisms and can take advantage of sets of rules and norms through which it can exercise influence over the IFIs. The USA nominates the World Bank president; it has by far the largest share of the votes and, on matters requiring special majority (e.g. constitutional matters), is the only country that has a veto power. It is the provider of one fifth of the International Development Association (IDA) funds (i.e. the single biggest contribution) and this gives it great influence not just on IDA but on the entire Bank.[1]

Even if, in practice, the Executive Boards both in the IMF and the World Bank work by consensus and formal votes are virtually never taken, work within the institutions reflects an awareness of member countries' relative voting strengths. Moreover, since the beginning of structural adjustment, the US Treasury has exercised a de facto veto on the appointment of the chief economist at the World Bank. This is a critical position, since the chief economist can shape what the Bank says by purposely using the findings of 'objective' research to underpin it.[2] In accordance with the Bank's president, the chief economist also appoints the director of the World Development Report, which is the Bank's flagship publication and reflects its ideological preferences.

Similarly, the USA has far greater influence than any other country in the IMF. As in the Bank, the USA is the largest single vote-holder in the Executive Board. While the IMF managing director is nominated by western Europe, the deputy managing director is always an American and most senior appointments are made only after US approval. In addition to this influence over appointments, the USA is able to exercise its authority through more indirect means. Woods (2002) reports that US representatives are the only ones to speak on all issues coming before the Executive Board and that the US representation comprises not one or two officials like many other countries but

> three dozen US Treasury officials [who are] regularly involved in working with, thinking about and offering advice concerning the IMF. As well as the Executive Director at the IMF ... there is also the Deputy Assistant Secretary of the Treasury for international monetary and financial policy office who presides over an office of the IMF within the Treasury ... Furthermore, most US Treasury country and regional offices spend time liaising with the IMF about analyses and programmes affecting their particular countries or regions. Additionally, staff working on G-7 coordination, as well as private sector involvement, capital account issues, crisis management, appropriate conditionality and so forth work regularly with the IMF. The US Federal Reserve also works closely with the staff and officials of the IMF.
>
> (pp. 959–960)

Despite the power of the USA in the IFIs, it would be too simplistic to conclude that the USA has the leverage to carry out its preferences. Even if signals of US displeasure have an impact on their staff, the USA may not enjoy full control over the IFI's activities, since the belief by member states that the institutions have a certain degree of independence is necessary for their legitimacy. Executive Directors are not only representatives of their countries but also officers of the IFI and, as such, do not take decisions only on the basis of narrow national interests. The provision that lending decisions should not be affected by political considerations is expressed in the IFIs' founding charters.

If changes in the IFIs' policies and priorities have been strongly affected by US interests and priorities and other external factors, such changes have also been a response to shifts in the understanding of economic development and in the preferences of their staff. The foundations of structural adjustment, for example, predated the Thatcher and Reagan elections, as internal evaluations at the Bank had already revealed disappointing results of poverty-oriented lending during McNamara's presidency and raised a radical criticism of state-led development and of poor institutions. Structural adjustment then moved to the top of the agenda with the appointment of conservatively minded staff in key positions. With structural adjustment and the increasing influence of neo-classical economists within the organization, the Bank became committed to the neo-liberal ideology and its policy came to coincide with the US agenda aimed at the liberalization of trade, foreign direct investment and portfolio flows. The IMF was less affected than the Bank by the shifting fashions of development theory and policy and its commitment to the neo-liberal model was in place long before 1981.

Moreover, the predominance of neo-liberalism and neo-classical economics in both IFIs has been institutionalized. Wade (2002) reports that in the World Bank pro-free market studies are rapidly disseminated while more critical studies are challenged and sent back for restudy. It is interesting to note in this context that the emergence of new policy agendas in the 1990s took place still within a general framework where the core principles behind macroeconomic stability, liberalization and privatization are reaffirmed and the new policies are seen as complements of adjustment.

The five chapters in this section of the book look at the influence of the USA and of neo-liberalism on the IFIs. The chapter entitled 'Voting power in the Bretton Woods institutions' by Dennis Leech and Robert Leech is an original investigation of the IFIs' systems of governance, which, despite substantial changes in the IFIs' roles and in the scale and scope of their activities, have remained basically unchanged.

Governance in the IFIs is based on a weighted voting system, according to which all member countries have the right to vote but cast different numbers of votes to reflect key differences between them. But the focus of the chapter is not on the allocation of voting weights or on the fact that often such weights do not reflect a country's importance in the world economy or population, resulting in a bias against developing and poor countries. Instead, the chapter introduces the distinction between voting weight and voting power. The former is simply the number of votes a country has the right to cast, while the latter is its capacity to be decisive in a decision taken by vote. Voting power can be measured by the frequency with which a country can change a losing vote to a winning one, which depends on all the other members' weights as well as the voting rule by which decisions are taken. A country's voting power, therefore, has a rather imprecise relation with its voting weight. Leech and Leech use Voting Power Analysis (a branch of the mathematical theory of games) to analyse power relations within the systems of governance of the IFIs.

This study shows that the system of weighted voting – both in the IMF and the World Bank – creates a bias that favours the USA at the expense of all other member countries, for the USA actually has much more voting power than its voting weight (which is already by far the largest of any other country) while all other countries have less power than their weight. Moreover, in the Executive Boards, the system of electing directors by constituencies increases the voting power of a few – mainly rich European – countries, while 41 countries – mostly in the developing world – are found to have no voting power in their constituencies.[3] Leech and Leech also show that this bias in the IFIs' weighted voting system would persist even if the basic votes were restored to their percentage level at the time of the foundation of the institutions.[4] Finally, Leech and Leech argue that the distinction between voting power and voting weight strengthens the argument for breaking the link between the allocation of votes on one side and both the provision of and access to finance on the other.

The chapter by Graham Bird and Dane Rowlands 'What determines IMF arrangements?' is a review of the literature that attempts to empirically identify the factors that determine the pattern of IMF lending. Generally, whether an arrangement with the IMF is finalized or not depends both on demand-side factors, representing a government's decision to turn to the Fund for assistance, and supply-side factors, representing the IMF's response to the request for financial support.

More precisely, Bird and Rowlands propose a multi-stage framework for thinking about the determinants of IMF arrangements. The first stage involves factors making a country's balance of payments position unsustainable, since it is mostly in such circumstances that countries will contemplate negotiating an arrangement with the Fund. Other explanations for entering an IMF arrangement are the government's attempt to shift the public's blame on the IMF for reforms that the government itself intends to implement (the so-called 'scapegoat theory') or the government's resolve to weaken the opposition by committing to reforms within the context of an IMF arrangement. The second stage involves domestic political factors, which for example determine how an agreement with the IMF might affect the government's chances of re-election. The third stage involves factors relating to the Fund's response. Such factors may have a bearing on whether the IMF decides to ration lending or to discriminate against certain political regimes.

Bird and Rowlands warn that, while econometric research may help identify a set of potentially relevant economic, political and institutional factors, it will not be possible to specify any single model which is able to explain all IMF lending. The reason is that countries' specific circumstances are different and specific variables may be relevant in certain cases but not in others. Anyhow, Bird and

Rowlands suggest, first, that the most common determinant of IMF arrangements in practice is the loss of balance of payments sustainability. Second, domestic political factors may not constitute a strong deterrent on a government's decision to refer to the Fund for assistance. This is because empirically governments have been able not to fully comply with conditionality without endangering their future access to IMF resources. Third, supply-side factors play a relatively limited role in explaining arrangements. Bird and Rowlands argue that an eventual institutional or political bias by the IMF is not likely to determine whether arrangements are reached or not. Such a bias will instead be reflected in the details of arrangements, the amount of finance provided and the specifics of conditionality.

The understanding of the circumstances under which countries enter into arrangements has implications for the granting of IMF assistance and for the design of conditionality. Bird and Rowlands suggest, firstly, that if IMF arrangements are largely demand-determined, the Fund may need to adopt a more active rationing policy in the future. By being more selective, the Fund could have a stronger catalytic effect on other capital flows into the programme country. Second, if different sets of circumstances lead governments to turn to the IMF, the Fund needs to ensure that it can offer a flexible response and, therefore, conditionality itself should be more flexible.

In the chapter 'The politics of IMF and World Bank lending: will it backfire in the Middle East and North Africa?' Jane Harrigan, Chengang Wang and Hamed El-Said assess the extent to which political factors have influenced the flow of funds from the IMF and the World Bank to the Middle East and North Africa (MENA) region.

While bilateral aid flows to the MENA region have been often influenced by donor interest, there is a question as to whether flows from the IMF and the World Bank are subjected to a similar influence. On the one hand, the Bank and the Fund Articles of Agreements explicitly state that lending decisions should not be influenced by political factors. On the other hand, it is often argued that these two institutions are strongly influenced by the economic and political needs of their major western shareholders, especially the USA. This may have even intensified after the terrorist attacks on September 11, since the USA has come to conceive the granting of aid and the fight against poverty as essential means in the War on Terror.

Harrigan, Wang and El-Said show that, although in some cases recipient economic need – as reflected by a deterioration in key macroeconomic variables – is a determinant of IMF and World Bank lending, political events in the recipients that carry favour with US policy in the region are also important. In particular, a shift towards a pro-western foreign policy, peace overtures to Israel, domestic political liberalization and the presence of strong Islamic opposition to the regime prompt an inflow of funds not just from the USA but also from the Bank and the Fund.

The allocation of aid funds according to donor interest rather than recipient need has, according to Harrigan, Wang and El-Said, two implications. First, it is likely to reduce the developmental impact of aid, for the countries that need aid the most or that can use aid to the best will not receive their due share. Second, it may well backfire, particularly in the MENA region. Harrigan, Wang and El-Said paint the prospect of a vicious circle in which the implementation of IMF and World Bank-supported reforms may lead in turn to declining social welfare, growing anti-reform movements opposing incumbent regimes and repression of such opposition by the regimes. This may enhance opposition movements' appeal to impoverished and disaffected groups and may lead to widespread unrest, not only directed at incumbent regimes but also anti-Western and more specifically anti-American and anti-globalization. Indeed, in some instances, such as in the case of riots in Jordan prompted by the IMF-induced lifting of price supports, the IMF and the World Bank have been viewed by many of the opponents of reform as synonymous with the American presence and interests in the region.

In the chapter 'A World Bank attempt to create a policy environment indirectly through an NGO support project: a case study of Palestine', John Cameron attempts to draw lessons for the World Bank's work with the NGO sector in a 'failing' state context. This case study focuses on a World Bank project, developed in the aftermath of the 1993 Oslo Accord, which intended to provide support to the Palestine NGO (PNGO) sector. This project was unusual in two interrelated ways. One, it was outside the framework of a Bank to sovereign state relationship, which is the normal protocol for World Bank assistance but cannot be followed when dealing with the people resident in the West Bank and Gaza. Two, it was designed so as to fund NGOs directly, while normally NGOs would receive Bank support indirectly, that is, from World Bank loans to the government, which in turn channels them to the NGOs.

The objectives of the project were threefold: to deliver services to the poor and marginalized in Palestinian society through NGOs; to provide financial and technical assistance to NGOs, increasing their capacities; to support efforts by the Palestinian Authority and the PNGO sector to strengthen their working relationship. The project, therefore, intended to address a wide range of needs, crossing the policy boundaries between welfare service delivery, developmental objectives and governance. If effective, it would have played a key role in setting the general policy environment in Palestine.

The chapter presents an analytical framework which was used for evaluation purposes in the Project Mid-Term Review and highlights some of the problems resulting from the World Bank 'involvement' in the project design. In particular, Cameron identifies two prerequisites that are essential to create the conditions for a suitable policy environment. The World Bank should be supportive of development of an effective Palestinian State and should be critical of States that by political acts damage livelihood opportunities for people who are not their citizens. However, for the Bank, meeting this condition is problematic, as the Article of Agreements forbids it to get involved in politics. Nonetheless, the World Bank may have to recognize that it cannot continue to conduct its policy under the pretence that States are equal in sovereignty, as demonstrated by the Israel/Palestine situation. A further difficulty for the Bank – for it inevitably raises the very issue of the Bank's governance – is that, as Cameron puts it, the State obstructing the

Palestinian people's self-determination to build a genuinely owned policy environment is 'the superpower or a close client state of the superpower'.

The second lesson identified by Cameron is that the Bank should have provided much greater support for the PNGO sector on many dimensions. The funding was relatively small and the project was based on a competitive model for grant allocation, which antagonized the PNGOs, while what was needed in order to encourage the development of a healthy civil society was to foster their cooperation. This severely hindered the project's role of developing the capacities of the sector as a whole and the attainment of the governance objective. Cameron argues that these lessons from the experience with the PNGO project could be relevant for building a policy environment in all 'failing' State contexts.

In the chapter 'The World Bank and good governance: rethinking the state or consolidating neo-liberalism?' Gordon Crawford addresses the question whether the World Bank's emphasis on good governance and the importance of an 'effective' state represents a fundamental rethinking of the role of the state in the development process. Views about this role have gone through radical changes since the foundation of the Bretton Woods institutions. In the 1950s and 1960s, the state was perceived as the key agent of growth and development. The statist strategy came later to be regarded as a failure and a new orthodoxy, based on neo-liberal theory and the 'rolling back' of the state emerged in the 1980s. Since the early 1990s, there has been reassertion of the state as a crucial actor, which emphasizes the complementarities between state and market. The World Bank has promoted good governance as a key area of policy reform but in fact good governance has been adopted as a policy objective almost universally by multilateral institutions as well as by most bilateral agencies (including the UK's Department for International Development). Does this post-Washington consensus represent a shift away from the state minimizing agenda of the 1980s?

Crawford argues that no such shift has actually occurred. In particular, in the World Bank's conception, the role of government remains limited and subordinate to that of the market. 'Good governance' becomes defined as the ability of the state to facilitate private entrepreneurship and promote institutions that support a free market economy. Interestingly, Crawford finds a significant degree of correspondence between this vision of governance and classical political liberalism, especially as articulated by Hayek. According to Crawford, this suggests that the World Bank's intention is to construct a liberal state and consolidate contemporary neo-liberalism, not to 'bring the state back in'.

That this interpretation is likely to be correct is illustrated by the World Bank's recommendations that the state should not intervene in business matters, especially those involving transnational corporations (for instance through regulations to protect the labour force and relatively small, indigenous firms) or play a redistributive role. The Bank has mostly addressed issues relating to economic efficiency and property rights, rather than distributional considerations, questions of access to justice, the enforcing of political and civil rights, and the strengthening of criminal law. While eliminating public corruption is a core element of the governance agenda, private sector corruption as a governance issue has remained largely ignored. Thus, in this chapter, Crawford reveals that notions such as 'good governance' and an 'effective state', while seemingly difficult to oppose, in fact perform an ideological role. The World Bank's worldview remains resolutely based on development as free market capitalism.

2   Poverty reduction strategies

An explicit focus on poverty reduction within the context of programmes supported by the World Bank and the IMF came in the aftermath of the East Asian crises (with the subsequent crisis contagion in other countries), which generated deep concern about the effect on poverty of their structural adjustment programmes.

The criticism that these programmes disproportionately hurt the poor is long standing. Throughout much of the 1980s the IFIs relegated the problem of poverty reduction to the background, as they embraced a new version of the 'trickle down' doctrine.[5] According to this, the only sustainable manner to reduce poverty is via economic growth. In turn, there can be a solid foundation for growth only with macroeconomic stability. The poor would automatically gain from adjustment not only through the aggregate growth process but also because devaluation and trade liberalization would remove the anti-export and the urban biases, which are deemed to hurt the poor for they are mostly in the rural sector.

However, despite the dominance of this neo-liberal economic doctrine, the promise of faster and sustainable economic growth did not materialize. Growth in developing countries has been not only disappointingly low but also lower than in the period between the 1950s and the 1970s, that is, a period dominated by interventionist policies that were supposedly inferior to the neo-liberal ones.[6]

Moreover, this low growth has been accompanied by growing inequality and increasing social problems, weakening of democratic consent, social unrest, and environmental degradation. Concerns about these issues led to a broadening of the development agenda. Poverty reduction, better health and education also become essential objectives, since human capital accumulation is an engine of growth.

Everyone welcomes the emphasis on poverty and most would accept that growth is necessary to reduce poverty in the long term. Nevertheless, there is still an acrimonious debate as to whether the policies advocated by the IFIs are the right ones to generate economic growth and whether the adoption of those policies is the right manner to set about reducing poverty. There is no convincing evidence that liberalization and structural adjustment – which still remain at the core of the Poverty Reduction Strategy Papers (PRSPs) – are the key to growth.[7]

The IFIs have maintained a firm commitment to macroeconomic stability and liberalization. Trade openness in particular continues to be seen as necessary to move economies on a higher growth path. On the basis of empirical research that has been widely disseminated by the World Bank showing that there is a one-to-one relationship between the growth rate of per capita income and the growth rate of income of the poor, it is concluded that increased trade is associated with improvements in the well-being of the poor (Dollar and Kraay, 2004). This argument has however been subjected to close scrutiny, as a result of which the optimistic conclusions about the effect of trade liberalization on poverty have been significantly weakened.

The positive relationship between trade and growth found in this study is blighted by serious methodological shortcomings that make this finding unconvincing (Nye *et al.*, 2002). In fact, the lack of robust evidence on this relationship is a rather typical result of the empirical literature in this area. Moreover, it is worth noting that the policy implication that trade reduces poverty would not necessarily stand even if trade increased economic growth and the one-to-one relationship between average income growth and the growth of income of the poor existed. First, the vast majority of countries deviate from the one-to-one relationship, which is only an average relationship. Therefore, growth would normally be associated with significant changes in income distribution, which depend on the structural characteristics of the individual countries. Second, since the incomes of the poor are lower than average incomes, their increase in proportion to the increase in average income would produce a smaller absolute income increase for the poor than for the non-poor. Consequently, income distribution would become more unequal. This raises legitimate doubts on the efficacy of promoting average growth as the core element of a poverty reduction strategy.

There is empirical evidence that since the 1980s there have been marked changes in world income distribution and that the increase in within-country inequality has been much more pronounced than the increase in between-country inequality. One possible explanation for these trends centres on the nature of the neo-liberal reform programmes, particularly the opening of the economy to free international movements of goods, services and capital (Cornia, 2004).[8]

Other empirical research fails to find any significant effect of IMF and World Bank programmes on poverty. Easterly (2003), however, also finds that these programmes have lowered the growth elasticity of poverty. While this implies that the programmes have somewhat protected the poor during economic contractions, it also means that periods of growth have contributed to worsen income distribution, at least for those near the poverty line. This is a matter for concern because in several countries the promotion of growth would reduce the stake of the poor in overall good economic performance and because high inequality might depress future growth. This is likely to prevent the achievement of halving world poverty.

One implication in terms of decision-making is that a certain policy cannot be justified simply on the basis of its mean outcome. The variance of outcomes must also be a relevant consideration in the policy-making process. The phenomenon of livelihood diversification, for example, is often explained by the presence of severe risk in the economic calculations of the poor. A second implication is that a Poverty Reduction Strategy (PRS) cannot be centred only on the promotion of growth. Poverty is not simply a low level of income or consumption. Poverty is also related, for example, to obligations arising from family and other social relations, access to assets and public services and the right to use common resources. It has been suggested in the literature that opportunity, security and empowerment are also central components of poverty reduction.

This is not to say that economic growth should be pushed to the background. On the contrary, the growth slowdown in developing countries since the 1980s requires an urgent answer to the question of how rates of return in agriculture, industry and services could be increased. Moreover, as Wade (2002) points out, there is not much evidence that economic growth and productivity are raised by changes in decision-making which give greater power to local groups.

This section of the book on 'Poverty reduction strategies' contains five chapters, each providing a different insight into the matter. The first, 'The effects of compliance with structural adjustment programmes on human development in sub-Saharan Africa' by Farhad Noorbakhsh and Shadan Noorbakhsh, investigates whether the extent to which different countries have implemented World Bank conditionality has led to different results in terms of human development. The contribution of this work should be seen in the context of the cross-country literature assessing the effects of World Bank (and IMF) programmes. A standard finding of this literature – no matter whether the focus of the analysis is on economic growth, poverty or other economic/social indicators – is that the programmes appear to have produced negligible effects. This literature, however, suffers from a shortcoming in the methodology employed, due to the equal treatment of all programme countries. In reality, programme countries have implemented reforms and met conditionality to very different degrees. It is likely, therefore, that the procedure of jumbling together countries with limited compliance with conditionality and countries with far more extensive compliance may have produced a large downward bias on the estimated coefficient of programme effectiveness.

While this argument cannot be faulted, it is not easy to account for the different degrees of conditionality implementation in practice due to the lack of suitable data. However, in a report on structural adjustment programmes in sub-Saharan Africa, the Operations Evaluations Department (OED) of the World Bank published a high-quality data set that evaluates programme countries' compliance with conditionality (World Bank, 1997). Using this data set, Noorbakhsh and Paloni (2001) find that indeed in sub-Saharan Africa the effect of structural adjustment programmes on economic growth depended on the degree of compliance. In this chapter, Noorbakhsh and Noorbakhsh use the same data set and methodology to analyse whether the importance of compliance with conditionality also extends to the case of human development. The results reported in this chapter suggest that it does not.

Over the medium to the long run (which is the horizon over which adjustment programmes are supposed to have their strongest effects) neither overall compliance nor compliance with conditions in various policy areas have any significant effect on changes in human development (as measured by the Human Development Index (HDI)). It is only in the short run that compliance appears to be associated with improvements in HDI. However, Noorbakhsh and Noorbakhsh comment that such positive effects may have more to do with the financial assistance accompanying the programmes than with the benefits deriving from the implementation of adjustment policies.

The chapter on 'Trade liberalization and economic reform in developing countries: structural change or de-industrialization?' by Mehdi S. Shafaeddin is an analysis into the first link in the chain running from trade liberalization to growth to poverty reduction. More precisely, this chapter gives an assessment of the effect of trade liberalization on growth and on the factors driving sustainable growth, such as investment and industrial development.

Shafaeddin finds that, following the structural reforms of the 1980s, only a small number of countries, mostly East Asian, saw fast and sustained growth in manufactured exports, rapid expansion of industrial supply capacity and upgrading of the industrial base. By contrast, in the vast majority of countries, the growth of manufactured exports was low and the structure of GDP did not change in favour of the manufacturing sector. The private investment response, particularly in the manufacturing sector, to reform programmes was weak. In fact, in many countries, the investment to GDP ratio was lower at the end of the reform period than at the beginning, in some cases even where the country recorded significant increases in FDI. Moreover, about half of the countries – mostly low income – were affected by the process of de-industrialization.

According to Shafaeddin, the explanation for such contrasting experience is in the different initial conditions at the time of trade liberalization and in the different characteristics of the trade liberalization process itself in these groups of countries. The East Asian countries had already a substantial industrial base and capabilities in the exports of manufactured goods before the implementation of the reforms. Furthermore, liberalization has been gradual and selective as part of a long-term industrial policy. By contrast, the other countries embarked on a process of rapid and across-the-board liberalization, which led to the development and reorientation of the industrial sector in accordance with static, rather than dynamic, comparative advantage, with the exception of industries that were near maturity.

This demonstrates that, while trade liberalization can be beneficial when an industry reaches a certain level of maturity, it should be selective and gradual, or it may lead to destruction of the existing industries – particularly those that are at early stages of infancy – without necessarily leading to the emergence of new ones. Moreover, the ones that emerge would be in line with static, rather than dynamic, comparative advantage.

In the chapter 'Integrating poverty reduction in IMF–World Bank models', Brigitte Granville and Sushanta Mallick extend the growth-oriented adjustment framework – originally proposed by Khan *et al.* (1990) to represent traditional IMF and World Bank supported programmes – in order to incorporate the analysis of the effects of such programmes on poverty reduction. Khan *et al.* integrated the IMF's approach to short-run economic stabilization (also known as 'Financial Programming') with the World Bank's Revised Minimum Standards Model, which focuses on medium-term growth and its financing through domestic savings and foreign assistance. This integrated framework illustrates the importance of both demand and supply constraints in countries undertaking adjustment programmes, which are normally operating much below their capacity output. Nevertheless, this framework, as it stands, is inadequate for an analysis of the recent IMF and World Bank programmes because it ignores the issue of poverty reduction. Granville and Mallick extend it so that the resulting framework can be used to model the links between macroeconomic policy and poverty and to evaluate the possible trade-offs arising from the implementation of poverty-reducing macroeconomic policy.

Their preferred strategy is to use consumption deprivation as a measure of poverty, which can be calculated from household surveys for different income groups. Assuming no change in income distribution, there is a well-defined inverse relationship between the change in income and consumption deprivation. Policies that are good for growth are good for poverty reduction. However, consumption deprivation depends on the price level and the distribution of income, which in turn are affected by IMF and World Bank programmes. Assuming that the distribution of income could be fully described by its mean and variance, one could quantitatively investigate how policy changes impact on the mean income of different income groups and then calculate the effect of such changes in mean income on consumption deprivation across income groups. This would also give an indication as to whether IMF and World Bank policies are associated with a simultaneous increase in mean income and a reduction in income variance or whether they give rise to a trade-off by increasing both the mean and the variance of income.

The chapter 'The contrasting effects of structural adjustment on rural livelihoods in Africa: case studies from Malawi, Tanzania and Uganda' by Kunal Sen addresses two questions concerning the observed rapid expansion of rural income diversification in sub-Saharan Africa in the 1980s and 1990s. Can this phenomenon be attributed to the effects of structural adjustment programmes (SAPs) undertaken in these countries? And, what has its impact on household welfare been?

According to Sen, the reasons for households to diversify their livelihoods may not have been well understood in the literature. The usual interpretation sees income diversification as a vital coping strategy by poor households in the face of increased uncertainty in their economic environment. Income Smoothing households – in Sen's terminology – diversify livelihoods to minimize the variance of their income. If this interpretation is correct, then such diversification is an unintended outcome of SAPs on two accounts. First, SAPs intend to give rise to a reallocation of resources from the non-tradeable and the import-competing sectors to the tradeable and the exportable sectors through changes in relative prices. If households 'straddle' sectors in their diversification strategies, changes in relative prices become internalized within households and will not act as a stimulus to resource reallocation. Second, income diversification from agricultural to non-agricultural sectors may be a contributing factor behind the stagnation of the agricultural sector if income diversification lowers rural productivity. It may be noted that if SAPs cause diversification into the informal sector, they may lead to a reduction in the growth elasticity of poverty compared to 'home-grown' reforms.

Sen suggests that an often overlooked motive for livelihood diversification is to increase household income. This motive is relevant for entrepreneurial households – or Wealth Accumulating households, as Sen calls them – who diversify into non-farm activities in order to build the capital required to invest in high-return production methods or activities in the farm sector. This alternative view of livelihood diversification is only sensible in the presence of a dynamic agricultural sector. If this interpretation is correct, then SAPs may provide an impetus for livelihood diversification by increasing the potential return to agricultural activities (e.g. through a shift in the terms of trade in favour of agriculture, particularly export crops, which creates further incentives for investment in export agriculture).

Sen provides some evidence that the increase in rural income diversification occurred in Uganda between 1992 and 1999 may have been caused by the attempt by rural households to take advantage of the economic reforms. Moreover, livelihood diversification may have been a causal factor in the observed fall in rural poverty. The beneficial effects of diversification could be related to the impact of SAPs in increasing the returns to farming. In contrast to the case of Uganda, SAPs do not appear to have been successful in Malawi and Tanzania. Sen suggests, however, that a variety of factors other than SAPs may have been responsible for the adverse outcomes in these countries. Thus, the analysis in this chapter suggests that rural livelihood diversification may or may not be linked to SAPs and that diversification may or may not adversely affect household welfare.

In the chapter 'The World Bank and the reconstruction of the "social safety net" in Russia and Eastern Europe', Paul Mosley discusses the World Bank's experience in transitional economies, particularly with regard to the Bank's objective of reversing the trend towards increasing poverty in the region. He notes that in practice this objective may have been overshadowed by the Bank's geopolitical role as an instrument of global governance. The percentage allocation of the Bank's financial assistance towards the social sectors was in fact insufficient for the task of reducing poverty. However, in Mosley's opinion, the major limitation of the Bank's social protection strategies was in their design, particularly the absence of any integration between social protection and policies to develop microfinance institutions.

Mosley presents an analytical framework for a government's decision-making and its choice of priorities when considering the implementation of economic reforms. In this framework, reforms bring long-term economic gain but, from the government's viewpoint, they also involve a short-term risk of political loss. Since both risk and return increase with the speed and extent of reforms, the government will choose these so as to attain the preferred combination of long-term gain and short-term risk. The trade-off worsens with negative shocks, such as natural disasters and market collapse, and improves with lower corruption, higher social capital and increased pro-poor expenditure, of which social sector expenditure is a component.

Mosley provides econometric evidence that indeed low levels of corruption and inequality, and high levels of social capital increase the effectiveness of aid and contribute to poverty reduction. The evidence with respect to pro-poor expenditure is more ambiguous, though it appears that its effectiveness is lower in Eastern Europe than in developing countries. According to Mosley, the implication of these results is that social protection policies should be assessed not only in terms of their direct impact on poverty, but also in terms of their ability to generate externalities involving other poverty-reducing factors. In other words, if a social protection policy represents also an investment in social capital, or if it raises the level of other pro-poor expenditures, it will reduce poverty both directly and indirectly, through the effects of these other factors. It is for this reason that Mosley criticizes the World Bank's social protection policies in Eastern Europe, that is, because they were not associated with policies to stimulate the bottom end of the financial sector, since microfinance has a proven ability to generate social capital and reduce the costs of corruption.

3   Borrower ownership and the reform of conditionality

It is not only IFIs' outsiders that disapprove of the use of conditionality, as insiders have also joined in the condemnation. It is important to recognize, however, that the criticisms raised by the insiders may have played an ideological role. As the second decade of structural adjustment policies was coming to a close without any major resumption of growth in the programme countries, the criticism of conditionality – that is, the view that conditionality was an ineffective mechanism for ensuring sustained reform implementation – shifted the blame for such lacklustre economic performance on the governments' lack of commitment to the reform policies rather than on the policies themselves. There appears to be some consensus now that reforms can be sustained and the reform programme successful only if governments have ownership of the programme. The important implication of this view is that it opens a completely new perspective on the role of conditionality. If a government owns a reform programme and can therefore be expected to implement it and sustain it, provided that the chosen policies are sound, conditionality is no longer required to ensure that the IFIs' financial assistance is not wasted.

A second implication concerns the role of donors. As reform programmes supported by the IFIs have failed to achieve good economic results because, despite the use of conditionality, they have not been implemented – and in turn this can be attributed to the recipient countries' lack of ownership – then donors should become more selective in providing their financial assistance. They should direct their assistance towards those countries where reform ownership is present, as this would ensure the implementation and sustainability of the programme.

Donors face a dilemma, however. Asymmetric information is intrinsic in all lender–borrower relationships, as inevitably only the borrowers know their true intentions concerning their actions after the loan has been disbursed. Lenders can only try to make an informed guess about them. A simple indicator of the government's true views about reform is the quality of the set of policy actions and institutions that are in place in the country. Such 'prior actions' can be seen as the best predictors of successful implementation available to lenders. Financial assistance would therefore be directed to already reformed policy environments. In other words, before obtaining financial support from the IFIs, governments should show their commitment to reform by starting to implement the reform programme and establishing a good policy environment. At a later stage, the IFIs would then provide support, but this would no longer be related to conditionality.

While this may be the end of traditional conditionality, it is not the end of conditionality per se. The point is not simply that, realistically, the use of conditionality in policy-based lending is unlikely to be stopped altogether. The more serious concern is that, rather than more conditionality being replaced by less conditionality, selectivity merely entails a change in the form of conditionality, that is, traditional conditionality is replaced by an *ex ante* conditionality, whereby the conditions about policy reforms must be implemented before the disbursement of financial assistance.

Selectivity is founded on two core beliefs. The first is that the IFIs know what the right policies are to set a country on a development course and lift it out of poverty. The second is that the policy environment, the opposition to (or support for) the reform programme and reform sustainability are exogenous with respect to the characteristics of the reform programme itself. Neither of these beliefs is realistic. Undoubtedly, conditionality has failed to turn reluctant governments into committed reformers; yet, this is not equivalent to saying that conditionality cannot have any effects. It is disingenuous to argue that, neither through their financial assistance nor through the design of policy reforms, the IFIs can influence the policy agenda in recipient countries.[9]

It should also be recognized that, despite the dominance of neo-liberal views in the economic and political discourse, there is an increasingly intense debate on what the right policies are with respect to macroeconomic stability, microeconomic efficiency, openness, economic growth and poverty reduction. This lack of consensus implies that the characterization of the relationship between the IFIs and recipient country governments as one where the IFIs know and support the correct policies while governments do not have such knowledge and implement the wrong policies is clearly inaccurate. In these circumstances, it would be unwise to impose one-size-fits-all policies on recipient countries. To the contrary, recipient countries should be encouraged to formulate their own development strategies. The IFIs could express their views on the basis of their experience with reforms in other countries as an input to the policy-making process. If ownership of reform matters and if ownership exists only when policies are 'home grown', then the role of the IFIs in the policy-making process should be confined to that of information providers. Since the IFIs' voice is one of the many from other development stakeholders, it is possible that the government would choose a policy that is not the IFIs' first choice. In an ownership regime, the IFIs should be prepared to lend their support to this home-grown development strategy.

A contrarian view is that ownership cannot be the sole criterion for providing financial assistance and that the soundness of the policies should also matter (e.g. Johnson, 2003). This view presupposes a hierarchical relationship between the IFIs and recipient countries, since it is the IFIs that have the power to decide whether the policies are sound and whether they deserve financial support and how much. This view may be inconsistent with ownership – if this is defined by the fact that the policy design is government-led – since the IFIs are assumed to have superior knowledge about what the correct policies are. The World Bank's new lending instrument – Development Policy Lending (DPL) – is ambiguous in this respect. On the one hand, DPL has the promotion of ownership as one of its key objectives. It envisages that the Bank would be involved in the consultation process on par with the other development stakeholders. On the other hand, however, the Bank will decide whether to support a country's reform programme on the basis of the evaluation of the country's macroeconomic, social and structural policies, its governance and its implementation capacity, taking into account the country's track record (which is regarded as one of the more robust indicators of commitment). The possibility of a conflict with country ownership is abundantly clear, as ownership must be more than the freedom to accept the IFIs' preferred policies.

But what is ownership? Research conducted within the IFIs but also by independent researchers finds ownership as the most important factor affecting the outcomes of IFIs-supported programmes. Despite the fact that the idea of promoting borrower ownership has gained widespread acceptance and seems to have natural appeal – who can possibly disagree with it? – it is striking that the concept of 'ownership' has not been clearly defined. For example, in one of the early studies on borrower ownership, Johnson and Wasty (1993) define it along four dimensions, namely, (i) the locus of initiative in programme design; (ii) the level of consensus among key policy-makers about the nature of the crisis facing the country and the necessary remedial policies; (iii) the expression of political will in support of reform by political leaders and (iv) the efforts towards consensus-building among various constituencies.

While this is a very useful framework of analysis, these four dimensions do not help define whether ownership is a static or dynamic concept. If ownership is seen in a dynamic perspective and reflects the determination by policy-makers to introduce and sustain policy reforms during the life of the programme, then it becomes conceptually very difficult to distinguish ownership from the willingness to implement the programme. It becomes tautological to refer to ownership to explain the implementation (or otherwise) of a reform programme. If, on the other hand, the concept of ownership is given a narrower interpretation and is taken to reflect a set of conditions at the outset of the programme – which together with other factors determine the decision to implement the programme – then this concept has a purely descriptive nature. While ownership is likely to give rise to at least the attempt to implement the reform programme, the concept is not particularly explicative. For example, it does not tell us why policy-makers may or may not identify themselves with the programme, or why there may or may not be consensus on the policies supported by the programme.

The emphasis on borrower ownership is often cast in terms of a direct conflict with the principle of conditionality. The latter could be seen as a means for the

IFIs to allow their views and priorities to strongly influence the recipient government's choice of development strategy. All chapters in this part of the book discuss the relationship between ownership and conditionality.

In the chapter 'Conditionality and IMF flexibility', Tony Killick argues that there is major disjuncture between, on the one hand, the empirical evidence of the ineffectiveness of conditionality as a mechanism for achieving policy change and, on the other hand, the practice of the World Bank and the IMF, which continue to rely on the use of conditionality. In his opinion, although the Fund has been more defensive than the Bank towards the critique of conditionality, one can expect a movement away from reliance on conditionality by both institutions. In the chapter, Killick assesses whether this is likely to be very significant and, in this context, he raises two points for concern.

The first is the depth of the Fund's response. This has concentrated on streamlining conditionality. This exercise, however, has been limited to structural conditionality (which is less binding) without significantly affecting other traditional areas of conditionality, particularly macroeconomic policies. Streamlining, therefore, may not mark any real move away from reliance on conditionality per se. It is also questionable whether streamlining is likely to have any impact on programme effectiveness, since the evidence on the effect of the number of conditions on programme outcomes is ambiguous. Killick also conjectures that any major attempt by the Fund's management to move away from the use of conditionality – even supposing it wished to – would be strongly resisted by influential members of the Board.

The second point for concern is the existence of an institutional gap, whereby no agency is responsible for maintaining an overall view of the conditions being required of a government, or of their internal consistency. The problem arises, for example, due to the Bank's tendency to include some of the structural conditions dropped by the IMF as a result of streamlining into its own conditionality. Another example is the increase in the extent of binding cross-conditionality between the two institutions. Killick remarks that, since streamlining is about focussing conditionality on the most critical areas, and since both institutions have tended to cut back most heavily the non-binding conditionality, governments are likely to find themselves in a more constrained situation, rather than an improved one. Thus, despite all the rhetoric on ownership, the Extended HIPC/PRSP arrangements may have provided a vehicle for further increasing conditionality.

The chapter 'Conditionality, development assistance and poverty: reforming the PRS process' by John Weeks discusses whether the use of conditionality by the IFIs can be consistent with ownership of the development process, which is a stated aim of the PRS process. Weeks starts by defining the terms of the problem. He distinguishes between a 'nationally owned' development strategy and it being 'country driven'. In the case of a government accepting the IFIs' conditionalities after a process of consultation with the public, the resulting development strategy could be said to be nationally owned, but not country driven. Having introduced this distinction, the precise question that Weeks addresses is whether the use of conditionality can be reconciled with country-driven national ownership of development policies. According to Weeks, this is possible but it all depends on the nature of the conditionalities themselves.

Weeks provides a typology of conditionality together with numerous examples of conditions which recipient governments would regard as legitimate, such as, for example, conditions that require accounting transparency to ensure an appropriate use of funds by recipients or, as another example, technical conditions. There are, however, other conditions, such as those involving macroeconomic stabilization, trade liberalization and privatization, which reflect the IFIs' desire to induce a recipient government to undertake their preferred policies. This type of conditions is inconsistent with national ownership, which requires, by contrast, that the assessment of policies should pass to the recipient government, in consultation with the IFIs. According to Weeks, it is only possible to talk of a country-driven, nationally owned development strategy if the IFIs and other donors are willing to accept recipient government policies with which they disagree.

In this chapter, Weeks also discusses several reforms of the PRS process that are necessary if this is to be consistent with national ownership. Most importantly, the PRS process should be established within existing national planning institutions and the PRS document should be a development strategy, that is, a political programme debated and endorsed by formal representative institutions, above all national parliaments.

In the chapter 'What does ownership mean in practice? Policy learning and the evolution of pro-poor policies in Uganda', Oliver Morrissey and Arjan Verschoor aim to clarify the concept of ownership of policy reform. In the literature, ownership is seen as necessary for the successful implementation of reform programmes but it is not clearly distinguished from the concept of commitment. The chapter provides a framework to distinguish between ownership and commitment. For commitment to reform, a government must prefer reform to the status quo and must feel it has the political capacity to advocate reform implementation. Naturally, commitment is only possible if the government can freely choose a particular policy, but this is not ownership. For ownership, the policy option itself and/or a significant part of the policy content must originate from the policy-makers. This distinction between ownership and commitment allows for the possibility that policy-makers could be committed to policies they do not own.

External agencies, such as the IFIs, can influence commitment by shaping policy-makers' preferences, contributing to their learning process and supporting their political capacity. Morrissey and Vershoor argue that probably the most important way for the IFIs to affect the willingness of governments to reform is by disseminating good policy experiences (i.e. policies that have been successful in other countries) and by providing evidence concerning the probable effects of alternative policies. The IFIs can also enhance political capacity in the recipient countries through the provision of technical and financial support. Whether the IFIs' influence is consistent with government ownership depends on the nature of the government's policy learning.

Morrissey and Verschoor use the example of policy reform in Uganda to illustrate this point and, more generally, the applicability of their interpretative framework. The Ugandan government was clearly committed to poverty reduction. Moreover, not only the government chose the policy direction but it also actively participated in policy design. Uganda could then be described as having ownership of the pro-poor policy even if it may not have owned all the details, since external agents played a role in policy design.

In the case of the strategic export promotion policy, its adoption by the Ugandan government was informed to some extent by the observation of the successful experience of East Asian economies. The policy was not owned, but was tailored and adapted to local conditions. This process of local adaptation confers ownership of the policy content, that is, the policy details.

In the case of economic liberalization, the government of Uganda did not design the reform strategy itself but largely followed donors' advice. Donors were able to influence the government's preferences and, through their continued support, they reinforced its political capacity. Thus, while the reform proposals and much of the policy detail originated from donors, the government demonstrated strong commitment to economic liberalization, without ownership of the economic reforms.

Morrissey and Vershoor suggest that, even when ownership is absent or limited, a government can be committed to reform if it believes that reform is superior to the current policy and can be implemented. Commitment drives implementation; ownership may be desirable but is not necessary.

The chapter 'Can conditionality improve borrower ownership?' by Alberto Paloni and Maurizio Zanardi is a theoretical contribution which discusses the conditions under which the use of conditionality may not be inconsistent with ownership. In practice, the latter cannot be defined unambiguously, since in a reforming country ownership is unlikely to be universal. This chapter considers the case where reforms are supposed to be welfare-improving for the population and the government is committed to them. However, there are also special interest groups which are opposed to the reforms and which the government cannot ignore. In circumstances such as these, conditionality need not be in conflict with ownership.

Paloni and Zanardi argue that whether there is a conflict between ownership and conditionality depends on the design of conditionality. If conditionality is not tailored to each country's special characteristics, a conflict is possible since conditionality may result in lower development and lower social welfare than in the case where the IFI does not provide financial assistance to the government's reform effort or where its conditionality is much looser. If, by contrast, conditionality is designed in a way that takes into account the country's circumstances, conditionality may lead to lower economic distortions and higher social welfare, even when the government is committed to the reform programme. This may imply that, in certain cases, the IFI may have to accept to support a reform process that proceeds at a slower pace than it wishes.

The design of conditionality is important because it affects the implementation and sustainability of reforms or the opposition to them. The strength of interest groups arises endogenously from the reform process. Paloni and Zanardi stress that this is a major criticism to the proposal that policy-based lending should be governed by the principle of selectivity, for the basic assumption underlying selectivity is that the responsibility for limited reform implementation rests with the recipient government's lack of commitment and inadequate institutions.

The results that Paloni and Zanardi present have two important policy implications. The first is that one-size-fits-all reforms are unlikely to succeed. Indeed, there is no single blueprint for reform that will work in all countries. The second implication is a consequence of the observation that the need to design reform policies which are appropriate to the specific circumstances of individual countries derives from a model where the recipient government and the IFI know the true economic model. The need for country-specific reforms must be even stronger when there are uncertainties about the true model and where the recipient government on the one side and the IFI on the other have different beliefs about what the correct model is.

4 Concluding remarks

The chapters in part three of the book point to what we regard as one crucial obstacle not only to the reconciliation between conditionality and ownership but also to the attainment of greater effectiveness of the IFIs' financial assistance. This obstacle is the role of the World Bank as 'The Knowledge Bank'. While in what follows we focus on the World Bank, many of the issues we raise concern the IMF as well.

The Knowledge Bank is a provider of knowledge with the self-given role of defining and disseminating a model of best development practice. As an integrated institution undertaking both research and lending operations, the World Bank can draw on unparalleled cross-country evidence and experience on the merits of policy experiments and project interventions. The dissemination of such knowledge, which no developing country would have the capacity to assemble, is invaluable for any country considering similar policy actions. It has been claimed that Bank and Fund research is an international public good, which justifies the establishment of an institution as a provider.

The issue at hand is not about the quality of Bank and Fund research (see Gavin and Rodrik, 1995; Stiglitz, 2000, for rather scathing remarks on this matter). The issue is whether one institution can at the same time be a Knowledge Bank and a lender for development policy support. The reorganization of the Bank as a knowledge institution can be seen as a response to the criticism about the limitations of conditionality. The Knowledge Bank disseminates development knowledge from which recipient countries can learn how to reform and develop. The Bank no longer needs to impose reforms through conditionality.

The problem of course is that there is not a single, consensual interpretative framework for the analysis of the development process and policy reform. The neo-liberal view of development may be the mainstream but there are certainly strong dissenting voices. To remain true to its founding objective of being a global catalyst for creating, sharing and applying the cutting-edge knowledge with which to inform recipient country policy-makers in their choice of policies, the Knowledge Bank ought to have an open attitude towards dissenting research and policies.

By contrast, the Bank appears to advocate a particular approach and seems to be unwilling to consider alternative views and policy advice. The Operations Evaluations Department itself recognizes that the policies that the Bank recommends are not adapted to individual country circumstances (World Bank, 2003). It is only a short step away from admitting that, despite its rhetoric about it recognizing the existence of alternative approaches to policy reform and development, in fact the Bank still regards the models and policies it presents as the only viable approach to solving economic and social problems in developing countries.

This prompts two observations. The first is that, so long as the research that the IFIs conduct remains partisan and aims to defend the IFI-supported policies, it is unlikely to be seen as objective and to be trusted by recipient country governments. If this is the case, such research and its dissemination cease to be international public goods.[10]

The second observation is that, so long as the IFIs see the policies they support as the only solution for developing countries' ills, the Knowledge Bank and the Conditionality Bank will remain complementary instead of substitutes. The distinction between *ex ante* and *ex post* conditionality is irrelevant: in either case the power to impose conditionality derives from the power over knowledge, that is, the power to decide what knowledge is and what is not. Until the Bank and the Fund are prepared to give up their claim to be guardians and disseminators of the world's development knowledge, there cannot be any true willingness on their part to accept alternative, home-grown development strategies and learn from them. Since the introduction of the PRS process – which, as said, was supposed to devolve policy-making to developing countries – the Bank has commissioned an increasing number of studies on current issues (from public spending to tariff reduction, from primary schooling to natural resource protection) in recipient countries. Some have commented saying that these countries are now 'flooded with expatriate consultants telling them how to make policy' (Bretton Woods Project, 2004). Without an acceptance by the IFIs that they do not have any hegemony over knowledge, the statement at the launch of DPL that the Bank believes that there is no single blueprint for reform is likely to be but a smokescreen and the IFIs will remain masters of illusion.

Notes

1 As IDA relies on periodic capital replenishments by member countries, the USA has sometimes threatened to reduce or even withhold its funding share in replenishments of the IDA fund in order to influence policy in the World Bank as a whole. The seriousness of such threat does not derive simply from the reduction in the US contribution but from the fact that the contributions of the other IDA members are often in proportion to that of the USA. Hence, if the USA diminishes its contribution, the effect becomes magnified through the reduction in everyone else's contributions.

2 For example, research underpins the World Bank's recommendations on policies that accelerate economic growth and/or reduce poverty. The chief economist also shapes the content of research and the extent of scrutiny of its results.

3 Some of the directors are appointed by their countries, but most are elected by groups of countries arranged in so-called constituencies.

4 The voting weight of each country is made up of two components: a fixed component (i.e. the basic votes), which is the same for all countries, and a variable component, which depends on the country's financial contribution. Over time, the basic votes, which represent a large fraction of the voting weight of the poor countries, have been eroded dramatically while the variable component has increased in importance.

5 What makes this version of the trickle down original is the causal factors of growth. While, in the previous version, growth was engineered by a state-led programme of industrial investments, growth under structural adjustment was seen to derive by macroeconomic stabilization together with supply-side reforms (such as liberalization and privatization) that aimed to significantly reduce the role of the state in the economy.

6 Neo-liberal defenders can argue that growth in the 1950s to the 1970s period was not sustainable because it was not based on a stable macroeconomic environment. Neo-liberal critics can retort that growth has eluded developing countries despite the dominance of adjustment policies since the 1980s.

7 A PRSP is a document associated with the PRS process, which is expected to be prepared by the countries themselves with the participation of civil society. In this document, countries are expected to provide an analysis of poverty and its determinants in the specific country context, and to define a specific strategy for poverty reduction. Preparation of a PRSP is a requirement not only for obtaining debt relief under the HIPC initiative but also for access to concessional lending from the World Bank and the IMF.

8 Domestic reforms – such as the reforms of the labour market, the financial sector and the tax system were often introduced to facilitate the international integration of poor countries.

9 A major criticism of conditionality-based lending is that recipient countries that failed to implement the conditionalities attached to the assistance they received were not punished for this failure and did not jeopardize their access to future borrowing from the IFIs. It is not clear, however, how the factors that are responsible for the IFIs' unwillingness to punish (e.g. geopolitical pressures and other organizational forces, such as the incentives for the IFIs to expand their lending) should stop exercising their pressure on the IFIs and allow them to deny financial assistance to countries that did not implement the *ex ante* conditions required for selective lending.

10 Moreover, questions have been raised about the legitimacy of the Bank carrying out studies involving cross-country regression analysis (Kanbur, 2003). In many cases, such studies do not rely on information that is solely available to the Bank because of its country operations and, therefore, the justification for this work on the basis of the Bank's alleged comparative advantage is weak.

Bibliography

Bretton Woods Project. (2004) *The World Bank's Knowledge Roles: Dominating Development Debates*. Available at http://www.brettonwoodsproject.org (8 November 2004).

Cornia, G.A. (2004) *Inequality, Growth and Poverty in an Era of Liberalization and Globalization*, Oxford: Oxford University Press.

Dollar, D. and Kraay, A. (2004) 'Trade, growth, and poverty', *The Economic Journal*, 114: 22–49.

Easterly, W. (2003) 'The effect of IMF and World Bank programs on poverty', in Dooley, M. and Frankel, J. (eds), *Managing Currency Crises in Emerging Markets*, Chicago, IL: University of Chicago Press.

Gavin, M. and Rodrik, D. (1995) 'The World Bank in historical perspective', *American Economic Review*, AEA Papers and Proceedings, 85: 329–334.

Johnson, J.H. and Wasty, S.S. (1993) 'Borrower ownership of adjustment programs and the political economy of reform', World Bank Discussion Paper 199.

Johnson, O. (2003) 'Country ownership of reform programs and the implications for conditionality', mimeo, Intergovernmental Group of Twenty-Four.

Kanbur, R. (2003) 'International financial institutions and international public goods: operational implications for the World Bank', in A. Buira (ed.), *Challenges to the World Bank and IMF: Developing Country Perspectives*, London: Anthem Press.

Khan, M., Montiel, P. and Haque, N.U. (1990) 'Adjustment with growth: relating the analytical approaches of the IMF and the World Bank', *Journal of Development Economics*, 32: 155–179.

Noorbakhsh, F. and Paloni, A. (2001) 'Structural adjustment programs and growth in sub-Saharan Africa: the importance of complying with conditionality', *Economic Development and Cultural Change*, 49: 479–509.

Nye, H., Reddy, S. and Watkins, A. (2002) 'Dollar and Kraay on "Trade, growth, and poverty": a critique', mimeo, Columbia University.

Stiglitz, J. (2000) 'What I learned at the World Economic Crisis: the insider', *New Republic*, 222 (16/17): 56–60.

Wade, R. (2002) 'US hegemony and the World Bank: the fight over people and ideas', *Review of International Political Economy*, 9: 215–243.

Woods, N. (2002) 'The International Monetary Fund and World Bank', *Routledge Encyclopedia of Politics*, London: Routledge.

World Bank (1997) 'Adjustment lending in sub-Saharan Africa: an update', Report No. 16594, Operations Evaluation Department, Washington, DC: World Bank.

—— (2003) 'Sharing knowledge: innovations and remaining challenges', Report No. 28040, Operations Evaluations Department, Washington, DC: World Bank.

Part I
Geopolitics and ideology

1 Voting power in the Bretton Woods institutions

Dennis Leech and Robert Leech

1.1 Introduction

Weighted voting is fundamental to the workings of the IMF and World Bank. The principle that all member countries have the right to vote but cast different numbers of votes to reflect key differences between them was enshrined in the original Bretton Woods constitutions and has dominated their work ever since. This has been shown to have resulted in practice in a severe democratic imbalance with a voting structure that is massively biased against the developing and poor countries. Many of the current calls for reform propose changes to the weights in order to increase the voice of the poor in decisions that affect their interests. Such proposals for reform are not the central concern of this chapter and we will avoid discussing them in as much detail as they deserve, leaving it to others who have done so more ably and persuasively.

Instead, this chapter will argue that a further bias exists, which results from the weighted voting system *itself*. It is possible to correct this bias by suitable choice of weights. However, in order to do so we must understand the characteristics of weighted voting systems in terms of their implications for voting power that derive, not directly from the weights, but from the system as a whole. It is first necessary to establish that a member country's voting *power* is not the same as its *weight*: its power is its ability to decide the issue when a vote is taken whereas its weight is just the number of votes it has the right to cast; the former is a fundamental property of the voting system and the weights that can only be revealed by suitable analysis, whereas the latter is a superficial feature. Because this distinction is often ignored, weighted voting often leads to undesired or unexpected properties. We analyse members' voting power and find that the Bretton Woods institutions (BWIs) are even more undemocratic than they are intended to be because the USA turns out to have much more voting power than its weight at the expense of the other members. This is another argument for reforming the weights. More generally the distinction between power and weight adds to the case for decoupling the allocation of votes from both the provision of and access to finance.

It is frequently suggested that the current system of weighted voting embodies democratic accountability if one accepts the principle that voting rights should be attached to the supply of capital in the form of quotas,[1] since it guarantees that voting power is allocated according to members' respective financial contributions. This argument has more force today than it has had in the past with the decline in the so-called 'basic votes' and increase in the variable component of voting weight to virtual dominance.[2] In fact the distorting effect of weighted voting that we describe here makes this claim far from being true, even in its own terms.

As a general principle weighted voting is an attractive idea because it offers the prospect of designing an inter-governmental decision-making body that could have a real claim to democratic legitimacy – for example, in an institution of world government where a country's voting power reflects its population. But it is important to be clear about what we mean by weighted voting. Systems based on the use of a bloc vote, where a country or group of countries acting together casts all its voting weight as a single unit, as in the BWIs, cannot be relied on to work like that and in general do not, as we will show. On the other hand if the system is one where a country is represented by a number of delegates each of whom has one vote that he is allowed to cast individually, rather than having to cast their votes as a unit, then there is no problem. The latter is simply a representative democracy and the number of votes or delegates is equivalent to the country's power. The argument we are advancing here holds only in the former case, when the votes cannot be split.

We will use the method of voting power analysis to explore the relationships between the voting weights, the decision rule and the resulting voting powers of the members. This requires us to analyse all the voting outcomes that can occur, and in each case to investigate the ability of every member to be decisive – that is to be able to decide whether the vote leads to a decision or not. An important aspect will be the use of voting power indices to make comparisons between the powers of the different members. Our principal result is that the voting power of the USA turns out to be far greater than its quota would warrant. We also use the method to investigate two important hypothetical scenarios. First, the power implications of a redistribution of voting rights that is being seriously proposed and enjoys widespread support, the restoration of the basic votes to their original 1946 level. The second scenario we consider is the Executive Board as a representative body in which the constituencies are really taken seriously as such. The main result here is that this system considerably enhances the power of the smaller European countries, especially Belgium and Netherlands.

We begin with an outline of the principles of voting power analysis in the next section. Then in Section 1.3 the system of governance of the IMF and World Bank is outlined, in Section 1.4 we present the analysis of the Board of Governors, and in Section 1.5 that of the Executive Board. In subsequent sections we use voting power analysis to study the effects of structural changes that have been proposed: reweighting by restoring the basic votes to their original 1946 level of 11.3 per cent of the votes, in Section 1.6, and in Section 1.7 we consider the voting power implications for making the constituency system of the Executive Board democratic by introducing formal voting within constituencies.

1.2 Weighted voting and voting power analysis

It is customary, in the language of the BWIs, to refer to the number of votes a member country has as its 'voting power'. No doubt this is what its voting power is *intended* to be, but it is certainly not its power in the true sense of the term, but its *weight*, in the sense of weighted voting. A country's power is its capacity to be decisive in a decision taken by vote, measured by the frequency with which it can change a losing vote to a winning one. In general this has a rather imprecise relation with its weight. In reality its power depends on all the other members' weights as well as the voting rule by which decisions are taken.

An important real-world example makes the point clearly and is worth considering here, even though it does not come from the BWIs. Between 1958 and 1972 the European Economic Community (EEC) comprised six countries: Belgium, France, Italy, Luxembourg, the Netherlands and West Germany. Although most decisions then were taken by unanimity, some were taken by qualified majority voting; that is a form of weighted voting, wherein France, Italy and West Germany had four votes each, Belgium and the Netherlands two, and Luxembourg one. Thus it was said that Belgium possessed half – and Luxembourg one quarter – as much voting power as West Germany, although their relative populations were only 16.7 and 0.6 per cent respectively of that of West Germany. It was often said that the smaller countries were over-represented in the voting system relative to their population sizes but that this was not a problem because they were sovereign states and voting power should reflect that as well as population sizes. But this was false as voting power analysis reveals.

Considering all possible voting outcomes shows that Luxembourg had no voting power whatever. The threshold number of votes for a decision to be taken by qualified majority voting had been fixed at 12. This decision rule meant that Luxembourg could only be decisive if the combined total of the votes cast by the other five members came to 11, which was impossible since they were all even numbers. Therefore the voting power of Luxembourg in any vote under qualified voting was precisely zero. We therefore have the significant finding that one of the six sovereign states that made up the EEC was in fact powerless[3] in qualified majority voting; this result should be more widely known than it is. It is important also because it illustrates the usefulness of voting power analysis in a real example, and moreover, the results do not depend on use of models or assumptions which might be open to question, but are simple arithmetical facts.[4]

By contrast, the same analysis shows that Belgium had some voting power. This can be measured by means of a power index as follows. Considering all voting outcomes that could theoretically occur, Belgium (equivalently Netherlands) could be decisive in 6 cases, while West Germany (equivalently France or Italy) could be decisive in 10 cases out of the 32 possibilities. Then the power index of Belgium (Netherlands) is $6/32 = 0.1875$ and that of West Germany (France, Italy) $10/32 = 0.3125$. Then we can say that Belgium has 60 per cent (i.e. its relative decisiveness, equal to $6/10 = 0.1875/0.3125$) of the power of West Germany. This result does support the idea that the weighted voting system did mean that Belgium was over-represented in relation to its population, compared with West Germany.

We use the voting power approach and power indices to study the BWIs in the next section. By considering all possible voting outcomes the method is technically that of a priori voting power: each member's power index is its decisiveness as a fraction of the possible outcomes. The method can be thought of as an analysis of the implications for power of the rules of decision-making, as giving what can be called constitutional power.[5] Probability calculus is used as a tool for calculating the power indices.[6]

The methodology of voting power analysis will be used in two ways in this study. First it will be used to analyse power relations in the existing structures of the IMF and World Bank. We will also consider the effects of restoring basic votes to their original level, aimed at increasing the power of poor countries. These will be the main empirical results of the chapter.

The methodology can also be used to study the properties of indirect procedures where there is first a vote in each of a series of groups, each containing a number of members, and then each of them votes as a bloc in the second stage. The power index described above provides a simple methodology for doing such analysis, since the power index for any member is simply obtained as the product of the two relevant power indices. This approach follows that proposed by Coleman (1973) to address the question of why social actors give up power to join groups. By joining with others in a group, an actor gives up his power as an independent voter but may gain by becoming a member of the group which is powerful because it possesses the power of combined forces. The use of power indices permits results to be obtained very easily since it allows us to combine the power of the actor within the group and the power of the group. This approach lends itself naturally to the analysis of inter-governmental weighted voting with accountability to a lower body, whether a country's electorate or a regional inter-governmental grouping. It is also useful for the analysis of voting power implications of changes to the architecture of voting in the international institutions.

The second use of voting power analysis in this chapter, then, as an application of this approach, is more methodological in focus, and speculative in context. The intention is to illustrate the approach, which has not been widely used. We will analyse the Executive boards of the BWIs treating them formally as constituent, representative bodies based on the existing constituencies and weights. We emphasize that such scenarios are very stylized and open to criticism.

1.3   Weighted voting in the IMF and World Bank

The IMF and World Bank have broadly similar constitutions, the main differences between them being relatively minor. All countries have direct representation at the highest level, as members of the Board of Governors, but the management of each of the institutions is done by its respective Executive Board, whose members are either appointed or elected. The voting weight of each country is made up of two components: a fixed component of 250 'basic' votes which is the same for each country, and a variable component that depends on the country's quota (IMF) or shareholding (World Bank).[7] When the BWIs were created, this arrangement was intended as a compromise between the equal representation of member countries (via the basic votes) and voting power based on contributions in the manner of a joint stock company. Over time the basic element has become eroded and the quota- or share-based votes have come to dominate. This is a major factor in the disempowerment of the poor countries, and the restoration of the basic votes to their original level is a main aim of the reform movement.

There are currently (in 2003) 184 members. The USA has by far the largest voting weight, with 371,743 votes, 17.11 per cent, in the IMF (and 16.41 in the World Bank, IBRD). This is followed by Japan with 6.14 per cent (7.87), Germany 6.00 per cent (4.49), France and UK with 4.95 per cent (4.31) and so on. The smallest member is Palau with 281 votes, representing 0.01 per cent (0.02).

The Executive Board consists of 24 members some of whom are appointed by their governments and some of whom are elected by member states. Five directors are appointed by the members with the largest quotas or shareholdings: USA, Japan, Germany, France and Britain. Three other members are appointed by Saudi Arabia, China and Russia. The remaining 16 directors are elected by the members. Executive directors use weighted voting exactly like the governors, the appointed directors exercising the number of votes of the member that appointed them, and the elected directors casting the combined number of votes of the countries that voted for them. There are elections for directors every two years. The rules for electing directors lay down strict limits on the sizes of the weighted votes that they can control in order to prevent any elected director becoming too powerful. The result is a pattern of voting power generally similar to that of the governors.

There are a variety of decision rules that are used for different types of decisions. Ordinary decisions are made by simple (weighted) majority of the votes cast (the quorum for meetings of the Board of Governors being a majority of members having not less than two-thirds of the voting weight; that for the Executive Board being a majority of directors having not less than one-half of the total voting weight). A number of matters require decisions to be taken by a super-majority of 85 per cent. This super-majority, taken in conjunction with the weight of the USA, 17.11 per cent in the IMF and 16.41 in the World Bank, mean that the USA is the only single member that possesses a veto.

It is well known that the American veto has always been an important aspect of the governance of the institutions, and continues to be so, the articles having been amended to increase the super-majority threshold for special decisions from 80 to 85 per cent when the USA wanted to reduce its contribution. The existence of this veto power does not mean that the USA can be said to *control* the institutions, however. On the contrary, although it gives it absolute unilateral blocking power, at the same time it also limits that country's power because it equally ensures a veto for small groups of other countries. Formally, in terms of Coleman's terminology,[8] while the super-majority rule gives the USA complete *power to prevent action*, it also limits its *power to initiate action*. Therefore its power – and its power index (which is an average of these two) – is limited. The existence of the 85 per cent super-majority can be seen to give a veto power to three other countries acting together (for example, Japan, Germany and France). The developing countries, if they acted as a bloc, or the EU countries, or many other similar small groups, obviously have a veto.[9] The 85 per cent rule effectively tends to equalize power to a considerable extent.[10] For these reasons the power analysis in this study considers only ordinary decisions that require a simple majority vote. Analysis of power under super-majorities (for the IMF) has been made in Leech (2002).

1.4   Power in the Board of Governors

Table 1.1 presents the results for the Boards of Governors of both the BWIs. The countries are arranged in order of their voting weight (and voting power) in the IMF. The table shows, for each of the main countries, in the respective columns, for the IMF, (1) its share of the total weighted votes, (2) its power index,[11] (3) its power index normalized such that it is expressed as a share of the total power; the equivalents for the World Bank are in columns (4), (5) and (6). The remaining three columns contain the shares of world GDP in terms of nominal dollars and purchasing power parity, and finally shares of world population, for comparison.

The table shows that the voting power of the United States is considerably more than its weight in both institutions. This result is a property of the weighted voting system with the given weights. All other members have less power than their weight. Thus we can say that the weighted voting system, as it is presently constituted, has a hidden tendency to enhance the power of the USA at the expense of all other countries.

The table brings out some of the inconsistencies that exist in the allocation of voting weights as well as voting power in the BWIs. The USA has a much smaller share of voting weight than its share of world GDP, over 32 per cent, would warrant; on the other hand it seems about right if its voting power is compared with its share of GDP in Purchasing Power Parity terms, and way too much compared with its population.

It also brings out a number of glaring anomalies. Canada and China have the same number of votes, and voting power, but on each of the three criteria, China is much bigger than Canada. This bias against developing countries is seen also, particularly in the IMF, in the comparison of the voting weight of countries like Belgium, Netherlands and Spain with India, Brazil and Mexico. A particularly glaring juxtaposition is that between Denmark and South Korea in the IMF, the former having more voting weight than the latter.

1.5   Power in the Executive Board

Table 1.2 shows the equivalent analysis for the Executive Board.[12] All 24 countries whose representatives are directors are listed. In the main these are the same for both institutions but, where they differ, as in the case of some elected directors,

Table 1.1 Voting weights and voting powers in the governors (selected countries)

	IMF				World Bank				Shares of World		
	Weight share (1)	Power index (2)	Power share (3)		Weight share (4)	Power index (5)	Power share (6)		GDP (7)	GDP(PPP) (8)	Population (9)
USA	17.11	0.7631	20.43		16.41	0.7471	19.49		32.90	21.88	4.71
Japan	6.14	0.2243	6.00		7.87	0.3014	7.86		13.54	7.13	2.10
Germany	6.00	0.2189	5.86		4.49	0.1669	4.35		6.04	4.66	1.36
France	4.95	0.1794	4.80		4.31	0.1598	4.17		4.28	3.17	0.98
UK	4.95	0.1794	4.80		4.31	0.1598	4.17		4.66	3.17	0.97
Italy	3.26	0.1169	3.13		2.79	0.1026	2.68		3.56	3.19	0.96
Saudi Arabia	3.23	0.1157	3.10		2.79	0.1026	2.68		0.61	0.64	0.35
Canada	2.94	0.1054	2.82		2.79	0.1026	2.68		2.27	1.88	0.51
China	2.94	0.1054	2.82		2.79	0.1026	2.68		3.79	11.42	21.00
Russia	2.75	0.0983	2.63		2.79	0.1026	2.68		1.01	2.30	2.39
Netherlands	2.39	0.0853	2.28		2.21	0.0812	2.12		1.24	0.97	0.26
Belgium	2.13	0.0761	2.04		1.81	0.0663	1.73		0.75	0.59	0.17
India	1.93	0.0687	1.84		2.79	0.1026	2.68		1.56	6.55	17.05
Switzerland	1.60	0.0572	1.53		1.66	0.0609	1.59		0.81	0.45	0.12
Australia	1.50	0.0535	1.43		1.53	0.0561	1.46		1.21	1.10	0.32
Spain	1.42	0.0504	1.35		1.75	0.0641	1.67		1.90	1.85	0.68
Brazil	1.41	0.0502	1.34		2.07	0.0762	1.99		1.64	2.83	2.85
Venezuela	1.24	0.0440	1.18		1.27	0.0467	1.22		0.41	0.31	0.41
Mexico	1.20	0.0428	1.15		1.18	0.0432	1.13		2.02	1.87	1.64
Sweden	1.11	0.0397	1.06		0.94	0.0345	0.90		0.69	0.48	0.15
Argentina	0.99	0.0351	0.94		1.12	0.0412	1.07		0.88	0.95	0.62
Indonesia	0.97	0.0345	0.92		0.94	0.0345	0.90		0.48	1.37	3.45
Austria	0.87	0.0311	0.83		0.70	0.0256	0.67		0.62	0.49	0.13
South Africa	0.87	0.0310	0.83		0.85	0.0311	0.81		0.37	1.09	0.71
Nigeria	0.82	0.0292	0.78		0.80	0.0292	0.76		0.14	0.25	2.14
Norway	0.78	0.0278	0.74		0.63	0.0232	0.60		0.54	0.30	0.07
Denmark	0.77	0.0273	0.73		0.85	0.0310	0.81		0.53	0.35	0.09
Korea	0.76	0.0272	0.73		0.99	0.0364	0.95		1.38	1.60	0.78
Iran	0.70	0.0250	0.67		1.48	0.0543	1.42		0.37	0.87	1.07
Malaysia	0.70	0.0248	0.66		0.53	0.0192	0.50		0.29	0.47	0.39

Note
Power indices calculations done using the program *ipmmle* available from the website http://www.warwick.ac.uk/~ecaae

Table 1.2 Voting weights and voting powers in the executive directors

Seat	Country of director[a]	No. of members (1)	IMF			World Bank		
			Voting weight (2)	Power share (3)	Power index (4)	Voting weight (5)	Power share (6)	Power index (7)
1	USA		17.11	21.50	0.64586	16.41	20.18	0.62311
2	Japan		6.14	5.83	0.17511	7.87	7.55	0.23323
3	Germany		6.00	5.69	0.17105	4.49	4.27	0.13198
4	France		4.95	4.70	0.14117	4.31	4.12	0.12716
5	UK		4.95	4.70	0.14117	4.31	4.12	0.12716
6	Belgium, Austria	10	5.14	4.88	0.14651	4.80	4.60	0.14196
7	Netherlands	12	4.85	4.60	0.13823	4.47	4.27	0.13190
8	Spain, Venezuela	8	4.28	4.06	0.12187	4.50	4.31	0.13294
9	Italy	7	4.19	3.97	0.11922	3.51	3.35	0.10337
10	Canada	12	3.71	3.52	0.10559	3.85	3.68	0.11351
11	Iceland, Denmark	8	3.51	3.33	0.09988	3.34	3.19	0.09851
12	Australia	14	3.33	3.16	0.09481	3.45	3.30	0.10176
13	Saudi Arabia	1	3.23	3.06	0.09179	2.79	2.66	0.08206
14	Indonesia, Thailand	12	3.18	3.01	0.09030	2.54	2.42	0.07487
15	Nigeria, Uganda	20	3.18	3.01	0.09029	3.41	3.26	0.10061
16	Egypt, Kuwait	13	2.95	2.79	0.08375	2.72	2.59	0.08011
17	China	1	2.94	2.79	0.08368	2.79	2.66	0.08207
18	Switzerland	8	2.85	2.69	0.08091	2.97	2.83	0.08739
19	Russia	1	2.75	2.60	0.07814	2.79	2.66	0.08206
20	Brazil	9	2.46	2.33	0.06990	3.60	3.43	0.10605
21	Iran, Pakistan	7	2.45	2.32	0.06969	3.38	3.22	0.09956
22	India	4	2.40	2.27	0.06814	3.40	3.24	0.10018
23	Chile, Argentina,	6	2.00	1.89	0.05674	2.32	2.21	0.06817
24	Guinea-Bissau, Equatorial Guinea	24	1.41	1.34	0.04024	2.00	1.90	0.05861
	Total	182	100.00	100.00	3.00404	100.00	100.00	3.08833

Note
a If the directors of a constituency on the two bodies are from different countries, that for the IMF is listed first. Power indices have been calculated using the method of generating functions using the program *ipgenf* on the website http://www.warwick.ac.uk/~ecaae

both countries are named. The directors of the first five countries listed are appointed and the rest are elected. For the latter countries, the number of members in the constituencies that elect them are given in column (1); apart from the three one-country constituencies which effectively appoint rather than elect, these vary from 4 to 20 and 24. As before the table shows the voting weight, power index and power share for both BWIs.

In so far as direct comparisons are meaningful, results are very similar to those for the Governors. Direct comparisons of power indices for the directly appointed directors are possible, but for some of the elected directors they are not so straightforward because it is necessary to take account of the power distribution within the constituency. We provide a fuller analysis of the Executive Board in Section 1.7.

The results show the same effect as before: a strong tendency for weighted voting to enhance the voting power of the USA at the expense of the other directors.

1.6   Restoring the 'basic' votes to their original level

One of the key proposals to improve the democratic legitimacy of the BWIs that has been made by the developing and poor countries, that has gained widespread support among industrial countries as well, has been the restoration of the basic votes to their level at the time of the foundation of the institutions in 1946 (Buira, 2002; Woods, 2001). Then each country was allocated 250 basic votes, which did not depend on its quota or shareholding. However, although these basic votes have remained unchanged and the number of member countries has increased more than fourfold, IMF quotas and World Bank shareholdings have grown more than 37-fold. The result has been that the basic votes, which represent such a large fraction of the voting weight of the poor countries, have been eroded dramatically limiting the voice of these countries in decision-making. The basic votes in the IMF have declined from their original level of 11.3 per cent (and their maximum level of 14 per cent in 1956) to 0.5 per cent now, and a similar pattern has occurred in the World Bank.

Table 1.3 reports the effect on voting power of restoring the basic votes to 11.3 per cent. We have assumed the basic votes of each member country of the IMF to become 1480, and in the World Bank to be 1088, instead of 250. The number of quota- or shareholding-based votes remains the same for each country but now these represent in total a smaller fraction than currently, 88.7 per cent. The effect is substantially to increase the voting weight of the poor countries and reduce the weight of the large industrial countries, but has little effect on the larger developing countries, some of whose weight shares fall.

The power analysis shows that, while the weights and powers of the smaller poor countries increase at the expense of the large and rich countries, the USA still has more power than weight, although the effect is smaller than before. It is therefore still the case that the system of weighted voting favours the USA, through its voting power being much greater than its weight.

Table 1.3 The effect of increasing the basic votes in the governors: weights and voting powers (selected countries)

	IMF				World Bank			
	Unchanged weights (1)	Power share (2)	Adjusted weights (3)	Power share (4)	Unchanged weights (5)	Power share (6)	Adjusted weights (7)	Power share (8)
USA	17.11	20.43	15.56	18.59	16.40	19.49	15.02	17.86
Japan	6.14	6.00	5.61	5.52	7.87	7.86	7.23	7.25
Germany	6.00	5.86	5.49	5.39	4.49	4.35	4.15	4.04
France	4.95	4.80	4.54	4.42	4.31	4.17	3.98	3.87
UK	4.95	4.80	4.54	4.42	4.31	4.17	3.98	3.87
Italy	3.26	3.13	3.00	2.90	2.79	2.68	2.59	2.50
Saudi Arabia	3.23	3.10	2.98	2.87	2.79	2.68	2.59	2.50
Canada	2.94	2.82	2.72	2.62	2.79	2.68	2.59	2.50
China	2.94	2.82	2.72	2.62	2.79	2.68	2.59	2.50
Russia	2.75	2.63	2.54	2.45	2.79	2.68	2.59	2.50
Netherlands	2.39	2.28	2.22	2.13	2.21	2.12	2.07	1.99
Belgium	2.13	2.04	1.98	1.90	1.81	1.73	1.70	1.63
India	1.93	1.84	1.80	1.72	2.79	2.68	2.59	2.50
Switzerland	1.60	1.53	1.50	1.44	1.66	1.59	1.56	1.50
Australia	1.50	1.43	1.41	1.35	1.53	1.46	1.44	1.39

Spain	1.42	1.35	1.33	1.28	1.75	1.67	1.64	1.58
Brazil	1.41	1.34	1.33	1.27	2.07	1.99	1.94	1.87
Venezuela	1.24	1.18	1.17	1.12	1.27	1.22	1.21	1.16
Mexico	1.20	1.15	1.14	1.09	1.18	1.13	1.12	1.08
Sweden	1.11	1.06	1.06	1.02	0.94	0.90	0.91	0.87
Argentina	0.99	0.94	0.94	0.91	1.12	1.07	1.07	1.03
Indonesia	0.97	0.92	0.93	0.89	0.94	0.90	0.91	0.87
Austria	0.87	0.83	0.84	0.81	0.70	0.67	0.69	0.66
South Africa	0.87	0.83	0.84	0.81	0.85	0.81	0.82	0.79
Nigeria	0.82	0.78	0.79	0.76	0.80	0.76	0.78	0.74
Norway	0.78	0.74	0.76	0.73	0.63	0.60	0.62	0.60
Denmark	0.77	0.73	0.75	0.72	0.85	0.81	0.82	0.79
Korea	0.76	0.73	0.74	0.71	0.99	0.95	0.95	0.92
Iran	0.70	0.67	0.69	0.66	1.48	1.42	1.40	1.34
Malaysia	0.70	0.66	0.68	0.65	0.53	0.50	0.53	0.51
Bangladesh	0.26	0.24	0.28	0.27	0.32	0.30	0.34	0.32
Jamaica	0.14	0.13	0.18	0.17	0.17	0.17	0.21	0.20
Guatemala	0.11	0.10	0.15	0.14	0.14	0.13	0.17	0.17
Ethiopia	0.07	0.07	0.12	0.11	0.08	0.07	0.12	0.11

Note
Power indices calculations done using the program *ipmmle*.

1.7   The Executive Board as a representative democratic body

Executive directors have two sets of roles; on the one hand they are professional members of the executive, working in a more or less continual session in a collegial relationship with their colleagues, as experts charged with implementing policies that are technically objective and politically neutral, and on the other they are appointed or elected representatives of the members who chose them and therefore political representatives. We are going to be concerned in this section with the latter set of roles, in particular those of the elected directors.

Although the Articles prescribe a set of formal rules for electing directors, in practice there is a constituency system in which the constituencies and their operation are said to be outside the scope of the BWIs, such that there are no formally laid down rules governing the relationships between directors and their electors that we can study. According to this those members who do not have the right to appoint their own director are arranged into rough geographical groupings. It is possible and natural to consider these constituencies as groups of electors which have a relationship with their elected representative director as any constituency does with its representative or delegate. The constituencies have no formal existence in the institutions and their workings are invariably referred to as being outside the institutions. However it seems natural to treat them for the purposes of understanding the power relations as electoral bodies.

Constitutionally constituencies are defined formally, not as geographical or other groupings of countries, but by the fact that all members voted for the director at the biennial election. This does not mean that there is general unanimity among them however and there is naturally considerable divergence of view, particularly in those constituencies containing both developing and industrial countries. Several commentators have pointed out that although directors are supposed to represent all their constituents equally, in fact they tend to give priority to the interests of their own country, and to regard attempts by other countries to become involved in decision-making as 'interference'. The suggestion has been made that, in the interests of greater transparency, the informal constituency consensus system be replaced with one of open voting with ordinary decisions taken by simple majority (Wood, 2001).

Many of the constituencies have a powerful dominant member whose director is invariably elected and so in effect these have become permanent board members. In some cases this member has an absolute majority in the constituency and therefore the other members would have no voting power if a vote were taken. This dominance means that the representatives of Australia, Belgium, Brazil, Canada, India, Italy, the Netherlands and Switzerland invariably chair their constituencies and are effectively permanent members of the board. Where the constituencies are mixed with both industrial and developing countries the chair is invariably the director from the industrial country. The other eight constituencies have no single dominant member and the chair rotates or changes otherwise.

As the institutions have grown with the addition of new members over the years, the size of the board has also grown but less than proportionately, with the result that the sizes of the constituencies have increased. Now there are an average of eleven members in each of the constituencies that elects its director. The size of constituencies varies enormously: from the 'Indian' constituency with only four members to the two enormous African constituencies, 'Anglophone Africa' which has 20 members and 'Francophone Africa' which is the largest with 24 members. The large size of these latter two constituencies representing many of the poorest countries, many involved with IMF/World Bank programmes, which have only one director each, is a major factor limiting the development and implementation of meaningful poverty reduction strategies. There is an urgent need to increase the representation of the African countries which has been widely acknowledged.

In the discussion of the BWIs it is customary to refer to the constituencies as if they operated just like any other in a representative democracy. Spokesmen for the IMF and World Bank often refer to constituencies in these terms. Directors meet their constituencies at the annual IMF/World Bank meetings.

However there appears to be issue of democratic legitimacy when one reads in the authoritative work on the governance of the IMF:

> When members belonging to a given constituency hold different views on a subject, the executive director can put differing views on record but cannot split his or her vote. The resolution of such conflicts is for each director to decide and any director remains free to record an abstention or an objection to a particular decision. The system has a tempering impact and evidence shows that the decisions that finally result may well be the best that could be taken under the circumstances.
>
> (Van Houtven, 2002)

We take the view that it would be appropriate, in the interests of greater transparency and democratic legitimacy, that decisions be taken in constituencies by majority vote. This argument gains particular force in view of the fact that IMF and World Bank conditionalities imposed on poor countries include 'good governance' and democratization requirements, and it seems not unreasonable that the same should apply to the BWIs themselves.

There is no presumption that all constituencies are alike in their composition or operation. We can distinguish two types of constituencies in terms of their composition by types of countries that make them up. Seven are mixed industrial, middle income and developing or transitional countries and nine are developing countries. Many of them, especially the mixed groups, have a member with a very large weight, usually an industrial country, which is dominant within the group and whose representative is invariably elected. Some constituencies have different arrangements for selecting their director and the office rotates; this may be the case where there is no one member who is dominant in terms of weight, such as the Nordic-Baltic constituency and also the two African constituencies; alternatively there may be two or three relatively dominant members among whom the office rotates but excluding the smaller members, for example the Mexican–Venezuelan–Spanish group where there are three dominant members.

The Articles do contain one provision for majority voting within constituencies: the procedure for a by-election for an executive director.[13] The members of the relevant constituency elect the replacement by a simple majority of the votes cast. There has been at least one case where a constituency has actually elected their director by simple majority voting rather than the consensus method.[14] We therefore feel it is of interest and appropriate to investigate the voting power of the member countries using voting power analysis on the stylized model of representative democracy suggested by the constituency system.

The first result is that, because five members have weights which give them a majority within their constituency, they are formally dictators and all the other members are powerless. This applies to Italy, Canada, Switzerland, Brazil and India. In effect this means just an increase in the voting weight for each one and a consequent big enhancement of its power: thus, Italy's IMF voting weight becomes 4.19 per cent, instead of 3.26, Canada's becomes 3.71 instead of 2.94, and so on. The country that benefits most from this effect is Switzerland whose voting weight goes up by 1.25 per cent of the votes, to 2.85 per cent.

The details are in Table 1.4 which also shows those countries whose weight does not make them 'dictators' but which are dominant in their constituencies: Belgium, Netherlands, Australia and Argentina. The table shows the relevant power shares as well as the voting weights of the countries and constituencies.

Table 1.4 Countries dominant in their constituency

	IMF			*World Bank*		
	Weight %	*Constituency weight %*	*Power share %*	*Weight %*	*Constituency weight %*	*Power share %*
	(1)	*(2)*	*(3)*	*(4)*	*(5)*	*(6)*
Countries with an absolute majority in their constituency: 'Dictators'						
Italy	3.26	4.19	100.00	2.79	3.51	100.00
Canada	2.94	3.71	100.00	2.79	3.85	100.00
Switzerland	1.60	2.85	100.00	1.66	2.97	100.00
Brazil	1.41	2.46	100.00	2.07	3.60	100.00
India	1.93	2.40	100.00	2.79	3.40	100.00
Countries dominant within their constituency but without an absolute majority						
Belgium	2.13	5.14	68.89	1.81	4.80[a]	59.79
Netherlands	2.39	4.85	98.94	2.21	4.47	98.94
Australia	1.50	3.33	49.97	1.53	3.45	48.63
Argentina	0.99	2.00	75.00	1.12	2.32	75.00

Notes
Columns (1) and (4) are the countries' weight shares in the institution; columns (2) and (5) the constituency shares; (3) and (6) are the power shares within the constituency.
a Votes cast by Austria.

The increases in weight are much larger for this group: Belgium's weight increases by over 3 per cent, the Netherlands by well over 2 per cent and Australia and Argentina gain almost 2 per cent. The power shares of these countries in their constituencies are less than 1 but they are dominant and would tend to win an election. For example, Netherlands has a power share of over 98 per cent, Belgium over 68 per cent, Argentina 75 per cent and Australia 49 per cent. Thus the weight and power of these countries in the executive is enhanced by the constituency system.

The second set of results is the list of those countries that are powerless. These include, not only all the remaining members of the five constituencies which have a dictator, but also – as revealed by the results of the voting power analysis – another six countries which have zero voting power although their constituencies do not have a dictator (analogous to the Luxembourg EEC example described in Section 1.2). These are Estonia in the IMF, and Costa Rica, El Salvador, Guatemala, Honduras and Nicaragua in both the IMF and the World Bank.

The case of Estonia is shown in the analysis of the Nordic-Baltic constituency in Table 1.5. This is illustrative of the value of the voting power approach because it has the interesting property that although it has no member so powerful as to be a dictator, there is one member, which has some votes but which is still powerless in the IMF. The voting weights of the eight members are such that Estonia, with its 902 votes, could never cast the decisive vote, and therefore its voting power is zero. On the other hand it should be noted that this is just a property of the voting weights used by the IMF, and does not apply in the World Bank where the weights are different. In that body Estonia could be decisive in 2 out of 128 voting outcomes and therefore has some power.

A second example of a constituency that does not have a dictator but does have a number of powerless members is the one that contains Spain, Venezuela, Mexico and most of Central America. There are three large members which share the power equally among them and all the five small members have no power at all. The analysis is presented in Table 1.6. Each of the three big countries has a power index of one half, and their power shares are all one third. The results are the same for the World Bank, although the voting weights are slightly different.

Therefore there are in total 41 member countries (22 per cent of the membership), in possession of some 4.3 per cent of the votes of the IMF (5.5 per cent of the World Bank) that would be powerless. They include some industrial countries but in the main they are developing countries. They are listed in Table 1.7.

Now we can analyse voting power of every member by considering an indirect voting system. Each member's power is the product of voting power in two voting bodies: first, in the constituency, then through the power of the constituency in the Executive. The member's voting power index is the arithmetic product of these two power indices. It is of interest to use this technique to investigate which members gain and which lose power from the constituency system. Obviously the 41 members who have been shown to be powerless lose from such a two-stage system. However it is not clear that the countries that dominate their constituencies, including the dictators listed in Table 1.4, necessarily gain since it depends on the

Table 1.5 Voting power analysis of the Nordic-Baltic constituency

Country	IMF						World Bank						
	Votes	Weight %	Weight share	Decisive	Power index	Power share	Votes	Weight %	Weight share	Decisive	Power index	Power share
Denmark	16,678	0.77	21.93	36	0.28125	17.64	13,701	0.85	25.35	54	0.42188	23.28
Estonia	902	0.04	1.14	0	0	0	1,173	0.07	2.17	2	0.01562	0.86
Finland	12,888	0.59	16.81	28	0.21875	13.72	8,810	0.54	16.30	22	0.17188	9.48
Iceland	1,426	0.07	1.87	4	0.03125	01.96	1,508	0.09	2.79	10	0.07812	4.31
Latvia	1,518	0.07	1.99	4	0.03125	01.96	1,634	0.10	3.02	14	0.10938	6.03
Lithuania	1,692	0.08	2.22	4	0.03125	01.96	1,757	0.11	3.25	14	0.10938	6.03
Norway	16,967	0.78	22.24	36	0.28125	17.64	10,232	0.63	18.93	42	0.32812	18.10
Sweden	24,205	1.11	31.73	92	0.71875	45.09	15,224	0.94	28.17	74	0.57812	31.90
Sum	76,276	3.51	100.00			100.00	54,039	3.33	100.00			100.00

Table 1.6 Voting power analysis of the Spanish-Central American constituency (IMF)

Country	Votes	Weight share	Decisive	Power index	Power share
Costa Rica	1,891	2.03	0	0	0
El Salvador	1,963	2.11	0	0	0
Guatemala	2,352	2.52	0	0	0
Honduras	1,545	1.66	0	0	0
Mexico	26,108	28.08	64	0.5	33.33
Nicaragua	1,550	1.67	0	0	0
Spain	30,739	33.06	64	0.5	33.33
Venezuela	26,841	28.86	64	0.5	33.33
Sum		100.00			100.00

Table 1.7 The countries with no voting power

Country	Weight IMF %	Weight WB %	Country	Weight IMF %	Weight WB %
Poland	0.64	0.69	Suriname	0.05	0.04
Philippines		0.44	Guyana	0.05	0.08
Portugal	0.41	0.35	Kyrgyz	0.05	0.08
Ireland	0.40	0.34	Tajikistan	0.05	0.08
Greece	0.39	0.12	Turkmenistan	0.05	0.05
Colombia	0.37	0.41	Barbados	0.04	0.07
Bangladesh	0.26	0.32	Estonia	0.04	
Serbia	0.23	0.11	Haiti	0.04	0.08
Sri Lanka	0.20	0.25	Albania	0.03	0.07
Trinidad Tobago	0.17	0.18	Belize	0.02	0.05
Ecuador	0.15	0.19	San Marino	0.02	0.05
Uzbekistan	0.14	0.17	St. Lucia	0.02	0.05
Jamaica	0.14	0.17	Antigua	0.02	0.05
Dominican Republic	0.11	0.14	Grenada	0.02	0.05
Guatemala	0.11	0.14	St. Kitts	0.02	0.03
Panama	0.11	0.04	St. Vincent	0.02	0.03
El Salvador	0.09	0.02	Dominica	0.02	0.05
Costa Rica	0.09	0.03	East Timor	0.02	0.05
Azerbaijan	0.09	0.12	Bhutan	0.01	0.05
Bahamas	0.07	0.08			
Nicaragua	0.07	0.05	Total votes	4.35	5.51
Honduras	0.07	0.06	Percentage of member		
Malta	0.06	0.08	countries	22.28	22.28

power of their constituency. Table 1.8 gives some results of this analysis for both institutions. Only the results for the countries that gain or lose most are presented. The power indices for the Governors, from Table 1.1, have been repeated, and these are used as the basis of comparison with the indices for the two-stage voting structure we have assumed.

Table 1.8 gives the results for the top ten gainers and the top ten losers, comparing the country's power in this two-stage voting procedure with its power

Table 1.8 Voting power indices for the Executive Board as a democratic representative body: biggest gainers and losers

	IMF			World Bank		
	Governors	Two-stage voting	Difference	Governors	Two-stage voting	Difference
Biggest gainers						
Belgium	0.0761	0.1356	0.0595	0.0663	0.1253	0.0590
Netherlands	0.0853	0.1381	0.0528	0.0812	0.1318	0.0505
Sweden	0.0397	0.0718	0.0321	0.0345	0.0570	0.0225
Indonesia	0.0345	0.0600	0.0255	0.0345	0.0563	0.0218
Switzerland	0.0572	0.0809	0.0237	0.0609	0.0874	0.0265
Kuwait	0.0231	0.0445	0.0214	0.0307	0.0547	0.0240
Australia	0.0535	0.0749	0.0214	0.0561	0.0846	0.0285
Brazil	0.0502	0.0699	0.0197	0.0762	0.1061	0.0299
South Africa	0.0310	0.0494	0.0184	0.0311	0.0545	0.0234
Mexico	0.0428	0.0609	0.0181	0.0432	0.0665	0.0233
Biggest losers						
Austria	0.0311	0.0109	−0.0202	0.0256	0.0166	−0.0090
China	0.1054	0.0837	−0.0217	0.1026	0.0821	−0.0205
Ukraine	0.0229	0.0001	−0.0228	0.0253	0.0001	−0.0251
Poland	0.0229	0.0000	−0.0229	0.0253	0.0000	−0.0253
Saudi Arabia	0.1157	0.0918	−0.0239	0.1026	0.0821	−0.0205
France	0.1794	0.1412	−0.0382	0.1598	0.1272	−0.0326
UK	0.1794	0.1412	−0.0382	0.1598	0.1272	−0.0326
Germany	0.2189	0.1711	−0.0478	0.1669	0.1320	−0.0349
Japan	0.2243	0.1751	−0.0492	0.3014	0.2332	−0.0682
USA	0.7631	0.6459	−0.1172	0.7471	0.6231	−0.1240

in the governors.[15] The results show that the countries which gain most (in some cases very substantially) tend to be dominant in their constituencies: Belgium, Netherlands, Switzerland, Australia and Brazil. It is not a universal effect, however, and notably neither Canada, Italy nor India are on this list. However it does tend to indicate another hidden source of bias towards the medium sized European countries. The biggest losers are all the members who are appointed.

1.8   Conclusions

This chapter has analysed the voting system of the IMF and World Bank using the method of voting power analysis and using power indices. It argues, and hopefully has demonstrated, that this approach provides valuable insights into understanding weighted voting systems such as this. The method has been applied in two ways: first in a straightforward analysis of power relations in the existing decision-making system, taking into account given structures in terms of voting weights; and second, more speculatively, to analyse scenarios of interest: the effect of increasing the basic votes as proposed as a means of increasing the voice of the poor and third, to investigate the implications of making the Executive Board into a representative body on transparent, democratic principles based on majority voting within constituencies. The principal finding – from the first analysis – is that the power share of the United States is always substantially much more than its share of voting weight, while for all other members, their power shares are slightly lower than their weight. Weighted voting is therefore a source of additional bias in favour of the USA in the BWIs. This bias would remain even after a redistribution of votes to restore the basic votes to their original level.

That there is such a pronounced difference between voting weight and voting power, particularly for the USA, as we have found, gives added support to arguments for breaking the link between the quotas or shareholdings and votes. If one wishes to argue that voting power should be based on the payment of financial contributions, then these ought to be related to voting power rather than only the weighted vote.

The second use of voting power analysis in this study has been to investigate the implications for voting power of the use of an indirect two-stage voting system that we have assumed to exist with the current voting weights. The results suggest that such a system would tend strongly to benefit the smaller European countries, especially Belgium and the Netherlands, but also other industrial countries as well.

Acknowledgements

The authors gratefully acknowledge the comments of participants to the Development Studies Association conference, the conference on 'International Financial Crises: What Follows the Washington Consensus', Warwick, July 2003, and seminars at Liverpool University and the CSGR, Warwick.

Notes

1 For example, 'I would also like to underline that still we are a financial institution, and a financial institution means you need also to have someone who provides capital, and I think there is a healthy element in the fact that the provision of capital and voting rights is, in a way, combined, because this is also an element of efficiency, of accountability.' Horst Köhler, Managing Director of the IMF, in evidence to the House of Commons Treasury Select Committee, 4 July 2002.
2 See Buira (2002), Van Houtven (2002).
3 The reader should note that there is nothing in this finding other than simple arithmetic.
4 See Leech (2003) on the relevance of voting power analysis.
5 No consideration is given here for the members' preferences, which would determine the likelihood of particular members voting in the same way as each other, which would produce an analysis of empirical voting power. Such an analysis is beyond the scope of the present study but would be useful in future work.
6 Technically these are Penrose indices (equivalently known as absolute Banzhaf indices or Coleman power indices). See Felsenthal and Machover (1998).
7 We take the IBRD votes and shareholdings to represent the World Bank, although it actually consists of four different bodies that have different voting weights. Studying the implications of these differences will be left for later work.

 8 Defined in Coleman (1971).
 9 This point about the difference between veto power and the power of control was made very clearly by Keynes in opposition to the proposed American veto based on super-majorities in his maiden speech to the House of Lords in 1943 at the time when the BWIs were being planned. See Moggridge (1980, p. 278); also his Letter to J. Viner (p. 328). Keynes advocated simple majority voting.
10 Taking the argument to its limit, the case of a unanimity rule (i.e. a super-majority requirement of 100 per cent) would give every member a veto and equalize power, making voting weight irrelevant.
11 These power indices have been calculated using the computer program *ipmmle*, which implements the algorithm for computing power indices for voting bodies.
12 It is customary for spokesmen for the BWIs to point out that decisions in the executive are normally taken by consensus and formal votes are avoided. However this claim has been questioned on the grounds that decision-making during a debate involves informally keeping a tally of the weighted votes held by the executive directors who speak on each side according to the sense of their contribution, a 'consensus' being deemed to have been found when the required majority has been reached. Thus although a formal vote is avoided, the system may be closer to weighted majority voting than consensus building. See Woods (2001).
13 Article XII, Section 3 (f): 'If the office of an elected Executive Director becomes vacant more than ninety days before the end of his term, another Executive Director shall be elected for the remainder of the term by the members that elected the former Executive Director. A majority of the votes cast shall be required for election'.
14 For example the Middle Eastern constituency in the IMF has selected its executive member by open election among candidates from different countries.
15 The ordering is in terms of the changes in the IMF powers.

Bibliography

Buira, A. (2002) *A New Voting Structure for the IMF*, Washington: G24, available at http://www.g24.org (1 July 2004).

Coleman, J.S. (1971) 'Control of collectivities and the power of a collectivity to act', in Lieberman, B. (ed.), *Social Choice*, New York: Gordon and Breach; reprinted in Coleman, J.S. (1986) *Individual Interests and Collective Action*, Cambridge: Cambridge University Press.

—— (1973) 'Loss of power', *American Sociological Review*, 38: 1–17.

Felsenthal, D.S. and Machover, M. (1998) *The Measurement of Voting Power*, Cheltenham: Edward Elgar.

Leech, D. (2002) 'Voting power in the governance of the IMF', *Annals of Operations Research*, 109: 373–395.

—— (2003) 'The utility of voting power analysis', *European Union Politics*, 4: 479–486.

Moggridge, D. (ed.) (1980) *Collected Works of John Maynard Keynes*, Vol. XXV Cambridge: Cambridge University Press.

Van Houtven, L. (2002) 'Governance of the IMF: decision making, institutional oversight, transparency and accountability', IMF Pamphlet Series No. 53, Washington, DC: IMF.

Wood, A. (2001) *Structural Adjustment for the IMF: Options for Reforming the Governance Structures*, London: Bretton Woods Project.

Woods, N. (2001), 'Making the IMF and the World Bank more accountable', *International Affairs*, 77: 83–100.

2 What determines IMF arrangements?

Graham Bird and Dane Rowlands

2.1 Background

Much of the early research into the operations of the International Monetary Fund (IMF) examined the effects of IMF-supported programmes and the impact of IMF conditionality. This research adopted various methodologies but always encountered the counter-factual problem; what would have happened in the absence of the IMF? Even so, a consensus emerged that IMF programmes tended to be associated with a reduction in current account balance of payments deficits, tended to be largely neutral in terms of inflation, and tended to have at least a negative short-run effect on economic growth.[1]

More recent research has begun to examine the implementation of programmes and the extent to which outcomes depend on the degree to which they are carried through to completion.[2] Increasing interest has also been shown in what happens after a programme has been completed or discontinued.[3] However, all of this research focuses on the latter stages in the 'life cycle' of IMF programmes. What about the earlier stages? What factors determine whether an arrangement with the IMF is reached in the first place? At any one time its Annual Report catalogues the countries with which the IMF has arrangements. What factors explain this pattern? The presumption must surely be that it is not purely random. But what explains whether or not a member country makes use of IMF resources?

Seeking to understand the determinants of IMF arrangements is important from a number of points of view. First, by better understanding the circumstances in which countries borrow from the IMF there may be a better chance of designing programmes to enable countries to graduate from the Fund. Second, a better understanding will allow us to assess whether there is a systematic political bias in IMF lending and the extent to which anecdotal explanations are generalizable. Third, it may become easier to predict the size and pattern of future claims on IMF resources and to evaluate their adequacy. Finally, through a greater understanding of the pattern of IMF lending it may be possible to deal with the problem of selection bias in evaluative studies.[4]

This chapter is essentially a review of the current state of knowledge pertaining to the pattern of IMF lending, although it also offers a commentary on the chances that we shall be able to improve our ability to explain it. Section 2.2

discusses, in principle, some of the demand and supply influences on IMF lending, suggesting that both economic and political factors are involved. Section 2.3 examines the existing literature on IMF lending that has gradually attempted to accommodate both economic and political factors. We unashamedly focus here on two recently published papers of our own. Section 2.4 discusses the prospects for improving on the current state of our understanding and offers an interpretation of the findings of empirical studies and an informal model of how arrangements with the IMF materialize. Section 2.5 offers some concluding remarks and in particular explores the policy implications of the findings reported.

2.2   IMF arrangements: demand and supply influences

2.2.1   Demand side influences: why do governments turn to the IMF?

For there to be an arrangement with the IMF, a government has to turn to it for assistance and subsequent negotiations have to result in an 'agreed' programme. There will therefore be influences coming both from the demand side, representing a government's decision to turn to the Fund, and the supply side, representing the IMF's response to the request for financial support.

What motivates a government to turn to the Fund? The short answer is that it perceives the benefits of the negotiated programme as outweighing the costs. An IMF programme comprises finance and conditionality. In principle, both components could be a source of benefit to a government. There may also be linkages between them. Countries will be in greater need of external financial assistance from the IMF where they are facing a shortage of foreign exchange. This will be the case where they have a current account deficit and poor or impeded access to other forms of international capital. However, they are more likely to attach a high value to finance from the Fund where they are also keen to defend the value of the currency and have depleted their reserves.

The conditionality component of the programme may enable governments to overcome a time consistency problem associated with economic reform outside the IMF. By agreeing to an IMF programme, the government may be able to signal its commitment to economic reform to capital markets and via this modality may be able to persuade foreign investors to lend more than they would otherwise have done.[5] In this way, conditionality may be seen as the catalyst for additional external finance. A government may also favour the imposition of conditionality as part of an IMF programme where it independently supports broadly similar policies but believes that the Fund's resources will 'tip the balance' in favour of reform or will enable it to escape domestic political costs by blaming the IMF. It may want to use the IMF as a 'scapegoat'. Governments may also, in effect, be forced to approach the IMF and negotiate a programme in order to persuade private and official creditors to reschedule debt.

Where the principal motivation for turning to the IMF is to secure additional financing, it may be assumed that a government's demand for a Fund programme will vary inversely with balance of payments sustainability. Factors contributing to a loss of sustainability, such as an adverse movement in the terms of trade combined with reluctance to alter the exchange rate, or the build up of external debt associated with enduring fiscal deficits, or a loss of market confidence, will serve to increase the probability that a country will turn to the IMF for financial assistance. Where the principal motivation is to import IMF conditionality in order to ease the adoption of a preferred programme of economic reform, factors related to the balance of payments may be expected to be less significant. Here it will be domestic political factors that dominate.

However, if governments disagree with the IMF's preferred programme of policies they will be discouraged from turning to it. In this case conditionality will be viewed as a cost. The size of this cost will depend on the size of the discrepancy between the policy preferences of the government and those of the Fund. The bigger the discrepancy the bigger the cost. Governments will be deterred from turning to the Fund where they anticipate being asked to pursue policies that, for economic or political reasons, they regard as unacceptable. Acceptability will be influenced by the distributional effects of policies, the time profile of the costs and benefits involved and the proximity of elections. Governments, it may be assumed, will want to avoid policies that impose severe costs on politically powerful groups and that involve short run costs (even when combined with longer run benefits) especially where the costs will be incurred ahead of elections.

A caveat is in order here since, where the balance of payments is unsustainable, governments will be forced to change policy irrespective of whether the Fund is involved. Implicitly the government therefore needs to compare the programme of policy reform it anticipates in conjunction with IMF conditionality with the one that it will have to pursue if it opts to by-pass the Fund. This leads to the possibility that governments may attach positive utility to 'sovereignty' over economic policy. Ceding the control of economic policy to the IMF may be perceived as a cost even where there is no significant disagreement about the design of economic reform.

So what follows from the above analysis? Countries with current account deficits are likely to turn to the IMF but not if they have access to private capital, have large international reserves or are prepared to let the value of their currency fall. It is the combination of a current account deficit, poor access to private credit, low reserves and a desire to moderate exchange rate depreciation that is likely to lead to referral. In these circumstances the balance of payments becomes unsustainable. This could be the consequence of a current account or a capital account shock, leading either to a weakening in the current account or to a decline in the capital inflows needed to finance a current account deficit. Such shocks may occur over different time frames. The current account may weaken secularly over a protracted period of time. The capital account may be affected by a short term and more immediate crisis.

However, some countries may still turn to the Fund even though their current account balance of payments deficits are relatively small. Here the benefits tend to lie in conditionality rather than in the additional finance provided. In contrast, governments that are strongly opposed to the policies favoured by the Fund or which place a high value on sovereignty will be reluctant to turn to the Fund.

2.2.2   Supply side influences: how will the IMF respond?

But how will the IMF respond to governments that approach it for financial assistance? Will it be prepared to supply the resources? A response to these questions requires us to know what it is that is motivating the IMF. This is a complex question and there are various ways of approaching it.[6] The first adopts a public choice interpretation of the Fund's operations. In this model, Fund staff and management are presumed to maximize an objective function that incorporates power, prestige, responsibility and remuneration. This approach views the Fund as keen to make loans but also to maximize conditionality.[7] The second approach involves agency theory and presents the IMF as acting as an agent representing the interests of the institution's major shareholders. Tough conditionality is a way of signaling to the principals that IMF resources are not being squandered. Using conditionality to promote policies of openness with respect to trade and investment could be seen as serving the commercial interests of advanced economies, while making loans to certain countries in economic distress could represent an attempt to bail out foreign investors with commercial interests in these countries.[8] Third, the Fund could be viewed as operating in a way that attempts to comply with an institutional agenda described in general by its own Articles of Agreement. In this context the design of conditionality reflects a desire by the Fund to offer good advice based on sound economic analysis and to work in the public interest.

The advice may not resonate with governments since the IMF will place a higher priority on strengthening the balance of payments and will be less directly concerned about the politics of economic policy in terms of its redistributive effects, except inasmuch as these affect the chances that programmes will be implemented. The Fund may also be working to a different time frame. Furthermore, the Fund provides financial support to help countries avoid having to place excessive emphasis on adjustment policies that are destructive of domestic and international prosperity; another objective to which the IMF lays claim in its Articles of Agreement.

The outcome of the negotiations between governments and the IMF depends on their respective bargaining strengths. Is the IMF the lender of only resort? Does the country have influential advocates within the Fund? However, the 'outcome' may be interpreted in two ways. First, there is the issue of whether or not an arrangement is made. There is a discrete distinction. The Fund may be reluctant to veto arrangements *ex ante* because of the club-like nature of the institution. 'Client' countries are also 'members.' It may be difficult for the Fund to say an outright 'no'. For this reason it may be more likely that bargaining strength is reflected in the amount of financial assistance offered and the nature of the conditionality embodied in arrangements rather than in terms of whether or not there is an arrangement. This gives us a second way of differentiating outcomes. If the Fund is reluctant to turn countries away, it follows that the first interpretation of outcomes – whether an agreement is signed – may be dominated by demand-side factors, whereas the second interpretation – the amount of finance and the design of the programme – may be more heavily influenced by supply-side factors. A problem is that it is difficult to test this idea since the data on the design of conditionality is, as yet, insufficiently rich. In what follows we therefore treat outcomes in a discrete fashion; is there or is there not an arrangement?

The above discussion suggests that whether or not we see an arrangement between a country and the IMF depends on a range of economic, political and institutional factors. It also suggests that there will be no one single model that explains all IMF lending. Different things will be important in different cases. For example, a given current account deficit, normalized for country size, may be sustainable in one set of circumstances but unsustainable in another. One would not therefore expect current account deficits to be a good predictor of whether or not a country borrows from the IMF. Even countries in similar economic circumstances may make different decisions about whether or not to turn to the IMF because of differences in domestic political circumstances.

The response of the IMF to requests for assistance may, in principle, influence the eventual outcome if there is a geopolitical bias within the Fund or if the Fund prefers to lend to previous client countries with whom a relationship has already been developed, or if the Fund only lends to countries that are perceived to be genuinely prepared to accept its policy advice. But our discussion suggests that there is reason to believe that the 'supply side' will exert greater influence over the nature of programmes rather than whether or not an arrangement is made. With a relatively passive supply side and a reluctance by the Fund to turn countries away, it is reasonable to assume that the existence of an arrangement will be more strongly influenced by demand-side factors. There is considerable evidence that the Fund is indeed reluctant to say no, that it does not discriminate against countries that have had programmes in the recent past even where these have been unsuccessful, and that it finds it difficult *ex ante* to distinguish between governments that are genuine in their commitment to reform and those that are not, tending, as a consequence, to give governments the benefit of the doubt (see, for example, Killick, 1995).

But what does the empirical evidence tell us about the determinants of IMF arrangements? The above discussion suggests that large sample regression analysis will tell us only a strictly limited amount. A large sample will include some cases where a particular variable is significant and others where it is not. We shall therefore get a picture of muted overall significance when the correct picture is one of strong significance in some cases and weak or no significance in others. In Section 2.3 we examine the empirical evidence and, in the light of this, move on in the following one to present a schema that summarizes the circumstances under which arrangements may (or may not) be made.

2.3   Empirical evidence

Early econometric research which set out to try and explain IMF arrangements tended to focus solely on their economic determinants. However, without exception, these studies left a large residual (Bird and Orme, 1981; Cornelius, 1987). Something was being missed. Later studies included a more comprehensive list of economic variables, with some of these, such as government expenditure relative to GDP, having a political dimension. But these augmented studies still left much unexplained (Joyce, 1992; Conway, 1994; Santaella, 1996; Knight and Santaella, 1997). Areas of consensus emerged suggesting that IMF lending was significantly related to poverty and growth, previous IMF involvement, the availability of alternative sources of external finance, exchange rate overvaluation and holdings of international reserves. But there was less agreement about how it was related to the terms of trade, external debt and the performance of macroeconomic and policy variables. While some progress was made concerning the significance of individual variables, the overall predictive power of the equations remained relatively weak (Bird, 1996).

At the same time, there appeared to be mounting anecdotal evidence that IMF lending was driven by political influences. The natural question was whether politics was the missing link. Would the inclusion of political variables improve the ability of large sample equations to explain the pattern of IMF lending? Certainly the influential Meltzer Report argued forcefully that IMF lending strongly reflected the influence of US political and economic interests, reinforcing the agency approach to IMF lending (IFIAC, 2000). Studies began to specifically include variables to try and capture such systematic political bias, and claimed to discover empirical support for it (Thacker, 1999; Barro and Lee, 2001). However, while there was now some evidence to suggest that including political variables improved our ability to explain the pattern of IMF lending, it could certainly not be claimed that we had discovered a satisfactory general explanation. In many respects this new research raised as many questions as it answered. Were the results robust across different methodological approaches and different time periods? Did a wider array of political variables beyond US influence exert a significant effect? Were institutional factors within the Fund important? Were political factors idiosyncratically rather than systematically significant? And was it possible to disentangle the demand-side and supply-side influences on IMF lending?

The authors of this chapter have an on-going programme of research designed to help provide answers to these questions. An initial phase of this research sought to extend existing large sample research to incorporate additional political and institutional variables, as well as to test the robustness of findings reported in the literature concerning a reasonably conventional range of economic variables as well as the 'US influence' hypothesis. Was there evidence that certain types of country were systematically favoured by the IMF? Moreover, was there evidence of hurry-up lending before a quota review? Did the Fund show a preference for large loans in an attempt to reduce average transactions costs? Was there a geographical bias in IMF lending? Did the Fund use arrangements as a way of maintaining a client–patron relationship?

The results of this research are reported in Bird and Rowlands (2001). The study covered all high conditionality lending by the IMF over the period 1974–94, and used Probit techniques in an attempt to explain the probability of there being an IMF arrangement in terms of economic, political and institutional variables. The economic variables were: per capita income, economic growth, the level of and change in international reserves, the current account balance of payments, changes in the real exchange rate, the level of and changes in the debt service ratio, the debt to GNP ratio, arrears, the level of and changes in global interest rates and future debt rescheduling. The political variables were: the economic interests of the US and France as measured by export penetration, and political conditions in potential recipients as measured by the nature of the regime, expected changes in government, the level of and changes in civil liberties and the frequency of coups. The institutional variables were: the incidence of failed IMF programmes over the previous five years, the imminence of a quota review, IMF liquidity, the size of the country as measured by GDP and the number of years spent in an IMF programme in the previous three years.

The results of the study are summarized in Table 2.1. These broadly confirm the significance of key economic variables in helping to explain IMF lending that had been found in previous studies. They also show that some of the additional political and institutional variables are individually significant. IMF arrangements appear to be negatively associated with the degree of socialism and, perhaps surprisingly, US exports, as well as with normal expected changes in government. A history of incomplete programmes seems to increase the probability of a new arrangement, although the significance of this variable disappears when the presence of past arrangements is added, suggesting that it is the existence of past programmes rather than the extent to which they are completed that is important.

The empirical model underlying Table 2.1 explained IMF lending better in the period after 1989, although the significance of individual coefficients also changed as between sub-periods, with civil liberties becoming insignificant after 1989. The research also tended to cast doubts about the 'US influence' claimed by other studies, even when similar variables designed to capture it (voting patterns in the United Nations) were added. It suggested that including a wider array of political influences did little to improve our ability to explain IMF lending overall as compared with more parsimonious models based on economic factors. Indeed, the predictive accuracy of the equations varied more with the sample than with the specification of the model.

In broad terms the exercise and the absence of robust coefficient estimates suggested that while several factors affect the pattern of IMF agreements they do this in an idiosyncratic rather than a systematic way.

The next stage in the research programme, reported in detail in Bird and Rowlands (2002b), used the large sample model to identify outliers; cases where the model failed quite badly to predict the actual outcomes. This involved some cases where there had been no arrangement with the Fund even though one was predicted by the model, and others where an arrangement was reached in spite of the model's failure to predict it. What was going on in these cases? What was the model failing to pick up? And could we learn from these cases in ways that would allow us to improve the general model? The cases where there were unpredicted arrangements included Argentina, 1984; Barbados, 1982 and 1992; Guatemala, 1992; Ghana, 1983 and 1984; Nepal, 1974 and 1992 and Uruguay, 1980 and 1981. The cases where arrangements predicted by the model did not happen were Brazil, 1987; Chile, 1976; Congo, 1989 and 1993; Egypt, 1990 and Nigeria, 1988.

Table 2.1 Estimation results for the two augmented models

Variables	Economic model	Supplemented model
Constant	−0.794*** (−5.31)	−0.962*** (−2.73)
GNP per capita	−0.101** (−2.13)	−0.0391 (−0.74)
GDP growth	−0.00186 (−0.49)	−0.00263 (−0.67)
Reserves/imports	−0.990*** (−4.14)	−0.904*** (−3.46)
Change in reserves	−0.218** (−2.27)	−0.264*** (−2.55)
Current account/GDP	−0.0124* (−1.66)	−0.0171** (−2.16)
Real exchange rate change	0.77*** (2.58)	0.234*** (2.89)
Debt–service ratio	1.41*** (3.72)	1.59*** (3.66)
Change in debt–service ratio	−0.000295 (−0.80)	−0.000288 (−0.72)
Debt/GDP	−0.257* (−1.83)	−0.307** (−1.98)
Arrears/debt	−0.485 (−0.72)	−0.0508 (−0.07)
Past reschedulings	0.338*** (4.64)	0.186*** (2.31)
Real LIBOR	−0.0279 (−1.31)	−0.036 (−1.39)
Change in real LIBOR	0.0759*** (3.02)	0.0929*** (3.16)
US exports	—	−0.813** (−2.10)
French exports (Africa)	—	−0.0113 (−0.84)
Socialist	—	−0.828** (−1.99)
Recent government	—	−0.392 (−1.34)
Civil freedom	—	0.0151 (0.378)
Change in civil freedom	—	0.122** (1.96)
Coup frequency	—	0.326* (1.73)
Past incomplete programmes	—	0.0443 (0.76)
Imminent quota review	—	−0.0358 (−0.27)
IMF liquidity	—	−0.229 (−0.49)
Gross real GDP	—	0.117 (1.03)
Imminent rescheduling	2.49*** (3.54)	2.63*** (3.61)
Imminent new government	—	0.234* (−1.74)
Past IMF agreements	—	0.0411*** (5.00)
Number of observations	1041	1041
% correct predictions	82.22	82.71
# of correct predictions	856	861
# of positive observations	189	189
R-squared	0.129	0.185

Notes
The *t*-statistics appear in parentheses. Coefficient estimates marked *, **, and *** are statistically significant at the 0.05, 0.025, and 0.01 levels of confidence for a one-tailed test. The dependent variable indicates a signing of an SBA (Stand-by Arrangement), EFF or ESAF (Enhanced Structural Adjustment Facility) arrangement.

Analysis of these cases helped to suggest extra variables that might be usefully added to the general model. The research identified deteriorating terms of trade, possibly in conjunction with export concentration, and budgetary imbalances as potentially significant explanatory variables that could be of general importance. These factors certainly appeared to have been important in Barbados and Guatemala (export concentration) and Argentina (budgetary imbalance). However, including them into the basic model and then re-running the regressions in fact did nothing to improve the model's predictive powers. The other case studies suggested that factors such as disagreement over key aspects of economic reform (wages policy in Chile), strong feelings of national sovereignty (Brazil and Nigeria) and changes in regime type or other political factors (Ghana, Nepal and Egypt) could help to explain prediction failures. However, it is difficult to capture these influences statistically in the context of large sample analysis because of the absence of satisfactory data, so it remains uncertain as to how important these factors are in general.

2.4   Interpretation, scenarios and a schema for discussing IMF arrangements

On the basis of the available evidence reported in Section 2.3, as well as our earlier discussion, can we offer an explanation of the pattern of IMF lending? What factors determine whether or not a country has an arrangement with the IMF?

As anticipated no straightforward answer is warranted. We can explain IMF arrangements only up to a point. Theoretical and empirical analysis has done a reasonable job in identifying a list of variables that may potentially exert a significant influence over IMF lending. We know what the determinants may be. However, these determinants will not be significant in each and every case. We have therefore been unable to move from the point where we have assembled a list of potentially important determinants to a point where we can specify an equation that explains all IMF arrangements. We have no satisfactory general model of the determinants of IMF arrangements.

But should we be surprised by this? Not really. Our theoretical discussion suggested that there are likely to be different combinations of factors that lead governments to turn to the IMF for assistance. Not all countries experiencing current account deficits or carrying high levels of external debt will, for example, need to involve the Fund, but some will. The challenge is to delineate the combinations of circumstances that make it more likely that countries will have an arrangement with the IMF. For example, one possible scenario could involve low income countries with poor access to private international capital experiencing current account balance of payments deficits as a consequence of adverse movements in their income terms of trade. Where international reserves are low and there has been a preference to maintain a pegged exchange rate, these circumstances may enhance the probability of turning to the IMF, especially where there are no binding political constraints and where future aid flows depend on the Fund's involvement. In another case it may be a loss of access to private capital markets in circumstances where there is a large amount of external debt and a low level of international reserves that drives a government to the Fund. In order to delineate a pattern of IMF lending, therefore, we need to delineate the most common combinations of factors that lead countries to apply to the Fund for financial assistance.

One could envisage a multi stage schema for analysing the determinants of IMF arrangements as depicted in Figure 2.1. The first stage involves factors affecting the sustainability of the balance of payments. Except in the cases of

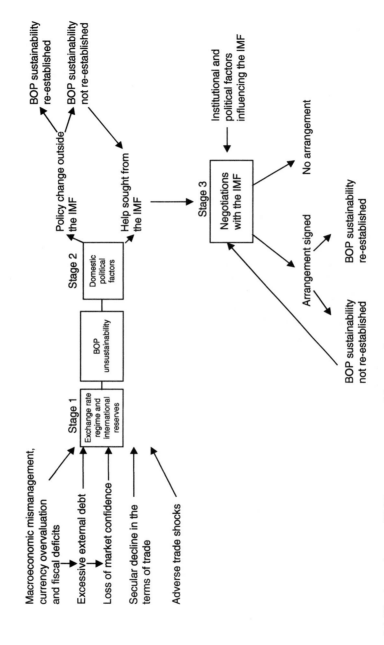

Figure 2.1 The determinants of IMF arrangements: a multi stages schema.

Note
BOP: Balance of Payments.

'tipping the balance' or 'scapegoating', countries will contemplate negotiating an arrangement with the Fund only when their balance of payments is unsustainable. However, as noted earlier, the causes of unsustainability are various, as shown in Figure 2.1. The second stage involves governments assessing the domestic political implications of involving the IMF; how, for example, will it affect their chances of re-election? Again circumstances will vary across countries. For some countries, politics will be a bigger hurdle than for others. The third stage involves the Fund's response. Does the Fund ration its lending in some way? Does it, for example, discriminate against certain types of political regime or does it favour countries that are 'friends' of the USA or other large advanced economies?

In terms of the first two stages there may be trade-offs. Thus a country with relatively few economic problems may still turn to the IMF if the domestic political environment is conducive. This would cover cases where IMF resources can be used to tip the balance or where the government needs someone else to blame. On the other hand, governments with significant political resistance to involving the Fund may still turn to it for assistance because of the severity of their economic difficulties. The evidence on IMF arrangements is consistent with this general description of the circumstances in which governments turn to the IMF.

The Fund's response may be influenced by a range of institutional characteristics. There may be a tendency towards overestimating what programmes will achieve. Mission chiefs may believe that their chances of promotion will be helped by negotiating an arrangement rather than by failing to agree on one. These characteristics will create a bias in favour of responding positively to requests for assistance (Independent Evaluation Office, 2002). At the same time there is, at present, little empirical evidence to support a public choice explanation of IMF lending, which is, in any case, better suited theoretically to explaining the total amount of IMF lending than its distribution across countries. There is mixed evidence relating to a US effect – the jury is still out on this agency approach as a systematic explanation of IMF lending. The supply side contribution to explaining IMF arrangements seems most likely to come in the form of the IMF setting certain preconditions for correcting the balance of payments. This may rule out some arrangements. The Fund's focus remains on the balance of payments, and IMF programmes seem to exert their principal effects on the balance of payments. They may even not uncommonly exceed expectations in terms of achieving balance of payments targets (Baqir *et al.*, 2003). But this orientation seems unlikely to severely or systematically constrain the probability of an arrangement being reached. After all, governments will in general terms know in advance what to expect in the form of IMF conditionality and will have factored this into their decision to turn to the Fund. However, they will be turning to the Fund at a time when they are also prioritizing the balance of payments. As already noted it therefore seems more likely that the supply side will influence the details of an arrangement rather than whether or not there is one. In any case, the Fund has to wait until it is approached by governments. Governments are the prime movers. It therefore seems reasonable to conclude that IMF arrangements are largely driven from the demand side with domestic politics and the supply side acting as filters.

2.5   Concluding remarks

The IMF has come under close scrutiny in recent years and its lending operations have been subject to considerable criticism. In order to assess the legitimacy of some of these criticisms it is important to examine the determinants of IMF arrangements. Can we explain their pattern? Empirical analysis designed to try and answer this question has taken the form of both large sample regression analysis and individual case study analysis. The former approach has looked for a general explanation of IMF arrangements while the latter has tended to imply that regression analysis may miss important nuances and that the explanation may vary from country to country.

There is sufficient evidence available to justify a review of what we know about the determinants of IMF arrangements. Our assessment of the evidence is that we know enough to make a list of economic, political and institutional factors that may potentially be significant. However, we also know that individual circumstances will differ and that the significance of specific variables will vary from case to case. The next challenge for research is to see whether we can identify reasonably common combinations of characteristics that lead to IMF arrangements. In this chapter we present a multi-stage schema which seeks to explore the routes that lead towards IMF arrangements. This schema appears to be consistent with available empirical evidence.

Our hypothesis is that IMF arrangements are largely determined from the demand side and that in turn the demand for IMF assistance is largely driven initially by economic factors that contribute in some way to cause a loss of balance of payments sustainability. Whether this results in governments turning to the IMF will then be moderated by domestic political factors. But given conditions of economic crisis, and given that governments can opt to not fully comply with conditionality at apparently little cost in terms of future access to IMF resources, the political constraints on referral to the Fund may be generally expected to be fairly weak. Similarly, and based on analysis and evidence, it seems unlikely to us that the Fund has a strong systematic institutional or political bias that is exhibited in terms of whether arrangements are reached or not. It seems more likely that such a bias will be reflected in the details of arrangements, the amount of finance provided and the specifics of conditionality.

If these observations are accurate they have important implications for policy. First, if different sets of circumstances lead governments to turn to the IMF, the Fund needs to ensure that it can offer a flexible response. This suggests that conditionality itself needs to be flexible and that it may be sensible for the Fund to have a range of lending windows. The question to be answered is whether the Fund's existing range of facilities matches the common combinations of circumstances which lead countries to seek assistance from the IMF and whether the move towards streamlining conditionality offers sufficient flexibility. Second, if, up until now, IMF arrangements have been largely demand determined, does the Fund need to adopt a more active rationing policy in future? The poor implementation of programmes and the existence of prolonged users may suggest that it does. By being more selective, the Fund could strengthen its catalytic effect since the successful negotiation of an arrangement would transmit a more powerful and well-defined signal.

In terms of future research our prediction is that large sample regression analyses will continue to fail to possess strong explanatory powers, even as more and more variables of both an economic and political nature are added. This is because there is no 'holy grail' when it comes to the determinants of IMF arrangements. Case studies will continue to provide useful insights into particular country experiences with the Fund but, unless combined in a systematic way, will fail to emphasize common characteristics. Instead it will be useful to build on the notion of balance of payments sustainability to see if empirical analysis can identify reasonably common combinations of country characteristics that increase the probability of an IMF arrangement. In this chapter we conjecture as to what some of these common combinations may be but future empirical work will be required to test for their significance.

Notes

1 These alternative methodologies are well described in Killick (1995) and in Haque and Khan (1999). These studies also summarize the results from cross section studies of the impact of IMF programmes. More recent evaluative studies which focus on the effects of IMF programmes on economic growth include Barro and Lee (2001), Hutchison (2003) and Przeworski and Vreeland (2000). Bird (2001) provides a broader assessment of the extent to which IMF programmes 'work'.
2 See, for example, Ivanova *et al.* (2001). The completion of IMF programmes is also discussed in some detail in Mussa and Savastano (2000) and in Bird (2002a).
3 This issue is discussed at some length in the first report of the IMF's Independent Evaluation Office (2002) which examines the prolonged use of IMF resources.
4 The concern here is that countries with IMF arrangements are significantly different from those without them so that the course of events after an IMF arrangement is put in place may be attributed to these differences rather than to the IMF programme.
5 We do not explore this signaling role and the related catalytic effect here, but see Bird (2002b) and Bird and Rowlands (2002a).
6 A problem is also associated with treating the IMF as a unified actor. Just as there may be factions within governments, different parts of the IMF may have different objectives or different points of view. A distinction may need to be drawn between the staff and the management or between the senior management and the Executive Board, or between different departments within the Fund. We do not pursue this issue in any detail in this chapter although we implicitly allude to it on occasions.
7 A strong version of this approach may be found in Vaubel (1991, 1994) although a softer version also exists (Willett, 2002) which emphasizes automony and a desire to avoid failure as determinants of actions by IMF officials.
8 This argument has often been made anecdotally. It was made in the context of the 1980s debt crisis by Finch (1989) and has been made more recently and with some force by Feldstein (1998) and by the Meltzer Commission (IFIAC, 2000).

Bibliography

Baqir, R., Ramcharan, R. and Sahay, R. (2003) 'IMF programme design and growth: what Is the link?', processed, Washington, DC: IMF.
Barro, R.J. and Jong-Wha Lee. (2001) 'IMF programs: who is chosen and what are the effects', paper presented at the second IMF Research Conference.
Bird, G. (1996) 'Borrowing from the IMF: the policy implications of recent empirical research', *World Development*, 24: 1753–1760.

Bird, G. (2001) 'IMF programs: do they work? Can they be made to work better?', *World Development*, 29: 1849–1865.

—— (2002a) 'The completion rate of IMF programmes; what we know, don't know and need to know', *The World Economy*, 25: 833–847.

—— (2002b) 'The credibility and signalling effect of IMF programmes', *Journal of Policy Modeling*, 24: 799–811.

Bird, G. and Orme, T. (1981) 'An analysis of drawings on the IMF by developing countries', *World Development*, 9: 563–568.

Bird, G. and Rowlands, D. (2001) 'IMF lending: how is it affected by economic, political and institutional factors?', *Journal of Policy Reform*, 4: 243–270.

—— (2002a) 'Do IMF programmes have a catalytic effect on other international capital flows?', *Oxford Development Studies*, 20: 229–249.

—— (2002b) 'IMF lending: an analysis of prediction failures', *Journal of Policy Reform*, 5: 173–186.

Conway, P. (1994) 'IMF lending programs: participation and impact', *Journal of Development Economics*, 45: 355–391.

Cornelius, P. (1987) 'The demand for IMF credits by sub-Saharan African countries', *Economics Letters*, 23: 99–102.

Feldstein, M. (1998) 'Refocusing the IMF', *Foreign Affairs*, 77: 20–23.

Finch, D.C. (1989) *The IMF: The Record and the Prospect*, Essays in International Finance, 175, Princeton, NJ: Princeton University Press.

Haque, N. and Khan, M.S. (1998) 'Do IMF-supported programs work? A survey of the cross-country empirical evidence', IMF Working Paper, 98/169.

Hutchison, M.M. (2003) 'A cure worse than the disease? Currency crises and the output costs of IMF-supported stabilization programmes', in Dooley, M. and Frenkel, J.A. (eds), *Managing Currency Crises in Emerging Markets*, Chicago, IL: University of Chicago.

Independent Evaluation Office (2002) Evaluation of the *Prolonged Use of IMF Resources*, Report, Washington, DC: IMF.

International Financial Institution Advisory Commission (2000) Report of the IFIAC (the Meltzer Report), Washington, DC: US Government Printing Office.

Ivanova, A., Mayer, W., Mourmouras, A. and Anayiotas, G. (2001) 'What determines the success or failure of fund-supported programs?', IMF working paper.

Joyce, J.P. (1992) 'The economic characteristics of IMF program countries', *Economic Letters*, 38: 237–242.

Killick, T. (1995) *IMF Programmes in Developing Countries*, London: Routledge.

Knight, M. and Santaella, J.A. (1997) 'Economic determinants of IMF financial arrangements', *Journal of Development Economics*, 54: 405–436.

Mussa, M. and Savastano, M. (2000) 'The IMF approach to economic stabilization', in Bernanke, B.S. and Rotemberg, J.J. (eds), *NBER Macroeconomics Annual, 1999*, Cambridge, MA: MIT Press.

Przeworski, A. and Vreeland, J.R. (2000) 'The effect of IMF programs on economic growth', *Journal of Development Economics*, 62: 385–421.

Santaella, J.A. (1996) 'Stylized facts before IMF supported macroeconomic adjustment', *IMF Staff Papers*, 43: 502–544.

Thacker, S.C. (1999) 'The high politics of IMF lending', *World Politics*, 52: 38–75.

Vaubel, R. (1991) 'The political economy of the International Monetary Fund: a public choice analysis', in Vaubel, R. and Willett, T. (eds), *The Political Economy of International Organisations*, Boulder, CO: Westview Press.

—— (1994) 'The political economy of the IMF: a public choice analysis', in Bandow, D. and Vasquez, I. (eds), *Perpetuating Poverty: The World Bank, the IMF and the Developing World*, Washington, DC: Cato Institute.

Willett, T.D. (2002) 'Towards a broader public choice analysis of the International Monetary Fund', in Andrews, D.M., Henning, C.R. and Pauly, L.W. (eds), *Governing the World's Money*, Ithaca, NY and London: Cornell University Press.

3 The politics of IMF and World Bank lending

Will it backfire in the Middle East and North Africa?

Jane Harrigan, Chengang Wang and Hamed El-Said

3.1 Introduction

The Middle East and North Africa (MENA) consists of the predominately Islamic cultures of the Gulf Arab countries, the Levant, the countries of North Africa, plus Iran and the more industrialized country of Israel.[1] MENA assumes both political and economic significance. Politically, it is arguably the epicentre of world crisis, chronically war-prone and the site of the world's most protracted conflicts (Hinnebusch, 2003, p. 1); economically, it owns the bulk of the world's oil reserves and as such serves as the petrol tank of the world economy, driving in particular the US economic engine. The region benefited immensely from the sharp increase in oil prices in the 1970s. The resulting wealth financed an explosion of investment and growth in the oil-exporting countries. This investment, in turn, spilled over into other non-oil countries in the region via worker remittances, trade and capital flows (IMF, 2003), such that Yemen is now the only remaining low-income country. However, the wealth derived from the boom in oil export revenues failed to bring peace, political stability and sustained economic growth to the region.

In light of the region's geopolitically and economically strategic position in the world economy it is clear that economic and political factors are inextricably linked when it comes to the manner in which the West, particularly the USA, responds to the region's needs. The aim of this chapter is to examine the flow of funds from the International Monetary Fund (IMF) and the World Bank to the MENA region in order to assess the extent to which political factors have influenced this flow. It is often argued, particularly by the anti-globalization movement, that these two Washington-based multilaterals are strongly influenced by the economic and political needs of their major Western shareholders, especially the USA. This influence can take two forms – determining the geographical flow of funds that is, who gets what from the IMF and the World Bank; and influencing the conditionality attached to such funds that is, programme loan[2] recipients are expected to undertake economic liberalization programmes, which help to open up their economies to the global economy and thereby extend the reach of Western pro-capitalist and pro-globalization ideology.

There is a long and rich theoretical and empirical literature on the determinants of the geographical allocation of foreign aid.[3] It is generally accepted that this allocation is influenced by both recipient need and donor interest and that multilateral aid is less susceptible to donor interest than bilateral aid (Maizels and Nissanke, 1984; Rodrik, 1995). In the past donor interest has often reflected the geopolitics of the Cold War, with pro-Western regimes, regardless of economic need and their record on human rights, being large recipients of Western aid.[4] Now that the Cold War has been replaced by the War on Terror a new emphasis on aid flows to pro-Western regimes in the Islamic world and MENA[5] may well emerge. For example, post 9/11 the USA has been increasingly up-front in suggesting that the War on Terror and US security are important reasons for foreign aid:

> The new century has brought new threats to US security and new challenges and opportunities for the national interest...Pre-empting threats and disasters is not the only reason that fostering development is in the U.S. interest. Successful development abroad generated diffuse benefits. It opens new more dynamic markets for U.S. goods and services. It generates more secure, promising environments for U.S. investment. It creates zones of order and peace where Americans can travel, study, exchange and do business safely. And it produces allies...
>
> (http://www.usaid.gov/fani/overview, p. 2)

Likewise, when President G.W. Bush proposed the first significant increase in US development assistance in a decade, he offered the following justification when speaking at the United Nations Financing for Development meeting in Monterrey, Mexico in March 2002: 'We fight poverty because hope is an answer to terror.'

The USA's concern with radical Islam considerably pre-dates 9/11. Even before the collapse of Communism in the late 1980s and early 1990s, a new theory was emerging to the effect that 'Islam [is] the new Communism and [hence represents] a grave threat to Western civilization' (Niva, 1998, p. 27). 'Rogue Sates', characterized by dissent from the 'Washington Consensus', were to be disciplined and contained: 'states that resist the Pan-Americana face economic and political isolation and no longer have a superpower sponsor to turn to for support', and, if they persist in their challenge, 'can expect to feel the sting of American military might' (Hubbell, 1998, p. 9). Obedient regimes or allies, on the other hand, particularly if they were threatened by Islamists, were to be rewarded for serving Western interests, and 'supported...in their brutal repression of all shades of Islamist activism in the name of eradicating terrorism' (Niva, 1998, p. 27). The upshot was a subversion and arrest of the region's nascent process of political liberalization. More importantly, the end of the Cold War replaced the old dichotomy in the Arab World between conservative pro-Western and socialist pro-Communist Arab regimes with a new and less covert formula based on 'friends or allies, or good or bad' regimes (Perthes, 1998, p. 30).

It is possible therefore that past aid allocations to MENA have been influenced by US foreign policy. Our interest is to see whether this has affected the flow of funds from the IMF and World Bank. In addition, we can speculate that if there is evidence that past financial flows into MENA have responded to donor interest rather than recipient need, then, given the post 9/11 foreign policy concerns of the West, this may well intensify in the future. This has two important implications, which go beyond the scope of this chapter. First, the allocation of aid funds according to donor interest rather than recipient need is likely to reduce the developmental impact of aid – the most needy countries or those that can use aid to the best of effect will not receive their due share.

Second, the politically motivated flow of funds to MENA may well backfire. The flows of programme aid funds from the IMF and World Bank almost always have economic liberalization conditions attached to them. Such reform conditions may well have negative social ramifications in the recipients. For example, reforms such as privatization, removal of state subsidies on foodstuffs, devaluation and trade liberalization can potentially increase unemployment and income inequality as well as reduce real incomes of the poor. This, in turn, may lead to the growth of anti-reform movements challenging incumbent regimes. There is already ample anecdotal evidence that this has occurred. The 1990s and the first four years of the twenty-first century have witnessed a rise in the number and forms of distributive conflicts in the Arab World, including riots, demonstrations, strikes, violence, assassinations, clashes with labour unions and university students in addition to an increase in crime rate (Ayubi, 1995; Richards and Waterbury, 1996; El-Ghonemy, 1998; Shafiq, 1998; *The Economist*, 2002). Quite often this unrest has an explicitly anti-Western and anti-IMF focus. For example, the IMF-induced lifting of price supports sparked rioting in Jordan in April 1989, August 1996 and again in early 2003. On each occasion, the rioters were trans-Jordanians (as opposed to Palestinians), the Hashemites' traditional backbone of support and once known for their unconditional loyalty to the regime (Brand, 1994; ICG, 2003).

Many such opposition movements have centred on Islamic-based political parties. Political Islam and Islamic fundamentalism should not be confused. But a vicious cycle of declining social welfare caused by possible effects of economic liberalization, increased domestic opposition to pro-Western local regimes implementing such programmes and repression of such opposition by the same regimes is likely to force frustrated religiously based political groups into increasingly extremist responses as well as enhancing their appeal to impoverished and disaffected members of society. Given that IMF and World Bank programme loans to developing countries are intimately associated with economic liberalization packages, an analysis of the past determinants of the flow of IMF and Bank funds into MENA is important.

The remainder of this chapter is divided up as follows. In the next section we provide background information on the general trends in aid flows to the MENA region. This is followed by an assessment of what is already known about the geo-political influences on aid flows to the MENA region and the potential for this to operate via the IMF and World Bank. From this we conclude that there is scope for IMF and World Bank lending in the region to respond to the political interests of their major shareholders, particularly the USA. We support these arguments with both a qualitative and a quantitative analysis of the determinants of World Bank and IMF programme lending to the region, focusing on both economic need in the MENA countries and the politics of donor interest before concluding.

3.2   Trends in aid flows to MENA

The MENA region has been the second largest regional recipient of aid in the period since 1960. From 1960 to 2001, the MENA region received nearly US$329 billion of aid (in 2000 prices), which only its poor neighbour sub-Saharan Africa exceeds by a large margin. By contrast, regions such as South and Central Asia have received less than MENA despite having larger numbers of their population below the poverty line.

The inflow of foreign aid to the MENA region has varied substantially with regard to historical period. Figure 3.1 depicts the trend of aid inflow since 1960. There are three distinct periods that can be identified: the downward trend of the 1960s, the boom of the 1970s and the contraction of the 1980s and 1990s with exception of the Gulf War period. This kind of trend is only partially in line with the world trend and two regional-specific factors help explain this. The oil boom years of 1973 to 1980 sparked large inflows of aid to MENA, especially in the form of non-DAC aid from the oil rich GCC countries, as shown in Figure 3.2. Similarly, the Gulf War accounts for the 1990–91 spike, which is purely a strategic and military consequence of the war.

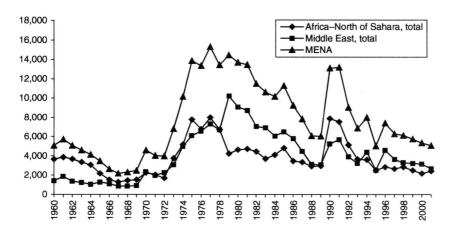

Figure 3.1 The trend of net ODA disbursement (all donors, US$ million – 2000 price).

Source: DAC online database.

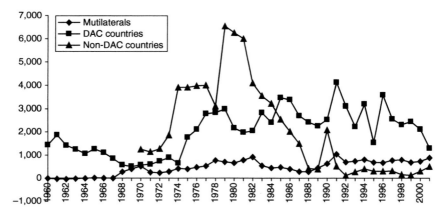

Figure 3.2 The source of net ODA disbursement (US$ million – 2000 price).
Source: DAC online database.

Table 3.1 US aid and World Bank aid to MENA

Middle East	USA	US share (%)	WB	WB share (%)	Total
Africa – North of Sahara					
1960–69	9,995.95	39	−49.3		25,610
1970–79	7,545.67	16	1,051.4	2	48,466
1980–89	16,303.53	42	1,191.7	3	39,084
1990–99	13,785.49	34	308.2	1	41,105
2000	629.13	29	22.8	1	2,184
2001	586.09	24	−1.0		2,403
Middle East					
1960–69	5,056.72	42	−76.4		11,969
1970–79	11,554.3	22	582.0	1	51,540
1980–89	19,787.32	33	691.3	1	60,860
1990–99	17,554.76	44	606.7	2	39,739
2000	1,216.42	39	47.3	2	3,141
2001	500.46	19	57.9	2	2,674

Source: DAC online database (in US$ million).

In terms of the importance of different donors to the region, the USA championed MENA in the 1960s, 1980s and 1990s, whilst the GCC was the largest donor in the 1970 (see Figure 3.2 and Table 3.1). The multilateral donors have been less important to the region than the bilaterals and although the World Bank is the largest multilateral donor its role pales into insignificance compared to that of the USA, as shown in Table 3.1. The same is true of the IMF (Appendix Tables 3A.1–3A.3 provide details of all IMF and World Bank programme loans to MENA countries as well as details of Paris Club debt arrangements). However, in

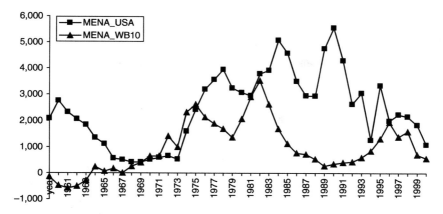

Figure 3.3 USA aid trend World Bank trend.

Source: DAC online database.

Note
US$ million – 2000 price and World Bank figures times 10.

the light of our question as to whether IMF and World Bank lending in the region is influenced by the political interests of the West, especially the USA, it is interesting to note that the World Bank's disbursement trend is quite similar to that of the USA, apart from early years and the Gulf War Period, as shown in Figure 3.3.

In terms of destination of aid in the MENA region, DAC aid is quite concentrated. Between 1961 and 2001 Egypt received 35.4 per cent of MENA aid and Israel 26.6 per cent. Hence, these two countries are by far the largest accounting for more than 60 per cent of DAC aid into the region, followed by Morocco 8.0 per cent, Jordan 5.3 per cent and Tunisia 4.5 per cent.

3.3   Politics, aid and MENA – what do we already know?

Three facts are already established in the literature – bilateral aid flows are influenced by donor political interest; flows into MENA, most notably Egypt and Israel, are partly politically determined; and the USA wields considerable power and influence in the IMF and World Bank.

Many aid allocation studies based on models which incorporate variables representing both donor interest[6] and/or recipient need have reached the conclusion that donor interest is an important determinant of the geographic allocation of aid, especially on the part of bilateral donors (Jalée, 1968; Frank, 1969; Hayter, 1971, 1981; Hensman, 1971; McKinlay and Little, 1977, 1978, 1979; Maizels and Nissanke, 1984; Berthelmy and Tichit, 2002; Feeny and McGillivray, 2002; McGillivray, 2003). Our own recent study, based on a mathematical model of the aid allocation process and employing a fixed effects model with panel data, produced a similar result (Harrigan and Wang, 2004).[7]

A number of the aid allocation studies also introduce dummies to reflect specific strategic links between donors and certain recipients. This is most common in the context of MENA, where dummies are often introduced for Egypt and Israel when the database includes these two countries. Many of these studies find these dummies to be positive and significant, for example, Alesina and Dollar (2002) among many others. The Egypt and Israel dummies reflect that fact that these two countries are key strategic allies to the West, especially the USA, such that donor interest is likely to have a positive influence on aid allocations. According to Feeny and McGillivray (2002, p. 14) 'Israel's relationship with the United States is arguably one of the most intense between a donor and a recipient'.

More recent and advanced aid allocation studies produce similar results. For example, Berthelemy and Tichit (2002) use three-dimensional panel data (recipient–year–donor) and a Tobit model with independent variables representing recipient need, recipient policy performance and donor interest. A dummy variable was introduced to reflect the US–Egypt link. The dummy parameter was particularly large in the 1980s sub-period following the Camp David Peace Accord with Israel. The analysis suggested the privileged assistance enjoyed by Egypt from the United States translates to an aid bonus of US$49 per capita. Alesina and Dollar (2002) likewise introduces special relationship dummies into their analysis in a donor interest and recipient need model. A special relationship dummy was introduced for the USA, which took the value of 1 for Egypt and Israel and zero for all other countries. The dummy was found to be statistically significant at the 95 per cent confidence level. Feeny and McGillivray (2002) apply a donor interest and recipient need model to data for 10 principal recipients of bilateral aid over the period 1968–99. They introduced a Gulf War dummy for Egypt (equals one for 1990–92 period) and a Camp David dummy for Israel (equals one from 1978 onwards) and again both were found to be significant.

Our own work (Harrigan and Wang, 2004) has enabled us to go beyond simple dummies for Egypt and Israel and to make more country specific observations regarding the influence of donor interest in aid allocations to MENA countries. In our base regression, we have applied a fixed effects model to panel data to analyse the determinants of aid allocations by various classes of donors (with 2,484 observations covering 32 years and 138 recipients). The donor–recipient fixed effects coefficients for MENA countries are reported in Table 3.2. These coefficients capture donor–recipient specific effects that is, they show the linkages between donor and specific recipients, which include long-term strategic relations, economic linkages, colonial ties, etc. As can be seen from Table 3.2, donor interest, as represented by the fixed effects coefficient, has a strong positive effect in the allocation of US aid (LUSMPC) to Israel and Jordan, two of the most strategically important US allies in the region, and a strong negative effect on US aid allocation to Iran, Sudan and Yemen, countries traditionally hostile to US foreign policy in the region. As expected, the fixed effects coefficients for multilateral aid (LMULTMPC) are much smaller, although links between

Table 3.2 Donor–recipients fixed effects coefficients for MENA countries

Country	USA	Non-USA	Multilateral
Egypt	0.87	1.56	0.72
Iran	−1.61	−0.21	−0.83
Israel	6.03	1.40	−1.22
Jordan	2.41	0.85	0.67
Lebanon	0.91	0.00	0.72
Morocco	0.35	1.23	0.25
Sudan	−1.90	−0.24	0.18
Syria	−0.34	−1.45	−0.49
Tunisia	0.65	1.34	0.39
Turkey	−0.60	1.46	0.15
Yemen	−2.24	−0.55	−0.23

Source: Harrigan and Wang (2004).

Table 3.3 Optimal versus actual 1996 aid allocation in selected MENA countries

Country	Poverty-efficient allocation	Actual aid
Jordan	0.0	3.26
Egypt	0.0	1.31
Morocco	0.0	0.70
Tunisia	0.0	0.29
Algeria	0.0	0.22

Source: Collier and Dollar (2002, table 3, in per cent of GDP).

multilateral aid and Egypt, as well as Jordan and Lebanon, are evident. Interestingly, Israel is not favoured by the multilaterals, in contrast to its special relationship with the USA.

Another recent study of aid allocation, which enables conclusions specific to some of the MENA countries is that of Collier and Dollar (2002). In their paper they compare the actual allocation of aid with an optimal poverty-efficient allocation of aid, with the latter assumed to depend on each recipient's level of poverty, the elasticity of poverty with respect to income, and the quality of its policies. Comparing actual 1996 aid allocations with the optimum they find that a large number of middle-income countries with poor policy receive excessive amounts of aid. The significance of their results in the context of MENA is that none of the MENA countries in their sample of 59 developing countries should receive any aid on the poverty-efficient criteria. Table 3.3 compares this optimal allocation with the actual aid receipts of such countries in 1996. Jordan in particular stands out as a country receiving aid equivalent to 3.26 per cent of its GDP as opposed to 0 per cent under the optimal Collier and Dollar allocation.

Although there seems to be ample evidence that bilateral aid flows to the MENA region are influenced by donor interest, a common view is that flows from multilaterals such as the IMF and World Bank are less likely to be influenced in this way since they do not represent the interests of any particular country. Indeed, the Bank and Fund Articles of Agreement explicitly state that lending decisions should not be influenced by political factors.[8] The IMF is supposed to limit itself to matters of macroeconomics in dealing with a country, namely, the government's budget deficit, its monetary policy, its inflation, its trade deficit, its borrowing from abroad; and the World Bank is supposed to be concerned with medium term structural economic issues (Stiglitz, 2002).

In theory, the clauses in the Articles of Agreement should rule out the possibility of IMF or World Bank involvement in political affairs. However, in reality, it seems that this has only reduced the level of politicization in their actions rather than removed it altogether. Therefore, it is possible that IMF and World Bank lending provide donors with another arms length instrument to pursue their own interests. Indeed, since IMF and Bank lending decisions are deemed less politically oriented, this may enable donors to pursue certain objectives through these two institutions that may be too costly or difficult to blatantly pursue via their own bilateral aid programmes.

Donors can employ multilateral lending to complement their own foreign aid strategy in several ways. The first way applies to the extreme situation when a donor's relations with a particular recipient are so strained that the donor is unable to exert any direct influence. For example, when Bangladesh was liberated on 16 December 1971, the World Bank was encouraged to provide funds to the new country by the US government whose own hostile posture towards the emergence of Bangladesh made it difficult to establish a presence or any sort of access to the political leadership and decision-makers. Hence, it was hoped that the Bank would establish itself in Bangladesh as a useful proxy for western interests (Sobhan, 1982, p. 170).

Second, the immense power of the IMF and World Bank, especially the former, means that their ability to influence developing countries with rewards and punishments is considerable. For example, an IMF agreement is the key to access to the international capital market for many developing countries – it is required for debt relief from the Paris Club and may facilitate the flow of funds from other official and commercial sources. Because the IMF can impose punishments or rewards which are much wider in scope than those which any single donor country can impose, Western donors may well try to influence the IMF stance in a particular country to consolidate or reinforce the existing commercial, strategic and political alignments which have already been pursued by their own bilateral aid policy.

The last and perhaps most important reason why individual donors might see the IMF and World Bank as productive avenues through which to pursue their own interests, arises from the conditionality attached to multilateral lending. This can be seen to serve the donor's objective of altering the behaviour of recipient governments. For example IMF and World Bank economic reform conditions encourage developing countries to adopt Western-style capitalism and open up their economies to the global economy and Western investors. Indeed, the acceptability of such extensive multilateral conditionality derives partly from the perception that the World Bank and the IMF operate somewhat autonomously from policy makers in Western capitals and in a relative non-political manner (Rodrik, 1995). Given the considerable power the IMF and World Bank can wield in developing countries, the Western member countries are likely to be keen to exercise leverage over both institutions in order to help pursue their own interests.

Analysis of the voting power of the USA in the IMF and World Bank clearly shows that the USA has the capacity to exercise such leverage. Indeed, a common criticism of the operation of IMF and World Bank is that their decision-making process is dominated by the G-7 countries, especially the USA. The Bretton Woods institutions have systems of governance based on weighted voting. Each member possesses a number of votes, which depends on its quota allocation and which must be cast as a bloc. Legally, general decisions require a simple majority (51 per cent) and fundamental decisions require a special majority of 85 per cent of the votes. This leads to a problem of democratic legitimacy since a member's influence or voting power within such a decision-making system does not in general correspond to its voting weight.

Using voting power analysis,[9] Dennis Leech and Robert Leech (2005) and Dennis Leech (2002) show that the USA possesses considerably more power than voting weight in relation to ordinary decisions requiring a simple majority.[10] They conclude 'Weighted voting tends to further enhance the power of the United States at the expense of all other members in both the board of Governors and the Executive board' (Leech and Leech, 2005) and 'Our principal result is that the voting power of the USA turns out to be far greater than its quota would warrant' (ibid., p. 3).

Given America's voting power advantage in the IMF and World Bank, Mckeown *et al.* (1999) have argued that there is no reason why American policy makers would not be expected to use this power in order to promote adherence to US alliances; to secure the strengthening of a regime friendly to the USA or to weaken a hostile regime by removing a source of support; and to win trade or investment concessions. Conteh-Morgan (1990) and Zimmerman (1993) have made a similar argument. The influence of the US government is further evidenced by the fact that the American Executive Director 'is ordered by law to clear his or her decision with the Secretary of the Treasury' (Swedberg, 1986, p. 379) and each major decision must have the approval of the US Senate and Congress (Smith, 1984).

In defence of its weighted voting system, the IMF argues:

> Most IMF decisions (the day-to-day decisions that require 51 percent majority) reflect not a formal vote but a consensus... since all decisions in IMF get broad support, indicating that if a vote were held, the majority would be much higher; clearly, the United States and/or a coalition of industrial countries could veto the important decisions (requiring a 70 percent or 85 percent majority), so could a bloc of developing countries since, as a group, these countries represent about 37 percent of voting power in the Executive Board.
> (http://www.imf.org/external/np/exr/ccrit/eng/crans.html)

However, such a defence ignores the process of how such consensus is reached and, in particular, who has the final say. For the day-to-day decisions, we know little about this process due to lack of scrutiny of IMF and World Bank behaviour and information closure.[11] Joseph Stiglitz's insight as a former Bank insider is illuminating:

> You won't find hard evidence of a terrible conspiracy by Wall Street and the IMF to take over the world.... The truth is subtler. Often it's tone of voice, or a meeting behind closed doors, or a memo that determines the outcome of discussion.
>
> (2002, preface p. xv)

In addition, although the developing countries represent 37 per cent of votes in the IMF and hence have a potential veto in major decisions, this ignores the fact that they are heavily dependent on industrialized countries for imports, exports, aid, technology, security etc. and so may end up compromising their interests.[12]

A number of empirical studies have attempted to provide more rigour to the above analysis by trying to identify and quantify the specific determinants of IMF lending.[13] These studies can be divided into two types: the first attempts to explain the amount of IMF lending; and the second approach seeks to explain whether or not countries had programmes rather than seeking to explain the amount of lending. In both approaches, four sets of variables can be introduced into the analysis with respect to four hypotheses: does IMF lending respond to recipient's economic need (variables include: GDP per capita, balance of payment, debt service ratio); do institutional factors influence IMF's lending activities (variables include: programme completion ratio, IMF liquidity, past IMF programme and imminent quota review); is IMF lending influenced by the major political powers, for example USA's political and strategic interests (variables include: UN general assembly voting pattern, colony history, recipient's trade relationship with major donors, bank exposure); and finally are the recipient's political conditions considered in the IMF's lending decision-making process (variables include: regime type and changes, election, civil freedom and so on).

Joyce (1992), Conway (1994), Knight and Santaella (1997) concentrated on economic determinants. Some consensus has emerged with respect to key economic variables, though they are not always measured in the same manner. Declines in export earnings, high debt service ratios and the presence of arrears on debts, as well as histories of other financial problems are all associated with a higher likelihood of an IMF agreement being signed. Many other economic measures, such as GDP per capita and the balance of payments have inconsistent effects across the different studies.

Based on a simple macroeconomic model, Thacker (1999) conducted a test on whether IMF lending is politicized by introducing variables of political proximity (UN voting pattern, similarity between USA and recipient) and political movement (the shift of recipient's voting pattern towards US voting pattern). His results show that movement toward the United States within a defined international political space can significantly increase a country's chances of receiving a loan from the IMF. The results from similar studies (e.g. Rowlands, 1995; Barro and Lee, 2001; Bird and Rowlands, 2001) are generally consistent with Thacker's findings, but divergent at the level of US influence intensity. For example, Rowlands (1995) concludes that the evidence for systematic US influence is less strong than that commonly expected.

It is not just the receipt of a loan that may be influenced by Western countries, the terms of the loan might also be affected. A series of case studies conducted for a project by Killick (1995, pp. 118–119) reveals that at least one-third of seventeen countries studied secured favourable loan terms on their IMF programmes due to the intervention of major shareholding countries on their behalf.

Regarding World Bank lending, Fleck and Kilby (2001) used panel data to examine the geographic distribution of the World Bank lending from 1968 to 1992 and conclude 'Countries with strong U.S trade ties received a significant share of the World Bank lending than comparable countries with weak ties; Countries which the U.S favoured with bilateral aid received a disproportionate share of the World Bank funds as well' and such effects 'vary across U.S presidential administrations' (Fleck and Kilby, 2001, p. 16). In a more qualitative analysis of the World Bank, Schoultz (1982) has documented that the World Bank's 'interests' in a given loan or aid package are often influenced by the US Executive and Congress.

IMF lending may also be influenced by political conditions in recipient countries, such as democratization or elections. For instance, as Vaubel suggested:

> The ruling politicians try to influence the domestic business cycle in their favour by generating a boom at the time of election and low popularity and by reversing the impulse thereafter. IMF lending facilitates the expansion. IMF conditionality facilitates the contraction. In this way, the IMF tends to contribute to the generation of political business cycles.
>
> (1991, p. 213)

Dreher and Vaubel (2002) conduct a formal test of the political business cycles using regression analysis. They found IMF credits in the more democratic recipient countries are larger in pre-election and post-election years, while the credits in more authoritarian regimes are marginally smaller in post-election years.

The above literature review has indicated that donor influence, including strategic geopolitical interests, influence aid allocations, especially allocations in the MENA region, and that the IMF and World Bank are not immune from the influences of their major shareholders, particularly the USA. We now turn to look more specifically at the determinants of IMF and World Bank programme lending in MENA in order to assess to what extent it has been determined by recipient need and to what extent by donor interests. We adopt two approaches – a qualitative analysis of the timing of Bank and Fund loans and a more formal quantitative analysis based upon a Probit model.

3.4   The timing of IMF and World Bank programmes in key MENA recipients: a qualitative analysis

3.4.1   Recipient economic need

Although IMF and World Bank programme loans have only been a small percentage of total aid flows into the MENA region they nevertheless have the capacity to profoundly influence the recipient economies via the loan conditionality. In the past such conditionality has brought with it economic reform via structural adjustment and stabilization programmes. A cursory glance at economic performance in the region makes it clear that reform was indeed needed in many MENA countries in the post-1980 period.

The overall growth performance of the MENA region since the 1960s has been disappointing. Table 3.4 compares MENA growth with other regions. The MENA growth performance in terms of real GDP per capita is only slightly better than sub-Saharan Africa and it is the only region that has experienced a contraction. The relatively better performance in the 1960s and 1970s is respectable and can be largely attributed to the favourable external environment in the form of high oil prices. Even so, the performance pales into insignificance compared with that of the most successful NICs in East Asia.

There are many factors contributing to this disappointing performance. Makdisi *et al.* (2000) conclude that in comparing the growth pattern of the MENA region within an international perspective, capital is less efficient; the natural resource curse more pronounced; trade openness less beneficial to growth; the impact of adverse external shocks higher and the effect of output volatility on growth more detrimental.

In order to fully understand economic performance in the region and the evident need for both financial support and economic reform from the mid-1980s onwards (and hence a role for the IMF and World Bank) it is necessary to divide performance into sub-periods.

The 20-year-long (1973–92) slow down of world economic growth is best understood in terms of two critical events: two massive oil price rises of 1973 and 1979–80; and the consequent developing country debt crisis which erupted in 1982. The lost decade of the 1980s and subsequent 1990s under-performance in

Table 3.4 Regional comparison of real GDP per capita growth

Region	1961–70	1971–80	1981–90	1991–2000
MENA	3.9	3.0	−1.3	1.4
East Asia	4.3	3.6	2.6	2.0
Latin America	2.7	2.3	0.5	2.0
Sub-Saharan	1.8	1.6	0.2	0.3
World	3.1	2.5	1.0	0.6

Source: WDI 2002 CD-ROM.

Table 3.5 Selected economic indicators of the MENA 1975–2000

Year	1975–79	1980–84	1985–89	1990–94	1995–99	2000
GDP growth (%)	6.2	2.3	1.3	4.4	2.96	3.9
GDP per capita (constant 1995 US$)	1,908.5	1,882.3	1,759.1	1,842.7	1,909.1	1,983.1
Gross domestic savings (% of GDP)	36.7	28.7	18.7	22.2	23.1	30.5
Gross capital formation (% of GDP)	29.5	27.4	23.6	24.6	21.7	20.4
Export (% of GDP)	42.0	36.2	23.9	32.0	30.7	37.9
Import (% of GDP)	34.8	35.0	30.1	34.5	29.3	27.9

Source: WDI 2002 CD-ROM.

the MENA region are also rooted in these two events. During the 1973–81 period, the region's wealth and industrial structure was concentrated on oil. During this period the region as a whole also enjoyed substantial inflows of so called Official Development Assistance (ODA) from DAC bilateral donors, non-DAC bilateral donors and multilateral donors. As shown in Table 3.5, the 1970s was a golden period for the MENA region. GDP growth averaged over 6 per cent per annum, gross domestic savings and capital formation were a respectable 37 and 29 per cent of GDP respectively and both export and import coefficients were high. On the back of this wealth public expenditure expanded with a strengthening of both state welfarism and state economic activity.

However, when oil prices softened in the 1980s, the structural weaknesses of the economies in the region, especially the over-reliance on oil, became apparent.[14] As can be seen from Table 3.5, growth declined and per capita GDP decreased by an average 1.0 per cent per year in the 1980s, a rate worse than any other developing region, except sub-Saharan Africa. Other economic indicators also pointed in the same direction: the saving rate and investment rate dropped to 18 per cent of GDP and 24 per cent of GDP in the late 1980s and the export/GDP and import/GDP ratios also declined to 24 and 30 per cent.

The disappointing economic performance of the MENA region in the 1980s can be attributed to a number of factors. Internally, a high population growth rate, poor economic management, corruption, and prolonged heavy protection led to high unemployment and economic inefficiency. It is also worth noting that during the oil boom years, despite having high domestic saving rates and high inflows of foreign aid, investment in the MENA region was well below the saving capacities. Consequently, resources were mostly diverted towards consumption as well as non-productive investment. Externally, the softening of oil prices and the increased competition against other MENA exporting industries,[15] especially from Southeast Asian countries, put the region's economy in a critical condition.

The extent of crisis can be seen when we look at key macroeconomic indicators for countries in the region who were to become major recipients of IMF and

World Bank programme loans. In the period since 1981 Egypt received one programme loan from the Bank and four from the Fund, Jordan received eight from the Bank and six from the Fund, Morocco eleven from the Bank and seven from the Fund and Tunisia nine from the Bank and two from the Fund. More recently from 1989 onwards Algeria has received four from the Bank and four from the Fund.[16] Hence, we concentrate our political economy analysis on these five countries. Details of the IMF and the Bank programmes implemented in the above countries are listed in Appendix Tables 3A.2 and 3A.3 respectively, and debt relief or rescheduling from the Paris Club is given in Appendix Table 3A.4. Macroeconomic indicators for the above five countries indicate that inflation and current account imbalances were built up in the 1970s and persisted throughout the 1980s, the central government debt and total debt service ratio were also high in the 1970s and became even worse in the 1980s. With the rising debt and high inflation, gross capital formation started to decline from the early 1980s and never looked like bouncing back to the peak level of the late 1970s. In light of this fall in investment, the decline in GDP per capita growth witnessed in all five countries during the 1980s seems inevitable.

However, a more nuanced analysis, which looks at the specific timing of loans and corresponding macroeconomic indicators in each recipient suggests that the determinants of lending often do not reflect recipient economic need. Table 3.6 provides macroeconomic data for each of the five countries for the year in which each received its first IMF loan and for the previous five years (Egypt received two distinct phases of loans and so is represented twice).[17] By looking at the macroeconomic variables for the year in which each country received the first of its series of IMF loans and comparing them with the previous period we can see if there is evidence that the granting of the first loan coincided with severe macroeconomic distress. The results are surprising.

Algeria

Algeria received its first IMF Standby Loan in 1989. Comparing 1989 with the previous five years it does not seem that Algeria was in exceptional distress in terms of inflation, the current account balance, gross capital formation or GDP growth. Indeed, GDP growth had bounced back after three years of negative growth. The only variable that shows any sign of significant deterioration is the debt service ratio, which had doubled compared to 1984. However, in the year in which Algeria was granted its first IMF programme the debt service ratio was already beginning to improve. This cursory glance at the type of macroeconomic variables that the IMF usually considers when deciding whether a country is in need of a loan seems to suggest that Algeria's first IMF loan in 1989 cannot be explained by the standard analysis of recipient need. As will be argued below, it is possible that important changes in Algeria's domestic politics and foreign policy provide an alternative explanation of the timing of the 1989 loan.

Egypt

Egypt received its first IMF loan in 1976 followed by a new phase of loans that commenced in 1987. The first 1976 loan does seem to coincide with a period of increased inflation and a deterioration in the current account. However, in terms of debt service, gross capital formation and GDP growth there is no indication of problematic performance. Given that inflation and the current account are often regarded as critical indicators by the IMF it would seem that the 1976 loan reflects a degree of recipient need. The picture, however, is very different for the 1987 loan. There is no indication of macroeconomic instability in 1987. Indeed, all variables apart from the GDP growth rate were improving in 1987. Although some of the improvement may be due to the IMF programme itself, given that the loan was signed in May, the previous year's data, apart from inflation, do not suggest any increase in macroeconomic distress. Again, it seems we must look for other factors, which go beyond recipient need to help explain the 1987 IMF loan.

Jordan

Jordan's IMF programmes began in 1989. In this case there is much more evidence of macroeconomic crisis. Inflation, the build up of central government debt and GDP growth all registered a significant deterioration in 1989. The previous two years had also seem escalation in the debt service ratio. However, as we will argue below, the 1989 economic crisis in Jordan was inextricably linked with changes in domestic politics and foreign policy, both of which may also have played a part in loan timing.

Morocco

Morocco commenced her IMF programmes in 1983 but on the macroeconomic data contained in Table 3.6 would not seem to be an obvious candidate for such programmes. Inflation, the current account and debt service ratio all improved in 1983 and this cannot be ascribed to the IMF programme itself, as the loan was not signed until September. The only variable that worsened dramatically in 1983 was the GDP growth rate, which is not a variable IMF programmes traditionally responded to in the 1980s.

Tunisia

Tunisia became an IMF Standby recipient in 1986. As with Morocco, there is little sign of recipient need in terms of the standard variables of concern to the IMF. Inflation, the current account and debt indicators were showing no notable deterioration. Again, evidence of need is limited and it seems, as with Morocco and Egypt in the 1980s, that the only obvious indicator of need contained in Table 3.6 is the decline in GDP per capita growth.

Table 3.6 Macroeconomic indicators for selected countries

Countries	1971	1972	1973	1974	1975	1976	1978	1979	1980	1981	1982	1983	1984	1985	1986	1987	1988	1989
Algeria																		
Inflation, consumer prices													8.1	10.5	12.4	7.4	5.9	9.3
Current account balance													0.1	1.8	−3.5	0.2	−3.5	−1.9
Central government debt																		
Total debt service													36.8	35.6	56.4	53.4	76.6	66.8
Gross capital formation													35.2	34.6	33.6	27.6	27.6	30.1
GDP per capita growth													2.2	0.5	−2.4	−3.5	−3.6	1.8
Egypt																		
Inflation, consumer prices	3.1	2.1	5.1	10.0	9.7	10.3					14.8	16.1	17.0	12.1	23.9	19.7		
Current account balance	−5.7	−5.3	−5.8	−17.7	−21.2	−10.2					−9.9	−5.4	−8.2	−9.3	−9.4	−2.3		
Central government debt															0.0	0.0		
Total debt service	21.8	32.5	31.1	11.9	10.3	6.4					19.3	20.1	21.4	25.8	27.0	17.9		
Gross capital formation	13.2	12.3	13.1	22.5	33.4	28.4					30.1	28.7	27.5	26.7	23.7	26.1		
GDP per capita growth	1.6	0.2	−1.1	0.5	6.8	12.2					7.1	4.6	3.4	3.9	0.1	0.0		
Jordan																		
Inflation, consumer prices													3.8	3.0	0.0	−0.2	6.6	25.7
Current account balance													−5.3	−4.9	−0.7	−5.4	−4.6	4.4
Central government debt													49.6	56.4	59.0	70.1	100.1	126.1

Total debt service	13.0	17.2	19.7	24.0	30.9	19.7
Gross capital formation	28.8	20.5	20.5	23.3	23.5	23.7
GDP per capita growth	4.6	-0.2	3.1	-0.8	-5.2	-16.5
Morocco						
Inflation, consumer prices	9.7	8.3	9.4	12.5	10.5	6.2
Current account balance	-9.9	-9.4	-7.5	-12.0	-12.1	-6.4
Central government debt	38.2	39.8	41.7	53.4	58.4	73.2
Total debt service	22.9	26.6	33.4	38.4	45.4	40.3
Gross capital formation	25.4	24.5	24.2	26.1	28.2	24.0
GDP per capita growth	0.0	2.5	1.3	-4.9	7.2	-2.7
Tunisia						
Inflation, consumer prices				8.9	7.3	6.2
Current account balance	-5.4	-8.1	-6.8	-9.3	-6.9	-6.7
Central government debt	35.1	38.2	41.5	42.3	45.5	56.5
Total debt service	15.2	16.2	19.3	22.7	25.0	28.4
Gross capital formation	32.3	31.7	33.5	35.9	30.2	26.6
GDP per capita growth	2.8	-3.1	2.0	3.7	2.5	-4.5

Source: GDI 2002.

Note
Inflation, consumer prices (annual %); current account balance (% of GDP); central government debt, total (% of GDP); total debt service (% of exports of goods and service); gross capital formation (% of GDP); GDP per capita growth (annual %).

In summary, the 1980s, when most IMF programmes in the MENA region commenced, was a period of generally deteriorating economic performance for the region as a whole. There was a clear need for both external finance to help with growing debt burdens as well as a programme of economic reform to restructure many of the economies in the region and generate sustainable economic growth. Hence, the stage was set for entry of the IMF and World Bank with their stabilization and structural adjustment loans and we cannot deny the element of recipient need in this respect. However, an analysis of the exact timing of the first IMF loan in the five major recipients provides only limited evidence that economic need, as illustrated by key macroeconomic variables, was a determinant. Although it seems that Egypt's loan of 1976 and Jordan's loan of 1989 were a response to clear macroeconomic difficulties the evidence for Algeria, Morocco and Tunisia's first loans as well as Egypt's 1987 loan is much less clear cut. Indeed, if anything, in Morocco, Egypt and Tunisia it seems that the IMF was responding to the growth rate variable rather than the standard macroeconomic variables one usually associates with IMF programmes.[18] This would suggest that in many instances other factors might well have influenced the decision as to when a country is eligible to commence a series of IMF and World Bank programmes. It is to this issue that we now turn.

3.4.2   *Donor interest and the influence of the USA*

We have argued in an earlier section that there are reasons to suspect that the political interests of their major shareholders, particularly the USA, may well influence the flow of funds from the IMF and World Bank. Hence, in this section we present a qualitative analysis of the timing of the signing of World Bank and IMF programme loans in the major MENA recipients in order to see whether there is any evidence that political factors have been influential.

Jordan

While the 1989 agreement with the IMF and World Bank largely reflected dire domestic economic conditions, Jordan's experience with both bilateral and multilateral aid, before and after 1989, presents an excellent example of the subjection of such flows to the political interests of and pressure from major Western donors. Following on from the 1973 Arab–Israeli War and an Arab oil embargo against the USA, Washington increased pressure on the late King Hussein to sign an individual peace treaty with Israel. But with more than half of his population being of Palestinian origin, and without tacit support, if not direct participation, of the PLO,[19] a separate peace treaty with Israel would have been tantamount to political suicide. The USA 'frustration with King Hussein' led to the suspension of American aid to Jordan in 1978[20] (Shultz, 1993, p. 454). During this period, Jordan was neither favoured by the IMF nor the World Bank.

Although US pressure on Jordan to join Egypt and sign a peace treaty with Israel intensified in the early 1980s, particularly following President Reagan's 1982 proposed Peace Plan,[21] which placed Jordan in the position of representing the

Palestinian people, Hussein continued to develop closer relations with the PLO.[22] However, in the second half of the 1980s tension between Hussein and Arafat led to a rift on who should really represent the Palestinians in any peace settlement with Israel. Hussein consequently reverted to an old and by now well documented approach of continuing secret cooperation with the Israeli state, further intensified following the collapse of negations with the PLO in 1985 (Dallas, 1999). Hussein's dogged refusal to allow Arafat to gain ground in the West Bank and Gaza Strip (WBG) led to a hastily and ill thought out plan in 1988, when Jordan severed all economic and administrative ties with the WBG. Although the move aimed at curtailing Arafat's increasing popularity in the WBG, it backfired and proved detrimental to the Jordanian economy. With Jordan's Palestinians dominating the private sector, severing ties with the WBG created uncertainty with regard to their political future and presence in Jordan. They thus engaged in extensive capital flight and curtailed their investment and economic activities in the country, leading to Jordan's first real banking and financial crisis in 1989. Within the space of six months, the Jordanian Dinar lost almost 50 per cent of its nominal value, Jordan's external debt reached unsustainable levels and per capita income was almost halved (Kanovsky, 1989). Riots in the streets, sparked by rumours that the government was about to sign an agreement with the IMF and World Bank that would raise prices of commodities and lift subsidies on basic staples, resulted in a tactical move by King Hussein; he restored parliamentary elections in 1989 (suspended since the 1976 war), and within a span of two years abolished martial law, legalized political parties and sanctioned greater freedom of press. In July 1989, the IMF granted Jordan an SDR 60 million Stand-By Agreement and the World Bank provided a US$160 million SECAL for the industrial and trade sector. It seems that a complex interaction of the stance towards Israel and the WBG, the ensuing economic crisis and the attempted panacea in the form of political liberalization, all played a role in qualifying Jordan for IMF and World Bank Support in 1989.

With strong domestic opposition to foreign intervention in the region, Jordan took a neutral stand in the 1990–91 Gulf war and refused to openly support US-led attacks against Iraq. This led to a complete halting of aid flows to Jordan from the USA and its Arab allies in the Gulf and the temporary suspension of the IMF and World Bank agreements with two-thirds of the IMF Standby funds not being drawn. Squeezed financially, isolated internationally and ostracized regionally, the US-led pressure had the desired effect of prompting an 'alliance shift' (Brand, 1994, p. 20). Hussein soon criticized Saddam Hussein and openly talked about regime change in Iraq, and went further by hosting Iraqi opposition leaders. Following this revised stance, a new SDR 44.4 million Stand-By Agreement was signed with the IMF in February 1992.

Since the mid-1990s Jordan has been further rewarded for her peace overtures to Israel. In 1993, Jordan started direct negotiations with Israel under the Oslo Accords of 1991–92, leading in October to a Common Agenda agreement on issues related to territory and water, refugees, and arms control. In the same month, the World Bank granted Jordan a second US$80 million SECAL for the energy sector. This was followed in May 1994 by a SDR 130 million IMF Extended Fund Facility. In 1994, Jordan formally signed a peace treaty with Israel in *Wadi Araba*, formally ending the 46-year-old state of war between the two countries. Since then, Jordan not only became one of the largest recipients of US aid in the world, but also the recipient of a further six World Bank loans and three IMF loans. The political timing of many of these loans deserves attention. The third World Bank US$80 million SECAL for the agricultural sector came only three months after the *Wadi Araba* Agreement was signed. In the same year, the USA wrote off US$833 million of Jordan's debt and began providing Jordan with advanced weaponry. The fourth SECAL for the same amount came in October 1995, less than a month after Jordan's support for the OSLO II Accord under which Israel agreed to a partial withdrawal from the West Bank with administrative powers to be given to the Palestinian Authority. This period was also associated with a lapse in the political liberalization movement that was initiated in 1989. A new electoral law in 1993 reduced the Islamist power in the parliament, and the regime intensified security measures against Islamists and nationalists opposed to the peace treaty with Israel and the regime's closer alliance with the USA. The regime was bolstered in February 1996 by a SDR 238 million Extended Find Facility from the IMF. Finally, it is possible that the June 2001 US$120 SECAL for public sector reform was influenced by the need to provide further financial support to a regime increasingly under pressure from Islamists as the region became unsettled with the escalation of the Israeli–Palestinian conflict following Sharon's assumption of power – in the same month that the loan was signed King Abdullah dissolved the House of Representatives and postponed the general elections by Royal Decree.

In light of the above analysis, it would seem that the timing of at least nine of the fourteen programme loans that Jordan has received from the Bank and the Fund since 1989 may well have been influenced by Jordan's stance on Middle East affairs as well as changes on the domestic political front.

Algeria

Throughout the 1970s and 1980s Algeria was considered a rogue state by the non-communist West. In 1974 the country firmly rejected the 'open door policy' (infitah) adopted by Egypt and much of the Arab world which involved a shift in the balance of domestic economic power to the private sector, opening up to Western investment and accepting the hegemony of the USA. Instead, in 1976 President Boumedienne adopted a new socialist constitution and Islamic state, with the Islamist movement further promoted by his successor President Chadli Benjedid. During this period, which witnessed rapid industrialization and the successful development of domestic oil and gas, the West remained hostile to Algeria's anti-American regime (Pfeifer, 1996; Swearingen, 1996). In 1980, Algeria embarked on a successful liberalization programme designed to overcome the inefficiencies created by the previous import substituting industrialization strategy. Although the programme was not dissimilar to a standard IMF and World Bank package, Algeria, unlike its Western friendly neighbours Morocco and Tunisia, received little assistance. Whilst Morocco and Tunisia had more than a third of their annual external debt on concessional terms, Algeria was forced to finance its reform programme in the early and mid-1980s with market-based loans with only 3 per cent of her debt on concessional terms.

But reforms, associated with external borrowing on unfavourable terms, induced a ballooning of foreign debt. The collapse of oil and gas prices in 1986 followed by a large devaluation in 1988 led to escalating inflation and unemployment, which triggered strikes, riots and growing domestic opposition to the regime. The economic and political crisis prompted a shift in both domestic and international policy. In 1988 a new constitution restricting the military and allowing opposition parties was introduced. In early 1989, Algeria joined the new Arab Maghreb Union (UMA) which was committed to preventing the spread of radical Islam and fostering closer links between the Maghreb and the European Union. As in Jordan, Algeria's new pro-Western stance combined with domestic political liberalization was a signal for the arrival of the World Bank and IMF. In May 1989 the Fund granted a SDR 156 million Standby followed in August 1989 by a US$ 300 million structural adjustment loan from the World Bank. In total between 1989 and 1999 Algeria received four IMF stabilization loans (as well as a Compensatory Financing Facility) and four World Bank adjustment loans. The timing of several of these, as argued below, is noteworthy.

President Benjedid's political liberalization backfired producing unexpected support for the Islamic opposition. The Bank and the Fund responded in June 1991 by offering the embattled regime a SDR 300 million Standby and a US$350 million structural adjustment loan (the largest ever Bank programme loan to any country in the MENA region). The army, shaken by the Islamists' overwhelming victory in local elections, stepped in on January 1992, deposed Benjedid himself and cancelled the elections. A retired army general, Liamine Zeroul, was appointed by the army as the head of the state in January 1994, and confirmed President after the 1995 elections. The disposition of Benjedid and cancellation of elections ushered in a new and bloody era in Algeria's history, characterized by two main features. First, brutal repression of Islamists and other opposition in what became known as the 'dirty war'. Second, the growth of a radical opposition Islamic movement coincided with the new post-Cold War American view of Islam as the new communism. Therefore, the new Algerian military-backed regime used the so-called war on terror to build closer relations and links with the USA. In March 1993, Algeria broke off diplomatic relations with Iran, after years of cultivating relations with Tehran, which it now blamed for exporting Islamic revolutions to the Arab World. At the same time, Algeria withdrew its ambassador from Sudan, another country described by the US officials as a rogue and anti-Western state (EIU, 2001, pp. 14–15). In May 1994, Algeria was rewarded with a SDR 457 million IMF Stand-By Arrangement.

In late 1994, Algeria also vigorously supported, along with Egypt, an anti-terrorist code of conduct at the Casablanca Islamic Summit. A few months later in January 1995, Algeria received a US$150 million World Bank Economic Rehabilitation Support Loan, followed in May 1995 by the largest ever IMF Extended Fund Facility in the region of SDR 1.2 billion. The latter came to an end in May 1998, and was associated with unexpected macroeconomic success, mostly caused by improved global prices and demand for gas.

In late 1998, President Zeroual announced that he would stand down and that elections would be brought forward to early 1999. One day before the voting began in the delayed April 1999 elections, all candidates, except Mr Abdelaziz Bouteflika, pulled out due to credibility problems. This left Mr Bouteflika, who is supported by a pro-Western, anti-Islamist powerful coterie of senior army officers and state officials, to become Algeria's seventh President. His first years of rule were marked by intensified violence and further crackdown on Islamists. To help bolster Mr Bouteflika's position, particularly following the decline in oil prices in late 1998 and the rise of debt service ratio to 46 per cent, the IMF extended a Compensatory and Contingency Financing Facility of SDR 223.5 million in May 1999. Since then Algeria has not resorted to either IMF or World Bank loans, bolstered by its rents from the largest liquefied natural gas facility in the world it developed in the 1990s (EIU, 2001, p. 52). Algeria is today viewed by the USA as a bulwark against the spread of radical Islam to North Africa.

Egypt

Egypt was the first Arab state to sign a peace treaty with Israel in 1978, hence formally ending the state of war between the two countries. Since then, Egypt has become a favoured recipient of US aid, despite its appalling human rights record. Although Egypt has had relatively few Bank and Fund programme loans,[23] what is noteworthy is that Egypt has continued to receive such loans despite the disappointing pace and quality of reform which falls significantly short of that in Morocco and Tunisia as well as in Jordan after 1999. The timing of two of these loans to Egypt is also noteworthy. Without Egypt, there would have been no Arab stance supportive of the US-led coalition in 1990–91. Egypt mobilized Arab support for the war against Iraq and held an emergency Arab Summit for that purpose in 1990. Unlike Jordan, Egypt also sent troops to fight alongside the American forces in liberating Kuwait. Three months after the war ended in May 1991, Egypt was rewarded with a SDR 234 million IMF Standby loan and a US$300 million Bank Structural Adjustment Loan. Egypt also received more than US$15 billion of debt write-off from the West for its efforts and strong support for the allies during the 1990–91 war, the highest level of debt forgiveness in the history of MENA.

Tunisia and Morocco

Tunisia, like Morocco, has long been regarded as a friendly pro-Western regime within MENA. Consequently, both Morocco and Tunisia have been treated favourably first by the EU, and later, by the IMF and World Bank. Between 1982 and 2003, Morocco had six debt rescheduling agreements with the Paris Club and three with private international banks, received 15 World Bank structural and sectoral adjustment loans and seven standby and extended facilities from the IMF. Morocco has also long been the recipient of generous American military support. Over the same period, Tunisia received nine World Bank structural and sectoral adjustment loans in addition to five years of continuous IMF financial support.

Such treatment compares very favourably with their less America-friendly neighbours such as Algeria 1980s and Libya in the 1980s and 1990s. Tunisia and Morocco were also the first countries in the region to sign Association Agreements[24] with the European Union in 1995 and 1996, respectively and were also among the first Arab states to join the WTO in 1995[25] (El-Ghonemy, 1998).

It has been argued that Washington not only used its influence inside international financial institutions to soften IMF and World Bank conditionality as well as the WTO's entry requirements, but also, along with the EU and Japan, 'repeatedly and generously lubricated' their reform efforts through 'financial assistance to ease the pain and political costs to the regime of early austerity phases of SALPs [Structural Adjustment Lending Programmes]' (Pfeifer, 1999, pp. 23, 25–26). It would seem that in these MENA countries US officials hoped, by providing friendly regimes with financial and military support and by developing them into regional showpieces of globalization, that this would stabilize and support the regimes of their Arab allies (Alexander, 1996; Waterbury, 1998).

Morocco has been such a massive and continuous recipient of Bank and Fund programme loans that it is difficult to link key domestic and international political events to the timing of such loans. However, its efforts in supporting the 1991 Gulf war, including sending 1,200 of its troops, was rewarded handsomely with more than US$5 billion in debt forgiveness from the USA and Arab oil-rich states. Political liberalization in late 1997 and early 1998, with parliamentary elections resulting in the first change over of political power in the Kingdom's history, was followed by three World Bank loans over the next year totalling US$450 million.

Tunisia has long pursued a pragmatic pro-Western foreign policy (Murphy, 2002). However, a significant shift in domestic politics occurred in late 1987 with the coming to power of General Zine Ben Ali. Ben Ali's new regime, claiming an attempted Islamic coup, rapidly cracked down on the Islamic movement, arresting the head of the main opposition, the Movement de la Tendance Islamique. In early 1989 the regime signalled a further shift against Islamic politics in favour of a pro-Western stance by joining the UMA designed to prevent the spread of radical Islam and foster closer links with the EU. The response of the Washington-based international financial institutions mirrors that in Algeria. The crackdown on Islam was followed by both a Bank and Fund loan the following year, whilst joining the UMA was followed within four months by two further Bank sectoral adjustment loans.

3.5 Loan timing: a more formal quantitative analysis

The above has provided a simple descriptive analysis of the timing of IMF and World Bank programme loans to MENA recipients in order to try and isolate the influence of both economic need and key domestic and international political events. The results suggest that although in some cases recipient economic need, as signalled by a deterioration in key macroeconomic variables, is a determinant of IMF and World Bank lending, such loans also seem to be influenced by political events in the recipients that carry favour with US policy in the region.

However, so far the analysis lacks rigour. In order to strengthen and advance our argument we now use a more formal quantitative approach.

In this section, we employ a Probit model to investigate what factors influence IMF loans to MENA countries.[26] The dependent variable is IMF coded, either 1 if a country signed an agreement (including Structural Adjustment Facility (SAF), Enhanced Structural Adjustment Facility (ESAF) and Poverty Reduction and Growth Facility (PRGF)) in year t, or 0 otherwise. Based on the previous discussion, three sets of variables are included in the regression: economic need, US influence and domestic political factors. Independent variables representing economic need consist of GDP per capita, GDP growth rate, debt service ratio, short term debt as percentage of total debt, balance of payments and changes in national reserves. US influence is captured by the dummy variable PEACE, which indicates whether a country signed a peace treaty with Israel or not. Two variables are used to capture the domestic political factors: DEM – the democracy index (ranging from 1 to 7, 1 is the highest level of democracy, 7 the lowest), and DELEC – the legislative election year.

The estimation is conducted in a pooled sample with 11 countries from 1975 to 2000. The detailed variable definition, data sources and the country list are reported in Appendix Table 5A.1. Following the standard procedure, the sample was limited to years in which a country was not under a previously agreed IMF programme, and the explanatory variables – LGDPPC, GDPG, CAB, TDEBTS and SDEBT are lagged by one year to avoid simultaneity bias.

The first stage of the analysis focuses only on the economic variables, which may reflect the presence of a financial or macroeconomic problem that might prompt the government to approach the IMF for resources and which may be used by the IMF to decide on loan eligibility. The results for the corresponding economic model are reported in Table 3.7. The coefficients on GDP per capita (LGDPPC[−1]), total debt service ratio (TDEBTS[−1]) and changes in net reserves (D(RES/GDP)) are all significant and with the expected signs indicating that a MENA country with low GDP per capita, high debt service ratio and experiencing a sharp decline in reserves is likely to receive IMF assistance. The coefficient on the current account balance (CAB[−1]) is not significant and the coefficients on GDP growth (GDPG[−1]) and short-term debt (SDEBT[−1]) are significant but with unexpected signs.

Although the above economic approach provides some useful insights into the determinants of IMF programmes, it suffers from specification error due to the omission of relevant variables (e.g. variables that capture political factors which we know from our above literature review and qualitative analysis are likely to be important). Consequently the economic model has low explanatory power (measured by an R^2 of 0.194) and a low correct prediction ratio. As can be seen from the bottom of Table 3.7 the number of observations for receipt of a loan is 23 but our economic model only correctly predicts 5 of these.[27]

In order to try and improve the model the two sets of political variables are added into regression. The results for corresponding supplemented model are reported in the third column of Table 3.7. The coefficients on GDP per capita (LGDPPC[−1])[28] and GDP growth (GDPG[−1]) are no longer significant; the coefficient on the current account balance (CAB[−1]) is still insignificant; and the coefficients on short term debt (SDEBT[−1])[29] and the change in reserves

Table 3.7 Probit analysis of the determinants of IMF agreements

Variables		Economic model		Supplemented model	
LGDPPC[−1]		−0.659		−0.337	
		(0.279)**		(0.445)	
GDPG[−1]		0.058		0.042	
		(0.033)*		(0.045)	
CAB[−1]		−0.015		0.038	
		(0.023)		(0.037)	
TDEBTS[−1]		0.039		0.033	
		(0.013)***		(0.017)**	
SDEBT[−1]		−0.060		−0.065	
		(0.023)***		(0.037)*	
D(RES/GDP)		−5.731		−6.972	
		(3.46)*		(4.426)†	
DEM[−1]				−1.008	
				(0.445)*	
DELEC[−1]				0.6000	
				(0.535)	
DELEC				0.694	
				(0.601)	
DELEC[+1]				0.832	
				(0.505)*	
PEACE				1.052	
				(0.481)**	
Constant		3.197		5.804	
		(1.941)*		(3.089)**	
Number of observations		165		154	
		Predicted		Predicted	
		0	1	0	1
Actual	0	139	3	125	6
	1	18	5	7	16
Log likelihood		−48.8***		−31.4***	
Chi squared		35.6***		67.1***	
R^2 (ML)		0.194		0.353	

Notes
Standard errors are in parentheses, and values of degrees of freedom are in square brackets. ***, **, *, † indicate that the coefficient is significantly different from zero at the 1, 5, 10 and 15 per cent levels respectively.

(D(RES/GDP)) changed slightly in terms of magnitude. For those political variables, the dummy PEACE is positive and significant, the democracy index DEM is negative and significant and the dummy for the year after a legislative election DELEC[+1] is positive and significant. This suggests that MENA countries who have signed a peace treaty with Israel, just had a legislative election and are democratic are likely to receive an IMF loan. In the supplemented model, the R^2 statistic is much higher at 0.353 and correct prediction ratio of the positive value (sign an agreement with IMF) is 16 out of 23, which is a big improvement, compared to the economic model.[30]

The above results clearly show that in trying to predict when the IMF will sign a loan agreement with a MENA country the model which incorporates both political and economic variables is superior to a purely economic model. Our supplemented model indicates that whether a country receives an IMF programme is influenced by both economic and political factors, particularly the latter. The only economic variables in the supplemented model that have the predicted sign and are significant are the change in foreign reserves and total debt service – a decline in reserves or a high debt service ratio are good predictors of an IMF programme. This finding can be further supported by the fact that 20 out of 28 IMF programmes in MENA were accompanied by a Paris Club debt relief or reschedule agreement (see Appendix Tables 3A.2 and 3A.4). Hence, IMF programmes seem to clearly coincide with debt problems and the need to save foreign reserves. Along with the two economic variables, signing a peace treaty with Israel and improving democracy also increase the likelihood of reaching an agreement with the IMF. The existence of political business cycle also plays its part in that we have found that MENA governments are more likely to enter into an agreement with the IMF in the year after the legislative election.

3.6   Conclusion

Our qualitative and quantitative analyses enable us to conclude that both recipient need and donor interest influence the granting of IMF and World Bank programme loans to countries of the MENA region. This is not surprising given that our literature review indicated that most empirical studies of aid allocation find that donor interest, including geopolitical interest, influences who gets what in terms of aid. The generally accepted view is that donor interest plays a more important role in bilateral aid allocation than in multilateral aid allocation. This may be so, but we have identified important reasons why the major Western shareholders might seek to influence the flow of funds from the two major Washington-based multilaterals. Given its voting power in both the Bank and the Fund, the USA is in a particularly influential position.

Our qualitative analysis focused on the five major MENA recipients of IMF and World Bank programme loans – Algeria, Jordan, Morocco, Tunisia and Egypt. Looking at each country's macroeconomic performance in the year in which they commenced their first of a phase of programme loans we see very little evidence of economic need. Only in the case of Jordan in the late 1980s and Egypt in its first phase of loans during the mid-1970s do we see any clear sign of recipient economic need in terms of a significant deterioration in the macroeconomic indicators the IMF is usually concerned with. It seems therefore that we must look to other factors to explain the IMF and World Bank engagement with Egypt in the 1980s and with Morocco, Tunisia and Algeria. In all cases a cursory political analysis would indicate that a shift towards a pro-Western foreign policy, peace overtures to Israel, domestic political liberalization and the often related challenge to the regime by Islamic opposition prompt an inflow of funds not just from the USA but also from the Bank and Fund. Even in the case of Jordan, who became a recipient of such loans in 1989, the severe economic crisis of that year was inextricably linked with foreign policy and domestic political events.

The above findings are further supported by our more formal qualitative analysis. Using a Probit model to estimate the determinants of IMF lending in the region we found that a model that only includes variables representing recipient need performs very poorly. However, once we include foreign policy and political variables the model performs extremely well. In this supplemented model the only economic variables that help to predict whether a MENA country will be granted an IMF loan are a change in foreign reserves and total debt service – a decline in reserves or a high debt service ratio are good predictors of an IMF programme. Signing a peace treaty with Israel improves a country's chance of a loan as does improving democracy. Related to the latter, we also found that holding an election is likely to be followed by an IMF loan in the post-election year.

The above findings are important, not just because they add to an already large body of empirical work on the determinants of aid allocation, but also because they have important policy implications. The fact that IMF and World Bank lending in MENA seems to be orientated towards pro-Western regimes that introduce Western-style democracy, and adhere to US foreign policy interests in the region suggest that factors other than recipient need are influencing global aid allocations. This may well reduce the developmental impact of a scarce resource, namely aid. As Collier and Dollar have argued (2002) a more poverty-efficient allocation of aid has the potential to double the number of people lifted out of poverty from 10 to 20 million.

Second, IMF and World Bank loans to MENA countries do not just provide finance, they also bring with them an extensive package of economic reform and liberalization. Many of these reforms, if correctly implemented, have the ability to bring tremendous gains to the region. Nevertheless, economic liberalization also brings risks and costs. Unemployment may increase, at least in the short term, income inequality may worsen and certain vulnerable groups, if not caught by social safety nets, will be harmed. In light of this there is the serious risk that US foreign policy in the region, including the encouragement of IMF and World Bank lending to pro-Western regimes, could catastrophically backfire. Economic and political liberalization by Western-supported MENA regimes, if it brings with it adverse social welfare effects combined with a backlash in the form of a crack down on often legitimate opposition groups, is likely to fuel the already growing unrest in such countries. Increasingly, such unrest is directed not just at incumbent regimes but also has anti-Western and more specifically anti-American and anti-globalization overtones. In some instances, such as in the case of past riots in Jordan prompted by the IMF-induced lifting of price supports, the IMF and the World Bank have been viewed by many of the opponents of reform as synonymous with the American presence and interests in the region. If this persists, the very regimes that America and the West are trying to support with funding and reform packages may well not survive. The welfare effects of IMF and World Bank programmes in MENA countries as well as local perceptions of these two institutions are hence an area that deserves further research.

Appendix

Table 3A.1 Variable definition and data source

Variable	Definition
D(RES/GDP)	Changes in net reserves (BoP, current US$)/GDP(current US$)
CAB	Current account balance (% of GDP)
TDEBTS	Total debt service (% of exports of goods and services)
GDPG	GDP growth (annual %)
LGDPPC	Log[GDP per capita (constant 1995 US$)]
SDEBT	Short-term debt (% of total external debt) (World Development Indicator 2002 CD-ROM)
DEM	Democracy index (1–7) (Freedomhouse: http://www.freedomhouse.org)
DELEC	Dummy, is there a legislative election? (1 if yes) (World Bank DPI database: Beck *et al.* (2001); the World Bank Economic Review)
PEACE	Dummy, the year that a country under peace treaty with Israel (1 if yes)
Countries	Algeria, Djibouti, Egypt, Iran, Jordan, Libya, Morocco, Oman, Syrian, Tunisia and Yemen
Years	1975–2000

Table 3A.2 History of IMF lending arrangements in MENA

	Date of arrangement	Date of cancellation	Amount agreed	Amount drawn	Amount outstanding
Algeria					
Extended fund facility	22 May 1995	21 May 1998	1,169,280	1,169,280	525,487
Standby arrangement	27 May 1994	22 May 1995	457,200	385,200	0
Standby arrangement	03 Jun. 1991	31 Mar. 1992	300,000	225,000	0
Standby arrangement	31 May 1989	30 May 1990	155,700	155,700	0
Egypt					
Standby arrangement	11 Oct. 1996	30 Sep. 1998	271,400	0	0
Extended fund facility	20 Sep. 1993	19 Sep. 1996	400,000	0	0
Standby arrangement	17 May 1991	31 May 1993	234,400	147,200	0
Standby arrangement	15 May 1987	30 Nov. 1988	250,000	116,000	0
Jordan					
Standby arrangement	03 Jul. 2002	02 Jul. 2004	85,280	10,660	10,660
Extended fund facility	15 Apr. 1999	31 May 2002	127,880	127,880	127,880
Extended fund facility	09 Feb. 1996	08 Feb. 1999	238,040	202,520	113,738
Extended fund facility	25 May 1994	09 Feb. 1996	189,300	130,320	35,205
Standby arrangement	26 Feb. 1992	25 Feb. 1994	44,400	44,400	0
Standby arrangement	14 Jul. 1989	13 Jan. 1991	60,000	26,800	0
Morocco					
Standby arrangement	31 Jan. 1992	31 Mar. 1993	91,980	18,396	0
Standby arrangement	20 Jul. 1990	31 Mar. 1991	100,000	48,000	0
Standby arrangement	30 Aug. 1988	31 Dec.1989	210,000	210,000	0
Standby arrangement	16 Dec. 1986	30 Apr. 1988	230,000	230,000	0
Standby arrangement	12 Sep. 1985	15 Dec. 1986	200,000	10,000	0
Standby arrangement	15 Nov. 1959	15 Mar. 1985	833,250	0	0
Standby arrangement	16 Sep. 1983	15 Mar. 1985	300,000	300,000	0
Tunisia					
Extended fund facility	25 Jul. 1988	24 Jul. 1992	207,300	207,300	0
Standby arrangement	04 Nov. 1986	31 May. 1988	103,650	91,000	0

Source: IMF (amount in thousands of SDR).

Notes
Seven cases are not reported here: Djibouti, 1996 SAF and 1999 PRGF; Yemen 1996 SAF and 1997 PRGF and ESAF; Egypt 1976, SAL and Morocco, 1980 SAL; and the date for Morocco second arrangement seems to be wrong in IMF Webpage.

Table 3A.3 History of World Bank lending arrangements in MENA

Project name	Commitment US$ million	Country	Date of approval
Economic reform support loan	300	Algeria	31 Aug. 89
Enterprise & financial sector adjustment loan	350	Algeria	21 Jun. 91
Economic Rehabilitation Support Loan	150	Algeria	12 Jan. 95
Structural Adjustment Loan	300	Algeria	25 Apr. 96
Agricultural Industrial Imports	70	Egypt	03 Dec. 74
Agricultural Industrial Imports (02)	70	Egypt	14 Jun. 77
Structural Adjustment Loan	300	Egypt	21 Jun. 91
Industry & Trade Policy Adjustment Loan	150	Jordan	14 Dec. 89
Energy Sector Adjustment Loan	80	Jordan	07 Oct. 93
Agriculture Sector Adjustment Loan	80	Jordan	08 Dec. 94
Economic Reform & Development Loan	80	Jordan	24 Oct. 95
Economic Reform & Development Loan (02)	120	Jordan	11 Dec. 96
Economic Reform & Development Loan (03)	120	Jordan	01 Jun. 99
Public Sector Reform Adjustment Loan	120	Jordan	21 Jun. 01
Public Sector Reform Adjustment Loan (02)	120	Jordan	02 Jul. 02
Industrial and Trade Policy Adjustment Loan	150.4	Morocco	31 Jan. 84
Agricultural Sector Adjustment Loan	100	Morocco	20 Jun. 85
Industrial and Trade Policy Adjustment Loan (02)	200	Morocco	16 Jul. 85
Education Sector Reform Program	150	Morocco	20 Mar. 86
Public Enterprise Rationalization Loan	240	Morocco	26 May 87
Agricultural Sector Adjustment Loan (02)	225	Morocco	24 Nov. 87
Structural Adjustment Loan	200	Morocco	01 Dec. 88
Financial Sector Development	235	Morocco	25 Jun. 91
Structural Adjustment Loan (02)	275	Morocco	30 Apr. 92
Financial Markets Development Loan	250	Morocco	27 Jul. 95
Contractual Savings Development Loan	100	Morocco	09 Jun. 98
Post Information Technology	101	Morocco	06 May 99
Policy Reform Support Loan (PRSL)	250	Morocco	01 Jun. 99
Information Infrastructure Loan	65	Morocco	31 May 01
Asset Management Reform Loan	45	Morocco	05 Jun. 03
Agricultural Sector Adjustment Loan	150	Tunisia	18 Sep. 86
Industrial and Trade Policy Adjustment Loan	150	Tunisia	24 Feb. 87
Structural Adjustment Loan	150	Tunisia	16 Jun. 88
Agricultural Sector Adjustment Loan (02)	84	Tunisia	01 Jun. 89
Public Enterprise Reform Loan	130	Tunisia	11 Jul. 89
Economic & Financial Reforms Support Loan	250	Tunisia	12 Dec. 91
Economic Competitiveness Adjustment Loan	75	Tunisia	25 Jul. 96
Economic Competitiveness Adjustment Loan (02)	159	Tunisia	20 Apr. 99
Economic Competitiveness Adjustment Loan (03)	252.5	Tunisia	20 Dec. 01

Source: World Bank Project Database.

Note
Six cases are not reported here: Iran, 1957 SAL; Lebanon, 1977 SAL; Djibouti, 2001 SAL; Yemen, 1996, 1997, 1999 SAL.

Table 3A.4 History of Paris Club lending arrangements in MENA

Country	Date of the treatment	Type of the treatment	Status of treatment	Amounts treated
Algeria	21 Jul. 1995	Classic	Active	7,320
	01 Jun. 1994	Classic	Active	5,344
Egypt	25 May 1991	Ad-Hoc	Active	21,164
	22 May 1987	Classic	Fully repaid	7,098
Jordan	10 Jul. 2002	Houston	Active	1,170
	20 May 1999	Houston	Active	821
	23 May 1997	Houston	Active	400
	28 June 1994	Houston	Active	1,147
	28 Feb. 1992	Classic	Active	771
	19 Jul. 1989	Classic	Fully repaid	586
Morocco	27 Feb. 1992	Houston	Active	1,250
	11 Sep. 1990	Houston	Active	1,390
	26 Oct. 1988	Classic	Fully repaid	940
	06 Mar. 1987	Classic	Fully repaid	1,000
	17 Sep. 1985	Classic	Fully repaid	678
	25 Oct. 1983	Classic	Fully repaid	1,210

Source: Paris Club.

Notes
Amount treated in US$ million; four cases are not report here: Yemen, 1996, 1997 and 2001, Djibouti, 2000.

Eligibility
Classic: any country which has an appropriate programme with the IMF that shows the need for Paris Club debt relief may benefit from classic terms.
Houston: eligibility for Houston terms is assessed on a case-by-case basis by Paris Club creditors, taking into account the track record of the debtor country with the Paris Club and the IMF and various other criteria.
Ad-Hoc: The Participating Creditor Countries reserve the right to review the implementation of the conditions stated in for the comparability of treatment between all external creditors; if the Participating Creditor Countries determine that these conditions are not substantially fulfilled the present Agreed Minute will become null and void.

Notes

1 The World Bank definition of MENA includes: Algeria, Djibouti, Egypt, Iran, Iraq, Jordan, Lebanon, Libya, Malta, Morocco, Oman, Palestine, Saudi Arabia, Syria, Tunisia and Yemen. It does not include the high income countries of the Gulf, nor Israel, nor Sudan and Mauritania which although predominantly Arab countries face challenges more typical of sub-Saharan Africa. In our general discussions of aid allocation we use the same country grouping as the Bank, although also include reference to Israel, a major recipient of US aid.
2 Programme loans divorce development finance from specific investment projects in the recipient and instead provide general support for the balance of payments and/or government budget in return for which the recipient agrees to undertake various economic reforms, which can often be far reaching. See Mosley *et al.* (1995).
3 For an excellent survey and methodological critique of this work see McGillivray and White (1993).
4 Western aid to Mobuto's Zaire or Marcos's Philippines designed to bolster anti-communist pro-Western regimes are good examples.

5 Within the MENA region there is ample anecdotal evidence of donor interest influencing past aid allocations to the strategically important state of Israel. Sierra Leone and Israel were both classified as developing countries by the OECD's Development Assistance Committee in 1995 and both had a similar population size. However, Israel is one of the USA's most strategically important allies. From 1969 to 1995, Sierra Leone received an annual average of ODA of US$74 million, while Israel received US$937 million which is roughly 13 times the amount allocated to Sierra Leone despite the fact that Israel's income per capita was 27 times that of Sierra Leone. Egypt, likewise, with its peace overtures to Israel since 1974 has also been a major recipient of US aid.

6 Donor interest includes pursuit of commercial interests via the promotion of donor trade or investment opportunities by allocating aid to countries most likely to absorb donor exports and investment. It also includes the pursuit of political, diplomatic and strategic objectives in order to create an international environment, which favours the donor. According to Feeny and McGillivray,

> This can involve allocating aid to countries which are in a strategic geographic location or which have particularly close diplomatic ties with the donor. It can even involve rewarding countries for particular actions with increased aid or punishing others with reduced or continually low or zero levels of aid.
>
> (2002, p. 3)

7 We ran our regressions for three dependent variables – US aid, bilateral aid excluding the US, and multilateral aid and found that donor interest has the strongest effect on the allocation of US aid, and also that non-US bilateral aid responded more to donor interest than did multilateral aid.

8 IBRD Articles of Agreement IV: operations, section 10; IDA Articles of Agreement V: operations, section 6.

9 A country's voting power is not the same as its voting weight: its power is its ability to decide the issue when a vote is taken whereas its weight is just the number of votes it has the right to cast. Voting power is calculated by analysing all the voting outcomes that can occur, and in each case investigating the ability of every member to be decisive – that is to be the one member who can decide whether the vote leads to a decision or not.

10 The distribution of power in relation to decisions requiring a special majority is, by contrast, relatively equal since although this majority requirement ensures the United States has a veto, it also limits that country's power to act within the organization.

11 The record of UN General Assembly voting patterns is supplied by the Bureau of International Organizations and Affairs in the US Department of State and can be accessed by the public, whilst, to the best of our knowledge there are no such public records regarding the World Bank and IMF.

12 It should also be noted that the Head of the IMF is always a European and that of the World Bank an American. They are chosen behind closed doors, and experience in the developing world does not seem to be a prerequisite.

13 The bulk of the studies have concentrated on the determinants of IMF rather than World Bank lending. The reason seems to be two-fold. Firstly, an IMF agreement is usually a prerequisite for a Bank programme loan and most IMF agreements are followed by such a loan. Hence, many of the determinants of an IMF agreement will also be determinants of the Bank's activities. Secondly, the aspects of recipient need that the IMF is meant to respond to, namely inflation, balance of payments and budget deficits are much easier to measure than the more medium-term supply-side determinants of World Bank programme loans (structural imbalance, developmental indicators etc.). Hence, from a methodological standpoint it is much easier to construct the independent variables in an equation estimating the determinants of IMF loans than those that would need to enter such an equation for World Bank programme loans.

14 Reliance on oil took two forms, direct and indirect. Direct reliance refers to the oil exporting countries including OPEC countries in the region, along with Egypt and Yemen.

Indirect reliance refers to those countries, especially Jordan, Egypt and Yemen, who received large remittances from the oil rich GCC countries.

15 The main exporting industries are petroleum refining, petrochemicals, textiles and clothing, engineering goods, food processing, iron and steel, and pharmaceutical sectors (see MENA Trends Report, 1996).

16 In addition, Djibouti received a SAL in 2001, Lebanon in 1977, and Yemen received three between 1996 and 1999.

17 We look at IMF loans rather than World Bank programme loans because the former are almost always a prerequisite for the latter.

18 The traditional division of labour in the 1980s was that the IMF would take care of balance of payments problems whilst medium term growth would be the concern of the World Bank (Mosley *et al.*, 1995, vol. 1, pp. 51–56).

19 In the 1974 Arab Summit in Rabat, Morocco, the PLO was declared as the 'sole representative of the Palestinian people', a fact which further weakened King Hussein's hand in negotiating a separate peace settlement with Israel.

20 Lost aid from the USA was more than compensated by the 1979 Arab Summit in Baghdad, which allocated US$1.25 million in annual grants to Jordan from oil-rich Arab states. This obviously weakened the USA's bargaining position in persuading King Hussein to sign a separate peace treaty with Israel and at the same time marked the beginning of stronger and long-lasting relations between Jordan and Iraq's Saddam Hussein. However, with the collapse of international oil prices in the early 1980s, Arab aid to Jordan was drying up. Only Saudi Arabia was able to continue to provide Jordan with grants over the ten-year period agreed upon during the 1979 Arab summit (see Brand, 1994).

21 This plan was based on the principle of peace for land formula, including the establishment of a self-governing authority in the WBG in association with Jordan, since the USA was strongly opposed to the idea of recognizing or negotiating with the PLO so long as the latter did not recognize Israel's right to exist (Lukacs, 1997).

22 This culminated in what became known as the Amman Accord in 1985. The Accord called for Israeli withdrawal from the occupied territories, the resolution of the refugee problem and Palestinian self-determination within a Jordanian–Palestinian confederation.

23 Egypt received only three World Bank SALs (two of which were in the 1970s) and four IMF programme loans.

24 These Association Agreements were part of the 1994 Barcelona Initiative, which aims at establishing a free trade area between the EU and 15 Mediterranean states by the year 2010, later modified to 2012.

25 Very few Arab states were members of GATT. Hence, when the WTO was established in 1994, and started its operations in January 1995, Arab countries that were GATT members became WTO members immediately. They consisted of Bahrain, Egypt, Morocco and Tunisia.

26 Again only IMF programs are considered here due to the fact that the World Bank's SALs or SECALs are generally preceded by an IMF programme. The Probit model can be used to determine the eligibility of receiving aid as opposed to the amount received. Hence the dependent variable takes the value of 1 or 0 depending on whether each country in the sample receives aid in a given year or not. In our case we use the Probit model to predict whether a country receives an IMF loan.

27 The actual number of observations for no IMF loan is 142 and of these the economic model correctly predicts 139 (and incorrectly predicts 3). But it should be noted that most Probit model analysis scores highly on predicting the zeros in the observations of the dependent variable.

28 The coefficient on LGDPPC[−1] is sensitive to whether we include a constant or not. When the constant is excluded, the coefficient is negative and significant.

29 Short-term debt as percentage of total debt has a negative impact on receiving an IMF loan, which is not expected. However, when we checked the debt structure of MENA

countries, we find short-term debt has been in decline since the early 1980s, and more than two-thirds of their long-term external debt is from official sources. If the government's desire to sign an agreement with IMF is designed to help initiate the process of long-term debt relief from major donors this would explain the negative coefficient on short-term debt. The smaller the percentage of short-term debt (and hence the larger the percentage of official long-term debt) the more likely it becomes that an IMF agreement will be signed.

30 Given this study is based on a relative small sample, those figures are very respectable. Bird and Rowlands (2003) have shown that a common feature of this genre of research is its arguably low explanatory power overall. Although the percentage of correct prediction was often 80 and 90 percent, it has to be recalled that these numbers corresponded roughly to the percentage of countries without agreements.

Bibliography

Alesina, A. and Dollar, D. (2002) 'Who gives foreign aid to whom and why', *Journal of Economic Growth*, 5: 33–64.

Alexander, C. (1996) 'State, labour and the new global economy in Tunisia', in Vandewalle, D. (ed.), *North Africa: Development and Reform in a Changing Global Economy*, New York: St. Martin's Press.

Ayubi, N. (1995) *Over-Stating the Arab State*, London: I.B Tauris.

Barro, R.J. and Jong-Wha Lee (2001) 'IMF programs: who is chosen and what are the effects', Paper presented at Second IMF Research Conference, Washington, DC: IMF.

Berthélmy, J. and Tichit, A. (2002) 'Bilateral donor's aid allocation decision', World Institute for Development Economic Research (WIDER) Discussion Paper, No. 2002/123, United Nations University.

Bird, G. and Rowlands, D. (2001) 'IMF lending: how is it affected by economic, political and institutional factors?', *Journal of Policy Reform*, 4: 243–270.

—— (2003) 'The demand for IMF assistance: what factors influence the decision to turn to the fund', Department of Economics Working Paper Series, University of Surrey.

Brand, L. (1994) *Jordan's Inter-Arab Relations: The Political Economy of Alliance Making*, New York: Columbia University Press.

Collier, P. and Dollar, D. (2002) 'Aid allocation and poverty reduction', *European Economic Review*, 46: 1475–1500.

Conteh-Morgan, E. (1990) *American Foreign Aid and Global Power Projection*, London: Dartmouth Publishing Co.

Conway, P. (1994) 'IMF lending programs: participation and impact', *Journal of Development Economic*, 45: 365–391.

Dallas, R. (1999) *King Hussein: A Life on the Edge*, London: Profile Books.

Dreher, A. and Vaubel, R. (2002) 'Does the IMF cause moral hazard and political business cycles? Evidence from panel data', Economic Working Paper Archive at WUSTL in its series International Finance, No. 0207002.

Economist Intelligence Unit (EIU) (2001) *Country Profile Algeria 2001*, London: EIU.

El-Ghonemy, M.R. (1998) *Affluence and Poverty in the Middle East*, London: Routledge.

Feeny, S. and McGillivray, M. (2002) 'Modelling inter-temporal aid allocation', CREDIT Research Paper No. 02/10, University of Nottingham.

Fleck, R.K. and Kilby, C. (2001) 'World Bank independence: a model and statistical analysis of U.S. influence', Vassar College Department of Economics Working Paper Series, No. 53.

Frank, A.G. (1969) *Latin American, Underdevelopment or Revolution*, New York: Monthly Review Press.

Harrigan, J. and Wang, C. (2004) 'A new approach to aid allocation among developing countries: is the US more selfish than the rest?', School of Economic Studies Working Paper, No. 0412, University of Manchester.

Hayter, T. (1971) *Aid as Imperialism*, New York: Penguin Books.

—— (1981) *The Creation of World Poverty: An Alternative View to the Brandt Report*, London: Pluto.

Hensman, C.R. (1971) *Rich Against Poor: The Reality of Aid*, London: Allen Lane.

Hinnebusch, R. (2003) *The International Politics of the Middle East*, Manchester and New York: Manchester University Press.

Hubbell, S. (1998) 'The containment myth: US Middle East policy in theory and practice', *Middle East Report*, Fall 1998: 9.

IMF Survey Supplement (2003), Vol. 32, International Monetary Fund.

International Crisis Group (ICG) (2003) *The Challenge of Political Reform: Jordan Democratisation and Regional Instability*, Middle East Briefing, Brussels, 8 October, available at http://www.crisisweb.org

Jalée, P. (1968) *The Pillage of the Third World*, New York: Monthly Review Press.

Joyce, J.P. (1992) 'The economic characteristics of IMF programme countries', *Economic Letters*, 38: 237–242.

Kanovsky, I. (1989) *Jordan's Economy: From Prosperity to Crisis*, Mosha Dayan Centre: Tel Aviv University.

Killick, T. (1995) *IMF Programs in Developing Countries: Design and Impact*, London: Routledge.

Knight, M. and Santaella, J. (1997) 'Economic determinants of IMF financial arrangement', *Journal of Development Economics*, 54: 405–436.

Leech, D. (2002) 'Voting power in the governance of the International Monetary Fund', *Annals of Operations Research*, 109: 375–397.

Leech, D. and Leech, R. (2005) 'Voting power in the Bretton Woods institutions', in Paloni, A. and Zanardi, M. (eds), *IMF, World Bank and Policy Reforms*, London: Routledge.

Lukacs, Y. (1997) *Israel, Jordan and the Peace Process*, Syracuse: Syracuse University Press.

McGillivray, M. (2003) 'Modelling aid allocation: issues, approach and results', *Journal of Economic Development*, 28: 171–188.

McGillivray, M. and White, H. (1993) 'Explanatory studies of aid allocation among developing countries: a critical survey', Institute of Social Studies Working Paper No. 148, The Hague: Institute of Social Science.

Mckeown, T., Pallansch, L. and Thacker, S. (1999) 'Political conditionality in US bilateral and multilateral foreign assistance', Paper presented at the 40th Annual Convention of the International Studies Association, Washington, DC, February 16–20.

McKinlay, R.D. and Little, R. (1977) 'A foreign policy of US bilateral aid allocation', *World Politics*, 30: 58–86.

—— (1978) 'The French aid relationship: a foreign policy model of the distribution of French bilateral aid, 1964–1970', *Development and Change*, 9: 459–478.

—— (1979) 'The US aid relationship: the test of recipient need and donor interest models', *Political Studies*, 27: 236–250.

Maizels, A. and Nissanke, M.K. (1984) 'Motivations for aid to developing countries', *World Development*, 12: 879–900.

Makdisi, S., Fattah, Z. and Liman, I. (2000) 'Determinants of growth in the MENA countries', Paper presented at the World Bank Sponsored Workshop on the Global Development Network in Prague, June 9–11.

MENA Trend Report 1996, available at http://www.erf.org.eg (19 July 2004).

Mosley, P., Harrigan, J. and Toye, J. (1995) *Aid and Power*, London and New York: Routledge.

Murphy, E. (2002) 'The foreign policy of Tunisia', in Hinnebusch, R. and Ehteshami, A. (eds), *The Foreign Policies of Middle East States*, London: Lynne Rienner.

Niva, S. (1998) 'Between clash and cooptation: US foreign policy and the spectre of Islam', *Middle East Report*, Fall 1998: 26–29.

Perthes, V. (1998) 'Points of differences and cases for cooperation: European critique of US Middle East policy', *Middle East Report*, Fall 1998: 30.

Pfeifer, K. (1996) 'Between rocks and hard choices: international financial and economic adjustment in North Africa', in Vandewalle, D. (ed.), *North Africa: Development and Reform*, New York: St. Martin's Press.

—— (1999) 'How Tunisia, Morocco, Jordan and even Egypt became IMF success stories', *The Middle East Report*, 210: 23–26.

Richards, A. and Waterbury, J. (1996) *A Political Economy of the Middle East*, Colorado, CO: Westview Press.

Rodrik, D. (1995) 'Why is there multilateral lending', NBER Working Paper, No. 5160.

Rowlands, D. (1995) 'Political and economic determinants of IMF conditional credit allocations: 1973–1989', Norman Paterson School of International Affairs Development Working Paper, Ottawa: NPSIA.

Schoultz, L. (1982) 'Politics, economics, and US participation in multilateral development banks', *International Organisation*, 36: 537–574.

Shafiq, N. (ed.) (1998) *Prospects for Middle Eastern and North African Economies: From Boom to Bust and Back?*, London: McMillan.

Shultz, G. (1993) *Turmoil and Triumph: My Years as Secretary of States*, New York: McMillan.

Smith, Jr F. (1984) 'The politics of IMF lending', *The Cato Journal*, 4: 211–247.

Sobhan, R. (1982) *The Crisis of External Dependence: The Political Economy of Foreign Aid to Bangladesh*, London: The University Press Ltd (Dhaka, Bangladesh) and ZED Press.

Stiglitz, J.E. (2002) *Globalisation and its Discontents*, New York and London: W.W. Norton.

Swearingen, W.D. (1996) 'Agricultural reform in North Africa: economic necessity and environmental dilemma', in Vandewalle, D. (ed.), *North Africa: Development and Reform*, New York: St. Martin's Press.

Swedberg, R. (1986) 'The doctrine of economic neutrality of the IMF and the World Bank', *Journal of Peace Research*, 23: 377–390.

Thacker, S.C. (1999) 'The high politics of IMF lending', *World Politics*, 52: 38–75.

The Economist, 'Revolution Delayed', 5 September 2002.

US Agency for International Development's (USAID) Website: foreign aid in the national interest: promoting freedom, security, and opportunity, available at http://www.usaid.gov/fani (19 July 2004).

Vaubel, R. (1991) 'The political economy of the International Monetary Fund: a public choice approach', in Roland Vaubel, Thomas D. Willett (eds), *The Political Economy of International Organisations*, pp. 205–245, Boulder, CO: Westview.

Waterbury, J. (1998) 'The state and economic transition in the Middle East and North Africa', in Shafik, N. (ed.), *Prospects for Middle Eastern and North African Countries: From Boom to Bust and Back?*, London: McMillan.

Zimmerman, R.F. (1993) *Dollars, Diplomacy and Dependency*, Boulder, CO: Lynne Rienner Publishers.

4 A World Bank attempt to create a policy environment indirectly through an NGO support project

A case study of Palestine

John Cameron

4.1 Introduction

Working in Palestine in the mid-1990s was a great challenge for any agency. The Oslo Accords, an Israel–PLO Declaration of Principles, signed in September 1993 were under continuous pressure, with large areas of the West Bank and movement between the West Bank and Gaza under de facto complete Israeli control.

The Palestinian situation can be characterized as one that challenged conventions of the World Bank protocols envisaged at Bretton Woods in the 1940s in which the World Bank deals with states that possess internal authority over citizens and territory and are externally recognized by other states. But such situations of strong sovereignty are arguably becoming less common in the post-Cold War period with perceptions of increasing numbers of so-called failed or failing states (Fukuyama, 2004). Such states are not so much inefficient in terms of neo-liberal preoccupations of the 1980s and 1990s but chronically ineffective.

The model for the World Bank in the Bretton Woods agreement was a Bank to sovereign state relationship. This system was confirmed as numerous new States emerged from colonial rule with well-defined territorial and citizenship boundaries. Border disputes were frequent, but the principle of a system of sovereign states dividing the whole global landmass and fresh-water lakes reaching out to include considerable areas of ocean was universally accepted.

The Cold War played a role in maintaining and reproducing this system, as both superpowers abhorred vacuums in the global order, shoring up and inventing states where necessary. The World Bank to sovereign state model was therefore, in principle, capable of virtually universal application from 1950 to 1990, even if many states had little effective relationship with the World Bank for much of this period.

From 1967, the World Bank was unable to use this model in relating to the people resident in the West Bank and Gaza. The Israeli conquest meant that these territories were no longer under the umbrellas of Jordanian and Egyptian State sovereignty, but were in limbo in relation to Israeli sovereignty (Davis, 1974). By the mid-1980s, international voices were making the case for a two-state 'solution' as offering the highest possibility of satisfying the parties and to do so in a conflict reducing way (Nordquist, 1985).

But the two-state 'solution' envisaged in the Oslo Accords appeared to permit de jure normalization of relationships between the World Bank and the people who claim Palestinian identity and the right to a state reflecting that identity. On '13 September 1993, the prospect of eventual Palestinian statehood became probable, if not virtually inevitable' (Sayigh, 1995, p. 5). But Sayigh then proceeds to reflect on the complexity of a two state solution and the need to include Jordan, possibly looking towards a tripartite Benelux or Nordic model.

In the wake of Oslo, the World Bank developed projects to support the Palestinian Authority (hereafter the PA) and also a project to support the Palestine NGO (PNGO) sector. This chapter is concerned with the PNGO sector project as a case study of what the World Bank can learn about working with the NGO sector in a 'failing' state context – though, in this case, the 'failure' is more a product of actions by a neighbouring state than internal processes. We shall return to this wider issue of the World Bank and sovereignty in the conclusion to this chapter.

The following sections will show how creating a policy environment drawing on strengths in Palestinian civil society that was conducive to reconstruction and development of the Palestinian economy and polity proved difficult to implement in practice.

4.2 The World Bank PNGO Project

The rationale for the establishment of the PNGO Project in the mid-1990s was that the World Bank was already developing a framework for working more directly with NGOs, albeit on a small scale. The World Bank

> sees an important role for NGOs in helping achieve each of its three main objectives – promoting equitable economic growth, reducing poverty, and protecting the environment. NGOs can help improve the quality of people's lives through project work and by representing the interest of the poor. In fact, their programmes are often more effective in reaching the poor in remote areas than those managed by the public sector.
>
> (1997, p. 1)

But the Bank was still rarely funding NGOs directly. Rather, NGOs usually received Bank support indirectly, from World Bank loans and credits that a borrowing government has channelled to them.

In the first intifada (1987–93), PNGOs played an important role in delivering economic and social services in the West Bank and Gaza Strip and experimenting in self-governance in Palestinian civil society. PNGOs were lead players in the internal resistance to Israeli occupation. This history meant that in the post-Oslo period, they were significant players in Palestinian society on the ground, to some degree rivalling the PA, which drew significantly on the previously exiled PLO leadership. Sullivan reports that an official with the UN Development Programme acknowledged that there has been a concerted effort to shift funds out of the hands of the PNGOs and into those of the PA (PNA in this quote):

> Our [UNDP] mandate is to work directly with governmental authorities. We are constantly under pressure by our bosses to give our money to the PNA. But we employees are not happy about this because we've worked closely with NGOs; we know what they can do. And we know the PNA can't replace NGOs.
>
> (1996)

With the establishment of the PA, PNGOs began to lose funding from international donors, both bilateral and multilateral. Some key World Bank officials accepted that:

- PNGOs were well positioned to provide help to Palestinian people, especially the poorest and most marginalized;
- PNGOs needed continuing financial and technical assistance for at least a transitional period;
- PNGO–PA relations had become acrimonious and in need of improvement.

In line with this perception, the PNGO Project was created. Its objectives were:

- to deliver services to the poor and marginalized in Palestinian society, using NGOs as the delivery mechanism;
- to increase the capacities of NGOs receiving grants under the project by using a competitive tendering approach to allocating funds;
- to support efforts by the PA and the PNGO sector to strengthen their working relationship, including support for the development of a positive legal framework for the sector.

The PNGO Project was unusual in being designed to work directly with NGOs independently of a notionally sovereign, if embryonic, State, though the PA was allowed a 'right of objection' to Project supported activities if the PA considered them to duplicate their own efforts or to be outside their own national development plan. But outside of this consultative role, the PA has no direct role in running this project and the limitations in the services it could provide meant that outright duplication was very unlikely. A consortium to run the Project Management Organization (hereafter PMO) was selected on a competitive tendering basis. But, given the unusual design, it was not surprising that World Bank officials had a very hands-on attitude to the PNGO project.

In a process of initial consultation with the PNGO sector, the PMO identified felt-needs as:

- The West Bank priorities were land reclamation, development of NGOs, income generation for target groups, housing, youth services, rehabilitation, early childhood education, and programmes to oppose confiscation of land.

- The Jerusalem priorities are legal services to protect Palestinians from Israeli measures, development of NGOs, schools, youth services, including drug control and prevention, housing, early childhood education, community empowerment, income generation and production, school health, management training.
- The Gaza priorities were in health and education – primary health care for under-served communities, early childhood education, adult formal and non-formal community education, vocational training for the disabled. Also, credit programmes for poor farmers and poor women; and medical financial assistance to the poor.

This mixture of needs crosses policy boundaries between welfare service delivery, developmental objectives and governance. Effective action across all these areas would inevitably play a key role in setting the general policy environment in Palestine.

With initial funding of US$12.5 million, provided by the World Bank and the Governments of Saudi Arabia and Italy, the PNGO project began to support development projects proposed by PNGOs on a competitive tendering basis. The first grants were approved and distributed in summer 1998. In that first round, 365 applications were submitted and 39 projects received funding with a total disbursement of US$1.8 million. The second round, in spring 1999, yielded 235 proposals, but only 34 were recommended by the PMO's project appraisal staff for approval by the consortium. The total to be disbursed was about US$3 million.

This disbursement was an attempt to meet the first two project objectives, albeit on a smaller scale than originally envisaged. The third objective to improve relations between the PA and PNGOs was surrounded by suspicion on both sides as the PA moved towards legislation seen as unduly intrusive by leading PNGOs.

4.3   The Project mid-term review

An analytical framework was developed jointly by a Project mid-term review team (hereafter MTR) in 2001 drawing on this author's earlier work evaluating the Project in 2000. The team consisted of four people: John Cameron, Team Leader and operation issues/administrative efficiency; Denis Sullivan, governance issues; Lisa Taraki, gender poverty and social exclusion analysis; Laurie Zivetz, impact assessment and capacity building.

The team met with members of the PMO staff, the World Bank, the Project governing consortium, the Project Governance Committee as well as key representatives from NGO networks and unions, the PA, and donor agencies. A total of 15 visits were undertaken to funded projects representing all of the geographic and sectoral areas covered by the project. In addition, 8 focus groups were undertaken: 6 with grant recipients (including 1 with block grant managers, and 1 all-women group focusing primarily on the capacity building aspect of the programme) and 2 with non-grant recipients. These focus group discussions were conducted with specific open-ended questions; participants also filled out a close-ended questionnaire (with 21 questions). In advance of the MTR, the PMO commissioned an in-depth study of 12 purposely selected projects.

The MTR team developed an analytical framework as a set of continua. This type of analysis offered the opportunity to think in terms of processes and directions of change and avoided dichotomous choices in a very tense, heated, highly politicized environment. Changing the balance significantly along a particular continuum was envisaged as creating a new milestone for the Project. The following analyses show how the Team saw the Project as having travelled from inception (I) to the time of the MTR (M) and how the Team saw a desirable movement over the next three years (F). The following is an edited version of the MTR report, though the present tense, referring to early 2001, has been maintained.

4.3.1   Should the Project treat the underlying situation as more 'emergency' than 'ongoing'?

As stated in the Conceptual Framework for the MTR, none of the socio-economic and political processes in force during the project development stage has been reversed in any fundamental sense. A borderline emergency situation prevails, and there are no concrete indications that the PA has adopted a comprehensive development strategy or has plans to put in place a programme of social assistance to the poor and marginalized. NGOs continue to provide critical services in major areas, especially in primary health care, disability and preschool education. This situation is likely to hold for the near future, given the intractability of the political situation (which has a high impact on the viability of the Palestinian economy), and the priorities of the PA in terms of spending on social services. Also the NGO sector itself is still under financial pressure and still adapting to the shocks of the early 1990s.

Therefore the PMO has been unable to move the Project very far away from the Inception position (position M).

Ongoing————————F——————————M——I——Emergency

This continuing situation limits the degree to which the future of the project in Phase II can move to the left of this continuum.

4.3.2   Should the Project be more concerned with outputs than processes?

An emphasis on procedural and accountability requirements of the Bank (and the accountability-conscious context), coupled by a decision on the part of the PMO to limit projects to one year (presumably to allow for a greater spread of resources) and an output orientation among 'charitable' organizations in Palestine, led to a disappointing preponderance of output-oriented projects among grant recipients. Block Grant managers, who enjoy more flexibility in disbursement, share more of a process orientation, although limitations on time and resources are likely to curtail the extent to which community participation and long-term programme impact can be achieved even for these agencies.

In its interactions with clients and segments of its capacity-building approach to date, the PMO has tended to be more process oriented, while at the same time generating rigorous statistical baseline and monitoring data.

Processes————————F——————————I———M——Outputs

A greater emphasis on projects designed to pilot and maintain processes which will mobilize ideas, networking, dialogue in support of service delivery to and participation of grassroots-based institutions that represent more marginal segments of society is highly desirable in future. Output-oriented funding may extend dependencies on external donors, dependencies more appropriately transferred to the state.

4.3.3 Should the Project be more concerned with welfare than sustainable development?

PNGOs relied on the generosity of expatriate Palestinians and Arab countries as well as a spirit of solidarity and voluntarism to support the basic needs of large segments of the society through the demanding conditions of the past 50 years. The flow of resources has dropped off, new demands for accountability from bilateral and multilateral donors have been introduced, and the spirit of voluntarism has waned in the wake of disappointments with national leadership. The Bank predisposed the Project towards a welfare orientation in the selection of the Welfare Association Consortium.

The service delivery objective has been operationalized in a welfare modality, with lower priority to cost recovery, sustainability, participation or cost/benefit. This was found in programmes visited by the MTR Team and documented in the case studies prepared for the MTR – it is a matter of concern that some grants spent as much as US$10,000 per direct beneficiary.

Sustainable
development————————F——————————I———M——Welfare

Although there may always be a role for NGOs in welfare programming for the poorest in Palestinian society, a future project seeking to support the transition and continuing relevance of the NGO sector in a Palestinian state needs NGOs who can leverage such services for the poor from government, recover costs for services they provide, and promote and model self reliance and democratic principles.

4.3.4 Should the Project be more concerned with including poor and marginalized people than targeting poor and marginalized people?

The Project Appraisal Document (PAD) conceptualized the Project as targeting the poor and marginalized. Project performance indicates, however, that the services provided tend to be of a 'community' nature and not specifically targeted (with the exception of services to the disabled).

Targeting——I——F——————————————M——Non-excluding

The Team sees the future as returning to a more focused targeting orientation, with special attention to identifying the more excluded and programmes that could promote their greater control over decision-making and resources as well as providing services. Given the general lack of such control experienced by women, gender will be an important explicit variable in this process.

4.3.5   *Should the Project emphasize poverty rather than marginality?*

The PAD does not distinguish between poverty and marginality, nor does it discuss the relationship between the two. In practice, the Project has seemed to focus on marginality rather than poverty, given the relative ease of identifying and isolating certain 'marginal' sectors of the population such as the disabled. Women, especially poor women, are not identified as a marginal group in the PAD, although project performance seems to indicate that an implicit notion of women as a marginal group has in fact been adopted.

Marginality————M——I——F——————————————Poverty

The key task for the future of the project is that it must ground itself in a more comprehensive understanding of the structural determinants of poverty, marginality and exclusion in Palestinian society. This would then inform an assessment of whether poverty alleviation is a realistic objective for this kind of Project, given the structural causes of poverty. Furthermore, a more studied consideration of marginality must also be attempted, one that examines the various types of marginality and identifies both the groups at most risk and those who can be most realistically served by this kind of project. A systematic monitoring of socio-economic data and analysis provided by the Palestinian Central Bureau of Statistics (PCBS), the National Poverty Eradication Commission, and other policy research institutes producing social and economic monitors should be an ongoing activity of the PNGO Resource Centre.

4.3.6   *Should the Project Development Grants be used for working with stronger rather than weaker PNGOs?*

The Team considered the issue of whether the Project should be working with stronger rather than weaker PNGOs. The question of whether stronger PNGOs were necessarily larger PNGOs was discussed. Overall it was felt that while some smaller NGOs could be strong in terms of rootedness in their communities, nevertheless, for project purposes the strongest PNGOs tended to be larger.

The Team viewed the positions on the spectrum at Project inception, at the time of the Review, and a desirable position in three years' time in the following pattern.

Weaker PNGOs—I——F————————M——Stronger PNGOs

The Inception position was based on the view that the whole NGO sector was vulnerable – an exaggerated perception even at the time in our view. Though the general continuing pressure on the sector cannot be underestimated, that did not mean all NGOs could be seen as equally vulnerable five years ago or today.

The conditionalities attached to Development Grants biased the allocation process in favour of less vulnerable NGOs (a position consistent with the perception at inception). This is being partially redressed at the time of the Review by the allocation of Block Grants that increase the opportunities for smaller NGOs/Charitable Societies to benefit from the Project.

In the future the team envisages the extension of much less competitive Block Grant type allocation, rather than Development Grants, and capacity building targeted specifically at smaller NGOs' needs. This should mean the Project comfortably working right across the range of NGOs.

4.3.7 Should the Project be developing competition rather than cooperation between PNGOs?

The Project was overwhelmingly based on a competitive model at its inception. Stronger NGOs thought they could live with this model providing they played on a level playing field. This competitive model for Grant allocation has coloured the whole Project – arguably distorting its efforts to play a role in developing the capacities of the sector as a whole and the governance objective. The PMO has had to expend much effort in administering the Grant allocation process as arm's length competitive 'tendering'. In a situation where applications were vastly more than the Project could accommodate, this has produced much ill will. The word 'rejection' has dominated the Grant allocation process and produced accusations that run from the relatively mild 'bias towards stronger NGOs' to accusations of outright 'discrimination'.

At the time of the MTR, the Team considers the PMO had moved the Project towards greater cooperation, partially through the introduction of Block Grants, and as a less intended outcomes of bringing NGOs together for training. The Bank does not seem to have been a positive force in this respect.

Co-operation——F————————————M—I——Competition

In order to encourage the development of a healthy civil society with a degree of autonomy from governmental and market processes, the Team thinks that the Project needs to move towards fostering cooperation as the dominant relationship between NGOs. The proposed development of a research and capacity building facility for the NGO sector is consistent with this vision.

4.3.8   Should the Project be more concerned with PNGO intra-sector relationships than PA/NGO sector relationships?

The project was designed to be very heavily engaged in promoting PA/NGO relations. The PMO has also focused on these relations primarily through informal contacts. The heavily competitive model of Grant Allocation has inhibited the role of PMO in developing intra-NGO relationships.

> PNGO Relations———F—————M—I——PNA/PNGO Relations

In Phase II, the project should focus its attention as much on intra-sector NGO relations as part of civil society development as on PA/NGO relations.

4.3.9   Should the Project seek to maximize its own value-added rather than seek funder coordination/synergy?

No specific activities in the area of donor coordination were built into Project design. The PMO rightly, therefore, focused its energies on maximizing its own value-added. The lack of contact with other funders is now appearing as a weakness as some of them create large NGO programmes of their own.

> Funder synergy/—————F—————I—M——Project
> co-ordination   value-added

Thus, in the future second phase, the PMO should focus much more of its energies on fundraising and donor coordination (which in itself could be of significant value to this Project in technical and financial terms).

4.3.10   Should the Project be more concerned with sectoral or multisectoral activities?

PNGO in its design and implementation understood service delivery in its broadest, most multisectoral meaning, stretching and possibly exceeding the technical capacity of the PMO. Although consultants were engaged on occasion to provide input into project appraisal, the small size and highly technical nature of many of the projects has made it impossible and inappropriate to actually appraise the technical soundness of any one proposal. The same is true for technical assistance and monitoring support rendered by the PMO to grantees. Personnel on the field with generic development skills will find it impossible to make any meaningful specialized input or indeed monitor impact across the variety of types of projects or assess the advice of sectoral technical specialists.

> Sectoral—————————F—————————M——I—Multisectoral

A future project should take this into consideration in the design including staffing considerations and the potential for synergies among projects. While the Project should engage with the priorities expressed by more excluded people, providing technical advice on sectoral matters is not where the comparative advantage of this Project lies.

4.3.11 Should the Project take risks or seek certainty?

The World Bank tends to be risk averse and work on minimizing down-side risk. The PAD's Risk Analysis demonstrates this approach. Not surprisingly, the PMO has remained close to this position. The proposal procedures and information system of the Project are designed to provide a comprehensive quantitative administrative record of activities and 'due process' is the guiding maxim. The choice of NGOs' projects starts from rejecting those without formal registration and two years of activity regardless of the potential of their ideas.

Risk- ————————F—————————————————M—I–Certainty-
taking   seeking

The Team sees the future Phase II as needing a more risk-accepting attitude. This is partially because of the Palestinian context and partially because of the risky nature of worthwhile NGO activity everywhere. Moving towards a more no-blame, risk management culture will be important for a successful Phase II.

4.3.12 Should the Project emphasize teaching or learning?

The Project was designed to teach the PNGO sector how to survive in a challenging context. The lessons to be learnt centred on writing proposals and having accountability procedures in place that would be acceptable to new, usually 'Western' funding agencies. MTR Team interviews with people from NGOs produced evidence that the PMO has successfully taught these lessons to a substantial number of NGOs, including those unsuccessful in their Grant applications.

Learning————————————————F————————————M—I——Teaching

The MTR Team thinks that the issue of teaching NGOs and learning from NGOs should be more balanced in the Resource Centre and in Phase II. NGOs can bring valuable inputs from grassroots experience and international contacts. The inception pattern of the 'I' is consistent with a classical World Bank view of the wider (indeed global) development challenge in the mid/late 1990s which has been transferred to the PNGO sector. The pattern of the 'M' represents the Team's view of the situation at the time of the Mid-Term Review. This shows elements of *ad hoc* adjustment in the light of pressures coming from the Palestinian context or pressures from the World Bank in the process of design and implementation of procedures. It is not a new vision of the Project, and has lost a little of the strong logical underpinning of the Bank's original vision. The pattern of the 'F' represents the Team's vision of where the Project could be looking towards 2006. It has a logic, but is also generally willing to engage with the tensions of working towards the centre of the continua.

The original World Bank vision has proven inappropriate for Palestinian NGOs in the challenges they face in working as civil society, rather than market or state, institutions – arguably it is an inappropriate vision for NGO sectors anywhere in the world. Moving from M to F positions can be seen as a movement that requires a Palestinian State creating a context in which NGOs should be able to play roles more conventional for a middle-income society. Such roles are not easy, but the parameters of successful performance for NGOs in politically democratic, middle-income societies are well known internationally. Large-scale external funding for the NGO sector over five years from an agency like the World Bank could play a useful role in this transition by strengthening civil society in the interests of the more excluded. But it would be important for the World Bank to also be supportive of development of an effective Palestinian State.

4.4   Sustainability and targeting issues

Sustainability in the Project was analysed with respect to activities, NGOs and the Project itself.

4.4.1   Activities

The one-year limit on activities acceptable as projects for funding has been a grave obstacle to sustainability. Some grant-supported projects have involved capital investment with little indication of where recurrent funding will be found to use the investment; some have had strong recurrent funding elements but with little indication of how they can be continued. Of course, it is in the beneficiary NGOs' interests to represent themselves as in a desperate financial plight. Team field visits suggested that, while Project Grants were appreciated, the activities being funded were at risk once Project funding ceased. It could be that the Project was adding to the portfolio of NGOs' activities and widening the choice of what activities could not continue in the year following the Project Grant. In this sense, the Project Grant could be seen as supporting experiments, though in many cases the Project was merely providing a respite from financial pressure on mainstream activities.

4.4.2   NGOs

The Project has sustained Grant receiving NGOs as organizations only as a by-product of supporting activities. The Project has tried to minimize provision of core funding (a common feature of funder support globally). NGOs have learned to tackle complex proposal procedures, which may be of some help in their sustainability and the general capacity-building efforts of the PMO were appreciated in terms of 'technical' sustainability. The Hardship Grant element would have focused on the survival of NGOs as organizations, but the concept was never properly developed and the sum of money, and target number of NGOs, was too small to be meaningful in terms of sectoral sustainability.

4.4.3 The Project

The Project has been sustainable in the simple sense that its contractual obligations were always limited to allow withdrawal from an activity or a NGO in a maximum of a year by the PMO, and total World Bank withdrawal after three or four years. The challenge of longer-term commitment has been put into the future and other agencies' hands.

The MTR team envisaged a future shifting in the target group from 'poor and marginalized' to 'more excluded'. This includes the identification of the target group from aggregate data for identifying localities for national and international NGOs. But it puts a major emphasis on locality level identification through participative methods and qualitative analysis of control over decision-making and resources. Any receiving NGO would produce an analysis of the heterogeneity of the population in its chosen catchment locality and a primary target group of around 25 per cent of the population as 'more excluded'. We would expect women always to be a majority of this group along with others (children, elderly people and even men), who are gender oppressed by the exercise of adult men's masculinity.

Given the lack of a clear and common understanding of who the more excluded people in Palestinian society are, the identification of the more excluded will be carried out by NGOs through a process of participatory investigations in the locations in which they are active, including consultations with other NGOs, and the monitoring of macro-level socio-economic trends in the West Bank and Gaza Strip. It would also include an on-going social policy dialogue with the PA. This process in itself should be a valuable means of building NGO capacity in the identification of social intervention priorities and contributing to creating a pro-poor, pro-excluded policy environment.

4.5 The World Bank, 'failing' states and the NGO sector

Even as the MTR team completed their report the political situation was deteriorating and the second intifada was developing (Diwan and Shaban, 1999; PCBS, 2000; PCBS, 2001). The PA was unable to develop any meaningful policy environment as the Israeli State exercised arbitrary, unaccountable authority over the lives of the residents of the West Bank and Gaza. Border closures now compounded by the construction of a wall crossing into the West Bank to protect Israeli settlements have caused chaos for many livelihoods (http://www.miftah.org, July 2004).

Nevertheless there are signs that the basic principles of the Oslo Accords on a two-state solution are still supported (Qurei, 2001). In 1999, in a small survey of 141 Palestinians accompanied by some intriguing testimony, Halkin found Palestinians strongly favouring a 'normal' democratic, armed state with only 32 per cent looking for a return to a strong Palestine–Jordan connection. In similar vein:

> For those Palestinians who share the vision of a two-state solution – and public opinion surveys consistently show this applies to a majority of Palestinians living in the territories – the starting point of their vision is a total Israeli withdrawal from the West Bank and Gaza.

(Green, 2003, p. 46)

The international focus is increasingly turning to the Israeli position:

> Israel's severe restrictions on drilling for water, planting, and irrigation placed on Palestinians have maintained at a low level the amount of water made available to the Palestinian population. Israeli policies ensure that most of the water of the west Bank percolates underground to Israel and that Israeli settlers are provided with preferential access to water resources.
>
> (International Debates, 2004, p. 133)

> For Israelis, it means no one can agree on the meaning of a security fence because they are unwilling to decide, once and for all, Israel's position on the future of the settlements, the territories, the borders and, in fact, the very nature of the Jewish state.
>
> (Green, 2003, p. 47)

> [Only] peace built on an equity of resources and rights will sustain and guarantee security for both sides.
>
> (Isaac and Rizik, 2002, p. 83)

> Israel must be transformed into 'a state for all its citizens'.
>
> (Bishara, 1999, p. 16)

So how can the World Bank work towards a suitable policy environment in this context? First the Bank must recognize that the world is not organized on the basis of a system of sovereign states tidily dividing up territory between themselves. In a global hierarchy with one overwhelming superpower, sovereignty is a property dependent on permission of that superpower, not a natural right.

In the case of Israel and Palestine this process is totally transparent. The sovereignty of Israel might be described as a super-sovereignty. The Israeli State gains strength from the acquiescence of the superpower in permitting claims to territory that makes Palestinian political and economic viability impossible. In the very delicate issue of the status of Jerusalem, symbolically precious to people of various faiths, the superpower does nothing to assist the clearly desirable solution of establishing a UN administration that could remove the issue of sovereignty, but implicitly supports Israeli government aspirations to making Jerusalem the capital of Israel.

In terms of global geopolitics, the Israeli government calls upon all people of a diaspora of people adhering to Judaism to support Israel as if they were de facto Israeli citizens. A cynic might argue that while all French 'Jews' are encouraged to come to Israel, it might be less desirable if all US 'Jews' decided to emigrate. The Palestinians also have a massive diaspora of economically highly productive people vital to the economic well-being of people in the West Bank and Gaza, but they have virtually no clout in the global political order. So while one diaspora weighs heavily in the sovereignty scale, the other weighs very lightly.

So the World Bank could develop a framework that weighed up relative sovereignty and develop criteria to assess whether a group of people with strong claims to self-determination to build a genuinely owned policy environment are being obstructed from exploring alternatives by another state. Of course, in many cases the state obstructing this self-determination will be the superpower or a close client state of the superpower. The World Bank clearly has its own dilemmas in terms of its own governance in this respect. But to continue to conduct World Bank policy as if the global system were organized on the basis of states meeting as equals in sovereignty is a fiction that is transparently exposed by the Israel/Palestine situation. The World Bank needs to build a sovereignty factor into its policy that explicitly acknowledges undue influence by other states and seeks to equalize sovereignty, not pretend independence or equality. The World Bank should be explicitly critical of states that by political acts clearly damage livelihood opportunities for people who are not their citizens and recommend sanctions against such states.

There are principles that could guide such criticism. Among thinkers in the Western European philosophical oeuvre, Heacock identifies a line running from Kant's categorical imperative to Habermas' deliberative democracy that supports Palestinian rights to resist in modernist terms:

> In the words of Jurgen Habermas 'Human rights and the principle of popular sovereignty still constitute the sole ideas that can justify modern law. These two ideas represent the precipitate left behind, so to speak, once the normative substance of an ethos embedded in religions and metaphysical traditions have been forced through the filter of post traditional justification.'
>
> (2003, p. 56)

But the World Bank responsibility in 'failing' states contexts goes beyond pointing the finger at those external agencies who are complicit in the failing. The Bank should not simply stop at pointing a finger and then refuse to deal with people who have the misfortune to be residents in territories with failed states – these people have rights to reconstruction and development activities. The Palestinian people had built a wide range of PNGO institutions crossing boundaries between service delivery and self-governance. These institutions merited support in terms of reconstruction and development objectives and would have benefited from encouragement to build more co-operative relationships. Instead the Bank instituted a relatively small Project based on competitive relationships that antagonized PNGOs and those who look to them for representation in the policy environment of a developing Palestinian sovereign state.

The World Bank can learn lessons from the early years of its PNGO project in terms of building a policy environment in all 'failing' state contexts. The MTR report finds across many dimensions that the World Bank project was failing the people of Palestine. First, weigh up imbalances of sovereignty and make clear statements on conditions to be met by other states necessary for a healthy policy environment. Second, treat organizations built by people in struggle with respect and do not reduce them to service delivery, neo-liberal competitors.

Bibliography

Bishara, A. (1999) '4 May 1999 and Palestinian statehood: to declare or not to declare', *Journal of Palestine Studies*, 28: 5–16.

Davis, R.W. (1974) 'Palestinian Arab sovereignty and peace in the Middle East: a reassessment', *Journal of Peace Research*, 11: 63–73.

Diwan, I. and Shaban, R.A. (1999) *Development Under Adversity: the Palestinian Economy in Transition*, Washington, DC: World Bank; Ramallah: Palestine Economic Policy Research Institute.

Fukuyama, F. (2004) *State Building: Governance and World order in the Twenty-First Century*, London: Profile Books.

Green, D.B. (2003) 'A wall of ambivalence', *Prospect*, August: 42–47.

Halkin, H. (1999) 'The state of the Palestinians', *New Republic*, 220: 1–12.

Heacock, R. (2003) 'Palestine, 1987–2000: from natural law to positive law', *Palestine–Israel Journal of Politics, Economics and Culture*, 10: 54–61.

International Debates (2004) 'The Palestinian question and the United Nations' (reproduced from UN Department of Public Information, March 2003), 2: 132–133.

Isaac, J. and Rizik, M. (2002) 'The viability of the Palestinian state and Israel's settlement policy', *Palestine–Israel Journal of Politics, Economics and Culture*, 9: 76–83.

Nordquist, K.A. (1985) 'Contradicting peace proposals in the Palestine conflict', *Journal of Peace Research*, 22: 159–173.

Palestinian Central Bureau of Statistics (PCBS) (2000) 'Poverty in Palestine' (January–December 1998).

—— (2001) 'Impact of Israeli measures on the economic conditions of Palestinian households'.

Qurei, A. (2001) 'A Palestinian State is a historical necessity', *Palestine–Israel Journal of Politics, Economics and Culture*, 8: 16–25.

Sayigh, Y. (1995) 'Redefining the basics: sovereignty and security of the Palestinian state', *Journal of Palestine Studies*, 24: 5–19.

Sullivan, D.J. (1996) 'NGOs in Palestine: agents of development and foundation of civil society', *Journal of Palestine Studies*, 25: 93–100.

World Bank (1997) 'Non-governmental organizations', available at http://www.worldbank.org/html/extdr/faq/97523 (23 August 1997).

5 The World Bank and good governance

Rethinking the state or consolidating neo-liberalism?

Gordon Crawford

5.1 Introduction

This chapter subjects the World Bank's alleged 'rethinking' on the role of the state to critical scrutiny. Rather than denoting a break with neo-liberalism, it is asserted that such rethinking entails the reconfiguration of neo-liberalism in a more hegemonic version that integrates both political and economic components. The chapter examines the rise of governance issues and the shift in catchword from 'minimal' state to 'effective' state, but concludes that there is more evidence of continuity than change, with the role of the state in economic development remaining firmly subordinate to that of the market.

Following this brief introduction, the chapter is organized into two substantive parts. The first traces the perceived shifts in World Bank thinking about the state from the early 1990s onwards. It examines the key documents that pertain to World Bank-state issues, namely those relating to governance, the presentation of a 'market-friendly' state, including in East Asia, the emphasis on state effectiveness in the *1997 World Development Report* and the focus on political institutions and markets in the *2002 World Development Report*. It questions the interpretation that such documents signal a significant change in direction, away from the state minimizing agenda of the 1980s and towards a greater recognition of the role of the state in development. In contrast, it demonstrates that the World Bank's conception of the role of government remains limited and subordinate within an overall free market model of development. The second part explores the theoretical influences that give rise to the Bank's model of the state. It finds a significant degree of correspondence with liberal political theory, suggesting that World Bank intentions are to construct a liberal state and hence to consolidate contemporary neo-liberalism. The chapter concludes that concepts like 'good governance' and 'state effectiveness' are very beguiling – who can possibly disagree with either? Yet both have an ideological content. The Bank's intent is not to 'bring the state back in' but to ensure that government remains limited and the scope of state power restricted. The beneficiaries of such a strategy are the capitalist class, with private profits enhanced through the state's limited but 'enabling' role.

5.2   The World Bank and the state: 1990s to the present

This section undertakes an analysis of the key World Bank documents that outline its alleged 'rethinking' on the state from 1990 onwards. In three sub-sections, the first investigates the rise up the Bank's reform agenda of the concept of governance (and 'good governance'); the second examines a 'market-friendly' approach, especially its controversial use to describe the state in East Asian development and the third explores the notion of an 'effective state'. In each sub-section, it is contested that these perceived policy shifts constitute a positive acknowledgement of the state's centrality to development, and, alternatively, it is asserted that there is evidence of the continued subordination of the state to market mechanisms. Preceding these discussions, a brief history of the World Bank and the state is provided, including an introduction to different interpretations of the Bank's recent publications.

5.2.1   *The Bank and the state: a brief historical overview*

From its establishment in 1944 at the Bretton Woods Conference to the end of the 1970s, the Bank did not take a strong pro-market line (Brecknock, 1997, p. 52). Indeed, during the 1950s and 1960s, consistent with the Keynesian consensus at that time, the Bank perceived the state as the key engine of development. The Bank saw itself primarily as assisting government in its role in raising and allocating capital resources, notably for infrastructural projects (ibid., p. 51). Further, during Robert McNamara's presidency of the Bank (1968–81), the emphasis on the realization of basic human needs, to be achieved through 'redistribution with growth' (Chenery *et al.*, 1974), entailed a top-down strategy in which government was responsible for public service provision and for development programmes targeted at the poor. The paradigm shift within the Bank to a market-led approach came in the early 1980s, co-inciding with the electoral triumph of the 'new right' in two of the Bank's largest shareholders, the UK and USA, with the coming to power of Prime Minister Thatcher and President Reagan respectively. The adoption of neo-liberalism as the Bank's driving ideology and the subsequent attack on the state was evident in documents such as the 1981 Berg Report on sub-Saharan Africa and the *World Development Report 1987* on *Trade and Industrialization*.[1] Under William Clausen's presidency (1981–86), Anne Krueger replaced Hollis Chenery as the chief economic theorist, with the research department characterized at that time by 'a particularly devout commitment to neo-liberalism and an intolerance to dissent' (Berger and Beeson, 1998, p. 490). The 'overgrown' state was now perceived as the major problem, and the solution was a fundamental reorientation of economic structures from a state-led to a market-led system. In developing countries, this meant the implementation of structural adjustment programmes, based on economic liberalization, deregulation and privatization. John Williamson (1990) famously dubbed this set of policy prescriptions, emanating from Washington-based institutions, as the 'Washington Consensus'.[2]

If the pendulum had already swung from one extreme to the other in the state versus market debate between the late 1970s and the late 1980s, World Bank thinking in the 1990s appeared to indicate movement in the opposite direction, with renewed emphasis on the quality of state capacity. Two concepts are particularly crucial, 'good governance' and 'state effectiveness', with the 'market-friendly' interpretation of East Asian developmental success also viewed by some as further recognition of the state's role. Yet, how significant was this movement of the pendulum? Some commentators thought it constituted a further break of paradigmatic proportions. For Archer, for instance, the governance agenda 'marks the demise of undiluted neo-liberalism' (1994, p. 13) and 'rehabilitates the state' (ibid., p. 7). For Evans, such rethinking marked a 'third wave' of theorizing about the role of the state in the development process: first, the state as the key agent of growth and development in the 1950s and 1960s; second, the perceived failure of the statist strategy leading to the new orthodoxy of neo-utilitarian (or neo-liberal) theory and the 'rolling back' of the state in the 1980s; third, a reconceptualization of the state's role and a reassertion of the state as a crucial actor in the early 1990s (Evans, 1992).[3] Such an interpretation is contested here.[4] Through analysis of key World Bank documents, it is argued that the theoretical and conceptual modifications remain firmly embedded within a neo-liberal paradigm. Indeed it is asserted that such modifications constitute a revised and strengthened neo-liberal framework, one in which the political dimension has been added, with the role of the state reformulated in the service of a free market economy.

5.2.2 *Governance and development*

The introduction of the concept of governance into development discourse is generally attributed to the World Bank and its 1989 *Long-Term Perspective Study* on sub-Saharan Africa (Nelson and Eglinton, 1992; Lancaster, 1993). In the context of poor results from structural adjustment programmes in Africa, a new departure was evident with the assertion that 'Underlying the litany of Africa's development problems is a crisis of governance' (World Bank, 1989, p. 60), and that 'Africa needs not just less government but better government' (ibid., p. 5). Yet the Bank's ongoing commitment to neo-liberal economic policies was evident in this initial shift – it was inconceivable that the set of policy prescriptions was wrong, therefore it had to be their *implementation* that was at fault. A paradox had emerged, clearly articulated by Evans as follows:

> orthodox policy prescriptions ... contained the paradoxical expectation that the state (the root of the problem) would somehow be able to become the agent that initiated and implemented adjustment programmes (become the solution).
>
> (1992, p. 141)

Therefore, whereas implementation had previously been regarded as simply a matter of political will (for instance, in the Berg Report), attention now shifted to the nature of government and to the introduction of political and administrative reforms that would *constrain* its ability to act in an arbitrary and unaccountable manner. From the Bank's perspective, to ensure that economic adjustment programmes were fully implemented, with reduced 'slippage',[5] it was necessary that the state acted in a more predictable, rule-based and transparent manner. Thus, in the early 1990s, the Bank vigorously pursued this new emphasis on governance, establishing a 'task force' on this subject. The outcome was its 1992 publication, entitled *Governance and Development*. Here, governance was defined as 'the manner in which political power is exercised in the management of a country's economic and social resources for development' (World Bank, 1992, p. 3). Four economic dimensions of governance were identified as of relevance to the Bank's work: public sector management; accountability; a legal framework for development and transparency and information. Improving public sector management pertained to pre-existing World Bank activities, for example, civil service reform, privatization of state-owned enterprises, and financial management, whereas the other three entailed new directions for the Bank's policy reform agenda. The latter three dimensions could involve an overlap with elements of democracy, for instance open and accountable government and the rule of law. However, in line with its mandate to remain apolitical, as laid down in its Articles of Agreement, the Bank restricted itself to consideration of the economic aspects of these concepts. Thus, its concern with the financial accountability of governments is said to entail strengthening accounting and auditing practices as well as improving capacity for economic policy management (ibid., pp. 13–28). Its interest in greater transparency and information provision is stated as involving: improving economic efficiency, preventing corruption and enabling greater dissemination of economic information, for example, by strengthening government statistical offices (ibid., pp. 40–47). Its concern for the rule of law is limited to establishing a legal framework for economic activity, for example, property rights, laws of contract and so forth (ibid., pp. 28–39).

The impression created is two-fold. First, governance reforms are presented as technical in nature, underpinned by the presumption of a neutral state. The idea of a neutral state is central to liberal political theory (discussed in more detail in part two) and would seem to have shaped the World Bank's thinking on governance (Williams and Young, 1994, p. 93). Yet, 'the notion of neutrality is unsustainable within liberal theory', with 'heavily loaded assumptions smuggled in' (ibid., pp. 93–94). In the Bank's case, Williams and Young argue, the supposedly technical reforms and the 'good' in 'good governance' are guided by pro-free market assumptions: in the Bank's own words, governments must provide 'rules to make markets work . . . and to ensure property rights' (World Bank, 1992, p. 6, cited in ibid., p. 94).

Second, at first glance the focus on governance reforms suggested a move away from the state shrinking agenda of the 1980s, and towards a greater emphasis on the importance of an efficient and effective state, albeit slimmed down from the previous overextended version. Considerations of whether the good governance agenda constituted a break or continuity with neo-liberalism had provoked divergent responses, however. As outlined earlier, for some it represented a paradigmatic break with neo-liberalism (Evans, 1992; Archer, 1994). In contrast, other analysts (Moore, 1993; Leftwich, 1994) maintained that governance initiatives remained enclosed within a minimalist conception of the state's role. In particular, Adrian Leftwich explained the rise of good governance as closely integrated with an overall neo-liberal agenda, again noting a close association between governance and liberalism. He reminded us that 'neo-liberalism is not only an economic theory but a political one as well', emphasizing 'democratic politics and a slim, efficient and accountable public bureaucracy [as] not simply desirable but *necessary* for a thriving free market economy, and vice versa' (1994, pp. 368–369). Thus it is precisely 'resurgent neo-liberal theory . . . [that] spurred western governments and international institutions to go on from promoting economic liberalization to making good governance (and democracy) a condition of development assistance' (ibid.). Such points will be expanded on in the second part of this chapter. Mick Moore also perceived a degree of continuity with state-scepticism, pointing to 'governance' as an expression of the doctrine of Anglo-American liberalism that dominates World Bank thinking. Consequently, in his view, the governance experience of East Asian countries with successful economic performance, 'appears to have been largely ignored' (1993, p. 41). In conclusion he asserted that the World Bank is willing 'to keep a close eye on the state . . . but . . . unwilling and unable to take state-building seriously' (ibid., p. 49).

Following its introduction by the World Bank, it is well known that good governance has been adopted as a policy objective almost universally by international development agencies, for example, by the regional development banks, by UN agencies such as UNDP, by the IMF since 1997, and by most bilateral agencies such as Danida (Danish International Development Assistance) and the UK's Department for International Development. One problematic issue, nonetheless, has been the varied and fluid definitions given to this rather slippery concept.[6] Additionally, good governance has been embraced, along with economic liberalization, by regional associations such as the New Partnership for African Development (NEPAD), though its introduction as an 'essential element' of the Cotonou Agreement between the European Union and African, Caribbean and Pacific group was contested and successfully resisted by the ACP nations.[7]

For over a decade, the World Bank has promoted good governance as a key area of policy reform. Although the terms governance and good governance were largely eschewed in the Bank's *World Development Report 1997* on the state (discussed later), despite covering the same terrain, they again featured more prominently in the *World Development Report 2002: Building Institutions for Markets*. The close association between notions of governance and a free-market economy is particularly evident in this later report, undermining the Bank's presentation of the state as a neutral instrument and its own approach as a technical one, while confirming the presence of the 'heavy-loaded' assumption that a free market system is both desirable and superior. The World Bank presents a picture of state neutrality within the framework of a market economy, for instance by not displaying bias to particular market actors, but disregards its own belief in a particular type of economy, and within that of a limited state. Thus, 'good governance' becomes defined as the ability of the state to promote the institutions that support markets (World Bank, 2002, p. 99), inclusive of four key characteristics that serve to consolidate and institutionalize a free market economy:

- the creation, protection and enforcement of property rights;
- the provision of a regulatory regime to promote competition;
- the provision of sound macroeconomic policies that create a stable environment for market activities;
- the absence of corruption.

(Ibid.)

Hence the rhetoric of 'good governance' – so alluringly positive – serves to disguise the reality of *pro-market governance*. This is verified by a brief look at World Bank activities. An examination of the Bank's legal reform activities concluded that

> The Bank has tended to place law on the side of markets rather than empowering individuals.... Law is viewed as a means of protecting businesses.... As such, the Bank has mostly addressed issues relating to economic efficiency and property rights, rather than distributional considerations, questions of access to justice, the enforcing of political and civil rights, and the strengthening of criminal law.
>
> (Collingwood, 2002, p. 11)

This approach, dubbed 'neo-liberal legalism' (ibid.), is confirmed by the Bank itself, giving the example of property rights as an illustration of the importance of effective legal institutions: 'Public officials cannot enforce property rights without the ability to try, judge, and punish those who do not respect those rights' (World Bank, 2002, p. 99). A similar pro-business orientation is evident in relation to anti-corruption activities, a core element of the governance agenda. Corruption is perceived as public corruption, defined as 'the abuse of public power for private gain' (World Bank, 1997, p. 102), caused by 'public officials hav[ing] wide discretion and little accountability' (ibid., p. 103). The outcome is the imposition of 'costs on private citizens and businesses' (ibid.), simultaneously undermining investment and economic growth. Anti-corruption activities are thus overwhelmingly directed at 'restraining arbitrary and corrupt behaviour [of state agencies] in dealings with businesses and citizens' (ibid., p. 99). Anti-corruption measures include contracting-out services to private companies, making rules more transparent, strengthening the legal framework, introducing market mechanisms into government, and limiting the discretion of regulators (ibid., chapter 6). In contrast, private sector corruption as a governance issue is relatively ignored, notably that associated with powerful transnational corporations. Clearly bribe-givers are required as well as bribe-takers, with benefits to firms, not costs, from corruptly securing lucrative deals.[8] Collusion between large corporations and their governments is also not unknown, with aid monies used to pressurize developing country governments to accept less favourable contracts, as allegedly happened in the Mozambique between US officials and the Mozambican government over a contract to an international oil company (Collingwood, 2002, p. 15, citing Hall and Bayliss, 2000, p. 20).

Thus, in such ways, the good governance agenda continues to display an unbalanced and asymmetrical response to state and market actors, amounting to pro-market governance.

5.2.3 A 'market-friendly' approach to development

An overlapping development in the early 1990s, consistent with the new emphasis on 'good governance', was the introduction by the World Bank of its 'market-friendly' approach. Initially outlined in the *World Development Report 1991: A Challenge to Development*, this approach focuses on state–market relations, with a claimed 'rethinking' and 'reappraisal' of the state (World Bank, 1991, p. 9). In attempting to present an approach distinct from the state versus market antagonism of the 1980s, the complementarities between state and market are emphasized for the first time, a theme repeated by the Bank during the 1990s. Interventions by the state become acceptable once again, though 'provided they are market-friendly' (ibid., p. 5). Yet little had changed in fact. The advice given to governments is to 'intervene reluctantly' and to 'let markets work', except where the private sector does not provide public goods such as basic education and infrastructure (ibid.). Essentially 'complementarity' means that the role of the state is to service the private sector. Thus the key feature of a 'market-friendly' state is the provision of an 'enabling environment' for private sector development, the lack of which is now perceived as the central problem of developing countries (Wade, 1996, p. 6). Five main components of such an 'enabling environment' are outlined: infrastructure; a well-educated workforce; macroeconomic stability; free trade and a regulatory framework favouring private sector investment and competition (ibid.). Core economic policy prescriptions remain within a neo-liberal framework, directed at getting the state out of the economy and allowing market mechanisms and the private sector to take over: 'Governments need to do less in those areas where markets work, or could be made to work, reasonably well' (World Bank, 1991, p. 9). National economies are to be opened up to international trade and investment (ibid., p. 11) and state-owned enterprises are to be privatized (ibid., p. 9). Thus, governments are given two sorts of tasks. One is to ensure that the 'right' policies are implemented with regard to macroeconomic management, inclusive of domestic, trade and financial liberalization. The other is to expend public monies on those 'public goods', such as infrastructure and education and health services, required by private firms in order to operate in an efficient and low-cost manner, hence 'enabling' private profits to be maximized.

Thus the claimed 'rethinking' and 'reappraisal' of the state (ibid.) is limited to according it a supportive role in market-led development, merely indicating a greater realization of how state powers can be utilized for private sector gain. There is no change in terms of the overall development model, with neo-classical economics remaining incontestable. There is an ideological function, however, with the Bank at pains to differentiate its new 'market-friendly' approach from both 'dirigisme' and 'laissez-faire' (ibid., p. 5). Nevertheless, the close association with free-market economics, and the continued distance from state interventionism, is clear. In Wade's view (1996, p. 10), the *World Development Report 1991* merely 'restated a largely free-market view of appropriate public policy for development, under the label "market-friendly"'.

5.2.3.1   Re-interpreting East Asian development

A more direct challenge to the World Bank's espousal of orthodox economic theory had come from the 'real world' experience of the East Asian NICs, especially as the Japanese government became more forceful in pressing the Bank to recognize the important role of state interventionism in general and of selective industrial policy in particular.[9] This challenge was undercut, however, by the publication in September 1993 of *The East Asian Miracle: Economic Growth and Public Policy*. Controversially, the Bank managed to interpret the undeniable *fact* of extensive government intervention being 'market-friendly' in character. Despite the concession (in the preface by Bank President Lewis Preston) that 'some selective interventions contributed to growth', the weight of the report is anti-statist. It is asserted that 'industrial policies were largely ineffective' (World Bank, 1993, p. 312) and concludes that the 'promotion of specific industries generally did not work and therefore holds little promise for other developing economies' (ibid., p. 354). Instead success is mainly attributed to export orientation and to 'getting the basics right', with the latter entailing six specific policies that conform to market orientation (ibid., p. 89).[10]

In this way, the threat of the East Asian experience to the World Bank's market-led approach was emasculated. Instead, by manipulating the evidence into a 'market-friendly' interpretation, the East Asian experience was accommodated into, and indeed presented as a vindication of, the Bank's orthodox policy advice to developing countries.[11]

5.2.4   State effectiveness

The publication of the *World Development Report 1997: The State in a Changing World* was received as evidence of a significant change of direction by the Bank. The UK's *Guardian* newspaper headlined a 'Sudden U-turn by the World Bank' and talked of an 'astonishing *volte-face*' with the Bank 'abandon[ing] its long-running support for minimal government in favour of a new model based on a strong and vigorous state', while Clare Short, the British government's Secretary of State for International Development, declared that 'the era of complete enmity to the public sector in general and state provision in particular is coming to an end', (both quotations cited in Hildyard, 1997, p. 40). The World Bank's own press department headlined the report as 'Rethinking the State' (*World Bank News*, 26 July 1997). Even the more measured response in a subsequent

IDS Bulletin suggested that it entailed 'a substantial shift in the public position of the World Bank in relation to the role of government in development... seen as a change from a state-sceptical to a state-friendly stance' (Evans and Moore, 1998, p. 3). It is argued here, however, that this is an overstatement. Rather it is claimed that the text reveals evidence of continued state scepticism and an ongoing intent to limit the scope of state activities, serving to maintain a neo-liberal paradigm. The main arguments of the *World Development Report 1997* are outlined here, along with a critique.

The Report's two main catchphrases are 'state effectiveness' and the 'complementarity of state and market', ostensibly replacing notions of a minimal state and of state-market antagonism. The central problem, according to the Bank, is the gap between demands on states and their capabilities. No longer is this to be resolved by simply reducing the state's role, it is claimed, but rather by increasing state effectiveness. This entails a two-part strategy:

- Matching the state's role to its capability;
- Increasing state capability by reinvigorating public institutions.

(World Bank, 1997, p. 3)

Both prongs require further examination, questioning the extent of alleged 'rethinking'. Particularly in the case of weak states, the first element implicitly entails a state-minimizing agenda, as their roles are shrunk to match their relatively low capacity. Martinussen (1998, p. 70) notes that an alternative strategy of strengthening the state's resource base, through taxation for instance, is not considered.[12] If the new catchphrase is 'state effectiveness', this still begs the question as to the exact role of the state, that is, what are the tasks that it should perform effectively? And, indeed, the Report does address this question, outlining five 'fundamental tasks' which all governments, including weak states, should concentrate on:

- establishing a foundation of law;
- maintaining a benign policy environment, including macroeconomic stability;
- investing in basic social services and infrastructure;
- protecting the vulnerable;
- protecting the environment.

(World Bank, 1997, p. 4)

There is little change here from the 'night-watchman' role of the minimal state, though the provision of a welfare safety net to protect the vulnerable and the protection of the environment does appear to entail some expansion. Yet, 'protecting the vulnerable' is not especially new, given UNICEF's critique (1987) of the need for 'adjustment with a human face' and the social dimension that was subsequently tacked on to structural adjustment programmes, while the seriousness of the commitment to environmental protection is questionable. Underlying state scepticism remains evident in the statement that 'Government intervention is not the only answer to pollution' (World Bank, 1997, p. 4), arguing vaguely for 'new tools' to induce improved environmental performance, including 'the power of public opinion' and the farce of 'self-regulatory mechanisms' (ibid.).

As with *World Development Report 1991*, what is clearly emphasized is the supportive role to be played by the state in promoting free-market development – 'the state is essential for putting in place the appropriate institutional foundations for markets' (ibid.) – a theme further re-emphasized in the later *World Development Report 2002*. Most fundamentally this entails providing a legal framework to satisfy and attract private investors, with enforcement by a predictable judiciary (World Bank, 1997, p. 4).[13] The underlying message that private is always better than public becomes immediately evident when 'Going beyond the basics', with the statement that 'the state need not be the sole provider' (ibid.). There follows the usual litany of opposition to 'monopoly public providers . . . [as] unlikely to do a good job' (ibid.) and the urging of a purchaser – provider split where government pays private companies to provide public goods and services.[14] With regard to welfare programmes, the state is advised to move from public to private provision of *social insurance* for all, limiting its own efforts to programmes of *social assistance*, targeted only at the poorest (ibid., pp. 58–59). Yet, even such public programmes of social assistance are not spared critique, with 'broad-based subsidies' said to benefit higher income households disproportionately, while 'means-tested programmes' are criticized as administratively costly. As alternatives, vague notions of 'self-targeted approaches' and 'giving voice to the poor' as 'self-advocates' are outlined (ibid.).

Regarding the second prong of the strategy, 'increasing state capability by reinvigorating public institutions', a paradoxically anti-state dogma is apparent from closer examination of the text. Under the heading 'Effective rules and restraints', and echoing the *World Development Report 1991*, the underpinning liberal fear of an arbitrary or capricious state is evident, with multiple references to 'checking arbitrary state action' (ibid., p. 7) and 'cutting back on discretionary authority' (ibid., p. 8). There is an underlying suspicion of the executive, with the strengthening of accountability mechanisms called for, both formal (legislative and judicial oversight) and informal (the private sector and civil society more broadly). Similarly, under the heading of 'subjecting the state to more competition', there is a focus on combating the arbitrary, discretionary and corrupt actions of state officials through the introduction of competitive market forces by two main means: the contracting out of public services to private and non-government providers; and the introduction of market mechanisms within state agencies (ibid., pp. 9–10). The overwhelming impression is of a state-scepticism that remains driven by neo-liberal ideology – fundamentally the state and public officials are not to be trusted and must be subjected to market forces. In contrast, there is little or no critique of private sector actors.

Under the seemingly innocuous heading of 'bringing the state closer to the people', the World Bank states that 'Governments are more effective when they listen to *businesses* and citizens and work in partnership with them in deciding and implementing policy' (ibid., p. 10, emphasis added), and recommends 'giving people a voice' and 'broadening participation' (ibid.). Taken at face value, such pronouncements suggest the implicit promotion of a democratic agenda, encouraging greater societal input into public policy making, though suspicions are raised by the apparent prioritization of businesses, a minority interest group, before citizens. Scratching the surface suggests that a veneer of political participation covers the underlying reality of undemocratic practices that 'lock-in liberalization' and 'lock-out society'. Profoundly undemocratic, the 'locking-in of good policies' is advocated by the Bank (ibid., p. 50), with ' "good policies" equated with neo-liberal policies' (Hildyard and Wilks, 1998, p. 51). Both internal and external 'lock-in mechanisms' are cited approvingly. Internally, an independent central bank and a 'conservative central bank governor' are strongly recommended (ibid., pp. 50–51). Externally, World Bank and IMF conditionality and WTO agreements serve to 'strengthen commitments' to policy 'rules' (ibid., p. 101), locking in nation states to economic liberalization and to opening up national economies to transnational actors. Simultaneously, citizens are effectively 'locked-out' (Hildyard and Wilks, 1998, p. 51), having little or no choice with regard to public policy making, at least in the economic sphere. This situation is confirmed by the Bank's own statement that key policy areas 'require insulation from political pressure' (World Bank, 1997, p. 117), and thus off-limits to public participation. The ostensible emphasis on 'voice' and 'participation' is therefore seen in a different light. Such rhetoric becomes a public relations exercise only, the appearance of a people-friendly Bank obscuring the reality of its intent to construct a neo-liberal state in which economic policy choices are excluded.

This is precisely the manner by which proponents of neo-liberalism, such as the World Bank, seek to construct hegemonic control. The attainment of hegemonic status by a particular body of ideas means that such is its dominance that it is subject to little questioning or challenge. Its proponents have been successful in presenting their ideas as rational, objective and universally beneficial, as 'good policies' for instance, to the extent that 'there is no alternative'. In neo-liberalism's case, its drive for hegemony entails creating the impression that there is no alternative to the politics of economic liberalization, trade liberalization and integration into the world economy. Cornia notes (1998, p. 33) that there are 'few changes from the orthodoxy evident in WDR97', with 'persistent dogmatism'.[15] It is *not* the task of state agents or the citizenry to question or challenge such neo-liberal assumptions, despite the rhetoric about 'voice' and 'participation'. The *World Development Report 1997* claims to present a new development model of 'good policies and more capable state institutions to implement them', which will in turn 'produce much faster economic development' (World Bank, 1997, p. 13). This merely amounts to a re-statement of the superiority of neo-liberal economic policies, with the task of a capable state being to implement such 'good policies' in an effective and efficient manner, not to subject them to democratic processes. Given this orientation, it is not surprising that the maintenance of such a policy environment is stated as one of the state's 'fundamental tasks'.

In the *World Development Report 1997*, what changed most was the rhetoric of an effective state, ostensibly placing more emphasis on the role of the state.

In fact, there was little difference from the 'market-friendly' state of the 1991 report in which a neo-liberal state was being constructed in the service of the private sector and a free market development model. As Hildyard and Wilks (1998, p. 49) pertinently ask, 'Effective for whom?'. The answer must be: effective for business. It is contended here that the capitalist class, notably international capital, benefits in two distinct ways from the World Bank's model of the state: from what it does and from what it does not. First, the business class gains from the reconfiguration of the state into the service of private capital, making available those 'public goods' that the private sector requires, such as transport and energy infrastructure and a healthy, educated workforce, thus providing the 'enabling environment' for private profits to be maximized. Second, the capitalist class also benefits from the state's continued withdrawal from intervention in a number of key areas. In the World Bank's model of an 'effective' state, it does *not* play a redistributive role, for instance through progressive taxation and improved welfare provision. Similarly the state is encouraged *not* to intervene in business matters, especially those involving transnational corporations, for instance through regulations to protect the labour force (such as minimum wages and working conditions, trade union representation) or to protect relatively small, indigenous firms (such as maximum levels of foreign ownership, minimum levels of local inputs).

5.3   The World Bank and liberal political theory

The World Bank tends not to specify the theoretical underpinnings of the strategies and policies that it advocates. Nevertheless, it is widely recognized that its economic policies are generally based on *laissez-faire* or neo-classical economics, stemming from the work of the classical liberal economists of the eighteenth and nineteenth centuries, as well as more contemporary influences, notably Milton Friedman and the 'Chicago School'. Such policies constitute the economic dimension of what is currently best known as neo-liberalism. The theoretical basis of the Bank's model of the state is less commonly discussed. It is argued here that the World Bank's recent thinking on the role of the state is strongly influenced by the political counterpart of classical economics, that is the classical political liberalism of the eighteenth and nineteenth centuries, especially as revived and re-articulated in the twentieth century by F.A. Hayek. It is contended in particular that classical liberalism's central concern to place constraints on state actions and limits on political power has been replicated in the Bank's recent doctrine. The association between liberal political philosophy and World Bank thinking on the state is explored here in three sections, focusing on the role of private property, the minimal state, and issues of democracy and participation. Preceding these discussions, very brief introductions to classical liberalism and to the work of Hayek are provided.

5.3.1   *Classical liberalism*

The emergence of liberal political thought from the seventeenth century onwards, notably through the work of theorists such as Locke, Montesquieu, Bentham,

James Mill and his son John Stuart Mill, complemented the free market economics of the classical economists of that period, most notably Adam Smith and David Ricardo. Together they provided a fully-rounded liberal theory of how economy–state–society relations should be conceived. From its inception, classical liberalism assumed the merits of a free market economy and was especially concerned with circumscribing the political parameters of the state, that is restricting it from interfering in the economy and in civil society. Classical liberalism presented the world as divided into the 'public sphere' of politics and the 'private sphere' of economy and family life, into which the state should not intervene. This overwhelming concern to delimit state activities stemmed from the notions of individual freedom and individual rights that were at the core of liberalism, and of the threat posed to such individual liberties by arbitrary and unrestrained state power. Classical liberal theorists believed in the rights of individuals (men) to act freely in an uncoerced manner, without state interference, in the domain of civil society, constituting both the economy and the family. The role of the state was to provide the rule of law in order to protect individual liberties against capricious and oppressive authority. Essentially, eighteenth- and nineteenth-century liberalism represented the interests of the bourgeoisie, the new property owning class, themselves benefiting most from the growth of the market economy, against the old powers of the monarchy, the feudal aristocracy and the church. In particular it represented the interests of bourgeois men, with patriarchy in both public and private life taken for granted. Despite variants of liberalism, in common classical liberal theorists advocated for: a constitutional state; private property and a competitive market economy (Held, 1996, p. 74).[16]

5.3.2   Hayek

With published work spanning from the 1940s to the 1980s, F.A. Hayek is widely regarded as the key academic influence on contemporary neo-liberal or 'new right' politics (Held, 1996, pp. 253–261; Pierson, 1996, pp. 81–83; Dunleavy and O'Leary, 1987, pp. 130–135), with Britain's Prime Minister Thatcher acknowledging him as her guiding influence (Wainwright, 1994, p. 45). Influenced himself by the Austrian School of Economics from his home country, Hayek was a forceful exponent and defender of liberalism, an opponent of both Eastern European socialism and of Western European Keynesianism (ibid., pp. 47–50). His aim was to return attention to the perceived insights of classical liberalism of the eighteenth and nineteenth centuries, and to restate these in a form appropriate for the modern world (Kukathas, 1989, pp. 4–5). Such a restatement was normatively based, intending to articulate his version of a 'good society', that is, one governed by liberal institutions, upholding a market economy and the rule of law (ibid.). He was particularly concerned to protect individual freedoms through limiting state activity, distinguishing not only what government should do but also what it should not (ibid., p. 9).

The following three sections demonstrate how key features of liberal political philosophy, both historically and more contemporaneously in the work of Hayek, correspond with current World Bank thinking on the state. It should be clarified here that no direct causal link between Hayek's writings and those of the Bank are being asserted.[17] Rather it is demonstrated that Hayek and the Bank hold common views on the role and nature of the state, suggesting a clear association between the opposition to arbitrary and unrestrained state power, most powerfully articulated by Hayek, and World Bank thinking on the state.

5.3.3   *Private property*

In asserting the interests of the new bourgeois class, a key feature of classical liberal political thought was the construction of a state that would ensure that ownership of the means of production remained in private hands and would protect such private property. Thus utilitarian theorists like Bentham and Mill discovered the paradox that the World Bank encountered in the early 1990s: the advocacy of a free market economy and minimal state in fact requires certain types of state intervention and a relatively strong state in order to safeguard the security of property and wealth, (see, for instance, J. Mill, 1828; Bentham, 1838; cited in Held, 1996, p. 96). J.S. Mill (1951, p. 355) outlined a primary task of the state as: 'Security of person and property and equal justice between individuals are the first needs of society and the primary ends of government'. He continued by saying that, 'there is nothing, except war and treaties, which requires a general government at all' (ibid.). As Held points out, such statements 'anticipated later 'neo-liberal' arguments' concerning free market political economy and minimal state interference (Held, 1996, p. 117).

Similar views on the inviolability of property rights were expressed by Hayek. In counterposing liberty with serfdom (Hayek, 1976), he offered a vigorous defence of a free market system and a hostility to any state interference that impinged on 'individual freedom' in economic activity and in private life. For Hayek, 'Almost any state interference with the economic realm is a first step on the "road to serfdom" ' (Dunleavy and O'Leary, 1987, p. 131). From this point of view, private property is perceived as 'the most important guarantor of freedom, not only for those who own property, but scarcely less for those who do not' (Hayek, 1976, p. 78). While recognizing that some government intervention is necessary to guarantee a free market system, this is limited to providing the legal framework for a competitive economic system. Legislative measures which attempt to 'alter the material position of particular people or enforce distributive or "social" justice' are examples of unwarranted intervention and coercive government (Hayek, 1960, p. 231).

Recent World Bank thinking on the state has also been shaped by New Institutional Economics (NIE), associated in particular with Douglass C. North, with its influence noted in particular in *World Development Report 1997* (Moore, 1998, pp. 40–41). In Kearton's (2003, p. 25) view, NIE's 'principal contribution was to encourage neo-classical economists to look again at the state.... Rather than regarding the state as a behemoth that prevents entrepreneurs from sponta-neously engaging in free markets, the state acquires coherence, purpose, and can play a positive role in unfettering markets'. Nevertheless, NIE shares underlying assumptions with neo-liberalism, notably the superiority of a free-market system and the importance of property rights. Indeed, from a NIE perspective, the role of the state is precisely to construct the type of polity that secures and enforces those economic rules, especially property rights, which simultaneously constrain its own activities. In North's view (1994, p. 366), 'Polities significantly shape economic performance because they define and enforce the economic rules. Therefore an essential part of development policy is the creation of polities that will create and enforce efficient property rights.'

The centrality of private property and property rights, as the key dimension of a free-market society, is clearly evident in the World Bank literature reviewed earlier. In the Bank's initial discussions on governance, laws guaranteeing property rights are regarded as a fundamental aspect of 'good governance'. As evidence, North's example is cited of the securing of property rights in seventeenth century England, including patent laws, leading to expanded economy activity, it is claimed (World Bank, 1992, p. 7). The ensuing publication, outlining the Bank's experience in the governance domain, cites 'laws on property rights' as the first example of Bank support to establish the legal framework for development (World Bank, 1994, p. xvii). The importance of secure property rights is a recurrent element of World Development Reports. In the 1996 report *From Plan to Market*, focusing on the transition countries of Central and Eastern Europe, there is a repeated emphasis on the legal definition and protection of property rights as a crucial element of market-oriented laws enforced by market-oriented institutions (World Bank, 1996, p. 44, 88, 102). In the 1997 report *The State in a Changing World*, the first 'basic task' of government, 'establishing a foundation of law', is primarily concerned with the institution of property rights – 'Markets cannot develop far without effective property rights' (World Bank, 1997, p. 41) – and the report continues by examining in some detail the necessary conditions for their effective protection (ibid.). In the 2002 report, *Building Institutions for Markets*, as outlined earlier, the first element of the Bank's updated definition of good governance is 'the creation, protection and enforcement of property rights' (World Bank, 2002, p. 99).

At no point does the World Bank express any qualifications or reservations about private ownership of the means of production. We are informed of the necessity for secure property 'rights', but not of the privileges and benefits enjoyed by the owners of private capital, at the expense of the rest of the population. The problem of excessive state power is repeatedly emphasized, including its 'arbitrary' and 'capricious' use by state officials and the opportunities thereby for corruption, but the economic and political power appropriated by the owners of private capital is never mentioned. An association between the strength of property rights and economic growth is claimed (ibid.), but massive inequalities in the accumulation of wealth are ignored, as is the potential role of the state in the redistribution of wealth through progressive taxation and welfare provision. In common with liberalism, the World Bank acts as if the issue that has divided political opinion for centuries is non-existent, that is whether private property is the solution or the problem to achieving sustained progress in socio-economic development.[18] Consistent with the maintenance of ideological hegemony, any problematic issues associated with the private ownership of the means of production are disallowed from entering the discursive paradigm.

5.3.4   Minimal state

Classical liberal theorists from John Locke (1632–1704) onwards have focused their concerns on the scope and powers of the state, with Held (1996, p. 81) describing as a central tenet of modern European liberalism that 'government must be restricted in scope and constrained in practice in order to ensure the maximum possible freedom of every citizen'. This central tenet has entailed securing limits to state activities, most fundamentally keeping the state out of the economy. The state's role is limited to 'ensur[ing] the conditions necessary for individuals to pursue their interests without risk of arbitrary political interference, to participate freely in economic transactions, to exchange labour and goods on the market and to appropriate resources privately' (Held, 1996, p. 95), described as the core of nineteen century English liberalism (ibid.). All the classical liberal theorists (Locke, Montesquieu, Bentham, James Mill, John Stuart Mill) have expressed a preference for this minimal, yet enabling state. The key mechanisms have been, first, constitutional rule to limit state power, and, second, the division of power within the state. In the eighteenth century, Montesquieu was an early advocate of the establishment of constitutions to set inviolable limits on state power, as well as the separation of powers between the executive, legislature and judiciary. In this respect, the strategy of liberal theorists was two-pronged, containing a certain paradox. While the principal drive has been to restrict the scope of state actions, in order to give full rein to a free-market society, this has required a 'strong' state and the strengthening of certain political institutions, notably constitutional rule, the legislature and judiciary, in order to keep a watchful eye on executive activities.

As stated, Hayek's intent was to revive and reassert classical liberal doctrine, though writing at the time of widespread state planning and of socialism, he was more aggressive in his anti-state stance than classical liberalism. In his wholesale opposition to Keynesian notions of state economic planning and management and the redistribution of economic resources, Hayek argued for the restoration of a liberal order in order to limit the scope of state power. Respect for the 'Rule of Law' becomes vital in his schema, with the power of the state circumscribed by law. 'General rules' are necessary which constrain the actions of governments, with 'the main applications of the Rule of Law laid down in a Bill of Rights or a Constitutional Code' (Hayek, 1976, pp. 62–63). As Held notes (1996, p. 258), Hayek makes an important distinction between *law* (fixed, general rules including constitutional rules) and *legislation* (routine changes in the legal structure), with 'the Rule of Law impl[ying] limits to the scope of [government] legislation' (Hayek, 1976, p. 62), especially in the economic domain.

In all, political liberalism's concerns have been less to increase the legitimate exercise of power by the state and more to limit the legitimate sphere of state activity. To what extent does the World Bank pursue the same objective? It is contended that the World Bank's emphasis on governance and an effective state stemmed from recognition of the same paradox that liberalism has addressed historically. That is, the minimal state also needs to be a 'strong' state in order to realize the (neo-)liberal project. J.S. Mill's (1861) concern with the possibility of an 'overgrown' state in the 1860s were replicated in the 1980s in the World Bank's arguments against the large, overextended state in many developing countries. The Bank's response at that time was a programme that intended to radically roll back the state and to shrink its spheres of influence, corresponding to the implementation of structural adjustment programmes in many developing countries. By the early 1990s, however, it was recognized that the strength and effectiveness of the state *itself* was crucial to the success of such neo-liberal reforms, including securing the state's own withdrawal from the economy. Consequently, the issue of governance rose up the agenda, representing an attempt to reconfigure the state in liberal form, that is both minimal and effective. In other words, the *scope* of the (neo-)liberal state's activities remain *limited* to providing an enabling environment for 'market-friendly' development, while its *capacity* to undertake that particular role is *strengthened*.

From the publications reviewed earlier, there is considerable evidence that circumscribing the state's scope, while strengthening its capacity to undertake limited activities, has been the main thrust of World Bank intentions since the early 1990s, a project influenced by classic liberalism, albeit indirectly and unacknowledged. One common element is the emphasis on the legal framework for development and the rule of law. It has been demonstrated that the Bank's activities in this area of governance are oriented strongly to providing the legal framework required by the private sector, that is property rights and security of contract, and the means of enforcing such laws, that is a relatively independent judiciary. In discussing the *World Development Report 1997*, Hildyard and Wilks (1998) remark that the emphasis on the rule of law:

> does not imply that citizens should have the right to promote legislation through their own democratic institutions which should in turn have the authority to enforce legislation. Rather, it is that the scope of state action should be limited through lock-in mechanisms.
>
> (p. 52)

Such an interpretation corresponds with the Hayekian notion of the 'Rule of Law', used to circumscribe the power of the state. It is also consistent with the pursuit of other 'lock-in' mechanisms, both internal and external, cited earlier.[19]

Further evidence confirms that, for the World Bank, the scope of political power (and democratic decision-making) is limited and not intended to extend into fundamental economic policy choices; see, for example, the statement that key policy areas 'require insulation from political pressure' (World Bank, 1997, p. 117). The underlying and unquestionable assumption is that all governments should implement 'good' policies (ibid., pp. 45–51), without explicit recognition that these constitute a particular ideological choice.

Additionally, there is commonality between liberal political theorists and the World Bank in terms of what the state should do and what it should not do. In the above dissection of various World Bank reports, it has been demonstrated that the scope of state action largely remains limited to providing the requisite framework to facilitate private enterprise. Yet, in the list of five fundamental tasks outlined in *World Development Report 1997*, the avowed commitment to 'protecting the vulnerable' appeared to be a step back from the harsh adjustment regime of the 1980s in which the poor and vulnerable were often hit hardest by World Bank and IMF policies (UNICEF, 1987). However, it is recalled that in the few paragraphs devoted to discussion of social insurance and social assistance policies (World Bank, 1997, pp. 58–59), any notion of an increased role for the state and for public provision was conspicuously absent. Cynically, one could think that the World Bank felt obliged to include 'protecting the vulnerable' as a 'fundamental task', given the presentation of poverty reduction as its overriding objective. Yet, in line with its pro-market ideology and its orientation to poverty reduction through economic growth rather than through reducing inequalities, it is unable to discuss a positive role for the state through social insurance provision, instead highlighting the 'role of private firms and other non-governmental providers' (ibid., p. 60). The commitment of the World Bank to poverty reduction would seem to be equivalent to that of the classical liberal theorist Jeremy Bentham regarding 'equality' (1838, part I, ch. 11). For Bentham, equality was stated as a goal of 'public good', yet readily abandoned when it became necessary to choose between 'equality' and 'security of individual goods and wealth', with the former having to yield to the latter (cited in Held, 1996, p. 96). In both cases, commitment is more evident to a pro-market ideology that limits and obstructs progress towards avowed objectives of socio-economic development.[20]

There is also accord in what is *not* included in the role of the state by both liberalism and the World Bank. In discussing the *World Development Report 1997*, Cornia (1998, p. 35) notes that there is a lack of prominence of the state's role in promoting social and economic equality, with words like 'equity', 'redistribution' and 'equal opportunities' either absent or underemphasized. Correspondingly, there is an ambivalence on taxation, with no mention of progression taxation as a means of redistribution of wealth and lessening inequalities (ibid.). This is consistent again with Hayek's strong opposition to state welfarism and poverty alleviation, opposed as encouraging dependency amongst recipients and involving 'coercion' of both beneficiaries and taxpayers forced to meet the cost of such state intervention (Dunleavy and O'Leary, 1987, p. 133). Further, on the World Bank's agenda, there remains *no* role for the state in terms of, for instance: labour rights, particularly in globalized production (e.g. Free Trade Zones); regulation of international trade, particularly controls on transnational corporations; and intervention in domestic economic planning (Hildyard, 1997, p. 41).

Perhaps the most telling feature is the common *attitude* towards the state held by many liberal theorists and the World Bank. Both share an essential negativity, captured in the same language of a deep-seated fear of an 'arbitrary' and 'capricious' state. Liberalism's overall fear of excessive and unrestrained state power is given contemporaneous expression in Hayek's intense hostility to bureaucratic government and administrative discretion. Similarly, the text of the World Bank reports examined earlier is littered with references to the arbitrary and capricious state, with a chapter dedicated to this subject in *World Development Report 1997* (ch. 6). Additionally, Hayekian language is used here, with 'cutting back on discretionary authority' as a key element of its anti-corruption strategy (World Bank, 1997, p. 105).

Therefore, even when devoting its annual showpiece report to 'the role and effectiveness of the state, what it should do, how it should do it and how it can do it better' (ibid., p. v), the Bank is unable to characterize the state as benign and portrays it far less positively. Despite the Bank's stated position regarding the complementarity of state and market, there remains a basic asymmetry in how the two institutions are treated, noted by Cornia (1998, p. 36). Markets are always more efficient than state agencies in distributing resources. Market failure is always preferable to state failure. State activities everywhere need to be circumscribed, restricted and constrained, while the extension of market relations in all areas of economic, institutional and social life is to be encouraged.

5.3.5 *Democracy, participation and the World Bank*

The histories of liberalism and liberal democracy are intertwined, with 'the tradition that became liberal democracy [being] liberal first...and democratic later' (Sorensen, 1993, p. 5). Classical liberalism's drive towards freedom from overarching and arbitrary political authority (as represented by monarchical rule) led inexorably to the establishment of democratic political institutions that would provide such protection, for instance, constitutionalism, the separation of powers between institutions and an elected representative assembly with legislative powers. In other words, what has become known as liberal democracy. Yet the discussions so far have also indicated the contradictions between liberalism and democracy, notably over the scope and power of democratic institutions, leading to questions such as: 'How much democracy should there be? How much of social and economic life should be democratically organized?' (Held, 1996, p. 107). This resulted in what David Beetham (1993, p. 56) has characterized as two centuries of 'almost continual struggle between liberals and various types of democrat over the extent and form that democratization should take'. Historically, such struggles were fought over the extension of the franchise from 'men of property' to universal suffrage. But the relationship between liberalism and democracy remains a 'deeply ambiguous' one (Beetham, 1993, p. 60), with tensions between the liberal and democratic components of liberal democracy. While the liberal component wishes to constrain and limit the scope of democratic decision-making, the democratic element wishes to extend it. In the contemporary era, Hayek has been a vigorous defender of liberal tenets and a highly restrictive model of democracy, one that excludes the economic domain from the sphere of democratic decision-taking. Although in principle a supporter of representative democracy as a safeguard against the arbitrary exercise of political power by the state, Hayek 'is primarily committed to the liberal in liberal democracy' (Dunleavy and

O'Leary, 1987, p. 94). His particular concerns have been two-fold: the perceived dangers of 'mass' democracy and unrestricted majority rule and of rule by administrative discretion, that is by state officials. Hayek has sought to substantially limit the scope of democratic decision-making, with the framework of 'general rules', established through a Constitutional Code or a Bill of Rights, designed to constrain the activities of majorities and of bureaucratic government. But such rules are not the type of minority rights that aim to protect vulnerable groups in society, but rather general rules that protect the wealth and privilege of the owners of capital through restricting the public domain of politics, disallowing any government 'interference' in the 'private' sphere of civil society, inclusive of business, private property and the market. In Hayek's view (1976, p. 172), 'politics' or 'state action' should be kept to a minimum, to the sphere of operation of an 'ultra-liberal state' (cited in Held, 1996, p. 260). As Held notes (1996, p. 259), 'Ultimately, Hayek's "legal democracy" sets the contours for a free-market society and a "minimal state" '.

Where does the World Bank stand in relation to issues of democracy and to the struggles between liberals and democrats over the extent and form of liberal democracy? Here the Bank is constrained, conveniently I would assert, by its own legal framework. Unlike bilateral aid agencies that are free to pursue a broader agenda of governance that includes issues of democracy and human rights, the World Bank proclaims that its mandate limits its attention to governance issues that promote economic and social development (World Bank, 1992, p. 5). The form of the political regime, it is stated, is outside its mandate not to interfere in the internal political affairs of borrowing countries (ibid., p. 58, note 1). Yet, although the Bank is able to conveniently hide behind its mandate, it can be deduced from its overall orientation to the political realm that its definition of what constitutes politics, and what is included within (and excluded from) the political sphere, is broadly in line with Hayek. Fundamentally, the Bank excludes broad economy policy-making from the orbit of democratic decision-making. We have seen how the World Bank, in conjunction with other multilateral organizations, is concerned to 'lock-in' nation states to a globalized free-market system in which the dominance of capital prevails. The nature of 'good' or 'sound' economic policies is pre-determined as neo-liberal policies, while remaining alluringly undefined in the Bank's governance literature (World Bank, 1992, 1997), seeking to create the impression that they are self-evidently and unquestionably superior. Thus, in Hayekian terms, such neo-liberal economic policies constitute 'general rules'. For all the Bank's avowed emphasis on 'participation' and 'voice', the crucial issue of economic policy-making is not one that can be contested, rather it has been spirited out of democratic politics. Further, if any challenge to neo-liberal economic orthodoxy emerges, the 'soft glove' of participation slips off to reveal the 'hard fist' of coercion, as shown by the Bank's opposition to Uruguay's system of referenda, an example of direct democracy. The outcome of two plebiscites in 1992 and 1989 in Uruguay was a challenge to neo-liberal policies, with citizens voting to reverse privatization and to link pensions to wage increases respectively (World Bank, 1997, p. 148). What was the Bank's response? Did it encourage a mechanism that supports its own avowed policy of 'Bringing the state closer to the people' (ibid., ch. 7), given that governments are 'more effective when they listen to . . . citizens and work in partnership with them in deciding and implementing policy' (ibid., p. 10)? In particular, isn't the case of the 1989 plebiscite, initiated by a pensioners' association, a prime example of 'giving voice to the poor' as 'self-advocates', as the Bank itself recommends (ibid., pp. 58–59)? It comes as no surprise that the Bank is in fact hostile to such a democratic mechanism, given that it has held back neo-liberal economic reforms. Such direct democracy is considered as an impediment, a problem of 'institutional design' (ibid., p. 148), implying the need for constitutional reform in order to 'rule out' the possibility of future popular control over economy policy-making. The Bank's evident disdain for direct democracy, and alternatively its support for political 'leadership' guided by (neo-)liberal principles, is comparable to Hayek's contempt for mass democracy and his statement that if democracy means 'the unrestricted will of the majority', then he is not a democrat (1982, p. 39). For both the World Bank and Hayek, democratic principles of 'popular control' and 'political equality' (Beetham *et al.*, 2002, p. 13) are subordinate to ensuring that liberal economic principles are observed by whatever means necessary.

5.4   Conclusion

This chapter has focused on the political dimension of World Bank policy reform, that is its views on the role of the state and what constitutes 'good governance'. One interpretation of the apparent changing character of the Bank's thinking on the state over the last fifteen years is that it entails 'bringing the state back in'. It has been suggested by some authors that the Bank's 'rethinking' on the state represents a paradigmatic break with the neo-liberal (or free market) fundamentalism of the 1980s, and a return swing of the pendulum towards renewed recognition of the role of the state in development. The Bank itself reinforces the notion that the old antagonism between state-led and market-led models of development has been transcended by this new synthesis where state and market are complementary. This author has long been unhappy with such an interpretation and this chapter has sought to challenge it.[21]

It is asserted here that there is more evidence of continuity with the neo-liberal paradigm than departure from it. Although the Bank has attempted to present itself as 'state-friendly', thus defusing critique of its pro-business and anti-state orientation, its thinking remains embedded within the paradigm of neo-liberalism and unimpeded free market operations. Evidence has taken two forms. First, an examination of the key World Bank texts on the state have shown that its role remains firmly subordinated to that of the market. The state is perceived as serving the market and providing the enabling environment for private sector development. The discomforting facts of the successful developmental state in East Asia have been reinterpreted, with success attributed to market-oriented policies rather than state-led industrial policies. The close association between governance and a free-market economy has been indicated. A state characterized by good governance is not only one where its scope is limited but also where its activities facilitate private entrepreneurship. This is achieved, for example, by provision of the legal framework required by the private sector, and by improved transparency mechanisms, enabling dissemination of useful economic information to business. The orientation of governance policies towards the consolidation and institutionalization of a free-market economy was most apparent in the *World Development Report 2002*. Undoubtedly, good governance equals neo-liberal governance. Similarly, an 'effective state' is predominantly effective for business, notably international companies, both in terms of what it does and what it does not do.

Second, this chapter has indicated continuity with a neo-liberal paradigm through showing a significant degree of correspondence between the Bank's contemporary views on the state and on state–economy–society relations and those of classical political liberalism, especially as revived by Hayek in the latter part of the twentieth century. The merits of a free-market economy, inclusive of private property and property rights, are a fundamental and unquestionable assumption for both. There is a celebration of the individual and of individual rights, especially those 'rights' of private entrepreneurs, with little acknowledgement that such 'individuals' constitute a social class whose interests are effectively being advanced. Conversely, a negative attitude towards the state is shared, with deep-seated fears of its 'arbitrary' nature, and a particular hostility to state interference in the economy. Thus the state remains minimal, yet also 'strong', with effective political institutions required both to contain executive powers and to implement its limited tasks efficiently. Finally, a shared ambivalence towards democracy is apparent, in which the liberal component of liberal democracy is emphasized and the scope of democratic decision-making circumscribed, notably excluding the sphere of economic policy. Thus it is suggested that the liberal political tradition, notably as reasserted by Hayek, has influenced World Bank thinking, directly or indirectly, on the role and nature of the state in a free-market economy.

Therefore, in conclusion, it is contended that World Bank's claimed 'rethinking' on the state in fact represents a revision and consolidation of neo-liberalism. In contrast to the first phase (1980s) of 'rolling back the state', the second phase of the neo-liberal project has entailed the crafting of the particular type of state, minimal but effective, that is required by a free-market economy. In effect, the World Bank is engaged in the construction of a liberal state, and thus, through attention to the political dimension, neo-liberal orthodoxy has been reconfigured in a more rounded and hegemonic version. It remains that it is *not* the task of the state or government to take a pro-active role in achieving socio-economic development. Instead, the state's role is limited to 'enabling' (servicing) the private sector through the provision of those 'public goods' that require significant expenditure, and to securing constraints on its own activities, notably in the economy. Yet who benefits from such a state and from the neo-liberal order more generally? Clearly, it is the capitalist class, particularly those who control large transnational corporations, that benefit most from the use of public monies to 'enable' private gain and from the state's continued withdrawal from a redistributive role and from the regulation of business activities. Notions such as 'good governance' and an 'effective state' may be beguiling and difficult to oppose. Yet they perform an ideological role. The World Bank's worldview (*Weltanschauung*) remains resolutely based on development as free-market capitalism, with 'good governance' and an 'effective state' firmly subordinated to that goal.

Acknowledgements

I would like to thank John Schwarzmantel for his helpful comments on political liberalism. Any errors or inadequacies are, of course, solely mine.

Notes

1 The Berg Report, officially titled *Accelerated Development in sub-Saharan Africa: An Agenda for Action* but best known after its author Elliot Berg, evaluated the development record of African governments and recommended a greatly reduced role for the state in the economy and a substantially increased role for the market in accelerating economic activity (Berger and Beeson, 1998, p. 490). The *World Development Report 1987*, entitled *Trade and Liberalization*, 'articulated a strong 'free market' or neo-liberal argument about the appropriate development approach' (Wade, 1996, p. 5).

2 The term 'Washington Consensus' was originally used by Williamson (1990) to describe a specific set of ten liberalizing economic reforms that were enforced on Latin American governments by Washington-based institutions, predominantly the World Bank, the IMF and the US Treasury Department. Subsequently the term became used in a broader, more populist way to describe neo-liberal or 'market fundamentalist' policies (Williamson, 2000, pp. 251–252).

3 This notion of three waves of post-1945 development theorizing is put forward by Ahrens (1999: pp. 18–19), with the governance agenda symbolizing the 'third wave' in which there is renewed appreciation of the role of the state and where the state and market are viewed as complementary and not dichotomous.

4 By implication, the chapter also questions the notion of a Post-Washington consensus. By introducing such a label, advocates are suggesting a shift of paradigmatic proportions (for instance, Stiglitz, 1998, 2001). Although there is not the opportunity to look in detail at this concept, the thrust of the argument here counters the idea that such a significant shift has actually occurred. See note 20.

5 Mosley *et al.* (1995, p. 141) found a high level of slippage on World Bank loan conditions, with only 60 per cent of policy changes agreed actually implemented.

6 Indeed, Doornbos (2001, p. 95) suggests that this lack of specificity is part of the attraction: governance is 'more like a flexible carrier which can be used to convey varying combinations of messages or consignments'.

7 The ACP objected to good governance as an additional 'essential element', alongside 'respect for human rights, democratic principles and the rule of law', and thus subject to a non-execution or suspension clause. Instead 'good governance' has been inserted as a 'fundamental and positive element' (Article 9), becoming a theme for regular dialogue and an area for positive support, but not subject to a non-execution clause (Salama and Dearden, 2001, p. 7). The ACP Group's reluctance to accept good governance as an essential element was due to its nebulous nature, with 'many meanings given to this concept' (Azor-Charles, 2000, p. 27).

8 For example, at the time of writing, a British newspaper published allegations that BAE Systems, Britain's largest arms company, had concealed evidence in Geneva of covert payments to foreign politicians, outside the jurisdiction of British legal authorities and

exploiting Switzerland's secrecy laws (*The Guardian*, 8 March 2004, p. 10). Further suspicions of large-scale corruption by BAE was reported in May 2004, with allegations of payments totalling over £60 million to prominent Saudi officials in attempts to secure arms deals from the Saudi regime (*The Guardian*, 4 May 2004, pp. 1–2). These are the latest in a number of allegations concerning corruption surrounding BAE's arms sales around the world. The international anti-corruption convention, making it illegal to bribe foreign public officials, was brought into force in Britain in February 2002, but it is alleged that payments to Saudi officials continued after this date (ibid.). BAE denies any allegations of wrongdoing (ibid.).

 9 Selective industrial policy refers to the selection and promotion of particular industries as key sectors for national economic growth through such instruments as concessional credit. Enterprises operating in such industries could be private-owned or, where necessary, state-owned.

10 These six 'basic' policies are: (a) maintaining macroeconomic stability; (b) maintaining an effective and secure financial system; (c) limiting price distortions; (d) investing in human capital; (e) opening the economy to foreign technology and (f) promoting agricultural productivity and not taxing it too much (World Bank, 1993, p. 89).

11 Wade (1996) has provided an insightful investigation into the process of researching, drafting and editing the report, described as 'the art of paradigm maintenance'.

12 Cornia (1998, p. 35) also notes the Report's general ambivalence towards taxation, silent about the need to increase tax ratios and tax rates.

13 Tellingly, this emphasis on a state that is oriented towards meeting the needs of business and capital is demonstrated by a specially commissioned survey of entrepreneurs in 69 countries regarding the 'core functions' of government in ensuring law and order, the protection of private property and the predictable application of rules and policies. Findings were that 'many states are performing their core functions poorly', thus suffering from low 'credibility' in investors' perceptions, with growth and investment suffering as a consequence (World Bank, 1997, p. 5, box 2).

14 Such policies are very familiar to readers in the UK, for instance, long implemented by successive Conservative administrations from 1979 to 1997, and subsequently adopted by the Labour governments from 1997 to date, yet with questionable success.

15 Cornia (1998, pp. 36–37) points out that among the 'good policies' discussed in the Report, despite 'their frequent failure in sub-Saharan Africa and Eastern Europe', are:

  • privatization presented as a universal panacea;
  • trade liberalization presented as a necessary measure for improved economic performance;
  • financial liberalization as necessary to attract foreign capital.

16 An important caveat here is to recognize that liberalism is a diverse and complex political philosophy and that there are different strands of liberalism. It is acknowledged that some strands entail a degree of critique of free market mechanisms, with qualified support for forms of state intervention such as welfare provision, for instance the work of L.T. Hobhouse (1911).

17 Indeed, I have found no references to Hayek in World Bank publications.

18 It could be argued that the current World Bank position is more extreme than that of some classical liberal theorists. James Madison (1751–1836), for example, expressed concern about the unequal distribution of property (Held, 1996, p. 90), though ultimately he believed in a natural right to private property (ibid., p. 94).

19 Further attempts to 'lock-in' developing countries to economic liberalization are evident through the economic conditionality associated with the HIPC (Highly Indebted Poor Countries) initiative and with the shift from SAPs (structural adjustment programmes) to PRSPs (Poverty Reduction Strategy Paper). The latter entails a significant development in the drive for neo-liberal hegemony, with the presentation of economic liberalization policies as poverty reduction measures and with PRSPs being

adopted, ostensibly, by borrower governments themselves. A further indicator of hegemonic success has been the endorsement of neo-liberalism, including 'good governance', within NEPAD (New Partnership for African Development), initiated by African leaders and supported by Northern bilateral and multilateral donors (Owusu, 2003).

20 In another interesting parallel, Holmes (1995, p. 15) argues for the compatibility of liberal democracy's concern with poverty and support for economic inequality. The latter is justified on the basis of increased economic efficiencies (through greater incentives, for example) which, through growth, leads to improvements in the absolute (but not relative) living standard of the least advantaged. Although Holmes has no connection whatsoever with World Bank or international development issues, the resonance with the World Bank perspective on poverty and inequality is again illuminating.

21 As stated in note 4, this chapter also challenges the notion of a paradigmatic shift from Washington Consensus to post-Washington Consensus, and suggests that the degree of actual change is exaggerated. Although a key element of post-Washington Consensus is a recognition that state interventionism is justified to correct market failings (Fine, 1999, p. 3), the state's role remains embedded within a market economy in which ongoing economic liberalization continues to be emphasized, including the introduction of competition and market-like relations into public institutions (Onis and Senses, 2003, p. 17). The post-Washington Consensus can be seen as an attempt by dominant actors to respond to deficiencies of neo-liberalism without threatening existing structures of power and inequality at both national and international levels (ibid., p. 27).

Bibliography

Ahrens, J. (1999) 'Towards a post-Washington consensus: the importance of governance structures in less developed countries and economies in transition', in Hermes, N. and Salverda, W. (eds), *State, Society and Development: Lessons for Africa?*, CDS Research Report No. 7, Centre for Development Studies, University of Groningen.

Archer, R. (1994) 'Markets and good government', in Clayton, A. (ed.), *Governance, Democracy and Conditionality: What Role for NGOs?*, Oxford: Intrac.

Azor-Charles, Y. (2000) Interview in *The Courier*, Special Issue on the Cotonou Agreement, September 2000, Brussels: European Commission.

Beetham, D. (1993) 'Liberal democracy and the limits of democratization', in Held, D. (ed.), *Prospects for Democracy: North, South, East, West*, Cambridge: Polity.

Beetham, D., Bracking, S., Kearton, I. and Weir, S. (2002) *International IDEA Handbook on Democracy Assessment*, The Hague: Kluwer Law International.

Bentham, J. (1838) 'Principles of the Civil Code', in Bowring, J. (ed.), *The Works of Jeremy Bentham*, Vol. 1, Edinburgh: W. Tait.

Berger, M.T. and Beeson, M. (1998) 'Lineages of liberalism and miracles of modernisation: the World Bank, the East Asian trajectory and the international development debate', *Third World Quarterly*, 19: 487–504.

Brecknock, J. (1997) 'The World Bank and the state: a brief history' (Appendix One), in Hildyard, N. (ed.), *The World Bank and the State: A Recipe for Change*, London: Bretton Woods Project.

Chenery, H.S., Jolly, R., Ahluwalia, M.S., Bell, C.L. and Duloy, J.H. (1974) *Redistribution with Growth: An Approach to Policy*, Washington, DC: World Bank.

Collingwood V. (ed.) (2002) Good Governance and the World Bank, unpublished paper based on research by LSE Masters students 2001–02.

Cornia, G.A. (1998) 'Convergence on governance issues, dissent on economic policies', *The Bank, the State and Development: Dissecting the 1997 World Development Report – IDS Bulletin*, 29: 32–38.

Doornbos, M. (2001) 'Good governance: the rise and decline of a policy metaphor?', *Journal of Development Studies*, 37: 93–108.

Dunleavy, P. and O'Leary, B. (1987) *Theories of the State: The Politics of Liberal Democracy*, Basingstone: Macmillan.

Evans, A. and Moore, M. (1998) 'Editorial introduction', *The Bank, the State and Development: Dissecting the 1997 World Development Report – IDS Bulletin*, 29: 3–13.

Evans, P. (1992) 'The State as problem and solution: predation, embedded autonomy and structural change', in Haggard, S. and Kaufmann, R.R. (eds), *The Politics of Economic Adjustment*, Princeton, NJ: Princeton University Press.

Fine, B. (1999) 'Neither the Washington consensus nor the post-Washington consensus: an introduction', paper available at http://www.globalpolicy.org/socecon/bwi-wto/wbank/2001/esrc.pdf (accessed 14 June 2004).

Hall, D. and Bayliss, K. (2000) *Privatisation of Water and Energy in Africa*, London: Public Services International Research Unit, University of Greenwich.

Hayek, F.A. (1960) *The Constitution of Liberty*, London: Routledge.

—— (1976, originally published 1944) *The Road to Serfdom*, London: Routledge.

—— (1982) *Law, Legislation and Liberty: A New Statement of the Liberal Principles of Justice and Political Economy*, London: Routledge.

Held, D. (1996) (2nd edition) *Models of Democracy*, Cambridge: Polity Press.

Hildyard, N. (1997) *The World Bank and the State: A Recipe for Change*, London: Bretton Woods Project.

Hildyard, N. and Wilks, A. (1998) 'An effective state? But effective for whom?', *The Bank, the State and Development: Dissecting the 1997 World Development Report – IDS Bulletin*, 29: 49–55.

Hobhouse, L.T. (1911) *Liberalism*, London: Williams & Norgate.

Holmes, S. (1995) *Passions and Constraints: On the Theory of Liberal Democracy*, Chicago, IL: Chicago University Press.

Kearton, I. (2003) 'Governance and development', unpublished paper, University of Leeds.

Kukathas, C. (1989) *Hayek and Modern Liberalism*, Oxford: Clarendon Press.

Lancaster, C. (1993) 'Governance and development: the views from Washington', *IDS Bulletin*, 24: 9–15.

Leftwich, A. (1994) 'Governance, the State and the Politics of Development', *Development and Change*, 25: 363–386.

Martinussen, J. (1998) 'The limitations of the World Bank's conception of the state and the implications for institutional development strategies', *The Bank, the State and Development: Dissecting the 1997 World Development Report – IDS Bulletin*, 29: 67–74.

Mill, J. (1828) 'Prisons and prison discipline', *Essays on Government*, London: J. Innis.

Mill, J.S. (1951[1861]) *Considerations on Representative Government*, in Acton, H.B. (ed.), *Utilitarianism, Liberty, and Representative Government*, London: Dent.

Moore, M. (1993) 'Declining to learn from the East? The World Bank on governance and development', *IDS Bulletin*, 24(1): 39–50.

—— (1998) 'Toward a useful consensus', *The Bank, the State and Development: Dissecting the 1997 World Development Report – IDS Bulletin*, 29: 39–48.

Mosley, P., Harrigan, J. and Toye, J. (1995) (2nd edition) *Aid and Power: The World Bank and Policy-Based Lending*, London: Routledge.

Nelson, J. and Eglinton, S.J. (1992) *Encouraging Democracy: What Role for Conditioned Aid?*, Washington, DC: Overseas Development Council.

North, D.C. (1994) 'Economic performance through time', *American Economic Review*, 84: 359–368.

Onis, Z. and Senses, F. (2003) 'Rethinking the emergent post-Washington consensus: a critical appraisal', ERC Working Paper in Economics 03/09, November 2003, Ankara: Economic Research Center, Middle East Technical University.

Owusu, F. (2003) 'Pragmatism and the gradual shift from dependency to neo-liberalism: the World Bank, African leaders and development policy in Africa', *World Development*, 31: 1655–1672.

Pierson, C. (1996) *The Modern State*, London: Routledge.

Salama, C.M. and Dearden, S.J.H. (2001) 'The Cotonou Agreement', Development Studies Association European Development Policy Study Group Discussion Paper No. 20, February 2001. Available at: http://www.edpsg.org/dp20.htm

Sorensen, G. (1993) *Democracy and Democratisation*, Boulder, CO: Westview Press.

Stiglitz, J. (1998) 'More instruments and broader goals: moving towards the post-Washington consensus', the 1998 WIDER Annual Lecture, 7 January, Helsinki.

—— (2001) 'An agenda for development for the twenty first century', in Giddens, A. (ed.), *The Global Third Way Debate*, Cambridge: Polity Press.

UNICEF (1987) *Adjustment with a Human Face*, Oxford: Oxford University Press.

Wade, R. (1996) 'Japan, the World Bank, and the art of paradigm maintenance: the East Asian miracle in political perspective', *New Left Review*, 217: 3–37.

Wainwright H. (1994) *Arguments for a New Left: Answering the Free Market Right*, Oxford: Blackwell.

Williams, D. and Young, T. (1994) 'Governance, the World Bank and liberal theory', *Political Studies*, 42: 84–100.

Williamson, J. (1990) 'What Washington means by policy reform', in Williamson, J. (ed.), *Latin American Adjustment: How Much Has Happened?*, Washington, DC: Institute for International Economics.

—— (2000) 'What should the World Bank think about the Washington consensus?', *World Bank Research Observer*, 15: 251–264.

World Bank (1981) *Accelerated Development in sub-Saharan Africa: An Agenda for Action*, Washington, DC: World Bank.

—— (1989) *Sub-Saharan Africa: From Crisis to Sustainable Growth – A Long-Term Perspective Study*, Washington, DC: World Bank.

—— (1991) *World Development Report 1991: The Challenge of Development*, Washington, DC: World Bank.

—— (1992) *Governance and Development*, Washington, DC: World Bank.

—— (1993) *The East Asian Miracle: Economic Growth and Public Policy*, Washington, DC: World Bank.

—— (1994) *Governance: The World Bank's Experience*, Washington, DC: World Bank.

—— (1996) *World Development Report 1996: From Plan To Market*, Washington, DC: World Bank.

—— (1997) *World Development Report 1997: The State in a Changing World*, Washington, DC: World Bank.

—— (2002) *World Development Report 2002: Building Institutions for Markets*, Washington, DC: World Bank.

Part II
Poverty-reduction strategies

6 The effects of compliance with structural adjustment programmes on human development in sub-Saharan Africa

Farhad Noorbakhsh and Shadan Noorbakhsh

6.1 Introduction

The ultimate goals of structural adjustment programmes (SAPs) were to improve standards of living through intermediate targets such as ensuring higher growth in the economy and maintaining its stability. The conditions attached to these programmes were aimed at reducing inflationary pressures and improving the efficiency of production in the economy and its management. These included promotion of free markets, tight fiscal and monetary policies, wage control, trade liberalization, devaluation and privatization amongst others.

Some scholars suggest that these programmes were initially designed by the World Bank to complement the poverty alleviation programmes (Summers and Pritchett, 1993; Please, 1996). Others conclude that the World Bank through these programmes attempted to move away, to some extent though not fully, from project lending to policy lending in order to reduce the economic distortions present in developing countries which were hampering the profitability of development projects (Kanbur, 1991).

There is little controversy in the literature on the aims of SAPs, however, there is no consensus on their achievements particularly in terms of their effects on poverty and standards of living. Some studies argued that conditionality has had adverse effects on standards of living in poorer countries (Cornia *et al.*, 1987; Stewart, 1995; UNRISD, 1995). Others suggested that high emphasis on structural adjustment conditions may lead to the misallocation of scarce resources and possibly waste of public funds (Killick, 1996). There is some evidence that these programmes also affected the aid provided by donor countries. According to Ehrenpreis (2003, p. 49) 'Over the 1980s, Swedish aid in many countries was redirected in order to ameliorate the negative effects of structural adjustment policies and ensure that important social development programmes could be maintained.' Some scholars have gone further and regarded these programmes as highly inappropriate particularly for African countries, and have suggested alternative approaches for attaining growth and stability in these countries (see, for example Cornia and Helleiner, 1994; Engberg-Pedersen *et al.*, 1996).

Van der Hoeven (2003) argues that in most *inefficient inegalitarian* societies the main policy aims are the resumption of positive economic growth and a reduction in inequalities allowing for the poor to benefit from growth where precisely in these countries SAPs fail to come out with the intended results. Almost all the sub-Saharan African countries, which undertook SAPs, have had poor economic growth combined with a high level of income inequality and would fall into this category.

Assessing the effects of SAPs is not a straightforward task. However, scholars have attempted to evaluate the effects of SAPs on poverty and standards of living. The effects on poverty have been mainly studied through country case studies (see, for example OECD, 1992; Stewart, 1995). Cross-country studies have mainly concentrated on evaluating the effects of conditionality in general and on standards of living by taking a temporal and/or comparative approach. The basic idea is to compare the level of a set of socioeconomic indicators in programme countries during the pre-adjustment period with the same for the adjustment or post-adjustment periods and/or compare the difference between the adjustment and pre-adjustment periods in programme countries with those of the non-programme countries, of broadly similar level, for drawing counter-factual conclusions (see, for example World Bank, 1992; Kakwani, 1995; Stewart, 1995; Noorbakhsh, 1999).

Basically there is a broad consensus that aiming for higher economic growth in programme countries is good, though there are some concerns on the ability of some countries in translating a higher rate of growth into higher standards of living (Dreze and Sen, 1989; Noorbakhsh, 1999). A recent report on chronic poverty, with reference to urban poverty in Ethiopia, states that improved macro-economic management in the mid-1990s did not result in a reduction in poverty, on the contrary the urban household welfare declined during this period (CPRC, 2004, p. 70). Other studies go further by pointing out the inconsistency between components of SAPs and the longer-term development policies of the programme countries. For example the public sector management component advocates cuts in public expenditure and often this takes place in terms of cuts in education, health and other pro poor social expenditures (Stewart, 1994). It is therefore suggested that as the main aim of aid and development loans is improvements in standards of living in the recipient countries, the conditions attached to aid and loans should take these objectives into account and indeed the effectiveness of the related programmes should be evaluated in terms of improvements in standards of living (Singer, 1995).

The World Bank, however, maintained that conditionality has had little adverse effect on standards of living in programme countries (see, for example World Bank, 1992). Despite widespread criticism of SAPs the World Bank has defended its position on a number of grounds of which the most logical one is that a number of countries, particularly in Africa, despite the conditionality imposed on their loans, did not comply with these conditions and in some cases they introduced other counter active measures or indeed reversed the reforms at a later stage. This means that a logical way of assessing the effect of conditionality is to differentiate between those countries which complied with conditionality, and those which did this partially or did not comply.

In fact most of the earlier studies of SAPs assessed and compared the situation in the so-called programme countries, regardless of compliance with conditions, with that of the non-programme countries, again regardless of reforms in the latter countries which took place on their own accord, independent of World Bank loans. In brief the earlier studies concentrated on the assessment of pay off to conditional loans rather than pay off to actual policy reforms. Mosley *et al.* (1995) suggest that it would be inappropriate to judge the effects of implementation in terms of recommended reforms even if these reforms are implemented. They note that a number of receivers of adjustment loans accepted the World Bank's conditionality only to receive the loan, to be followed by either reversing the conditions or taking counteractive measures to neutralize them.

In brief two types of errors may be associated with the early studies of the effects of SAPs. First that conditions attached to SAPs were assessed regardless of being implemented or not. Second that the control group of countries, which were supposed to be non-reformers, may have adopted similar reforms on their own accord. In this article we attempt to correct for such errors and evaluate the effects of compliance with conditonality on a set of socioeconomic indicators and the composite index of human development.

6.2 Data and methodology

The World Bank in a report (1997) provided an assessment of the extent of compliance of sub-Saharan African countries with conditionality of their loans. Countries were assessed with respect to the full range of policy reforms in their programmes taking into account all policy actions taken during the programme including actions of reversal or counteractive nature. The result of this study was an index of compliance which was based on the implementation of three groups of measures included in conditional loans.

The first group, Macroeconomic Stabilization, included measures such as fiscal deficit reduction, control of public expenditure level, increase in fiscal revenues, and exchange rate adjustment. The second group, Public Sector Management, concerned measures such as civil service reforms, public expenditure reforms, public enterprise restructuring and privatization. The third group, Private Sector Development, included measures such as financial sector reforms, trade policy reforms, pricing policies and incentive and improvements in regulatory environment. Countries were subsequently rated according to their level of compliance with each of these measures from 1 (the highest) to 4 (the lowest); the country's overall index for compliance was then the average of the scores for these three dimensions. The final result is the classification of countries into groups of *good, weak* and *poor* compliers according to their compliance score. The classification of countries is presented in Appendix 1.

Noorbakhsh and Paloni (2001) and Mosley *et al.* (2003) discuss the problems associated with this index and conclude that, despite its shortcomings, this is the best index of compliance available for sub-Saharan African programme countries. Noorbakhsh and Paloni (2001) use this index for investigating whether compliance has had any effect on growth. In this chapter we adopt a similar approach, though with a broader view, to assess the effects of compliance with SAPs on a number of socioeconomic indicators of standards of living in sub-Saharan African countries.

For our analysis we have selected a number of indicators. They consist of economic indicators reflecting broad economic aspects, which are expected to be affected by compliance and also social indicators, which as the literature argues, should be the appropriate measures for testing the ultimate success or failure of SAPs.

These are real GDP per capita (GDPPC), gross domestic investment as a percentage of GDP (GDIGDP), annual growth rate of agricultural value added (GAGRVA), expenditure on education as a percentage of GDP (EUEXP), primary school enrolment rate (PENROL), secondary school enrolment rate (SENROL), infant mortality rate (IMR) and human development index (HDI). The first three indicators measure the per capita income and its growth and growth in investment. Growth in agricultural value added has been selected as it is often argued that growth in agriculture has impact on poverty reduction for the poor who mostly live in rural areas and are active in this sector. Expenditure on education, enrolment ratios and infant mortality rate are to reflect the related social aspect and finally the composite measure of HDI has been selected to reflect the state of human development as defined by this index. Ideally we would have selected an indicator of poverty but this was not possible due to the non-availability of data in the periods required for our analysis.

The period of analysis selected for this study is of special interest. While most of the earlier analyses used a particular date as the beginning of the adjustment period, which was fixed for all countries (usually 1985 or 1986), we have taken the actual dates of the adjustment programmes which varies for different countries. Pre-adjustment period is defined as the five-year period prior to the actual date of adjustment and the adjustment period is five years after the start of the programme.[1] In order to evaluate the medium term effects of compliance with SAPs we also have a second five-year period after the immediate adjustment period. All indicators are averages for the five-year pre-adjustment and for the respective adjustment periods. The actual pre-adjustment and the short term and medium term adjustment periods (Adj1 and Adj2 respectively) for all countries in the sample are in Appendix 2.

6.3   Compliance with conditionality and standards of living in the short run

Following the approach adopted by Noorbakhsh and Paloni (2001) we start with employing two types of analyses: temporal and comparative temporal. In the temporal analysis for each indicator we look at the difference in the pre-adjustment and adjustment periods and test the mean of differences for these periods statistically in order to see if the improvement is significantly different from zero. This analysis is done for different groups of compliers. Two types of tests are employed: the standard parametric *t*-test and Wilcoxon Matched–Pairs

Signed–Ranks test which is a non-parametric test allowing us to relax the assumption of normal distribution in the samples.[2]

In the comparative temporal analysis we compare the difference between the adjustment and pre-adjustment periods in good and weak compliers with that of the poor compliers. We test the mean of difference where the group of poor compliers are the control group. Again two tests are employed for this purpose the standard parametric *t*-test and the Mann–Whitney U test which is a non-parametric test allowing for the relaxation of normality assumption in the samples, which in this case are independent.

Table 6.1 shows the temporal differences and their significance for our selected indicators and groups of compliers. That is the difference between the first adjustment period (Adj 1) and the pre-adjustment period for groups of good, weak, good and weak and poor compliers.

For all groups of compliers ΔGDPPC shows a drop. However, the only differences in means significant are those of Good and Weak group of compliers (*t*-test at the 10 per cent level) and that of Poor compliers (Wilcoxon test at the 5 per cent level).[3] The results for ΔGDIGDP are mixed and not significant. However, the drop in GAGRVA for the Poor group is highly significant according to both tests. Temporal mean differences for EUEXP, PENROL and SENROL are mixed and not significant for any group by any of the tests. The results for ΔIMR indicate that all groups, regardless of their level of compliance have experienced a drop in IMR and these differences in means are all significant. ΔHDI shows a significant temporal difference for Good, and Good and Weak groups.

Table 6.2 shows the comparative temporal differences and their significance for our selected indicators. The control group is the group of Poor compliers. Consequently the results show the comparative difference in performance (as measured by the mean of temporal differences for each group) between other groups and the group of Poor compliers. Again the parametric *t*-test and the non-parametric Mann–Whitney tests are employed for the reasons mentioned earlier.[4]

Mean differences in ΔGDPPC between the groups in Table 6.2 and the Poor group are positive but not significantly different from zero according to both parametric and non-parametric tests. The only exception is that of the *t*-test for Good and Weak compliers which is significant only at the 10 per cent level. The results for ΔGDIGDP are mixed and non-significant while there are significant differences for ΔGAGRVA indicating a higher rate of growth in agricultural value added in groups of Weak, and Good and Weak compliers as compared to that of the Poor compliers. Good compliance, however, is not associated with higher rate of growth in agricultural value added. The results for ΔEUEXP, ΔPENROL and ΔSENROL are not significant though the negative signs are notable. The differences in ΔIMR are negative and significant in the case of Weak group and the ΔHDI results are not significant.

Overall the results of temporal and comparative tests seem to suggest that in the short-run compliance with SAPs may have had effects on some indicators of standards of living, namely, GDPPC, GAGRVA, IMR and HDI, although the evidence is far from conclusive.

Table 6.1 Average differences in performance during the adjustment and pre-adjustment periods

Compliers/ variable	Good		Weak		Good and weak		Poor	
	t-test	Wilcoxon	t-test	Wilcoxon	t-test	Wilcoxon	t-test	Wilcoxon
ΔGDPPC	−8.343 (−0.89)	0.968	−29.318 (−1.80)*	1.682	−18.83 (−2.00)*	1.867	−80.823 (−2.07)	1.992**
ΔGDIGDP	2.155 (0.63)	0.561	−1.816 (−0.91)	0.357	0.169 (0.09)	0.075	−1.310 (−0.74)	0.722
ΔGAGRVA	0.822 (0.47)	0.561	2.020 (1.21)	1.172	1.421 (1.20)	0.859	−1.700 (−3.49)***	2.746***
ΔEUEXP	2.086 (1.25)	1.572	−1.294 (−0.90)	0.169	0.396 (0.35)	1.153	−0.820 (−0.43)	0.000
ΔPENROL	−2.528 (−0.87)	0.533	−3.525 (−0.87)	0.459	−3.053 (−1.23)	0.161	1.922 (0.45)	0.296
ΔSENROL	−0.467 (−0.58)	0.296	−1.063 (−0.69)	0.070	−0.747 (−0.91)	0.000	0.138 (0.07)	0.735
ΔIMR	−6.990 (−4.27)***	2.402***	−12.034 (−8.58)***	2.936***	−9.632 (−8.12)***	3.808***	−6.018 (−2.56)**	2.296**
ΔHDI	0.021 (5.30)***	2.521***	0.002 (0.31)	0.663	0.011 (2.29)**	2.200**	0.009 (1.46)	1.274

Notes
*** Significant at the 1% level. ** Significant at the 5% level. * Significant at the 10% level.

Table 6.2 Average difference in performance in good and weak compliers as compared with poor compliers

Compliers/ variable	Good		Weak		Good and weak	
	t-test	MW	t-test	MW	t-test	MW
ΔGDPPC	72.480 (1.59)	1.30	51.505 (1.09)	0.56	61.992 (1.86)*	1.11
ΔGDIGDP	3.465 (0.98)	0.89	−0.506 (−0.19)	0.29	1.480 (0.60)	0.70
ΔGAGRVA	2.519 (1.50)	1.32	3.717 (2.32)**	2.37***	3.118 (1.97)*	2.18**
ΔEUEXP	2.906 (1.09)	1.52	−0.474 (−0.19)	0.12	1.216 (0.58)	0.98
ΔPENROL	−4.450 (−0.86)	0.09	−5.447 (−0.92)	0.16	−4.975 (−1.07)	0.05
ΔSENROL	−0.605 (−0.32)	1.01	−1.201 (−0.50)	0.81	−0.885 (−0.51)	1.05
ΔIMR	−0.972 (−0.31)	0.50	−6.016 (−2.05)**	1.98**	−3.614 (−1.51)	0.93
ΔHDI	0.013 (1.60)	1.25	−0.007 (−0.76)	0.61	0.002 (0.22)	0.29

Notes
*** Significant at the 1% level. ** Significant at the 5% level. * Significant at the 10% level.

Table 6.3 Regression of the selected dependent variables on compliance scores

Explanatory variable	Dependent variable			
	ΔGDPPC	ΔGAGRVA	ΔIMR	ΔHDI
Constant	59.465 (0.90)	4.851 (1.57)	8.169 (1.70)*	0.041 (2.83)***
Compliance	−40.062 (−1.64)	−1.745 (−1.51)	−0.022 (−0.01)	−0.013 (−2.28)***
N	31	30	33	26
R^2	0.09	0.08	0.00	0.18
F-statistics	2.68	2.29	0.00	5.19***

Notes
*** Significant at the 1% level. ** Significant at the 5% level. * Significant at the 10% level.

6.4 Regression analysis

We extend our analysis by attempting to find out the effects of compliance on those indicators above, which are likely to be susceptive to compliance with SAPs. We start by regressing the temporal differences in variables which seem to be associated with compliance, namely GDPPC, GAGRVA, IMR and HDI, on the overall compliance scores. Table 6.3 depicts the results.

The regressions in Table 6.3 do not support a link between change in GDP per capita and compliance. Nor do they support the proposition of a link between growth in agricultural value added and compliance. The same can be said for a link between the change in IMR and compliance. However, the coefficient of compliance variable in the regression for HDI is significant at the 1 per cent level. The F-statistics for this regression is also highly significant. The sign of compliance in this regression is negative, indicating that the higher the degree of compliance the higher the improvement in HDI.[5] That is compliance is associated with higher level of improvement in HDI.

The above results suggest that compliance seems to be associated with a change in HDI far more than with changes in other selected variables. For this reason the rest of this study focuses on the effects of compliance on a change in HDI. As discussed in previous sections, the literature on the effects of SAPs on standards of living and poverty often quotes specific conditions being responsible for adverse effects, such as cuts in government expenditure and the vulnerability of expenditures in social sectors to such cuts. Other examples discussed in the literature often refer to the positive effects of financial and trade liberalization on the economy, which are expected to lead to higher standards of living. Therefore, it would be interesting to see the association between the change in HDI and compliance with various components of SAPs.

As indicated above, conditions attached to loans have been classified into three groups of (i) Macroeconomic Stabilization policies (MSP), (ii) Public Sector Management (PSM) and (iii) Private Sector Development (PSD). Table 6.4 shows the results of regressing the temporal change in HDI on the compliance scores for these groups of policies.

Model 1 in Table 6.4 shows the results for regressing short-run temporal change in HDI on all components of SAPs together. Compliance with MSP has

Table 6.4 Regression of temporal change in HDI on compliance with different components of SAPs

Variable/model	1	2	3	4
Constant	0.043	0.031	0.048	0.012
	(2.88)***	(2.66)***	(3.60)***	(0.92)
MSP	−0.002	−0.007		
	(−0.29)	(−1.87)*		
PSM	−0.016		−0.014	
	(−1.94)**		(−2.97)***	
PSD	0.006			−0.001
	(1.00)			(−0.20)
N	26	28	27	27
R^2	0.33	0.12	0.26	0.00
F-statistics	3.55**	3.51*	8.81***	0.04

Notes
*** Significant at the 1% level. ** Significant at the 5% level. * Significant at the 10% level.

the right sign but is not significant. While compliance with PSM has the right sign and is significant at the 5 per cent level, compliance with PSD is neither significant nor has the expected sign.

It would be also interesting to see if compliance with the individual components groups of SAPs have affected short run change in HDI independently. Models 2 to 4 show the results for these regressions. These results indicate that compliance with MSP has improved human development in sub-Saharan programme countries albeit that the coefficient is significant only at the 10 per cent level. More specifically compliance with measures such as fiscal deficit reduction, increase in fiscal revenues, public expenditure control and devaluation has been associated with an improvement in HDI.

Compliance with PSM measures such as civil service and public expenditure reforms, public enterprise restructuring and privatization seem to be highly significant in terms of their effects on improving HDI. However, compliance with PSD measures (including financial sector reforms, trade policy reforms, pricing policies) have not been associated significantly with changes in HDI.

A number of possible criticisms may apply to our analyses so far. The temporal analysis has an implicit assumption that all changes that occurred in the adjustment period, as compared to the pre-adjustment period, are due to SAPs. This is clearly an unrealistic assumption, in particular when one takes into account the varying sample periods. The comparative analysis may also be criticized as it implies that only compliance would differentiate between the country groups. Clearly there may be other factors responsible for the perceived differences. The regression analysis is also limited to the compliance variables without taking into account other possible variables. It may well be the case that in the presence of other relevant explanatory variables the significance of compliance variable would simply vanish.

To overcome these possible criticisms we have included a set of control variables in our regression for changes in HDI. A number of factors could affect the change in HDI. These could be the initial conditions, economic, social and also external factors. One suspects that the role of external factors, given our varying sample period could prove to be important.

We have chosen four control variables to reflect these factors. The level of HDI in the pre-adjustment period (HDIPA) was selected to reflect the initial conditions. GDP per capita in the adjustment period (GDPPCAD1) and growth rate of gross domestic investment in the adjustment period (GGDIAD1) were included to reflect the economic factors influencing HDI. Tertiary enrolment in the pre-adjustment period (TERPA) was selected to reflect the flow of highly educated human capital with potential future feedback to the society as well as to the future education. The external conditions, in the varying sample period years, were to be reflected by the growth rate of real world GDP in the adjustment period (WGGDPAD1).[6]

Table 6.5 shows the results for regressing temporal change in HDI on compliance with conditionality in the presence of control variables. We are interested to see if the significance of compliance in the presence of control variables would be diminished or remain as before.

Table 6.5 Regression of temporal change in HDI on compliance with SAPs and associated components and control variables

Variable/model	1	2	3	4	5
Constant	0.032	0.041	0.015	0.030	0.027
	(1.31)	(1.38)	(0.67)	(1.36)	(0.87)
HDIPA	−0.097	−0.082	−0.089	−0.065	−0.126
	(−2.38)**	(1.59)	(−2.07)**	(−1.64)	(−2.42)**
GDPPCAD1	0.0001	0.00004	0.0001	−0.0001	0.0001
	(3.61)***	(2.62)**	(3.32)***	(2.85)***	(3.68)***
GGDIAD1	0.001	0.001	0.001	0.001	0.001
	(1.40)	(1.46)	(1.21)	(1.54)	(0.98)
TERPA	−0.003	−0.004	−0.003	−0.004	−0.004
	(−1.60)	(−1.37)	(−1.66)	(−2.16)**	(−1.50)
WGGDPAD1	0.011	0.009	0.012	0.009	0.012
	(2.07)**	(1.67)	(2.20)**	(1.87)*	(2.14)**
Compliance	−0.012				
	(−2.43)**				
MSP		0.002	−0.006		
		(0.29)	(−1.93)*		
PSM		−0.012		−0.012	
		(−1.73)*		(−2.78)***	
PSD		−0.005			−0.009
		(−0.61)			(−1.40)
N	21	21	21	21	21
R^2	0.71	0.74	0.68	0.74	0.64
F-statistics	5.74***	4.34***	4.84***	6.48***	4.13***

Notes
*** Significant at the 1% level. ** Significant at the 5% level. * Significant at the 10% level.

The results in Table 6.5 support our previous results. All our models exhibit good fits as judged from R^2 and F-statistics. In model 1, where we use the overall compliance scores, the initial economic and external factors are significantly related to changes in HDI. The negative sign of HDIPA in the context of convergence literature, suggesting that the lower the initial level the higher the rate of growth, is justifiable.[7] GDP per capita and the world growth rate in the adjustment periods are also significant. Over all the empirical results seem to support the theoretical considerations for selecting the control variables.

As can be seen from model 1, in the presence of control variables the effect of compliance still remains significant with the correct sign, implying that compliance with conditionality has been associated with a higher change in HDI. Model 2 examines the effects of complying with various components of SAPs collectively. The results are ambiguous and less supportive. This may be because compliance with various components of SAPs has produced different outcomes. For example, PSM measures may affect HDI positively while PSD measures may have the opposite effect. It would be, therefore, interesting to see if compliance with different categories of SAP conditions have affected short-run change in HDI individually.

Model 3 examines the effect of MSP in the presence of our control variables. The same control variables are significant and the effect of complying with MSP is still significant, though at the 10 per cent level. In this respect there is no change to our previous results in Table 6.4 for compliance with MSP. The effect of complying with PSM policy conditions on ΔHDI, as shown in model 4, remains as highly significant as before even in the presence of the selected control variables. Finally the result for model 5, related to the effect of compliance with private sector management policy conditions on ΔHDI, remains insignificant.

6.5 Medium-term effects of compliance

So far we have considered the short-run effects of compliance. The World Bank often argues that it takes time for adjustment policies to work their way through the economy. While the short-run effects of fiscal deficit reduction is expected to have adverse effects on composite measures such as HDI, the World Bank argues that in the medium run such effects turn to be positive through the better finances of the public sector. Similarly it takes some time for the public sector reforms and trade and financial liberalizations to generate positive effects and affect productivity in the economy.

In order to investigate this we looked beyond the first five years of adjustment period and extended our analysis into the second five-year period after adjustment. Table 6.6 shows the preliminary results.

The top part of Table 6.6 shows the average HDI values for relevant groups and different periods. From an almost equal HDI in the pre-adjustment period various groups have made progress but to a different extent. During the first adjustment period the group of good compliers have done better than others followed by the group of poor compliers. What is of particular interest to us is that the group of good compliers have continued to increase their HDI in the second adjustment

Table 6.6 Compliance and medium-term change in HDI

Compliers/variable	Good	Weak	Good and weak	Poor
Average HDI for				
Pre-adjustment period	0.393	0.394	0.394	0.408
First adjustment period (Adj1)	0.415	0.396	0.404	0.417
Second adjustment period (Adj2)	0.429	0.399	0.413	0.425
Temporal tests				
t-test	0.036	0.005	0.019	0.017
	(11.10)***	(0.34)	(2.13)**	(1.67)
Wilcoxon	2.53***	0.87	2.20**	1.68*
Comparative temporal tests				
t-test	0.019	−0.012	0.002	Control
	(1.65)	(−0.67)	(0.14)	group
Mann–Whitney	1.16	0.11	0.70	

Notes
*** Significant at the 1% level. ** Significant at the 5% level. * Significant at the 10% level.

period. It is notable that, in the second adjustment period, good compliers have continued to do better than other groups; however, the poor compliers have done better than weak compliers.

The fact that poor compliers have done better than weak compliers raises the question as to whether good compliance and no compliance are equally effective. For compliance to be effective, one would have expected the weak compliers to have done better than poor compliers. In addition we are interested to know if any of the mean differences are significant. The lower parts of Table 6.6 are related to the temporal changes in HDI in the medium term and show the temporal and comparative temporal differences in HDI means between the second adjustment period (Adj2) and pre-adjustment period. Once again we have used *t*-test and Wilcoxon test for the temporal and *t*-test and Mann–Whitney test for comparative temporal differences in means for all our groups. In the comparative temporal comparison once again the poor group of compliers is the control group.

As can be seen from Table 6.6, both parametric and non-parametric tests indicate that the temporal differences in means for the group of good compliers is highly significant. The magnitude of the difference with respect to the mean of HDI for this group is also high. As for the group of weak compliers, the difference is low and not significant. The same for the group of good and weak is also relatively high and significant. However, the fact that the temporal difference for the poor group of compliers is also relatively high and significant, albeit at the 10 per cent level, suggests that the pattern may be the same for the good and poor groups; hence it seems that compliance does not clearly differentiate amongst these groups in terms of their HDI performance. The results of both parametric and non-parametric tests for comparative temporal differences in means at the bottom of Table 6.6 do not throw more light on this ambiguity, as none of these is significant for our groups.

To investigate this further and to attend to the possible criticisms of temporal and comparative analyses as outlined before, we regress the medium term temporal change in HDI on the overall compliance scores and also on the scores for various components of compliance. The results are shown in Table 6.7.

Model 1 indicates that the overall compliance has a significant effect on the medium term temporal change in HDI. Model 2 shows no association between compliance with MSP and a change in HDI in the medium term. However, compliance with PSM policy measures seems to have a positive effect on change in HDI, though significant at only the 10 per cent level. The effect of PSD measures on change in HDI is insignificant.

Once again it would be interesting to see if compliance with the individual component groups of SAPs have affected medium run change in HDI independently. Models 3 to 5 in Table 6.7 show the results for these regressions. Model 3 shows no significant association between compliance with MSP measures and the change in HDI. Model 4 shows a significant association between compliance with PSM measures and the change in HDI while compliance with PSD measures seems to have no significant effect on the change in HDI.

Table 6.7 Regression of medium-term temporal change in HDI on overall compliance and its components

Variable/model	1	2	3	4	5
Constant	0.065	0.070	0.045	0.075	0.019
	(2.42)**	(2.49)**	(2.08)**	(3.01)***	(0.82)
Compliance	−0.019				
	(−1.90)**				
MSP		0.000	−0.009		
		(0.00)	(−1.30)		
PSM		−0.027		−0.022	
		(−1.79)*		(−2.41)**	
PSD		0.008			−0.001
		(0.72)			(−0.11)
N	26	26	28	27	27
R^2	0.13	0.25	0.06	0.19	0.00
F-statistics	3.59*	2.42*	1.69	5.79**	0.01

Notes
*** Significant at the 1% level. ** Significant at the 5% level. * Significant at the 10% level.

Table 6.8 Regression of medium-term temporal change in HDI on overall compliance and its components with control variables

Variable/model	1	2	3	4	5
Constant	0.124	0.128	0.112	0.125	0.123
	(2.66)***	(2.26)**	(2.58)**	(2.90)***	(2.30)**
HDIPA	−0.386	−0.331	−0.396	−0.335	−0.419
	(−3.68)***	(−2.54)**	(−3.74)***	(−2.93)***	(−4.17)***
GDPPCAD2	0.00006	0.00005	0.00006	0.00005	0.00006
	(2.58)**	(1.75)*	(2.62)***	(1.95)*	(3.32)***
GGDIAD2	0.002	0.002	0.002	−0.002	0.002
	(2.26)**	(1.80)*	(2.42)**	(2.03)*	(2.36)**
TERAD1	0.005	0.003	0.006	0.004	0.001
	(1.09)	(0.48)	(1.15)	(0.73)	(1.14)
WGGDPAD2	0.009	0.008	0.011	0.009	0.009
	(0.73)	(0.55)	(0.86)	(0.72)	(0.67)
Compliance	−0.008				
	(−0.86)				
MSP		0.005	−0.004		
		(0.42)	(−0.58)		
PSM		−0.017		−0.013	
		(−1.16)		(−1.30)	
PSD		−0.001			−0.004
		(−0.07)			(−0.50)
N	22	22	22	22	22
R^2	0.64	0.66	0.63	0.66	0.62
F-statistics	4.35***	3.17**	4.17***	4.67***	4.14***

Notes
*** Significant at the 1% level. ** Significant at the 5% level. * Significant at the 10% level.

As we argued before, the results in Table 6.7 are subject to the criticisms that change in HDI in the medium term is exclusively attributed to compliance with conditionality. To overcome this problem, as before, we introduce a set of control variables which explain the changes in HDI. These are the same variables as we employed before, except that they are now relevant to the second period of adjustment where appropriate.[8] Table 6.8 shows the results for these regressions.

The results in Table 6.8 indicate that the effect of overall compliance on changes in HDI in the medium term, in the presence of control variables, vanishes (model 1). The same is the case for compliance with various components of conditionality, collectively (model 2) and separately (models 3–5). The selected control variables are by and large sensible as indicated by the results.[9] The least we could say is that there seems to be little to suggest that the effect of compliance with conditionality on HDI is persistent over time.

6.6   Concluding discussion

Some socioeconomic aspects seem to have changed differently in countries which complied with SAPs. In the first instance it seems that a high degree of compliance with conditionality was associated with positive changes in some socioeconomic aspects as reflected by our selected indicators in the short run. Out of the four indicators, which seemingly were mostly affected by compliance, the change in HDI appears to stand the vigorous and stringent test of association. Categories of policy conditions were associated with the change in HDI in the short-run differently. The change in HDI was affected significantly by the PSM policy measures, less significantly by the MSP measures and not affected by the PSD policy measures. This was if we assumed that the changes in HDI were due to these measures only. However, when a set of relevant control variables were introduced, the effect of the above categories of policy measures remained more or less the same with a drop in the significance of MSP measures. In the light of these results it is reasonable to conclude that in the short run, compliance with the PSM and to some extent the MSP policy measures did lead to a positive improvement in HDI, while compliance with PSD policy measures had no effect.

The medium-run effects are somewhat more ambiguous. If changes in HDI are to be attributed to compliance, only the effect of compliance seems to remain significant. However, out of the categories of policy measures, only compliance with the PSM measures seems to be significant. Moreover, when control variables are introduced into the model, the significance of compliance with PSM measures disappears in the medium run. These results are in line with the outcome of a number of studies, including those by Noorbakhsh and Paloni (1998) on the export supply response to SAPs.

In brief the short-run effects are more pronounced than the medium-run effects. Bearing in mind that in the case of sub-Saharan African countries conditionality was packaged with substantial soft loans, the remaining question is whether the short run significant effects are purely the effect of spending the loan money and are unsustainable. Indeed, Mosley *et al.* (2003) conclude that the size of the loan has had a significantly positive effect on the recipient country's willingness to comply with conditionality. This is a question worthy of further research.

Appendix 1 Country typology by the level of compliance

Good compliers: Benin, Gambia, Ghana, Malawi, Mali, Mauritania, Mauritius, Mozambique, Sierra Leone, Tanzania.
Weak compliers: Burkina Faso, Cote d'Ivoire, Guinea-Bissau, Madagascar, Niger, Senegal, Togo, Uganda, Zambia, Zimbabwe.
Poor compliers: Burundi, Cameroon, Central African Republic, Chad, Congo, Gabon, Kenya, Nigeria, Rwanda, Sao Tome, Somalia, Sudan, Zaire.

The average score for the three components of Macroeconomic Stabilization, PSM and PSD constitutes the overall compliance score. The overall compliance scores for the *good* compliers range from 1.1 to 2.2 with an average of 1.7. The same for *weak* compliers range from 2.5 to 2.9 with an average of 2.7. The ratings for the poor compliers range from 3 to 4 with an average of 3.4.

The data for the selected indicators were not available for all the above countries, therefore some countries are excluded from the relevant analysis for this reason.

Appendix 2 Actual pre-adjustment, short- and medium-term adjustment periods

Table 6A.1 Actual pre-adjustment, short-term and medium-term adjustment periods

	Pre-	*Adj1*	*Adj2*		*Pre-*	*Adj1*	*Adj2*
Benin	1984–	1989–	1993–97	Mauritius	1976–	1981–	1986–90
Burkina	1986–	1991–	1996–	Mozambiq	1983–	1988–	1993–97
Burundi	1981–	1986–	1991–95	Niger	1981–	1986–	1991–95
Cameroon	1984–	1989–	1994–98	Nigeria	1982–	1987–	1992–96
CAR	1982–	1987–	1992–96	Rwanda	1986–	1991–	1996–
Chad	1984–	1989–	1994–98	Sao Tome	1982–	1987–	1992–96
Congo	1983–	1988–	1993–97	Senegal	1981–	1986–	1991–95
Cote	1977–	1982–	1987–91	Sierra	1987–	1992–	1997–
Gabon	1983–	1988–	1993–97	Somalia	1981–	1986–	1991–95
Gambia	1982–	1987–	1992–96	Sudan	1975–	1980–	1985–89
Ghana	1978–	1983–	1988–92	Tanzania	1982–	1987–	1992–96
Guinea-	1980–	1985–	1990–94	Togo	1978–	1983–	1988–92
Kenya	1975–	1980–	1985–89	Uganda	1983–	1988–	1993–97
Madagascar	1980–	1985–	1990–94	Zaire	1981–	1986–	1991–95
Malawi	1976–	1981–	1986–90	Zambia	1986–	1991–	1996–
Mali	1983–	1988–	1993–97	Zimbabwe	1987–	1992–	1997–
Mauritania	1981–	1986–	1991–95				

Notes

1 This approach was adopted by Noorbakhsh and Paloni (2001) for studying the effect of compliance on growth.
2 Wilcoxon test is an appropriate non-parametric test as samples are related.
3 Noorbakhsh and Paloni (2001) analyse the effect of compliance on the rate of growth of real GDP extensively using the same data set. We have not included this indicator in our list in order to avoid duplication and the reader is referred to this article for details.
4 Mann–Whitney test is a more appropriate non-parametric test in the case of comparative analysis as samples are independent.
5 The reader is reminded that the low (high) score for compliance indicates a high (low) degree of compliance.
6 Number 1 in the name of a variable indicates adjustment period 1 as described in the text. The relevant dates can be found in Appendix 2.
7 For a summary of the literature of convergence and its application see for example Noorbakhsh (2003).
8 Number 2 in the name of a variable refers to adjustment period 2 as explained in the text.
9 We tried the same regression excluding TERAD1 and WGGDPAD2 and there were no improvements in the results.

Bibliography

Cornia, G.A. and Helleiner, G. (eds) (1994) *From Adjustment to Development in Africa: Conflict Controversy, Convergence, Consensus?*, New York: St Martin's.

Cornia, G.A., Jolly, R. and Stewart, F. (1987) *Adjustment with a Human Face: Protecting the Vulnerable and Promoting Growth*, Oxford: Oxford University Press.

CPRC (Chronic Poverty Research Centre) (2004) 'The chronic poverty report 2004–05', Institute for Development Policy and Management, Manchester: University of Manchester.

Dreze, J. and Sen, A. (1989) *Hunger and Public Action*, Oxford: Clarendon Press.

Ehrenpreis, D. (2003) 'Poverty reduction in Swedish development cooperation: policies and practice', in Booth, A. and Mosley, P. (eds), *The New Poverty Strategies: What Have They Achieved? What Have We Learned?*, Basingstoke: Palgrave Macmillan.

Engberg-Pedersen, P., Gibbon, P., Raikes, P. and Udsholt, L. (1996) (eds) 'Limits of adjustment in Africa: the effects of economic liberalization 1986–94', Copenhagen and Oxford: Centre for Development Research in Association with James Currey, Oxford, Heinemann, Portsmouth, NH.

Kakwani, N. (1995) 'Structural adjustment and performance in living standards in developing countries', *Development and Change*, 26: 469–502.

Kanbur, R. (1991) 'Project versus policy reform', Proceedings of the World Bank Annual Conference on Development Economics 1990, Washington, DC: The World Bank.

Killick, T. (1996) 'Principals, agents and failing conditionality', Annual Conference of Development Studies Association, University of Reading.

Mosley, P., Subasat, T. and Weeks, J. (1995), 'Assessing adjustment in Africa', *World Development*, 23: 1459–1473.

Mosley, P., Noorbakhsh, F. and Paloni, A. (2003) 'Compliance with World Bank conditionality: implications for the selectivity approach to policy-based lending and the design of conditionality', CREDIT research paper, No. 03/20, University of Nottingham.

Noorbakhsh, F. (1999) 'Standards of living, human development indices and structural adjustments in developing countries: an empirical investigation', *Journal of International Development*, 11: 151–175.

—— (2003) 'Spatial inequality and polarisation in India', CREDIT Research Paper, No. 03/16, University of Nottingham.

Noorbakhsh, F. and Paloni, A. (1998) 'Structural adjustment programs and export supply response', *Journal of International Development*, 10: 555–573.

—— (2001) 'Structural adjustment programs and growth in sub-Saharan Africa: the importance of complying with conditionality', *Economic Development and Cultural Change*, 49: 479–509.

OECD (Organization for Economic Co-operation and Development) (1992) *Adjustment and Equity in Developing Countries*, Paris: OECD.

Please, S. (1996) 'Structural adjustment and poverty – blunting the criticisms', *Development Policy Review*, 14: 185–202.

Singer, H. (1995) 'Aid conditionality', Institute of Comparative Culture, Tokyo: Sophia University.

Stewart, F. (1994) 'Are adjustment policies in Africa consistent with long-run development needs?', in van der Geest, W. (ed.), *Negotiating Structural Adjustment in Africa*, London: James Currey and Heinemann.

—— (1995) *Adjustment and Poverty: Options and Choices*, London: Routledge.

Summers, L. and Pritchett, L. (1993) 'The structural adjustment debate', *American Economic Review*, 83: 383–389.

UNRISD (United Nations Research Institute for Social Development) (1995) *Adjustment, Globalization and Social Development: Report of the URISD/UNDP International Seminar on Economic Restructuring and Social Policy*, Geneva: UNRISD.

van der Hoeven, R. (2003) 'Poverty and structural adjustment: some remarks on tradeoffs between equity and growth', in Booth, A. and Mosley, P. (eds), *The New Poverty Strategies: What Have They Achieved? What Have We Learned?*, Basingstoke: Palgrave Macmillan.

World Bank (1992) *Adjustment Lending Revisited: Policies to Restore Growth: A World Bank Symposium*, Washington, DC: The World Bank.

—— (1997) 'Adjustment lending in sub-Saharan Africa: an update', Report No. 16594, Operations Evaluation Department, Washington, DC: World Bank.

7 Trade liberalization and economic reform in developing countries

Structural change or de-industrialization?

Mehdi S. Shafaeddin

7.1 Introduction

The purpose of this chapter is to analyse the performance of a sample of developing countries which undertook trade liberalization and economic reform since the early 1980s. It will be argued that the failure of traditional import substitution (MS) strategies of 1950s–1970s has been followed by the lack of success, in most cases, of export promotion (EP) strategies of the 1980s–1990s by countries which implemented the reform programmes and trade liberalization policies designed by international financial institutions (IFIs).

The process of trade liberalization and market-oriented economic reform that had started in many developing countries in early 1980s intensified in the 1990s. The reform undertaken varied in ownership and contents in different countries. The reforming countries can be classified into three groups. The first group consists of a number of countries in East Asia which continued their own dynamic industrial and trade policies initiated in the 1960s. The second group includes a large number of countries, mostly in Africa, which have gone through the reform programmes designed and dictated by the IFIs. The third group comprises a number of Latin American countries that undertook economic reform since the early 1980s, initially under pressure from IFIs. Nevertheless, in the 1990s they intensified their reform process without having been necessarily under pressure of those institutions in all cases. The contents and philosophy of their reform programmes were, however, similar to those designed by the IFIs which in turn have been referred to as the 'Washington Consensus' since the early 1990s. Universal and uniform trade liberalization was a part of that 'Consensus'. 'Universal' implies that all developing countries are to follow the same trade policy regime/trade liberalization irrespective of their levels of development and industrial capacities. 'Uniform' implies that all sectors and industries are to be subject to the same tariff rates, preferably zero rate, or low rate. Apart from trade liberalization, such reform programmes included mainly: capital account liberalization, devaluation at the early stages of reform to compensate for trade liberalization, fiscal and financial reform through contractionary macroeconomic policies such as budget cuts, increase in interest rates and privatization.

Trade liberalization measures, in particular, are believed to be a reaction to the failure of traditional MS policies of the 1950s–1970s. The philosophy behind the reform programmes was that the role of government in making decisions on resource allocation should be minimized and the incentive structure should change in favour of exports through import liberalization in order to follow an EP path instead of MS. It was argued that private agents, guided by the operation of market forces, would better achieve the objectives of growth and diversification of exports and output structure in favour of manufactured goods. Such objectives would in turn be attained through the expansion of investment, better channelling of resources and allocation of investment outlays to productive sectors. The change in the structure of incentives would not only lead to growth and diversification but also to the upgrading of the production structure, facilitated by imported technology and improved skills enhanced by trade.

To what extent have the objectives of reform been achieved? Has growth of exports of manufactures accelerated? If it did, has it been accompanied with growth of manufactured value added (MVA), structural change in exports and output and upgrading of the export structure necessary to sustain export expansion? Has investment been stimulated?

As the performance of countries varies, there is a controversy in the literature on the causes of failure in attaining the objectives of reform. Some scholars attribute the lack of success to improper implementation or incompletion of the reform programmes (e.g. Baumann, 2001). Others have cast doubts on the rationale and 'the same-size-for-all approach to reform' (e.g. Garrido and Peres, 1998; Katz, 2000a; Krugman, 2002; Lora *et al.*, 2002; Weisbrot, 2002). On the particular issue of trade liberalization,[1] Krueger (1998), Ben-David and Loewy (1998) and Greenaway *et al.* (1998) continue to argue in favour of the positive impact of trade liberalization on growth and industrialization. Greenaway *et al.* (1998) further believe that there is a lag response to liberalization. By contrast, Ocampo and Taylor (1998), Rodrik (1998), Shafaeddin (1995) and Weisbrot and Baker (2002) are doubtful.

Although the origin of the literature on trade liberalization and economic reform goes back to the publication by Little *et al.* (1970), followed by Krueger (1974), in the 1970s, the process of the reform was started by the introduction of the Structural Adjustment Programmes (SAPs) and Stabilization Programmes (SPs) of the World Bank and the IMF in the early 1980s. Therefore, we first briefly review the development in the views expressed by the World Bank, which has been the main advocate and implementer of SAPs, on the issue. Growth and structural changes in exports and output will be dealt with in the next section and the section following that. An analysis of the impact of liberalization on industries, which are near the stage of maturity is dealt with in Section 7.5. Changes in investment and vulnerability of the economies of the exporting countries will be discussed in Sections 7.6 and 7.7. As some countries in Latin America and Africa show severe patterns of de-industrialization we will subsequently review the debate on the subject before concluding the study.

7.2   Evolution of the World Bank's approach

The work of the World Bank on trade policy and economic reform has been dominating the field in recent decades. It started with the study on trade policy reform in *Word Development Report* (1987). This study takes outward orientation and liberal trade regimes as synonymous and shows that countries that followed outward orientation succeeded better. The study placed the countries of East Asia in the category of outward oriented regimes and attributed their success to liberal trade regimes. The study was attacked on methodological deficiencies, particularly definition of outward orientation, treatment of statistics and failure to distinguish among countries according to their level of development (e.g. Singer, 1988; Singer and Gray, 1988; Shafaeddin, 1991a). The World Bank study, as well as many other Banks' studies (see e.g. Papageorgiou *et al.*, 1990) take neutrality of a trade regime, that is, zero rates of protection for importables and exportables, and liberal trade regimes as synonymous. 'Trade liberalization is defined as any act that would make the trade regime more neutral – nearer to a trade system free of government intervention' (ibid., vol. 7, p. 13). Nevertheless, one should note that a neutral trade regime could be achieved at positive, but equal, rates of protection for exports and imports. Hence, outward orientation does not necessarily imply a liberal trade regime (Shafaeddin, 1991a).

This point is later on well recognized by the staff members of the Bank in their study of *Best Practices in Trade Policy Reform* (Thomas and Nash, 1991). Nevertheless, the authors still consider that 'relatively low and relatively uniform tariffs are preferable for reasons of efficiency and political economy', even though they agree that 'uniformity of import tariffs cannot be demonstrated in theory to be optimal in many circumstances' (ibid., p. 214). In other words, despite the fact that in practice the selective trade policy has been successful in East Asia and that 'uniformity of tariffs cannot be demonstrated to be optimal', the authors' value judgment tilts in favour of uniformity of the incentive structure. Further, they attribute the lack of success of many countries which followed uniform trade policy regimes to other factors, including the lack of proper implementation. This line of argument has more or less continued in other empirical studies of the Bank, including the *East Asian Miracle* (1993).

This study is a breakthrough in the work of the Bank on industrial policy. Generally speaking, it recognizes the fact that trade policy regime alone is not sufficient for rapid growth. It appreciates the importance of the institutional factors in success, or failure, of policies. Further, it advocates that interventions are required to enhance investment in physical and human resource capacities. More importantly, it recognizes, for the first time, that 'economic policies and policy advice must be country-specific, if they are to be effective' (World Bank, 1993, p. iv).

Nevertheless, the study suffers from a few important weaknesses including the contradictions between its recommendations and its general findings. Here, we refer to a few of these inconsistencies. First, despite the fact that the authors recognize the importance of country specific policies, they advocate almost universal trade and industrial policies for all developing countries during the process of their development. Second, they advocate that government involvement in the economy should be limited to functional, not selective, intervention. The functional intervention should concentrate on 'getting the fundamentals right'. By fundamentals it is meant good macroeconomic management, stable macro-economic policies, measures to enhance savings and investment and avoidance of excessive distortions. Otherwise, 'our assessment is that promotion of specific industries generally did not work and therefore holds little promise for other developing countries' (ibid., p. 32). It is concluded that: 'We find little evidence that industrial policies have affected either the sectoral structure of industry or rate of productivity change' (ibid., p. 30), and that: 'Indeed industrial structure in Japan, Korea, Taiwan, and China has *evolved* [my italic] during the past thirty years as we would expect on the basis of factor-based comparative advantage and *changing factor endowments* [my italics]' (ibid., p. 21). The authors of the report do not however take into account the fact that the industrial structure did not evolve automatically through market forces in these countries. It was the result of selective and 'careful policy interventions' which, elsewhere in the text, they admit to have been effective.

Third, the success of the East Asian countries was attributed to their low level of general 'nominal' tariff rates, 'the fact that East Asia's relative prices of traded goods were closer, *on average*, to international prices than those of other developing countries' (ibid., p. 29). Nevertheless, the figures on tariff rates refer to those of the 1980s and the early 1990s, that is, the end period. The dimension of time for each country, and the difference in stages of development of various countries in each period is not appreciated in this statement. Considering that, at the time of publication of the Report, East Asian countries were at, or close to, maturity in most industries, it was in fact essential that their trade regime would be, *on average*, more liberal than other developing countries. Otherwise they had been strongly, although on selective basis, protective of their importables and exporta-bles in the past. In fact, in the same study it is admitted that 'Most HPAEs [High Performing East Asian Economies] began industrialization with a protectionist orientation and gradually moved towards increasingly free trade'[2] (ibid.). Moreover, it should be mentioned that neither nominal rate nor average rate of protection is a good indication of selective protection policies. As recently as the mid-1980s, the effective rate of protection for consumer goods and machinery industries of the Republic of Korea was 135 per cent (Arndt, 1987).

Fourth, it is concluded that protection of domestic market coexisted with promotion of exports through countervailing subsidies in most East Asian countries (World Bank, 1993, p. 31). However, a similar policy is not advocated for other developing countries because it is believed to be difficult to manage and is incom-patible with the changing world trade environment (ibid., p. 33). While there is some truth in this statement, there are still ways to promote exports through government intervention (Amsden, 2000). Further, the rules are not god given; they can be changed.

Fifth, it is also recognized that 'externalities are an important source of rapid productivity growth' particularly through the spillover effect to the rest of the economy of exports of manufactured goods (World Bank, 1993, pp. 31–32). Nevertheless, the fact that certain industries, whether for export or domestic production, involve more externalities than others is not appreciated.

Another feature of the empirical studies undertaken by the Bank in general is that they attribute the failure of the trade liberalization to achieve development objectives, particularly in the case of Africa, to insufficient liberalization and inappropriate implementation of liberalization and adjustment programmes. Often the government is blamed for the lack of appropriate sequencing and speed of liberalization or inappropriate macroeconomic policies (see e.g. World Bank, 1994; Husain Faruqee, 1994). In the latter study by the staff members of the Bank, it is admitted that 'Import liberalization, if done too rapidly, will reduce the profitability of domestic firms competing with imports....' (ibid., pp. 435–436). Nevertheless, the appropriateness of universal trade liberalization to all countries at different stages of development is never seriously questioned and uniform liberalization of different activities within a country at any point in time is never questioned. The critics of the neo-liberals also often neglect this factor, with few exceptions. The exceptional cases include Singer and Gray (1998), Helleiner (1986), Michaely (1977), Wheeler (1984) and Shafaeddin (1991, 2005) who make some allowance for countries at different levels of industrialization and development. Further, Lall *et al.* (1994) are among those who distinguish four groups of activities within a country as far as the impact of trade liberalization is concerned. The first group includes those with strong resource advantage or well-developed capabilities so that they are already competitive internationally, and those that enjoy natural protection because they are heavy and difficult or expensive to transport, or require close producer–buyer interaction. They all benefit from liberalization. The second group consists of those which are in 'a short distance from the technological frontier', that is, those which are near the stage of maturity. They may also benefit from liberalization. The third group include activities which are potentially viable, but require time to learn, that is, are still at the stage of infancy. Sudden liberalization of imports will hurt them. Finally, there are activities, which are not economically viable currently, or potentially, so they suffer from liberalization but they should be allowed to die. Such categorization would imply that protection/liberalization should take place on selective basis.

7.3   Growth in exports and output

7.3.1   Methodology and data

To analyse the performance of developing countries we have used the data for a sample of countries reported in Shafaeddin (2005). The sample includes three different categories of countries. The first consists of countries which have already developed their industrial capacity and have substantial capabilities in exports of manufactured goods. This group includes mainly East Asian countries and other NIEs. The second group covers countries which have developed some industrial capacity through import substitution, with some export capabilities.

When they started liberalization, some of their industries were near maturity but not all. Further, they had developed a large number of industries due to balance of payments restrictions and not as a result of a designed industrial strategy. They include many Latin American, Middle Eastern and North African countries. The third group includes countries with little industrial base which are located mainly in Africa. The period used for the analysis is that of the 1990s, when the reform process intensified in most countries.

Figures on growth of exports are inflated by increases in import intensity of exports in recent years due to import liberalization and changes in the organization of production towards networking and assembly operation, particularly in export processing zones (see Buitelaar and Pérez, 2000, table 2; Palma, 2002, table 2; Shafaeddin, 2005). The data on the purchasing power of exports, rather than export value, are used for the analysis, as they better represent the ability of the country to acquire imports of manufactured goods, but the figures on the value of exports are also reported for comparison.

The expansion of exports does not necessarily indicate the growth in production capacity. If export expansion is not accompanied by a corresponding expansion of MVA and investment, it is either because resources are diverted from domestic markets to exports, or because the import intensity of exports has increased for the reasons mentioned earlier. Therefore, we have studied changes in MVA as well as investment and absorptive capacity of the sample countries. The data on MVA are derived from World Bank sources that are based on the UNIDO's definition of manufactured goods which include all processed and semi-processed primary products.

Despite all these shortcomings, Tables 7.1–7.5 provide some information on relative performances of the sample countries over the period 1989–2000. In these tables, countries of the sample are classified into three groups, according to their rate of growth of purchasing power of exports of manufactured goods: high (I), moderate (II) and low (III) as defined in the Appendix. Within each group they are classified according to their rate of growth of MVA and shown as subgroups.

7.3.2 Performance of the sample countries

Table 7.1 indicates first that rapid expansion of exports of manufactured goods has not been widespread. Only group I, which includes 20 of the 46 countries in the sample, shows high rates of growth of exports of manufactured goods;[3] the rest show moderate (group II), low, or negative, export growth (group III). For group I, rapid growth of exports of manufactured goods has also corresponded to rapid growth of total exports except for subgroup 'c'. The base of manufacturing exports, thus their weight in total exports, has been small for most countries in this subgroup.

Second, in group I only for subgroup 'a' (11 countries) rapid expansion of exports of manufactured goods has been accompanied with rapid growth in production (MVA, GDP) and domestic absorption.[4] With the exceptions of Costa Rica and El Salvador, the countries in subgroup 'b' are among those that had

Table 7.1 Average annual growth rates of output and trade, 1989–2000

Country with	Purchasing power of exports		Value added		Domestic absorption	Export value	
	Manufactured goods	Total	Manufactured goods	GDP		Manufactured goods	Total
I High export growth (20)	17.0	10.6	5.2	4.8	4.8	16.7	10.0
a High output growth (11)	16.6	12.3	7.6	5.9	5.5	16.7	11.6
b Moderate output growth (2)	21.5	12.4	4.5	5.0	5.3	21.4	11.8
c Low output growth (7)	16.3	7.5	1.6	2.9	3.4	15.2	6.9
II. Moderate export growth (20)	7.7	7.2	3.1	4.0	3.9	7.8	6.6
d High output growth (5)	8.3	8.4	6.8	4.8	3.9	8.8	7.8
e Moderate output growth (6)	7.7	7.4	4.2	4.7	4.7	7.9	6.8
f Low output growth (9)	7.4	6.3	0.0	3.1	3.2	7.1	5.7
III. Low export growth (6)	−1.5	3.7	0.7	2.4	3.6	−1.2	3.1
g High output growth (1)	3.2	−1.4	6.2	4.5	4.1	3.1	−1.9
h Moderate output growth (3)	1.5	5.4	3.5	3.1	3.9	1.8	4.8
i Low/negative output growth (2)	−8.2	3.7	−4.9	0.3	3.1	−7.8	3.1
Total sample (46)	10.6	8.2	3.8	4.1	4.3	10.5	7.6

Sources: World Bank, *World Development Indicators* and UNCTAD, *Handbook of Development Statistics* (various issues).

Notes

1 The notations for growth rates are as follows: Exports: high – more than 10; moderate – between 10 and 5; low – less than 5; MVA: high – more than 5; moderate between 5 and 3; low – less than 3.

2 Exports and output in the first column (*Country groups*) refer to purchasing power of exports and MVA, respectively.

3 Purchasing power of manufacturing exports was calculated by deflating the export value by the unit value of manufacturing exports of developed countries.

4 The figures in brackets in the first column refer to the number of countries in each group.

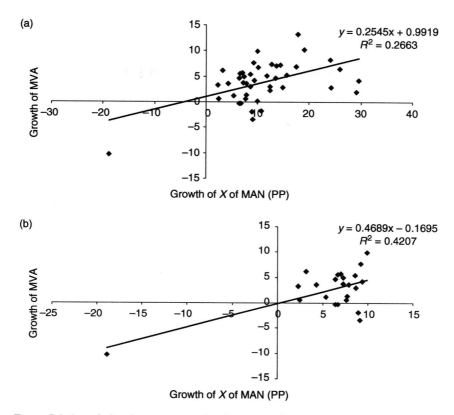

Figure 7.1 Association between growth of exports of manufactured goods and MVA
(a) all countries; (b) groups II and III.

Source: Based on UNCTAD database.

Note
PP, MAN, X and MVA stands for purchasing power, manufactures, exports and manufactured value added, respectively.

already shown rapid growth in exports and output in the 1980s and are mostly located in East Asia (see Appendix).

Third, the association between growth of export of manufactured goods and growth of MVA is reasonably high, particularly when group I is excluded from the sample (Figure 7.1); nevertheless, the direction of causation is not clear. The fact that assembly operations and export processing zones are very important in export operations of many of the countries in this group (e.g. Mexico, Costa Rica, Sri Lanka, Bangladesh, Bolivia and the Philippines) may explain, at least partially, the weaker association in the first group. In fact, in a few countries (Jamaica, Ghana, Colombia, Uruguay and Paraguay), high or moderate growth rates of exports of manufactured goods are accompanied with negative growth rates of MVA (Shafaeddin, 2005). By contrast, some countries have managed to achieve relatively fast expansion of their MVA with little or moderate export growth (e.g. subgroup 'g' and 'd').

Fourth, the performance of Mexico, Brazil and Ghana, is worth mentioning.[5] Mexico was among one of the top reformers in Latin American countries in areas of trade liberalization and economic reform and received significant inflows of foreign direct investment (FDI) (see ECLAC, 2001, table 11.3; Shafaeddin, 2005). It achieved a rate of growth of exports of manufactured goods of nearly 30 per cent. Yet, its growth rate of MVA was not particularly impressive – over 4 per cent as against 7.6 per cent for subgroup 'a'. Brazil's growth rates of exports of manufactured goods and MVA were 5.4 and 1.1, respectively, in spite of its deep reforms and significant inflows of FDI. Notwithstanding two decades of reform, Ghana's growth in MVA added was significantly negative (−3.5 per cent) during the 1990s, implying severe de-industrialization.

An important characteristic of the 1990s is that the rate of growth of absorption grew faster than GDP in most countries, that is, for the subgroup of countries with moderate or low output growth (Table 7.1).[6] On average, during the 1990s groups II and III not only did not manage to increase their exports substantially, but they also suffered from increases in their current account deficits in relation to their total exports of goods and services (Table 7.2). Many Latin American countries are in this category (see Appendix). The debt service ratios increased for some countries in these subgroups substantially. For example, the ratios for Brazil and Argentina were, on average, 92.8 and 68.3 per cent, respectively for 1998–2000. In many countries, capital flows played an increasing important role in financing the current account deficits. This is in contrast with the situation in the 1980s when export expansion was at the cost of domestic absorption, which grew slower than GDP. During this period, export expansion together with import compression was used to repay debts (Shafaeddin, 1991b). In the 1990s, capital flows allowed the expansion of domestic absorption, but not necessarily investment (see Section 7.6).

7.4   Changes in the structure of production and exports

One argument used in favour of universal and uniform trade liberalization is that it would help diversification of the structure of exports and output in favour of manufactured good. Has it happened?

7.4.1   *Diversification*

We have used the change in the share of manufactures in total exports of goods and the change in the ratio of total exports of goods and services to GDP as indicators of the reorientation of the structure of exports and output. The change in the MVA/GDP ratio is instead taken as a general indicator of diversification of output in favour of manufactured goods. The necessary data are provided in Table 7.3. Accordingly, first of all, the diversification of exports in favour of manufactured goods is very impressive for all groups, particularly Group I.

Table 7.2 Changes in debt and current account indicators for selected countries, 1979–2000

Country with	Debt service/exports of goods and services			Current account/exports of goods and services		
	1979/81	1989/91	1998/2000	1979/81	1989/91	1998/2000
I High export growth (20)	23.4	25.2	19.1	−35.1	−15.9	−7.0
a High output growth (11)	16.7	21.0	14.3	−27.5	−15.6	1.4
b Moderate output growth (2)	51.4	25.5	24.0	−45.8	−11.7	−9.7
c Low output growth (7)	24.1	31.2	24.5	−42.9	−17.4	−19.6
II Moderate export growth (20)	19.3	21.7	23.0	−23.7	−7.7	−12.2
d High output growth (5)	9.3	14.0	12.2	−12.6	−14.8	−4.0
e Moderate output growth (6)	20.2	19.5	20.5	−20.2	−17.0	−19.4
f Low output growth (9)	25.8	28.7	32.4	−31.8	1.3	−12.8
III Low export growth (6)	11.5	16.2	9.5	−22.4	−5.7	−11.0
g High output growth (1)	12.3	21.6	9.7	−23.0	7.7	−12.8
h Moderate output growth (3)	12.9	17.5	9.8	−20.8	−8.7	−6.0
i Low/negative output growth (2)	7.8	7.9	8.5	−24.5	−7.8	−17.7
Total sample (46)	20.4	22.8	19.8	−28.4	−11.1	−9.7

Sources: World Bank, *Global Development Finance (2002)* and *World Development Indicators* and UNCTAD, *Handbook of Statistics* (various issues), and UNCTAD database.

Table 7.3 Changes in indicators for manufacturing sector and total exports for selected countries, 1979–2000

Country with	Exports of goods and services to GDP			Export of manufactures to total exports			Share of manufacturing value added in GDP		
	1998–2000	Change over		1998–2000	Change over		1998–2000	Change over	
		1979–81	1989–91		1979–81	1989–91		1979–81	1989–91
I High export growth (20)	41.5	9.8	7.3	64.8	35.8	16.8	21.4	2.6	1.5
a High output growth (11)	52.5	12.5	10.9	76.6	40.8	16.9	25.0	5.7	3.4
b Moderate output growth (2)	30.1	14.3	3.8	50.7	39.4	21.7	17.1	−1.5	−0.6
c Low output growth (7)	27.5	4.1	2.8	49.4	25.4	14.6	16.4	−2.5	−1.8
II Moderate export growth (20)	36.7	7.3	3.2	55.4	19.9	4.9	16.0	−1.3	−1.3
d High output growth (5)	46.5	11.3	4.9	83.6	23.6	6.4	17.0	2.3	2.1
e Moderate output growth (6)	34.2	1.1	1.9	70.2	22.8	6.4	15.8	−1.1	−1.0
f Low output growth (9)	33.0	9.1	3.2	36.1	16.1	3.5	15.6	−3.8	−3.7
III Low export growth (6)	52.7	5.8	1.6	67.8	13.1	1.8	11.6	−3.6	−2.3
g High output growth (1)	15.8	−15.4	−6.1	40.5	27.3	3.1	17.9	n.a.	2.3
h Moderate output growth (3)	78.9	23.6	4.7	95.0	−1.0	0.4	13.6	2.0	0.3
i Low/negative output growth (2)	32.0	−10.2	0.7	n.a.	n.a.	n.a.	7.4	−6.5	−5.8
Total sample (46)	40.9	8.2	4.8	61.3	28.2	11.0	18.0	0.3	−0.2

Sources: World Bank, *World Development Indicators* (various issues), and United Nations COMTRADE database and estimates.

Nevertheless, once again the increase in the share of manufactured goods is partly due to assembly operations and increased import intensity of exports. Further, for all subgroups the diversification has taken place mainly during the 1980s rather than the 1990s. This is not unexpected as the introduction of trade liberalization and other reform measures in the 1980s provided a once-and-for-all shift in incentives in favour of exports. Except for the first group, the reform measures have failed to sustain fast growth in exports of manufactures in the 1990s.

Second, dependence on external markets has increased substantially during the last two decades, particularly for the first group during the 1990s, as indicated by the ratio of total exports of goods and services to GDP. Yet, such dependence has generally not been accompanied by diversification of output structure in favour of manufacturing sector, even when manufactured exports expanded fast. In fact, for groups I and II which have shown high and moderate export growth, only I.a and II.d (15 countries out of 31, mostly in East Asia) show increases in MVA/GDP ratio over 1980–2000. For the rest, MVA/GDP ratio declined continuously in 1980s and 1990s. For the whole sample, 20 countries out of 40 for which data are available (Singapore and Hong Kong excluded),[7] show decline in their MVA/GDP ratio, without recovering, implying a sort of premature de-industrialization.[8]

Most countries that experienced de-industrialization are among those with initial low levels of development and industrial bases (e.g. Ghana, Guatemala, Peru, Panama, Zimbabwe, Paraguay, Barbados and Haiti). In other words, the industrial sector has been more vulnerable to trade liberalization in countries at lower levels of development and low industrial bases. Nevertheless, de-industrialization has not been confined to low-income countries. A number of other countries, particularly in Latin America, have also suffered from premature de-industrialization. Such countries as Chile, despite its long period of reform, Argentina, Jamaica, Colombia, Venezuela, Uruguay, Brazil, the Philippines and Tunisia provide examples in this respect. Some of the countries with declining MVA/GDP ratio also show negative growth rates of manufacturing sectors over 1990s. They include, for example, Jamaica, Ghana, Colombia, Uruguay, Paraguay and Haiti.[9]

7.4.2 Upgrading of the production and export structure

Upgrading of the production capacity and export structure is necessary for a number of reasons. First, it is essential for sustainability of exports. Second, it helps technological development and spillover effects of the export sector to the rest of the economy. Third, it reduces the vulnerability of the economy to external factors, balance of payments crises, the fallacy of composition and terms of trade losses.

Most countries in Africa have achieved little in exports of manufactured goods to speak of upgrading; their structure of exports is still concentrated in primary commodities, particularly in sub-Saharan countries (see Lall and Stewart, 1986; Lall *et al.*, 1994; Shafaeddin, 1995; UNCTAD, 1999). In the case of East Asia, the first-tier NIEs have managed to continue to diversify and upgrade their manufactured exports mainly by pursuing their own selective industrial policy (UNCTAD, 1996).

Most Latin American countries had already developed some industrial capacity through MS when they initiated structural reform. Nevertheless, one criticism of MS strategies implemented in Latin America was that they failed to upgrade the industrial and export structure (Hirschman, 1992). Let us see what they have achieved after going for an outward-orientation strategy.

With a few exceptions, there has been a major regression, rather than upgrading, in the structure of production and exports in Latin American countries. Regarding the production structure, there has been a significant shift in favour of some non-tradable items, natural resource-based industries and food processing during the last two decades. Assembly operations in electronics and automobile industries have grown rapidly, mainly by TNCs, in a few countries. By contrast, labour-intensive industries (except assembly operations in electronic products), engineering and R&D-intensive sectors producing capital goods, fine chemicals and scientific instruments have shrunk in most countries (Benavente *et al.*, 1997b; Katz and Vera, 1997; Katz, 2000a). The relative expansion of non-tradables and the decline of labour intensive items are contrary to the claims made by the proponents of 'Washington Consensus', as liberalization was supposed to favour tradable goods. Nevertheless, they are not unexpected as non-tradables were not subject to competition from imports.

The change in the pattern of specialization in exports is by and large in conformity with the change in pattern of production. Following OECD, one may distinguish five categories of goods according to the nature of input intensity, skill, technology and scale requirement as follows:[10]

- Primary commodities and processed food
- Labour-intensive and resource-based industries with low skill/capital intensity
- Products with low-to-medium level of skill/technology and scale requirement
- Those with medium-to-high level of skill/technology and scale requirement
- Products with high level of skill/technology and scale requirement.

A study of a sample of ten countries with different initial industrial bases (MVA/GDP ratio) in 1989–91 (Brazil, Mexico, Chile, Colombia, Argentina, Venezuela, Bolivia, Haiti, Costa Rica and Uruguay) has shown that there has been a significant diversification away from group I, but it was mainly due to the decline in the price of primary commodities (Shafaeddin, 2005, chapter 2). Otherwise, according to the same study almost all countries, particularly those with a lower initial industrial base, for example, Bolivia and Haiti, concentrated in exports of resource-based industries, such as wood and paper products and/or non-metallic mineral products (in group II). Further, with the exception of Mexico, Colombia, Bolivia and Haiti, their main labour-intensive exports (textiles, clothing, footwear, toys and sports products) have suffered. Mexico enjoyed improved market access to the United States through NAFTA. However, a couple of countries (Costa Rica and Mexico) enjoyed rapid expansion of assembly operations figured under group V.

In the case of Chile, after 25 years of economic reform and liberalization, primary products constitute over 81 per cent of its exports; it shows little upgrading beyond the expansion of its natural resource-based industries – namely wood and wood products and chemicals. In fact, in the case of copper, which constitutes the bulk of export of the country, the share of refined product declined in favour of primitive copper concentrates (Palma, 2002, p. 24 and the sources therein).

The expansion of the car industry, in group IV, is noticeable in large countries (Brazil, Mexico, Argentina and Venezuela) and Uruguay due to three main factors: arrangements through MERCOSUR, the attraction of a large domestic market for TNCs and the high rate of tariff protection. Nevertheless, in most cases, particularly Mexico and Argentina, assembly operations dominated the industry (see UNCTAD, 2002). Only Brazil has important production capacity in this industry.

7.5 Liberalization helps industries that are near the stage of maturity

Despite the fact the Brazil did not perform well in expansion of exports of manufactured goods as a whole, the rapid expansion of exports of vehicles and machinery, particularly non-electric, in group IV and 'other' items – mainly aircraft – in group V, are noteworthy. These industries were near the stage of maturity and trade liberalization helped them to become more efficient. The spectacular performance of the aerospace industry of Brazil is in fact an example of the success of 'targeting' and 'selectivity'. It also proves that liberalization can be effective to make an industry competitive when it is near the stage of maturity[11] – while it harms infant industries or inefficient industries subject to prolonged protection. The aerospace industry is highly technology and skill intensive. Yet although faced with a crisis of competitiveness after the shock of liberalization and privatization, it soon recovered and became the most important exporter of manufactured goods in Brazil. The value of exports of Brazilian aircrafts increased from US$182 millions in 1995 to US$1.7 billions in 1999 and US$2.7 billions in 2000. In 1998, Embraer, the Brazilian aircraft manufacturing company became the world leader in commuter and regional jet market.

If a country can succeed in such an industry, it can succeed in any industry provided the industry enjoys dynamic industrial and trade policies. The aerospace industry of Brazil was established in 1945. Throughout its operation until its privatization, in the mid-1990s, it received government support through tax incentives, budgetary allocation, financial benefits, procurement, etc. Both the government policy and the company's strategy were coherent, cumulative and continuous and targeted. In particular, the company concentrated on the technology of system integration and developed local designs for a family of aircrafts to become independent and produce a differentiated product suitable for regional flights. To acquire the necessary technology, it focussed on organizational and technical training, both know-why and know-how, through learning by doing, by training, by adapting, by interacting, by using and by hiring.

After facing liberalization in the mid 1990s, the company went through some restructuring and innovation, in its organizational and institutional strategy, to consolidate its technical knowledge. It also established partnership and strategic alliance with other local and international companies. In addition, the Federal Government continued its support of the industry through export financing, and the Programme for the expansion of Brazilian Aerospace industry.

In short, the impact of structural reform on the structure of output and exports has so far been disappointing for the majority of countries which undertook trade liberalization and economic reform designed by the IFIs and through the 'Washington Consensus'. De-industrialization has taken place in a large number of countries, including some of those with high rates of export growth. Moreover, little upgrading took place except in industries which had been dynamic during the import substitution era and were near the stages of maturity. Has investment for the expansion of the production capacity and upgrading been encouraged?

7.6   Investment

Creating production capacity for sustaining export and upgrading its structure requires investment. In fact, investment has been the main contributory factor in structural change and competitiveness of NIEs in the international market.[12] Similarly, capital accumulation played a key role in relatively rapid growth of Africa during the 1960s and 1970s (Berthélemy and Södering, 2001). The inter-relation between investment and exports are strong and complicated. On the one hand, investment is the main factor for the growth of exports and supply capacity and for upgrading (Amsden, 2001, chapters 4 and 5). On the other hand, exports can have positive effects on investment through their 'income effects' and 'supply effects' and 'vent for surplus effects'. However, under certain circumstances, the expansion of exports may even depress investment, for example, if it diverts material inputs from investments to exports and/or if 'supply effects' of exports are not present due to 'import compression' needed for payment of debts.[13] It is also possible that liberalization policies which are pursued to encourage exports may not necessarily encourage private investment. Rather than providing incentives to investors, the structural reform may change the perception of investors regarding the balance between risks and return on investment particularly against the manufacturing sector (Shafaeddin, 2005).

One needs also to distinguish between domestic investment and FDI. The latter often facilitates export expansion as TNCs have better export marketing and distribution channels. Nevertheless, FDI may not necessarily always contribute to the expansion of production capacity when the inflow is spent on the purchase of existing assets.

A reform programme succeeds in accelerating growth of total output/or MVA if it achieves, *inter alia*, greater I/GDP ratio, and/or leads to changes in the structure of investment in favour of the manufacturing sector. Comprehensive data on the sectoral allocations of investment are not readily available for all countries.

Therefore, we analyse the data on total investment for the sample countries before referring to some evidence at sectoral and industry levels. Table 7.4 provides some indicators of investment. The data on FDI should be interpreted as reflecting sources of investment funds rather than additions to the stock of capital. According to the table, despite recovery for some subgroups over the 1990s, the reform and liberalization programmes have not been able to lift investment. On the contrary, the I/GDP ratios at the end of the period are lower than in the period 1979–81, that is prior to reform.

Further, investment seems to have had a strong influence on growth of both export and MVA at the group level. The group with the highest growth rate of exports (i.e. group I) shows the highest growth rate of investment and the greatest I/GDP ratio, followed by group II. Within each group, higher rates of growth of MVA are associated with higher growth rates of investment and I/GDP ratios. Moreover, the correlation between I/GDP ratios and growth of MVA is stronger than that between the ratio of exports of manufactures to GDP and growth of MVA (Shafaeddin, 2005, chapter 3). Furthermore, the direction of causality seems to be from investment to MVA leading to exports of manufactured goods rather than the other way round (ibid.).

Finally, the relation between FDI and GDFC is not clear. When one compares the figures for the 1979–81 period to those for the 1998–2000 period, the table indicates that, in all subgroups, the increase in the FDI/GDP ratio was not accompanied by an increase in the I/GDP ratio. At the level of individual countries, only in a few cases both ratios increased (particularly for China, El Salvador, Chile, Bolivia and Jamaica in group I and Panama in group II) (ibid.). In a large number of countries, particularly in Latin America, the I/GDP ratio fell despite increases in the FDI/GDP ratio (ibid.). In other words, the attraction of FDI has been accompanied by crowding out of investment by national entrepreneurs (see also Agosin and Mayer, 2000). For the 1990s the situation is only slightly better.

With the exception of Mexico, which is a member of NAFTA, the significant attraction of FDI to most Latin American countries could be in most part a once-and-for-all phenomenon, since the flow of FDI was allocated mainly to purchases of national plants rather than to greenfield investment. Foreign investors so far have shown little interest in investing in new capacity, except for raw materials, simple processing and some assembly operations.

The allocation of investment to productive activities, particularly manufacturing sector, also suffered from the reform. In most Latin American countries that started their reform programmes, or intensified them, in the early 1990s, private investors revealed a greater preference than before for investment in residential construction, which usually involves less risk than investment in plants. The structure of investment also changed against the manufacturing sector and infrastructure; infrastructure suffered as public investment was drastically cut in most countries. In countries where the share of public investment in total investment and GDP did not decline, or regained ground after a period of decline

Table 7.4 Changes in investment indicators for selected countries, 1989–2000

Country with	Domestic investment Average growth rate 1989–2000	Investment/GDP ratio 1998–2000	Change over 1979–81	Change over 1989–91	FDI net (million US$) 1998/2000	FDI net/GDP in % 1998–2000	Change over 1979–81	Change over 1989–91
I High Export Growth (20)	5.7	23.2	−1.0	1.2	4,045.0	2.9	2.0	1.2
a High output growth (11)	5.8	24.9	−1.7	−1.0	4,736.7	2.5	1.5	0.6
b Moderate output growth (2)	7.0	25.9	−0.5	4.4	6,742.6	2.4	1.4	0.5
c Low output growth (7)	5.2	19.9	−0.3	3.8	2,187.3	3.6	2.8	2.4
II Moderate Export Growth (20)	4.7	21.6	−4.2	0.3	1,976.0	2.8	2.0	2.2
d High output growth (5)	5.5	24.0	−4.6	−1.7	843.4	2.8	1.9	2.0
e Moderate output growth (6)	6.9	23.6	−1.9	3.3	54.1	1.5	0.9	1.6
f Low output growth (9)	2.6	18.6	−5.6	−0.6	3,886.6	3.6	2.9	2.8
III Low Export Growth (6)	3.3	17.8	−7.0	1.2	605.1	0.6	−1.5	−0.1
g High output growth (1)	4.9	21.7	−15.1	0.2	1,683.3	1.9	−2.2	0.1
h Moderate output growth (3)	3.2	20.1	−5.7	3.3	637.7	0.1	−2.1	−0.4
i Low/negative output growth (2)	2.6	12.4	−2.5	−1.9	17.0	0.5	−0.2	0.1
Total sample (46)	5.0	21.8	−3.1	0.8	2,696.7	2.5	1.5	1.5

Sources: World Bank, *World Development Indicators* (2003) and *Global Development Finance* (2003). FDI data are from UNCTAD, op.cit.

(Colombia, Chile and Costa Rica), the infrastructure did not suffer (Shafaeddin, 2005, chapter 3).

Within the manufacturing sector, during the post-reform period almost all countries consolidated their industrial base, established during the period of MS, with little upgrading. In most cases the industries which attracted investment during MS continued to be dynamic in terms of investment during the 1980s and 1990s. In those rare cases where a new product figures in the list, it is simple processing and/or labour-intensive products in which the country concerned has static comparative advantage, for example, metal in Chile and Colombia, press and publications in Chile and clothing in the case of Peru. Otherwise, in all other cases, the share in total investment of the previous dynamic industries, as a group, has increased sharply. The food industry, which produces mainly for the domestic market and involves little processing, remains the most favourite industry in the post-reform period in Chile, Colombia and Mexico, and iron and steel in Brazil. Nevertheless, certain items, most notably transport equipment in Mexico and Brazil, have been targeted for expansion for the reasons mentioned earlier.[14] Generally speaking, the gains attained in allocative – temporary – efficiencies in resource-based industries as a result of trade liberalization have been limited, and whether this has led to dynamic efficiencies is doubtful (Dijkstra, 2000).[15]

In short, investment, rather than exports, has been the main factor in the expansion of industrial capacity. Changes in economic policies have so far depressed the investment environment in most countries despite some temporary improvements during the second half of the 1990s. In many cases, particularly in Latin America, I/GDP ratios are lower than in the pre-reform period despite significant increases in FDI because of a deteriorating investment environment for domestic investors.[16] Public investment was cut and private investors shifted to less risky investment. Nevertheless, the dynamic industries of the import substitution era continued to attract investment.

7.7 Increase in vulnerability

What has been the implication of reorientation of production towards exports for the vulnerability of the economy, particularly the manufacturing sector, to external factors? If a country cannot finance its imports because of disruption in the flow of foreign capital and/or borrowing, or because of changes in external demand due to changes in world economic conditions, growth of MVA and GDP will be seriously affected.

Export expansion has been accompanied with mounting vulnerability of the exporting countries to external factors. Reliance on external markets is reflected in the exports to GDP ratio (X/GDP) already shown. Moreover, the vulnerability to the external markets, as a source of supply, has increased significantly, particularly for the manufacturing sector. We have shown data on the imports to GDP ratio (M/GDP) and the ratio of the trade balance[17] of the manufacturing sector [$(X-M)$ man.] to GDP as indicators of the vulnerability of the economy as a whole, and of the manufacturing sector, respectively, in Table 7.5. Accordingly, the import to GDP ratio has

Table 7.5 The ratios of trade balance of manufactures and total imports to GDP, 1979–2000

Country	Trade balance of manufactures to GDP			Imports/GDP	
	1979/1981	Change over		1979/81	Change over
		1989/91	1998/2000		1989/91
I High Export Growth (20)	−5.8	9.0	3.3	42.3	5.6
a High output growth (11)	−1.2	15.6	6.9	49.5	5.1
b Moderate output growth (2)	−8.0	n.a.	0.8	31.2	6.3
c Low output growth (7)	−12.2	1.3	−1.6	34.5	6.1
II Moderate Export Growth (20)	−11.6	1.2	−2.1	40.3	4.1
d High output growth (5)	−8.2	8.1	0.6	49.7	2.0
e Moderate output growth (6)	−9.3	−1.6	−1.8	36.2	1.1
f Low output growth (9)	−12.6	0.3	−1.9	37.7	7.3
III Low Export Growth (6)	−34.8	−8.1	−3.2	57.4	2.7
g High output growth (1)	−9.3	10.8	−0.1	24.3	−9.3
h Moderate output growth (3)	−51.6	−38.0	−16.9	78.7	6.0
i Low/negative output growth (2)	−26.7	−1.4	−7.0	42.1	3.9
Total sample (46)	−11.0	3.2	0.3	43.4	4.6

Sources: World Bank, *World Development Indicators* (various issues), and UNCTAD, op.cit.

increased substantially during the 1990s in all groups, particularly in group I where exports of manufactured goods expanded the fastest. Further, for 1997–99, the $[(X-M)$ man.$]$/GDP is substantially negative for all groups. In fact, it is also negative in all individual countries with the exception of a few countries in Group I.a, and in the Republic of Korea, Taiwan and Pakistan (Shafaeddin, 2005, table 3.4).

Except for Group I.a, during the 1990s, when reform was intensified in most countries, the $[(X-M)$ man.$]$/GDP ratio deteriorated for most subgroups. The decrease in the ratio is due to two main factors resulting from trade liberalization and FDI. One factor is the competition of imports in the domestic market for capital goods and consumer products. Another factor is the increase in import intensity of production of manufactured goods. According to the available data for 1990–94, the import intensity of the industrial sector as a whole increased from 54.4 to 60.4 per cent for Chile, from 23.9 to 35.9 per cent for Colombia, from 10.3 to 19.9 per cent for Peru and from 6.7 to 11.5 per cent for Brazil (UNCTAD, 2000, table 7). Since then, the import intensity of production must have increased further due to import liberalization through the Uruguay Round and the expansion of FDI in assembly operations. For example, in the case of Mexico, the share of Maquila Industry in total manufactured exports increased from 38 per cent in 1991 to 48 per cent in 2000. Over the same period the share of Maquila Industry in total imports of the manufacturing industry increased from 24 to 36 per cent. While exports in the Maquila sector increased by 4.01 times, its imports increased by 4.19 times. By contrast, in the non-Maquila sector, exports and imports increased by 2.59 and 2.36 times, respectively (Palma, 2002, table 2). In the particular case of Maquila industry for exports, the percentage share of imported inputs in gross production has been continuously increasing from 64.3 in 1974 to 74.4 in 1990 and 78.3 in 1998 (Buitelaar and Pérez, 2000, table 2).

7.8   The debate on de-industrialization

One would expect that in the process of economic development of a county, first the share of the manufacturing (secondary) sector in GDP would increase (and the share of the primary sector decline) up to a certain point before it declines (Chenery and Syrqin, 1985). Such a decline, together with the fall in the share of the sector in employment, normally takes place when a country reaches a certain level of development in terms of per capita income (around US$12,000). In such cases '...de-industrialization is simply the natural outcome of successful economic development and is generally associated with rising living standards' (Rowthorn and Ramaswamy, 1997, p. 5).[18] There is no general agreement also on the causes of de-industrialization in developed countries. For example, the following factors are regarded the main cause by different authors:

- Differential growth rates of productivity in the manufacturing and services sectors, resulting from innovation, in favour of the former as well as shift in the income elasticity of demand in favour of services (Craft, 1996; Rowthorn and Ramaswamy, 1997).
- Competition of imports from the South, relocation of industries to developing countries and outsourcing (Saeger, 1997).
- Underinvestment in the particular case of Britain (Kitson and Michie, 1996).
- Dutch disease.

In the cases studied in this chapter, the situation is different: de-industrialization is premature. We have defined de-industrialization as a premature decline in MVA/GDP ratio without recovering. It is due to the reorientation of the production structure of the economy from import substitution strategies towards production on the basis of static comparative advantage due to trade liberalization. In addition, in some developing countries, a commodity boom, resulting from a price jump, for example, the case of oil-exporting countries in the 1970s and the early 1990s, has led to the decline in the share of manufacturing in GDP and employment due to the so-called Dutch disease.

In the case of developing countries, there is controversy in the literature on this type of de-industrialization as there is no general agreement on the definition of the term. Consequently, the empirical results are mixed. For example, in the case of sub-Saharan Africa, Bennell (1988), Shafaeddin (1995), Noorbakhsh and Paloni (2000) and Thoburn (2001) concluded that trade liberalization has led to de-industrialization in many countries. Stein (1992) also argued in favour of the hypothesis. By contrast, Tribe (2001b), Jalilian and Weiss (2000) and World Bank (1994) argued against the hypothesis.[19]

In a study of 34 sub-Saharan countries for 1980–97, Tribe uses the evidence of a recovery in production of manufactured goods in Ghana and Uganda over 1985–96 as an argument against 'the hypothesized "de-industrialization" based on the liberalization process' (Tribe, 2001b, p. 279). Nevertheless, apart from the fact that temporary recovery in production alone cannot be taken as an indication of the lack of de-industrialization, his conclusion is dubious and is not supported by the data. On the one hand, generalizing the case of Ghana and Uganda, he maintains that: 'the overall conclusion must be that the case for the existence of sub-Saharan African de-industrialization in the 1990s and into the twenty-first century is not strong...' (ibid., p. 280). On the other hand, his final verdict is that 'claims that liberalization has "worked" supported by reference to evidence of short-term recovery in the manufacturing sector without consideration of the more significant long-term prospects are seriously deficient' (ibid., p. 280). Three points need to be emphasized with respect to his conclusion. First, the data he provides on the performance of the 34 countries included in his study cannot support his generalized conclusions. He uses the ratio of value added in the whole industrial sector, rather than in manufacturing alone, to GDP as an indicator of structural change. The figures on the industrial sector include such non-tradables as construction and utilities as well as mineral industries. These activities have been affected less adversely than the manufacturing sector, if at all, by liberalization. Therefore, the negative impact of liberalization is understated. Notwithstanding this caveats the data provided by him for the period 1990–97, in fact, indicate that the share of the industrial sector to GDP fell in 16 out of 32 countries for which data were available and did not change in other two cases (based on ibid., table 15.1). Further, in seven out of the 16 cases where the ratio fell, the growth of the sector was negative, in two cases was zero, in three cases between zero and one per cent and in four cases between one and two per cent. Overall, the average rate of growth of the industrial sector for the region fell from 2.7 per cent in the 1980s to 1.6 per cent during 1990–97 (based on ibid.). The comparable growth rate for the 1970s was 11.4 in current terms and 7.7 per cent in constant 1995 prices.[20] Further, even for countries which have shown positive growth rates in MVA, the expansion was in most cases mainly due to simple processing of primary commodities such as precious metals and food and wood processing (Lall *et al.*, 1994; Shafaeddin, 1995).

Second, in the case of Ghana, the increase in production was mainly due to capacity utilization, rather than capacity expansion as investment did not increase much. This is, in fact, acknowledged by Tribe himself (Acheampong and Tribe, 1998, p. 39; Tribe, 2001a, p. 279). It is obvious that the ample foreign exchange provided to the economy by the IFIs and foreign borrowing – allowed by the resulting improvement in the country's creditworthiness in international financial market – facilitated imports and eased production through capacity utilization. Despite such availability, considerable excess capacity still existed in the manufacturing sector by the end of the 1990s as shown in the previous section. Further, the increase in capacity utilization took place mainly in such natural-resource based industries as metals, non-metallic minerals, rubber, wood processing, or industries with local markets such as tobacco and beverages, food processing, and paper and printing. Otherwise, the rate of capacity utilization declined considerably in the case of electrical products, bicycles and motor cycles, cosmetics and leather, and remained almost stagnant in the case of textiles (Tribe, 2001b, table 6.6, p. 90). Both of these industries are labour intensive with potential for exportation. According to the same source, the total number of people employed by the manufacturing sector dropped from 51.7 thousands in 1985 to 20.6 thousands in 1991 (ibid., p. 91).[21] Moreover, the structure of exports further changed in favour of gold, other primary commodities and a few simple processing and resource-based items, rather than labour intensive items and other manufactured goods (Shafaeddin, 2005, chapter 3).

Third, it is true that MVA increased in 1997 as compared with 1985, but even at the end of the 1990s it was still lower than in the early 1970s (see Section 7.3). Overall, the short and temporary recovery of the manufacturing sector in a couple of countries is not an argument for long-term industrialization of the country, let alone generalizing it to the sub-Saharan countries as a whole.

Jalilian and Weiss (2000), using a different definition of de-industrialization, for the 1975–93 periods, concluded that: 'In general, our results provide no support for the general proposition that as a region Africa has been experiencing a degree of de-industrialization not found elsewhere'. The main issue, however, is not whether Africa as a *region* shows more de-industrialization in response to trade liberalization or not. As we have shown in the previous section countries at early stages of industrialization and development, whether they are located in Africa or not, are more vulnerable to import competition resulting from trade liberalization. In Africa, industries are more likely to be at earlier stages of infancy than elsewhere. Interestingly, Jalilian and Weiss found that, in the period 1975–93, about 44 per cent of the African countries included in their sample experienced de-industrialization: 'We find seven countries where we can identify a pattern of de-industrialization and nine where there is no evidence of such a trend' (ibid., p. 154). Furthermore, their time and country coverage is such that it underestimates the incidence of de-industrialization. Their sample does not include all the 37 sub-Saharan countries, many of which have low levels of development and industrialization, but includes two North African countries and South Africa, which are at higher level of development and industrialization. Moreover, had the time period of analysis been extended to the late 1990s, they would have possibly noticed more instances of de-industrialization.

The World Bank's view on the subject is theoretical and ideological. Accordingly, the sort of de-industrialization which has taken place in developing countries is welcome. It is argued that where the manufacturing sector had expanded excessively in relation to its comparative advantage as a result of protection, de-industrialization is justified if it is transitory, improves efficiency and promotes growth. The World Bank's implicit assumption in this argument is that SAPs improve efficiency, promote growth and, as inefficient industries disappear, efficient ones emerge. In fact, these are explicit arguments and objectives of SAPs. It is not unexpected that sudden and drastic trade liberalization under SAPs would lead to destruction of some industries as they become subject to severe competition from imports. Nevertheless, while these industries disappear, there is little evidence that new and efficient ones emerge to replace those destroyed. It is true that, under traditional MS strategies, excessive and prolonged protection was provided to some industries, which rendered them inefficient. But other industries were at the stage of infancy and, under certain conditions, could have been developed in accordance with the principle of *dynamic* comparative advantage, as has been the case in East Asian countries. Similarly, some inefficient industries were more likely to become gradually efficient, given time, if trade liberalization were undertaken selectively and gradually. The problem is that it is static comparative advantage, rather than dynamic comparative advantage, which is at the back of the mind of the designers of SAPs. In other words, the issue of de-industrialization arises from the intensification of specialization in accordance with the static comparative advantage. As shown in the previous section, even in some Latin American countries where export expanded and MVA showed noticeable growth, let alone in sub-Saharan countries, the expansion took place to a large extent in resource-based industries, simple assembly operation and, in some cases, in traditional labour intensive industries with little upgrading.

7.9 Conclusions

The analysis of a sample of developing countries in this study indicates that the structural reforms that have been undertaken in developing countries since the early 1980s have shown different results. Forty per cent of the sample countries have shown rapid expansion of exports of manufactured goods. In a minority of these countries, mostly East Asian, rapid export growth was also accompanied by fast expansion of industrial supply capacity and upgrading of the industrial base. These countries were among those with a substantial industrial base and capabilities in exports of manufactured goods already in the early 1980s, not to mention the early 1990s.

By contrast, the experience of the majority of countries, with or without industrial capacity, has not been promising. In most African and Latin American countries, growth of exports of manufactures was slow or moderate and the structure of GDP has not changed in favour of the manufacturing sector. More importantly, half of the sample countries for which data are readily available face de-industrialization. Most of them are low-income countries, which are more vulnerable to liberalization. Some countries experienced high growth rates of manufactured exports. Chile and Argentina in Latin America are notable examples in this respect. Brazil did not achieve acceleration of exports, and faced considerable de-industrialization. In the important case of Mexico, where exports grew extremely fast, the acceleration of manufactured exports was not accompanied by an acceleration of MVA. Little upgrading of the industrial base took place and the non-maquila industries which performed better were those that had enjoyed high investment during the import substitution era.

Slow growth of exports and de-industrialization have also been accompanied by a heightened vulnerability of the economy – particularly the manufacturing sector – to external factors. The reliance of this sector on imports has increased first and foremost because of greater import intensity of production and consumption, especially in cases where no upgrading of exports has taken place. In Latin America, the expansion of exports has taken place mainly in resource-based industries, in labour-intensive stages of production (i.e. assembly operations) and, in a few cases, in the automobile industry. A number of industries which had been dynamic during the MS era continued to be dynamic in terms of production, exports and investment. It appears that industries which were near maturity when the reform started, such as Aerospace in Brazil, benefited from liberalization as the emerged competitive pressure made them more efficient. By contrast, inefficient ones, or those at infancy stage, could not survive well. In a number of countries, some industries – including those labour intensive – suffered due to severe import competition.

The reform programmes designed by the IFIs also failed to encourage private investment in general, particularly in the manufacturing sector. Despite substantial increases in FDI in some Latin American countries, the I/GDP ratio was by the end of 1990s lower than before the reform period. Trade liberalization changed the structure of incentives. Nevertheless, the balance between risks and return in manufacturing activities also changed in favour of residential construction and other non-tradeables. A major difference between the 'minority' and the 'majority' groups is that in the case of the former, that is, East Asian NIEs, at least until recently, economic reform, particularly trade liberalization, has taken place gradually and selectively as part of a long-term industrial policy. Nevertheless, before they reached a certain level of industrialization and development, expansion of supply capacity whether aimed at domestic markets or exports played a significant role. By contrast, the 'majority group' embarked, in the main, on a process of rapid structural reform including uniform and across-the-board liberalization. Therefore, the pattern of industrial development that emerged in Latin America and Africa is not unexpected. Trade liberalization has led to the development and reorientation of the industrial sector in accordance with static comparative advantage with the exception of industries that were near maturity.

In short, no doubt trade liberalization is essential when an industry reaches a certain level of maturity, provided it is undertaken selectively and gradually. Nevertheless, the way it is recommended under the Washington Consensus, it is more likely to lead to destruction of the existing industries, particularly those that are at early stages of infancy, without necessarily leading to the emergence of new ones. Some have argued that there is a lag between trade liberalization and emergence of new and efficient industries. How long such a lag could be is not clear. Nevertheless, one thing is clear: any new industry that emerges would be in line with static, rather than dynamic, comparative advantage. In the particular case of low-income countries, this implies that they would be locked-in production and exports of primary commodities, simple processing and at best assembly operation or other labour intensive activities with little prospects for upgrading. Consequently, they would be subjected to the fallacy of composition.

Appendix

List of countries in the sample:

(a) Costa Rica (25.9), Sri Lanka (24.1), Malaysia (19), China (17.8), Bangladesh (17.5), El Salvador (15.5), Thailand (14.4), Singapore (13.7), Indonesia (12.8), Turkey (11.8), India (10.2).
(b) Mexico (29.6), Chile (13.4).
(c) Bolivia (29.2), Philippines (24.3), Guatemala (14.8), Kenya (12.4), Argentina (12.4), Jamaica (10.8), Madagascar (10).
(d) Nepal (9.9), Republic of Korea (9.2), Trinidad and Tobago (8.6), Mauritius (7.1), Jordan (6.7).
(e) Tunisia (9.4), Peru (7.9), Panama (7.9), Taiwan Province of China (7.3), Pakistan (7.3), Papua New Guinea (6.4).
(f) Ghana (9.1), Colombia (9), Morocco (8.7), Venezuela (7.8), Zimbabwe (7.7), Uruguay (6.7), Paraguay (6.4), Malta (6.2), Brazil (5.4).
(g) Egypt (3.2).
(h) Senegal (4.3), Fiji (2.3), China, Hong Kong SAR (−2.2).
(i) Barbados (2.5), Haiti (−18.9).

In this list, countries within each subgroup (formed according to the criteria explained in the text), are ranked according to the growth rates of purchasing power of exports of manufactured goods during 1989–2000, which are reported in brackets.

Acknowledgements

The opinions expressed in this chapter are my own and do not necessarily reflect the views of the United Nations. I benefited from comments of the participants to the Development Studies Association Conference. I would also like to thank Y. Akyüz and M. Tribe for their comments on the draft. M. Tribe also drew my attention to certain literature on de-industrialization. Any remaining shortcomings are my responsibility. Sections 7.3–7.6 are drawn, to a large extent, on my book: *Trade Policy at the Crossroads*, Shafaeddin (2005).

Notes

1 See Greenaway *et al.* (1998), for a short review of the literature.
2 It should be mentioned however that liberalization of the trade regime is taken as an indication of reversal of protectionist policies of the past (ibid., p. 33–34). This is not the case. Selective liberalization was the evolution of protectionist policies as the industries concerned became mature; it was not an indication of the past mistakes.
3 In the analysis related to Table 7.1, exports refer to purchasing power of exports.

4 Chile in subgroup 'b' shows the same picture (see Shafaeddin, 2005).

5 The situation in both Ghana and Brazil has somewhat improved recently; the sustainability of the recovery is, however, questionable.

6 Some African and East Asian countries had to run surplus to repay their debts. China ran a surplus in its current account for most years.

7 For Singapore and Hong Kong, the decline in MVA/GDP ratio is due to the expected change in the structure of output from the secondary to the service sector beyond a certain level of development à la Chenery (see Section 7.7). In the case of Hong Kong, the exceptional expansion of financial services has been also a contributory factor as Hong Kong has become a regional financial centre.

8 The corresponding figures are in constant prices. If one uses current prices, the number of countries that have been victims of de-industrialization increases. Nevertheless, as the relative price of manufactured goods has declined in relation to average price of total output due inter alia to trade liberalization, constant prices were used to avoid the impact of relative changes in the deflators for MVA and GDP.

9 Haiti's situation was, however, partly due to the political unrest in the country.

10 For details of the methodology, see UNCTAD (1996, pp. 115–121).

11 The following paragraphs are based on UNCTAD (2003).

12 For details and references, see Shafaeddin (1995) and UNCTAD (1996).

13 For details see Shafaeddin (1991a).

14 The differential changes in productivity at the industry level are in conformity with changes in the structure of exports and investment within the manufacturing sector (Benavente *et al.*, 1997a). Further, the increases in productivity were mostly due to 'labour saving', labour shedding, restructuring and displacement efforts rather than being the result of growth in manufacturing production (Katz, 2000b).

15 While this study concentrated on the manufacturing sector, the failure of the adjustment programmes is not confined to the manufacturing sector. The experience of the agricultural sector is not any better. For example, in the case of Mexico 'the hoped-for benefits first of sectoral reform, then of macroeconomic reform, have not materialized' (Davis, 2000).

16 For the explanation of the behaviour of investors see Shafaeddin (2005, chapter 3).

17 Goods and services.

18 According to Rowthorn and Ramaswamy (1997), the share of MVA in GDP, in constant prices, did not decline in advanced countries during 1970–94, which the authors studied. The decline in MVA/GDP ratio in current prices was due to the relatively higher productivity growth in the manufacturing sector as compared with services.

19 For a short review of the literature see Tribe (2001a). See also Jalilian *et al.* (2000) and Palma (2003).

20 Deflated by price index of exports of manufactured goods from developed countries based on UNCTAD (1994).

21 See also Thoburn (2001) for the case of Zimbabwe.

Bibliography

Acheampong, I.K. and Tribe, M. (1998) 'Sources of industrial growth: the impact of policy on large and medium scale manufacturing performance in Ghana' in Morrissey, O. and Tribe, M. (eds) (2001) *Policy Reform and Manufacturing Performance in Developing Countries*, Cheltenham: Elgar.

Agosin, M.R. and Mayer, R. (2000) 'Foreign investment in developing countries: does it crowd in domestic investment?', UNCTAD Discussion Paper 146.

Amsden, A.H. (2000) 'Industrialization Under New WTO Law', Paper prepared for UNCTAD X, High-level Round Table on Trade and Development on Directions for the Twenty-first Century, Bangkok, 12 February 2000.

Amsden, A.H. (2001) *The Rise of 'the Rest', Challenges to the West from Late Industrializing Economies*, Oxford: Oxford University Press.

Arndt, H.W. (1987) 'Industrial policy in East Asia', *Industry and Development*, 22: 1–66.

Baumann, R. (2001) 'Brazil in the 1990s: an economy in transition', *CEPAL Review*, 73: 147–169.

Ben-David, D. and Loewy, B.M. (1998) 'Free trade, growth and convergence', *Journal of Economic Growth*, 3: 143–170.

Benavente, G., Katz, G., Crespi, G. and Stumpo, G. (1997a) 'Changes in industrial development in Latin America', *CEPAL Review*, 60: 49–72.

——(1997b) 'New problems and opportunities for industrial development in Latin America', *Oxford Development Studies*, 25: 261–278.

Bennel, P. (1998) 'Fighting for survival: manufacturing industry and adjustment in sub-Saharan Africa', *Journal of International Development*, 4: 83–114.

Berthélemy, J. and Södering, L. (2001) 'The role of capital accumulation, adjustment and structural change for economic take-off: empirical evidence from African growth episodes', *World Development*, 29: 323–343.

Buitelaar, R.M. and Pérez, R.P. (2000) 'Maquila, economic reform and corporate strategies', *World Development*, 28: 1627–1642.

Chenery, H. and Syrqin, N. (1985) *Pattern of Development 1950–1970*, Oxford: Oxford University Press.

Craft, N. (1996) 'Deindustrialization and economic growth', *Economic Journal*, 106: 172–183.

Davis, B. (2000) 'The adjustment strategies of Mexican ejidatrios in the face of neo-liberal reform', *CEPAL Review*, 72: 99–118.

Dijkstra, A.G. (2000) 'Trade liberalization and industrial development in Latin America', *World Development*, 28: 1567–1582.

ECLAC (2001) *Economic survey of Latin America and the Caribbean*, New York and Santiago: United Nations Economic Commission for Latin America and the Caribbean.

Garrido, C. and Peres, W. (1998) 'Big Latin American industrial Companies and groups', *CEPAL Review*, 66: 129–150.

Greenaway, D., Morgan, W. and Wright, P. (1998) 'Trade reform, adjustment and growth: What does the evidence tell us', *Economic Journal*, 108: 1547–1561.

Helleiner, G.K. (1986) 'Outward orientation, import stability and African economic growth: an empirical investigation', in Lall, S. and Stewart, F. (eds) (1986) *Theory and Reality in Development*, London: Macmillan.

Hirschman, A.O. (1992) 'Industrialization and its manifold discontents: West, East and South', *World Development*, 20: 1225–1232.

Husain, I. and Faruqee, R. (1994) *Adjustment in Africa, Lessons from Country Case Studies*, Washington, DC: World Bank.

Jalilian, H. and Weiss, J. (2000) 'De-industrialization in sub-Saharan Africa: myth or crisis', *Journal of African Economics*, 9: 24–43.

Jalilian, H., Tribe, M. and Weiss, J. (eds) (2000) *Industrial Development and Policy in Africa: Issues of De-industrialisation and Development Strategy*, Cheltenham: Elgar.

Katz, J. (2000a) 'Structural change and productivity in Latin American industry, 1970–1996', *CEPAL Review*, 71: 63–81.

——(2000b) 'Structural change and labour productivity growth in Latin American manufacturing industries 1070–96', *World Development*, 28: 1583–1596.

Katz, J. and Vera, H. (1997) 'The ongoing history of a Chilean metal products and machinery firm', *CEPAL Review*, 63: 129–146.

Kitson, M. and Michie, J. (1996) 'Britain's industrial performance since 1960s: underinvestment and relative decline', *Economic Journal*, 106: 196–212.

Krueger, A.O. (1974) 'The political economy of the rent-seeking society', *American Economy Review*, 64: 291–303.

—— (1998) 'Why trade liberalisation is good for growth', *Economic Journal*, 108: 1513–1522.

Krugman, P. (2002) 'The lost continent', *The New York Times*, 9 August.

Lall, S. and Stewart, F. (eds) (1986) *Theory and Reality in Development*, London: Macmillan.

Lall, S., Navaretti, G.B., Teitel, S. and Wignaraja, G. (1994) *Technology and Enterprise Development, Ghana under Structural Adjustment*, London: Macmillan.

Little, I.M.D., Scitovsky, T. and Scott, M. (1970) *Industry and Trade in Some Developing Countries*, Oxford: Oxford University Press.

Lora, E., Panizza, U., Herrera, M. and Pérez, N. (2002) 'The future of reform', *Latin America Economic Policies*, 17: 1–8.

Michaely, M. (1977) 'Exports and growth: an empirical investigation', *Journal of Development Economics*, 4: 49–53.

Noorbakhsh, F. and Paloni, A. (2000) 'The "de-industrialisation hypothesis", structural adjustment programmes and the sub-Saharan dimension', in Jalilian, H., Tribe, M. and Weiss, J. (eds) (2000) *Industrial Development and Policy in Africa: Issues of De-industrialisation and Development Strategy*, Cheltenham: Elgar.

Ocampo, J.A. and Taylor, L. (1998) 'Trade liberalisation in developing economies: modest benefits but problems with productivity growth, macro prices, and income distribution', *Economic Journal*, 108: 1523–1546.

Palma, G. (2002) 'The Mexican economy since trade liberalisation and Nafta on the 'de-linking' of a dynamic export expansion and the collapsing of export multiplier', mimeo, UNCTAD.

—— (2003) 'Three origins of the process of "de-industrialisation" and a New Concept of the "Dutch Disease" ', mimeo, UNCTAD.

Papageorgiou, A., Choksi, A.M. and Michaely, M. (1990) *Liberalizing Foreign Trade in Developing Countries*, Washington, DC: World Bank.

Rodrik, D. (1998) 'Globalization, social conflict and economic growth', *Journal of Economic Perspective*, 6: 87–105.

Rowthorn, R. and Ramaswamy, R. (1997) 'Deindustrialization–its causes and implications', IMF, Economic Issues Series No. 10.

Saeger, S. (1997) 'Globalization and deindustrialization: myth and reality in OECD', *Weltwirshaftliches Archiv*, 4: 579–608.

Shafaeddin, S.M. (1991a) 'Trade policies and economic performance of developing countries in the 1980s', in Pendergast, R. and Singer, H.W. (eds), *Development Perspective for the 1990s*, London: Macmillan.

—— (1991b) 'Investment, imports and economic performance of developing countries in the 1980s' in Singer, H.W., Hatti, N. and Tandon, R. (eds), *Adjustment and Liberalization in the Third World*, New Delhi: Indus Publishing Company.

—— (1995) 'The impact of trade liberalization on export and GDP, growth in least developed countries', *UNCTAD Review*, 1–16.

—— (2005) *Trade Policy at the Crossroads: Recent Experience of Developing Countries*, London: Palgrave, Macmillan.

Singer, H.W. (1988) 'The world development report 1987 on blessing of outward orientation: a necessary correction', *Journal of Development Studies*, 24: 232–236.

Singer, H.W. and Gray, P. (1988) 'Trade policy and growth of developing countries: some new data', *World Development*, 3: 395–403.

Stein, H. (1992) 'Deindustrialization, adjustment, the World Bank and the IMF in Africa', *World Development*, 20: 83–95.

Thoburn, J. (2001) 'Could import protection drive manufacturing exports in Africa?', in Belshaw, D. and Livingston, I. (eds), *Renewing Development in Sub-Saharan Africa; Policy, Performance and Prospects*, London: Routledge.

Thomas, V. and Nash, J. (eds) (1991) *Best Practices in Trade Policy Reform*, World Bank Publication, New York: Oxford University Press.

Tribe, M. (2001a) 'An Overview of manufacturing development in sub-Saharan Africa', in Belshaw, D. and Livingston, I. (eds) (2001) *Renewing Development in Sub-Saharan Africa; Policy, Performance and Prospects*, London: Routledge.

——(2001b) 'A review of recent manufacturing sector in sub-Saharan Africa', in Jalilian, H., Tribe, M. and Weiss, J. (eds) (2000) *Industrial Development and Policy in Africa: Issues of De-industrialisation and Development Strategy*, Cheltenham: Elgar.

UNCTAD (1994) *Handbook of Statistics*, Geneva: United Nations.

——(1996) *Trade and Development Report*, Geneva: United Nations.

——(1999) *African Development in a Comparative Perspective*, Geneva: United Nations.

——(2000) *The Interaction between Macroeconomic Reform and Micro-level Industrial Activities*, UNCTAD/GDS/Misc.2, Geneva: United Nations.

——(2002) *Trade and Development Report*, Geneva, United Nations.

——(2003) *Transfer of Technology for Successful Integration into the Global Economy*, Geneva: United Nations.

Weisbrot, M. (2002) 'Failure in developing world', *International Herald Tribune*, 7 August.

Weisbrot, M. and Baker, D. (2002) 'The relative impact of trade liberalization on developing countries', Briefing paper, Washington, DC: Centre for Economic and Policy Research.

Wheeler, D. (1984) 'Sources of stagnation in sub-Saharan Africa', *World Development*, 12: 1–23.

World Bank (1987) *World Development Report*, Washington, DC: World Bank.

——(1993) *The East Asian Miracle: Economic Growth and Public Policy*, Washington, DC: World Bank.

——(1994) *Adjustment in Africa: Reform, Results, and the Road Ahead*, New York: Oxford University Press.

8 Integrating poverty reduction in IMF–World Bank models

Brigitte Granville and Sushanta Mallick

8.1 Introduction

Concerns remain about IMF–World Bank policy prescriptions, which have been evidenced to contribute to a temporary economic downturn, rising unemployment and poverty.[1] Fund programmes seem to have more success in lowering inflation than in achieving growth targets (Edwards, 1989). Khan and Knight (1981) formulated a structural version of the monetary model with endogenous inflation, balance of payment (BOP) and output; they found fluctuations in money playing an important role in explaining inflation movements but not real output variations. At the same time, growth has been evidenced to be negatively associated with inflation and large budget deficits (Easterly and Rebelo, 1993; Fischer, 1993). And while stabilizing the price level has been labelled as 'super-pro-poor' (Dollar and Kraay, 2002), questions remain about first, whether participation in an IMF or World Bank programme contributes to promoting higher growth in the long run and second, whether these contributions to growth reduce poverty.

Scholarly opinion seems to converge to the conclusion of Przeworski and Vreeland (2000) that 'if growth is the primary objective then IMF programmes are badly designed'.[2] Using cross-country data, Barro and Lee (2002) find that an increase in IMF lending has been associated with a reduction of economic growth over the time period 1975–99. After controlling for endogeneity with instrumental variables for the size of IMF lending, they find no statistically significant impact of IMF lending on economic growth in the contemporaneous five-year period but a statistically significant negative effect in the subsequent five years. Evrensel (2002) finds that Fund programmes solve BOP problems during programme periods, but are unable to bring about any statistically significant and lasting changes in programme countries' macroeconomic policies. While Taylor (1988) points to inefficient institutional and market structures as reasons for failure of Fund- and Bank-supported programmes, Romer and Romer (1999) contend that inconsistent macroeconomic policies[3] are among the factors preventing programme countries from encouraging investment and realizing growth. Fund-supported stabilization is generally achieved by lowering investment via a squeeze in domestic liquidity, rather than by increasing savings. Tanzi (1989) finds that because IMF programmes induce governments to save on public investment, this has negative consequences for growth. Investment carries the main burden of reduced absorption – private and public consumption are apparently little influenced by the negotiation of a programme with the Fund. This has some bearing on the debate over the effects of IMF-backed programmes on the poor (Bird, 2001).

The next critical issue is whether growth benefits the poor. Dollar and Kraay (2002), using a sample of 80 countries covering 40 years, find that there is a one-to-one relationship between income of the bottom fifth of the population and per capita GDP. In other words, average incomes of the poor increase *pari passu* with overall growth. For Agenor (2002), growth is not neutral and is accompanied by changes in income distribution.[4] Moreover Dollar and Kraay find no evidence that economic crises affect the income of the poor disproportionately. This of course does not mean that an identical proportional decline in income has the same impact on the rich and the poor if social safety nets are weak. Easterly (2003) suggests that government transfers may actually go to the middle income segment rather than the poor who in any case depend more on the informal sector for survival.[5] The poor lack assets, such as land or other bank collateral-suitable assets, and have little access to credit markets (Agenor, 2002; Easterly, 2003).[6] Easterly (2003) finds that IMF and World Bank adjustment lending lowers the growth elasticity of poverty, that is, the amount of change in poverty rates for a given amount of growth. This means that economic expansions benefit the poor less under structural adjustment, but at the same time economic contractions hurt the poor less. Moreover, while Easterly found some evidence that adjustment lending has counter-cyclical effects which may smooth the consumption of the poor, there is little evidence that any of the variables – inflation, the black-market premium, and fiscal transfers – for which adjustment lending altered the cycle, are responsible for smoothing the consumption of the poor. The author is careful to note that this result does not contradict the findings that a relatively low inflation rate[7] is good for the poor.[8]

If the new explicit focus of the IMF's concessional lending, as introduced in September 1999, is poverty reduction, then the IMF model is 'badly designed'.[9] Taylor (1983) and others in the literature go as far as arguing that, without country-specific structural features, poverty[10] cannot be incorporated in the IMF–Bank model. To address poverty, the IMF established the Poverty Reduction and Growth Facility (PRGF), which is based on a regular Poverty Reduction Strategy Paper (PRSP), replacing the Enhanced Structural Adjustment Facility (ESAF). Aside from key macroeconomic policies, PRGF-supported programmes differ from ESAF programmes by identifying and prioritizing social, sectoral programmes and structural reforms aimed at poverty reduction and growth.[11]

The aim of this chapter therefore is to attempt to include an explicit focus on poverty reduction in the context of a growth-oriented strategy reflecting the new objectives and procedures introduced by the IMF in September 1999. We first provide an explicit treatment of the demand side along with the standard supply-driven neoclassical framework. Second, we include poverty reduction as an objective with consumption deprivation as a measure of poverty. The remainder of this chapter is in three sections. Section 8.2 reviews the Fund–Bank models and points to the limitations of these frameworks, briefly discussing some conceptual and empirical issues. Section 8.3 develops an integrated model of poverty reduction within the framework of macroeconomic adjustment provided in Section 8.2. Concluding remarks follow in Section 8.4.

8.2 A digest on Fund–Bank models

The IMF and the World Bank have relied on their 'financial programming' and 'financing gap' exercises to design a policy framework prioritizing macro-economic stability and growth respectively. Both models however have been extensively questioned as long-term policy models.[12] Khan and Montiel (1989), and Khan *et al.* (1990) integrated the two approaches to provide an eclectic policy model known as 'growth-oriented adjustment' programme. A growth-oriented adjustment programme has three objectives: treatment of economic growth, BOP improvement, and price stability. The task became to determine a set of demand management policies (domestic credit ceilings and reductions in the fiscal deficit), exchange rate, structural (policies to increase savings and the level and efficiency of investment) and external financing policies to stabilize inflation and improve BOP, while maintaining stable growth.

8.2.1 The IMF monetary model

The Fund's approach to economic stabilization is known as 'Financial Programming' (FP) that links the monetary sector with the BOP (IMF, 1987). Polak's (1957) model forms the cornerstone of Fund programmes. It attributes BOP disequilibria to excessive credit expansion.[13] The model comprises the following relations

$$dM^s \equiv e\,dR + dDC \tag{8.1}$$

The first relation is derived from the consolidated balance sheet of the banking system including the Central Bank. It states that the change in assets ($e\,dR + dDC$,[14] that is, the increase in the stock of international reserves of the monetary system expressed in domestic currency, plus the increase in domestic credit) is eventually equal to the change in liabilities (dM^s, that is, the increase in the nominal supply of money). e is the nominal exchange rate expressed as units of domestic currency per unit of foreign currency. Both M and R are endogenous, while DC is exogenously fixed by the monetary authorities.

$$dM^d = \frac{1}{v}\,dY \tag{8.2}$$

The second equation states the increase in the nominal demand for money (M^d), with v defined as the income velocity (Y/M) and Y the nominal value of output aggregate (GDP).

In the simplest version of the model, both e^{15} and v are supposed constant.[16] Given a target value for the change in reserves (i.e. the overall BOP), and projections for dY, then the equilibrium expansion in the stock of credit is derived from money-market equilibrium $dM^d = dM^s$ as:

$$dDC = \frac{1}{v}\,dY - e\,dR \tag{8.3}$$

In the Polak model, real output (y) is exogenous ('natural rate output' in the classical tradition), while the price level and thus nominal output is endogenous: $Y = Py$, or, $dY = P_0\,dy + y_0\,dP$, where P_0 and y_0 stand for the initial period price level and real income respectively. P, which is endogenous, can be expressed as a weighted average of the price of importables (P_Z) and the price of domestic output (P_D), and written as $dP = \theta\,dP_Z + (1 - \theta)\,dP_D$ and $dP_Z = P_Z^*\,de = de$, where P_Z is the price of foreign goods measured in foreign currency. It is assumed for convenience that $P_Z^* = 1$. θ is the share of imports in the price index. Substituting the above relations in equation (8.3) and solving the resulting expression for the change in reserves yields:

$$e\,dR = \frac{1}{v}\,[P_0\,dY + \theta y_0\,de + (1 - \theta)y_0\,dP_D] - dDC \tag{8.4}$$

This relationship shows the change in reserves from the monetary side, where the desired change in reserves as well as the change in the domestic price level will be influenced by exchange rate[17] and credit policies.[18] Given two unknowns (dR and dP_D), an additional relationship is needed to determine the values of two endogenous variables. This is obtained from the external sector. The BOP identity is written as

$$\begin{aligned} dR &= X - m\,dY + dF \quad 0 < m < 1 \\ &= X - m(P_0 dy + \theta y_0 de + (1 - \theta)y_0 dP_D) + dF \end{aligned} \tag{8.5}$$

where m is the marginal propensity to import, X represents exports, and dF is the change in net foreign assets excluding monetary reserves. Equations (8.4) and (8.5) can be simultaneously solved to obtain the values of the endogenous variables: reserves and inflation. Alternatively, given target values for those two variables, two of the policy instruments (de and dDC) can be obtained from the equations (8.4) and (8.5), with an exogenous dy.

8.2.2 The World Bank growth model

The Bank's concern in its Revised Minimum Standards Model (RMSM) is with medium-term growth and its financing through domestic savings and foreign assistance. Assuming σ as the historically or technologically given incremental capital–output ratio (ICOR), the growth of output becomes a linear function of the level of investment. This relationship allows one to obtain either the growth of real GDP based on the available level of investment, or the level of investment required for a specified rate of growth. The growth of real output (or in equilibrium capacity output, which has long-term properties) is assumed to be a linear function of real investment, treating the increases in the factor productivity and the size of the labour force as exogenous.

$$dy = \alpha_0 + \alpha_1 dK \tag{8.6}$$

with $dK = \sigma \, dy$ and $dy = dy^*$ where $\alpha_1 < 1$ and dy denotes the change in real output (GDP), dK the change in real capital stock or investment (I), and dy^* the change in potential or capacity output.

The other element in the simple growth model is the identity of aggregate investment and aggregate savings. Private savings behaviour can be defined by making real private saving proportional to real private disposable income:

$$S = s(y - T) \tag{8.7}$$

where T represents net taxes and s is the marginal propensity to save with $0 < s < 1$. Using the savings-investment identity in an open economy ($S = I + X - Z$) with constant terms of trade, investment can be written as

$$I = s(y - T) + (my - X) \tag{8.8}$$

where Z is imports, which is taken to be a function of income. Combining this relation with $I = \sigma \, dy$, and using $y = y_0 + dy$, we obtain an expression for real GDP growth as follows:

$$dy = \left(\frac{1}{\sigma - s - m}\right)[(s + m)y_0 - sT - X] \tag{8.9}$$

This relationship implies that the denominator ($\sigma - s - m$) has to be positive for sustained long-term growth. For this to hold, ICOR (σ) needs to be greater than the sum of the marginal propensities to save and import ($s + m$).[19]

8.2.3   The merged Fund–Bank model

As discussed in the previous sub-sections, in the simple Fund model, real output is determined outside the system, whereas in the Bank model inflation is not determined because the price level is exogenously given and monetary variables play no active role. The merged model – an expositional conceptual framework by Khan *et al.* (1990) integrating the basic models of the Fund and the Bank – determines growth, inflation and the BOP simultaneously. In equations (8.4) and (8.5), dy was exogenous. With an additional relationship for dy as in equation (8.9), the values of three endogenous variables (growth, inflation and reserves) can now be determined simultaneously. The merged model is solved by condensing it into three relationships between dy, dP_D and dR. The key advantage of this merged framework is its simple structure, linking the macroeconomic targets mentioned earlier to government policies and determining the extent of foreign financing gap. The framework is summarized in Table 8.1.

The results of the merged model are summarized in Table 8.2. This table shows the signs of the impact effects of changes in the various policy instruments, behavioural parameters, and exogenous variables upon prices, real output and the BOP.

The behavioural equations in the merged model are primarily based on *ad hoc* rules. Trade and financial liberalization are included in a policy package for structural adjustment, but they are not explicit in the analytical models. The model also assumes away any role for the public sector in the generation of national output and investment, thus disregarding the fact that public policy to encourage investment – in firms, in labour, in infrastructure – may be important in promoting growth and alleviating poverty (Morrissey and Filatotchev, 2000).

In the merged model, monetary policy has a positive impact on output while fiscal and exchange rate policies have a negative impact. Although money growth in excess of output growth drives inflation, the degree of excess capacity in an economy or the gap between actual and potential output will decide the degree of growth rate of an economy or the 'real pricing power'. The combined approach does not incorporate macro features such as interest rate effects and price–wage

Table 8.1 Structure of the merged framework

Endogenous variables	Exogenous and predetermined variables	Policy instruments	Parameters
dy	dF	dDC	α_0 and α_1
dP_D	X	de	σ, v and θ
dR	Y_0 and P_0	T	s and m

Table 8.2 Impact effects of changes in instruments, parameters and exogenous variables

Change (Increase) in	Impact effects on		
	Domestic prices (dP_D)	Real output (dy)	Balance of payments (dR)
Domestic credit (dDC)	> 0	> 0	< 0
Exchange rate (de)	> 0	< 0	> 0
Net tax revenues (T)	< 0	< 0	> 0
Private saving rate (s)	< 0	> 0	< 0
ICOR (σ)	< 0	> 0	< 0
Velocity of money (v)	> 0	> 0	> 0
Capital inflows (dF)	> 0	> 0	> 0

determination. Money is the only financial asset. By excluding the interest rate the model leaves out a potentially important channel through which monetary policy could affect the economy. In Section 8.3, we address this issue by focussing on the role of credit in facilitating economic activities by making a distinction between credit supply to the government and to the private sector. It is the supply of loanable funds to the private sector that matters for greater economic activity, when there exist negative output gaps as in many developing countries.

8.3   An expanded model with poverty reduction

Although the merged model reflects the official policies or approaches of the IMF and the World Bank in a growth-oriented adjustment programme, it still cannot address the difficult issues that countries face in putting together a poverty reduction strategy. Thus the design of programmes supported by the IMF's PRGF is derived from a country's own poverty reduction strategy. Such a strategy is based upon fully integrated macroeconomic, structural and social policies.[20] Accordingly, we address this link by integrating poverty into a growth-oriented merged model, incorporating a clear distinction between public and private investment and identifying policies that influence private investment so as to accelerate the rate of private capital accumulation and thereby potential output growth.

In formulating the theoretical core of an extended model, we look first at the demand side. The national income identity is written as:

$$y = C_p + C_g + I_p + I_g + I_f + X - Z \tag{8.10}$$

where C is consumption, and subscripts p, g, and f denote private, government and foreign sectors, respectively. All variables are measured in real terms.

Substituting equation (8.7), private saving is given by:

$$y - C_p = S_p = s(y - T) \tag{8.11}$$

Fiscal deficits – the difference between total government expenditures $(G = C_g + I_g)$ and total government revenues (T) – are financed by either money creation (dDC_g), or net borrowing from abroad (dF_g), or through a rise in net indebtedness to the domestic private sector (dB). Since many developing economies do not have a well-developed domestic government bond market,[21] we may for simplicity ignore dB, and express the budget constraint for the government as:

$$C_g + I_g - T = dDC_g + dF_g \tag{8.12}$$

The supply of credit comes from the expansion of the banking system's balance sheet:

$$dDC = dDC_g + dDC_p \tag{8.13}$$

Substituting (8.11–8.13), $Z = m * y^{22}$ and $I_p = k * I_g^{23}$ into (8.10) and deriving dy by using $y = y_0 + dy$, we obtain

$$dy = \frac{1}{s + m}\{-(s + m)y_0 + (1 + s)C_g + (1 + s + k)I_g$$
$$- s\,dDC + s\,dDC_p - s\,dF_g + I_f + X\} \tag{8.14}$$

Substituting (8.4) into (8.14), the above equation can be written as:

$$dy = \frac{1}{s + m}\Bigg\{-(s + m)y_0 + (1 + s)C_g + (1 + s + k)I_g$$

$$- \frac{s}{v}[P_0\,dy + \theta y_0\,de + (1 - \theta)y_0\,dP_D]$$

$$+ se\,dR + s\,dDC_p - s\,dF_g + I_f + X\Bigg\} \tag{8.15}$$

Solving for dy, we obtain:

$$dy = \frac{v}{v(s + m) + sP_0}\Bigg[(s + m)y_0 + (1 + s)C_g + (1 + s + k)I_g - \frac{s\theta y_0}{v}\,de$$

$$- \frac{s(1 - \theta)y_0}{v}\,dP_D + se\,dR + s\,dDC_p - s\,dF_g + (I_f + X)\Bigg] \tag{8.16}$$

Equation (8.16) provides a formulation of demand-side factors influencing output growth, including policies towards investment. Provision of public infrastructure services as reflected in I_g has a positive impact on private investment and thereby aggregate demand growth. Poor complementary public capital can significantly reduce private investment.[24] Equation (8.16) also suggests that credit to the private sector has a positive impact on demand growth.[25] Importantly, the lack of property rights or perceptions of risk plays an important role in access to credit. Basu (2002) argues that since the loan market operates in the presence of uncertainty, two additional factors – credit standard and credit risk – are the most important in determining borrowers' access to the loan market. Indeed, at the interest rates prevailing in credit markets, there may be excess demand for credit by small enterprises to whom the banks are unwilling to lend because of perceptions of risk. Governments could prioritize the financing of SMEs. Caution however should be exercised, as credit allocation in favour of priority sectors such as agriculture has been the traditional instrument for monetary policy to play a redistributive role; but it has the disadvantage of distorting the credit market.

A country's potential output growth, or productive capacity (dy^*) is determined by supply-side factors, summarized as growth in capital (dK), in labour (dL) and in total factor productivity (TFP). TFP may increase as a result of improvements in production technology.[26] The endogenous growth approach postulates a positive feedback mechanism, captured by use of an augmented aggregate production function such as:

$$y^* = AK^\gamma(\mathrm{HL})^\delta \quad \text{and} \quad H = E^\eta$$

where K is the physical capital stock including both private and public fixed capital, L is the raw labour input, HL the average level of human capital indicating skilled labour – which is likely to improve productivity – and A is an index of TFP. E is a measure of the education level, and η is the economic return to education. Upon substitution and differentiation, we obtain

$$dy^* = dA + \gamma\, dK + \delta\, dL + \eta\delta\, dE$$

where dA is the exogenous TFP growth and dE is the growth of educational attainment or human capital formation. The growth of productive capacity (dy^*) depends on the rate of net investment in the current period, which together with updated values of total factor productivity determine the next period's level of productive capacity. Endogenous growth – which implies increasing returns to scale – would require $\gamma + \delta + \eta\delta > 1$. Assuming $\gamma = 1 - \delta \Rightarrow 1 + \eta\delta > 1$.

Demand conditions affect investment spending, which in turn affects the rate of labour augmenting technical progress; this affects the rate of output growth, which then feeds back on demand growth.[27] The investment function can be thought of as a relationship transforming desired gross additions to capacity output into the capital accumulation process. Thus to stimulate growth, private investment spending in the next period can be expressed as:

$$I_p = \omega_0 + \omega_1 dy + \omega_2 du + \omega_3 p$$

$$du = dy - dy^*$$

where the intercept ω_0 reflects the state of business confidence, dy is demand growth, du refers to change in the rate of capacity utilization and p is the expected rate of profit/return on new investment (or market capitalization as percentage of GDP). Policy interventions can affect the growth process by directly impacting public investment spending as in equation (8.16) and consequently influencing private demand conditions as in this formulation via the extent of the output gap or capacity utilization.

Assuming that higher growth leads to a decline in poverty, the relation between real GDP growth and change in poverty (dPV) can be written as:

$$dPV = -\beta_1 dy = -\beta_1(dY - dP) = -\beta_1[dY - \theta\, de - (1 - \theta)dP_D] \quad (8.17)$$

where PV stands for the poverty ratio or head-count ratio (HR) defined as the proportion of individuals or households earning less than a given absolute level of real income – the poverty line. Poverty is measured by consumption, hence the term poverty line, which is an amount of income needed to purchase a certain amount of goods.[28]

To link poverty reduction with output growth, equation (8.16) for dy can be substituted into (8.17) to get a dynamic relation for the poverty rate:

$$\begin{aligned}
dPV = -\beta_1 \Bigg\{ &\frac{v}{v(s + m) + sP_0}\Big[-(s + m)y_0 + (1 + s)C_g \\
&+ (1 + s + k)I_g - \frac{s\theta y_0}{v}de - \frac{s(1 - \theta)y_0}{v}dP_D \\
&+ se\, dR + s\, dDC_p - s\, dF_g + (I_f + X)\Big]\Bigg\}
\end{aligned} \quad (8.18)$$

Alternatively, to answer the concerns in the literature about the notion of poverty[29] and its measures,[30] we follow Kumar *et al.* (1996) in opting for a measure of poverty grouping people according to their consumer behaviour.[31] From the observed behaviour, one can define objectively a measure of consumption deprivation. Deprivation can be measured in terms of nutritional or consumption norms.[32] Kumar *et al.* use the consumption expenditure on food-grains and derive a non-linear consumption function of the form:

$$C = \frac{Vy}{K + y}$$

where C is the consumption expenditure on food-grains and y is the total expenditure (a proxy for income that is not observed). This is the equation for a rectangular hyperbola with V and K as its parameters, where V represents the saturation level of food-grain consumption expenditure and K is interpreted as the level of income needed to consume one half of the saturation level. In other words, V and K are parameters of a concave Engel curve. Consumption deprivation (CD) or poverty can be defined as the shortfall of actual consumption expenditure (C) relative to saturation level V, or $CD = V - C$. So from the above non-linear equation we derive the CD function:

$$CD = \frac{VK}{K + y}$$

This function, being a convex decreasing function of income, provides a direct measure of poverty based on nutritional norms. Differentiating this function with respect to y, we get:

$$dCD = -\frac{VK}{(K + y)^2} \, dy \tag{8.19}$$

Equation (8.19) provides a direct link between change in income and consumption deprivation or poverty without any reference to a subjective poverty line. When C approaches its saturation level V, at that point there will be no deprivation or poverty. People who are deprived of that saturation level of food-grains consumption will be considered to be in poverty.

Equation (8.16) for dy can be substituted into (8.19) to reflect the impact of macroeconomic policies on CD. Growth in y, *ceteris paribus* or with no change in income distribution, reduces poverty measured as CD, in this case, for food-grains. The food-grain CD index can be employed as a poverty index for this homogenous group.

Extending this approach to the entire economy means assessing the impact of programmes targeted for poverty alleviation, both direct and indirect, using total household consumption expenditures collected through household surveys for different income groups. Homogeneity of consumption bundles is feasible in case of each income group. For different income groups, there would be a different saturation level of consumption, from which the deprivation or shortfall of consumption below the saturation or bliss or critical level can be derived for each income group. Once we have obtained the food-grain deprivation function, the next step would be to aggregate these deprivation values across income groups to devise a poverty index. This type of index is different from the conventional poverty indices in the sense that (1) CD index does not depend on an arbitrarily chosen poverty line, (2) it depends on the observed and measurable consumption behaviour of people and (3) the index satisfies the standard axioms of a poverty index.

Given that consumption depends on income and the price level, the relationship between IMF–World Bank policy instruments and poverty could be examined through the impact of the programmes upon consumption deprivation via the general price level and the distribution of income. Assuming that the income distribution can be characterized by a two-parameter function, such as a log–normal distribution, the effect of these programmes on poverty can be examined via the mean and variance of income distribution. The mean and variance of income can be regressed simultaneously on the Fund–Bank policy instruments *ex post* to examine whether the policies simultaneously increase mean income and reduce income variance, or whether there is a trade-off in that they increase average income but also the variance. Thus dy can be substituted to reflect changes in policies in the above formulation either as a measure of aggregate demand growth or as changes in distribution of income via changes in mean and variance of the distribution in order to assess their impact on poverty reduction.[33] As mean income of the income distribution increases, the number of people below a fixed cut-off point will be reduced. Also, there could be a trade-off between mean income and deprivation with reduced variance in the sense that, if the variance of income shifts upwards, then the inverse relationship between mean income and deprivation might break down. In order to have a quantitative measure of welfare gains from income growth in terms of reduction in CD, the policy maker could use a fixed target of a particular percentage reduction in poverty or CD, given an initial level of deprivation. First, there is a need to examine quantitatively the possible impact of policy changes on mean income of different income groups, and, second, the possible impact of such changes in mean income on CD as a measure of poverty.

8.4 Conclusion

This chapter first reviews the Fund–Bank analytical frameworks and then attempts to integrate poverty reduction into a merged policy framework. Within a merged framework, the demand and the supply sides are integrated into a consistent framework linking macroeconomic policies to targets. It provides an explicit treatment of the demand side in addition to the standard supply-driven neoclassical framework. Poverty reduction has never been part of the Fund–Bank analytical model. Their integration can be attained via the mean and variance of income distribution as opposed to aggregate GDP, as the relationship between aggregate growth and poverty is not so simple.

The chapter suggests targeting public investment spending growth to overcome infrastructural deficiencies (that hold back private production and investment) for higher output growth, while reducing government consumption spending or minimizing the size of government operations could help achieve fiscal stability. Government's infrastructure, public utility and even manufacturing projects are likely to 'crowd in' investment by the private sector by making it more profitable, instead of crowding it out through the mechanism of higher government borrowing putting pressure on financial markets (Taylor, 1993). Taylor (1988) argued that public and private investments are complementary. Given the complementarity of public and private sector investment, particularly with regard to public investment in infrastructure, Agenor (2002) emphasizes that a cut in public investment expenditures may reduce the productivity of the private capital stock at the margin, and thus reduce private expenditure and aggregate demand. During fiscal contractions, government capital spending seems indeed to be reduced more than other categories of spending. For instance, in India, following the stabilization programme in 1991, a sizable portion of the adjustment came from a reduction in government capital expenditure including cutback in agricultural capital formation, while the growth in government current expenditures (such as wages and operational expenses, interest payments and defence spending) remained unaffected. Such decline in public capital spending particularly in public infrastructure could have growth retarding effects.[34] In turn, poor infrastructure just exacerbates the fact that the poor may find themselves isolated from the formal sector of the economy.[35]

We then link our integrated model to poverty measured as CD. One could analyse, first, how Fund–Bank policy instruments affect not only the mean but also the variance of income and, then, how these changes in income in turn have an effect on poverty.

Notes

1 See Easterly (2003, p. 1) for examples of criticisms of Bank and Fund structural adjustment programmes as disproportionately hurting the poor. For a historical review of the roles of the Fund and the Bank, and the choices that confront them for the future see Krueger (1998). For literature on stabilization and structural adjustment, see Edwards and Wijnbergen (1989) and Corbo and Fischer (1995). For a heated polemic on the IMF, see Stiglitz (2002).
2 Przeworski and Vreeland (2000, p. 403). On p. 386 the authors review some of the literature on whether the IMF programmes have positive effects on growth.
3 See also Agenor and Montiel (1999).
4 Dagdeviren *et al.* (2002) find that redistribution, either of current income or of the growth increment of income, is more effective in reducing poverty for a majority of countries than growth alone.
5 See Easterly (2003): the author takes the example of Zambia and Burkina Faso where he shows that 'self-unemployment is extremely important for the poorest deciles in Zambia. The bias is less extreme in Burkina Faso, but the poorest still have their earnings skewed towards self-employment income. These surveys are suggestive of the importance of the informal sector for the poorest households, lending credence to the relative insulation of the poor from structural adjustment measures'.

6 Das and Mohapatra (2003) find no evidence of any statistical association between financial liberalization and lowest income quintile's share of mean income.

7 Pooling information from 87 countries for the years 1970–90, Sarel (1996) discovered a structural break in the relationship between rates of economic growth and inflation. The break is estimated to occur when the annual inflation rate is 8 per cent. Between 0 and 8 per cent, Sarel found that the inflation rate either has no effect or even has a slight positive effect on economic growth. Once inflation rises above 8 per cent per annum, a significant negative effect on growth rates emerges. Easterly *et al.* (1995) found the costs more seriously and lastingly damaging when inflation is above 40 per cent a year.

8 Blank and Blinder (1986) found that inflation increases poverty rates, but also slightly increases the income shares of the bottom two quintiles. On balance they found little evidence that inflation hits the poor harder than the rich. Cardoso (1992) found that in Latin America the inflation tax does not affect those already below the poverty line, because they hold little cash. Cardoso also found that higher inflation is associated with lower real wages. In Granville *et al.* (1996), high inflation in early transition Russia seems to increase poverty through the inflation tax on cash and also wages and pensions, since they were not systematically indexed to inflation. Agenor (1999) finds that inflation always increases the poverty rate, using a cross-section of 38 countries. Easterly and Fischer (2000) found that the poor tend to rate inflation as a top concern, using survey data on 31,869 households in 38 countries. Using data for Indian states, Ravallion and Datt (2002) find some evidence that inflation is significant in explaining poverty.

9 See Easterly (2003, p. 1). Easterly also quotes the IMF web-site which says:

> In September 1999, the objectives of the IMF's concessional lending were broadened to include an explicit focus on poverty reduction in the context of a growth oriented strategy. The IMF will support, along with the World Bank, strategies elaborated by the borrowing country in a Poverty Reduction Strategy Paper (PRSP).
> (http://www.imf.org/external/np/exr/facts/prgf.htm)

See also www.imf.org (accessed 12 July 2004) for a fact-sheet on PRSPs.

10 See Addison *et al.* (2002).

11 Mosley (2001) makes a case for the IMF's long-term lending function being a precondition to the success of its short-term standby arrangement, arguing that a long-term presence is needed to achieve effective leverage in short-term operations. He also argues against transferring the long-term role to the World Bank, which has less credibility in global financial markets and less comparative advantage in macroeconomic management.

12 See Edwards (1989) and, for a survey of the controversial analytical issues in the design of IMF programmes, see Killick (1995, chapter 4).

13 See Polak (1998) for a comprehensive description of the FP framework and IMF (1977, 1987).

14 Here the symbol d is used to denote the change in a variable from the last period (y_0) to the present (y); that is, $dy = \Delta y = y - y_0$ and so on.

15 Recently, emerging market economies such as Brazil, when faced with credibility problems, have abandoned their fixed exchange rate (currency board) arrangements and have moved to a flexible system (in some countries with implicit inflation targets). The question remains as to how to adapt the traditional quantitative monetary conditionality (a ceiling on domestic credit) to the specific features of monetary policy under inflation targeting. When inflation is the overriding objective, having a credit ceiling may be considered somewhat superfluous, or at least, a non-binding constraint (see Blejer *et al.*, 2002).

16 Easterly (2002) finds that the assumption of constant velocity fails in the data and velocity is found to be non-stationary. Easterly finds the programming approach as

flawed, because it does not take into account the endogeneity of virtually all the variables in each macroeconomic identity, the instability of its simple behavioural assumptions, and the large statistical discrepancies in all the identities.

17 The financial programming approach is conditional upon the assumptions regarding the exchange rate regime. Polak (1998) quotes Schadler *et al.*'s (1995) study covering 36 countries under IMF programmes: 'targets for broad money growth were overshot by wide margins in approximately two thirds of the program years; in most countries this reflected mainly larger-than-expected increases in foreign assets.... These developments illustrate the power of financial programs in general, and credit restraint in particular, for building reserves but [equally] their weakness for curbing money growth and, ultimately, inflation, particularly when the exchange rate is not used as a nominal anchor'.

18 See Polak (1998, pp. 404–405): 'The combination of monetary instruments used in Fund programs to guard against an unfavorable development in the balance of payments does not provide protection against deviations from the program in the opposite direction. A more favorable balance of payments than envisaged at the time of the program could lead to over-performance on the reserve target and hence, unless the level of domestic credit creation was kept correspondingly below ceiling, to a larger increase in the money supply than had been programmed.'

19 There have been several attempts of extending the standard growth models by incorporating dynamics and building more economic structure. But very little of these have been reflected so far in the Bank model (Easterly, 1999).

20 See Key Features of IMF's PRGF Supported Programmes at http://www.imf.org/external/np/prgf/2000/eng/key.htm (accessed 12 July 2004).

21 By the end of 2001, only 20 emerging economies had outstanding domestic government bonds ranging from a maximum market capitalization of US$340 billion in case of Brazil to a minimum of US$5 billion in Chile (source: JP Morgan Local Markets Guide, 2002).

22 A structural export relation can also be incorporated, with exports being a positive function of world output (y_w) and a negative function of the terms of trade (px/pm).

23 We assume that private investment and public investment on infrastructure are complements, with private-investment being bounded above by the level of public-investment, with k as the ratio of private to public capital in the composite capital stock. Actual output will rise, through Keynesian demand effects via higher levels of both private and public investment, thereby bringing the economy closer to full capacity utilization.

24 Reinikka and Svensson (2002) find that despite recent successes in stabilization and structural reforms in many developing countries, the private investment response to date has been mixed, even among the strongest reformers. This disappointing result can be partly explained by the continued poor provision of public capital and services.

25 Levine (1997) and Levine *et al.* (2000) have convincingly documented a positive long-run relationship between financial development and economic growth. Moreover, Jalilian and Kirkpatrick (2002) suggest that financial sector development policy can contribute to poverty reduction in developing countries via growth.

26 Young (1995) provides evidence of the fundamental role played by factor accumulation in explaining the extraordinary postwar growth of Hong Kong, Singapore, South Korea, and Taiwan. Young finds that while the growth of output and manufacturing exports in the newly industrializing countries of East Asia is virtually unprecedented, the growth of TFP in these economies is not. In contrast, Chand and Sen (2002), in the context of Indian manufacturing, find that trade liberalization has raised TFP growth.

27 See Arestis and Sawyer (1998) for the role of aggregate demand in setting the level of economic activity, and Setterfield (2002) for a detailed exposition on demand-led growth models.

28 Kumar *et al.* (1996, p. 55): 'The standard approach which goes as far back as Rowntree (1901) is to define a poverty line in terms of a minimum level of income needed to purchase the basic necessities of life and use the income distribution to see what percentage of the people have an income less than such a poverty line. This measure is called Head Count Ratio (H).'

29 Kumar *et al.* (1996, p. 54): 'Poverty connotes the notion of a poor state of economic well-being or a state of economic ill-being. It connotes a state of economic deprivation. Deprivation can be based on comparing an individual's economic state with either an absolute norm, in which case it is called an absolute deprivation, or a normative or relative norm, in which case it is called a relative deprivation.'

30 See Ravallion (1994) for a discussion on measures of poverty.

31 In general, since the income-based method falls short in situations where for some attributes markets do not exist, Mukherjee (2001) examined analytically the problem of measuring deprivation in an economy with more than one attribute. However, given the importance of nutritional needs for survival, we focus on the deprivation of essential food-grains as a proxy for poverty.

32 Sen (1976) introduced the notion of deprivation in the income distribution literature, but focused on the head-count ratio as a measure of poverty. Rao (1981) suggested broadening the scope of poverty measurement to nutritional norms as opposed to monetary measures. Rao suggested that data on the proportion spent on food (PSF) per capita can be exploited to measure the incidence of deprivation and poverty. Assuming that, until the food needs are satisfied, people spend relatively more of their incremental income on food, this behaviour reveals itself as an increasing or invariant PSF, as income (or expenditure) increases up to a critical level. In other words, the proportion of people up to that critical level are deprived of the required food and the proportion constitutes the incidence of deprivation and the average expenditure at the deprivation point can be used to develop a poverty line.

33 Kumar *et al.* (1996, pp. 68–69): 'The real problem with poverty, is not the mean level of consumption deprivation, but it is the variability of the consumption deprivation. The lower income persons are more susceptible for deprivation as the spread of actual consumption is so wide due to high variance that it can go below the consumption requirements more frequently. Even if the variability is same at different income levels the probability that a person's consumption falls below the minimum required consumption is more for a lower income person than for a higher income person. This is because the mean deprivation is a decreasing function of incomes at all levels of income. It is the variability in consumption deprivation, and the possibility of differential variability at different income levels, that causes a major problem for the poor.'

34 See Mallick (2001) for a policy simulation exercise on this issue. For example, in the case of India, compression of government consumption expenditure over the years has been made difficult by the contractual nature of much of current expenditures and rigidities in the expenditure pattern (Economic Survey 2001–02, Government of India: http://www.finmin.nic.in). Ghatak and Ghatak (1996) find significant crowding-out effects of government consumption on private consumption.

35 Easterly (2003) notes that the urban informal sector is documented to be very large in most developing countries, especially the very poor ones. One can deduce that the rural informal sector is even larger.

Bibliography

Addison, T., Chowdhury, A.R. and Murshed, S.M. (2002) 'By how much does conflict reduce financial development?', WIDER Discussion Paper No. 2002/48: UNU, Helsinki.

Agenor, P.R. (1999) 'Stabilization policies, poverty, and the labor market', in Thorbecke, E. (ed.), *Poverty in sub-Saharan Africa*, Cornell: Cornell University Press.

Agenor, P.R. (2002) 'Macroeconomic adjustment and the poor: analytical issues and cross-country evidence', World Bank Working Paper No. 2788, Washington, DC: World Bank.

Agenor, P.R. and Montiel, P.J. (1999) *Development Macroeconomics*, 2nd edition, Princeton, NJ: Princeton University Press.

Arestis, P. and Sawyer, M. (1998) 'Keynesian economic policies for the new millennium', *Economic Journal*, 108: 181–195.

Barro, R.J. and Lee, J.W. (2002) 'IMF programs: who is chosen and what are the effects?', NBER Working Paper No. 8951.

Basu, S. (2002) *Financial Liberalization and Intervention: A New Analysis of Credit Rationing*, Cheltenham: Edward Elgar.

Bird, G. (2001) 'IMF programs: do they work? Can they be made to work better?', *World Development*, 29: 1849–1865.

Blank, R.M. and Blinder, A.S. (1986) 'Macroeconomics, income distribution, and poverty', in Danziger, S.H. and Weinberg, D.H. (eds), *Fighting Poverty: What Works and What Does Not*, Cambridge, MA and London: Harvard University Press.

Blejer, M.I., Leone, A.M., Rabanal, P. and Schwartz, G. (2002) 'Inflation targeting in the context of IMF-supported adjustment programs', *IMF Staff Papers*, 49: 313–338.

Cardoso, E. (1992) 'Inflation and poverty', NBER Working Paper No. 4006.

Chand, S. and Sen, K. (2002) 'Trade liberalization and productivity growth: evidence from Indian manufacturing', *Review of Development Economics*, 6: 120–132.

Corbo, V. and Fischer, S. (1995) 'Structural adjustment, stabilization and policy reform: domestic and international finance', in Behrman, J. and Srinivasan, T.N. (eds), *Handbook of Development Economics*, Vol. III, Amsterdam: North-Holland.

Dagdeviren, H., van der Hoeven, R. and Weeks, J. (2002) 'Poverty reduction with growth and redistribution', *Development and Change*, 33: 383–413.

Das, M. and Mohapatra, S. (2003) 'Income inequality: the aftermath of stock market liberalization in emerging markets', *Journal of Empirical Finance*, 10: 217–248.

Dollar, D. and Kraay, A. (2002) 'Growth is good for the poor', *Journal of Economic Growth*, 7 September: 195–225.

Easterly, W. (1999) 'The ghost of financing gap: testing the growth model used in the international financial institutions', *Journal of Development Economics*, 60: 423–438.

—— (2002) 'An identity crises? Testing IMF financial programming', Working Paper No. 9, August, Center for Global Development.

—— (2003) 'The effect of IMF and World Bank programs on poverty', in Dooley, M. and Frankel, J. (eds), *Managing Currency Crises in Emerging Markets*, Chicago, IL: University of Chicago Press.

Easterly, W. and Fischer, S. (2000) 'Inflation and the poor', Working Paper No. 2335, The World Bank.

Easterly, W. and Rebelo, S. (1993) 'Fiscal policy and economic growth: an empirical investigation', *Journal of Monetary Economics*, 32: 417–458.

Easterly, W., Mauro, P. and Schmidt-Hebbel, K. (1995) 'Money demand and seigniorage-maximizing inflation', *Journal of Money, Credit and Banking*, 27: 583–603.

Edwards, S. (1989) 'The International Monetary Fund and the developing countries: a critical evaluation', in Brunner, K. and Meltzer, A. (eds), Carnegie-Rochester Conference Series on Public Policy, 31: 7–68.

Edwards, S. and van Wijnbergen, S. (1989) 'Disequilibrium and structural adjustment', in Chenery, H. and Srinivasan, T.N. (eds), *Handbook of Development Economics*, Vol. II, Amsterdam: North-Holland.

Evrensel, A.Y. (2002) 'Effectiveness of IMF-supported stabilization programs in developing countries', *Journal of International Money and Finance*, 21: 565–587.

Fischer, S. (1993) 'The role of macroeconomic factors in growth', *Journal of Monetary Economics*, 32: 485–512.

Ghatak, A. and Ghatak, S. (1996) 'Budgetary deficits and Ricardian equivalence: the case of India, 1950–1986', *Journal of Public Economics*, 60: 267–282.

Granville, B., Shapiro, J. and Dynnikova, O. (1996) 'Less inflation, less poverty: first results for Russia', Discussion Paper No 68, London: RIIA.

International Monetary Fund (IMF) (1977) *The Monetary Approach to the Balance of Payments*, Washington, DC.

—— (1987) 'Theoretical aspects of the design of fund-supported adjustment programs', Occasional Paper No. 55, Washington, DC.

Jalilian, H. and Kirkpatrick, C. (2002) 'Financial development and poverty reduction in developing countries', *International Journal of Finance & Economics*, 7: 97–108.

Khan, M.S. and Knight, M.D. (1981) 'Stabilization programs in developing countries: a formal framework', *IMF Staff Papers*, 28: 1–53.

Khan, M.S. and Montiel, P.J. (1989) 'Growth-oriented adjustment programs: a conceptual framework', *IMF Staff Papers*, 36: 279–306.

Khan, M.S., Knight, M.D., Montiel, P.J. and Haque, N.U. (1990) 'Adjustment with growth: relating the analytical approaches of the IMF and the World Bank', *Journal of Development Economics*, 32: 155–179.

Killick, T. (1995) *IMF Programmes in Developing Countries: Design and Impact*, London: Routledge.

Krueger, A.O. (1998) 'Whither the World Bank and the IMF?', *Journal of Economic Literature*, 36: 1983–2020.

Kumar, T.K., Gore, A.P. and Sitaramam, V. (1996) 'Some conceptual and statistical issues on measurement of poverty', *Journal of Statistical Planning and Inference*, 49: 53–71.

Levine, R. (1997) 'Financial development and economic growth: views and agenda', *Journal of Economic Literature*, 35: 688–726.

Levine, R., Loayza, N. and Beck, T. (2000) 'Financial intermediation and growth: causality and causes', *Journal of Monetary Economics*, 46: 31–77.

Mallick, S.K. (2001) 'Dynamics of macroeconomic adjustment with growth: some simulation results', *International Economic Journal*, 15: 115–139.

Morrissey, O. and Filatotchev, I. (2000) 'Globalisation and trade: the implications for exports from marginalised economies', *Journal of Development Studies*, 37: 1–12.

Mosley, P. (2001) 'The IMF after the Asian crisis: merits and limitations of the long-term development partner role', *The World Economy*, 24: 597–629.

Mukherjee, D. (2001) 'Measuring multidimensional deprivation', *Mathematical Social Sciences*, 42: 233–251.

Polak, J.J. (1957) 'Monetary analysis of income formation and payments problems', *IMF Staff Papers*, 5: 1–50.

—— (1998) 'The IMF monetary model at 40', *Economic Modelling*, 15: 395–410.

Przeworski, A. and Vreeland, J.R. (2000) 'The effect of IMF programs on economic growth', *Journal of Development Economics*, 62: 385–421.

Rao, V.V.B. (1981) 'Measurement of deprivation and poverty based on the proportion spent on food: an exploratory exercise', *World Development*, 9: 337–353.

Ravallion, M. (1994) *Poverty Comparisons*, Chur, Switzerland: Harwood Press.

Ravallion, M. and Datt, G. (2002) 'Why has economic growth been more pro-poor in some states of India than others?', *Journal of Development Economics*, 68: 381–400.

Reinikka, R. and Svensson, J. (2002) 'Coping with poor public capital', *Journal of Development Economics*, 69: 51–69.

Romer, C. and Romer, D. (1999) 'Monetary policy and the well-being of the poor', *Economic Review*, Federal Reserve Bank of Kansas City, First Quarter: 21–49.

Rowntree, B.S. (1901) *Poverty: A Study of Town Life*, London: Macmillan.

Sarel, M. (1996) 'Non-linear effects of inflation on economic growth', *IMF Staff Papers*, 43: 199–215.

Schadler, S., Bennett, A., Carkovic, M., Dicks-Mireaux, L., Mecagni, M., Morsink, J.H.J. and Savastano, A. (eds) (1995) 'IMF conditionality: experience under stand-by and extended arrangements', Part II: Background Papers, IMF Occasional Papers No. 129, Washington, DC.

Sen, A.K. (1976) 'Poverty: an ordinal approach to measurement', *Econometrica*, 44: 219–231.

Setterfield, M. (ed.) (2002) *The Economics of Demand-led Growth: Challenging the Supply-side Vision of the Long Run*, Cheltenham: Edward Elgar.

Stiglitz, J. (2002) *'Globalization and Its Discontents'*, New York: W.W. Norton.

Tanzi, V. (1989) 'Fiscal policy, stabilization and growth', in Blejer, M.I. and Chu, K.-Y. (eds), *Fiscal Policy Stabilization and Growth in Developing Countries*, Washington, DC: IMF.

Taylor, L. (1983) *Structuralist Macroeconomics*, New York: Basic Books.

—— (1988) *Varieties of Stabilization Experience: Towards Sensible Macroeconomics in the Third World*, WIDER studies in Development Economics, Oxford: Clarendon Press.

—— (1993) 'A three-gap analysis of foreign resource flows and developing country growth', in Taylor, L. (ed.), *The Rocky Road to Reform: Adjustment, Income Distribution, and Growth in the Developing World*, Cambridge: MIT Press.

Young, A. (1995) 'The tyranny of numbers: confronting the statistical realities of the East Asian growth experience', *Quarterly Journal of Economics*, 110: 641–680.

9 The contrasting effects of structural adjustment on rural livelihoods in Africa

Case-studies from Malawi, Tanzania and Uganda

Kunal Sen

9.1 Introduction

There has been an apparent rapid expansion of rural income diversification in sub-Saharan Africa in the 1980s and 1990s. During these two decades, several countries in this region have undergone structural adjustment programmes (SAPs) and significant economic reforms. An influential body of thought argues that these two features are causally linked and that SAPs initiated in these countries can be taken to be the key contributing factor behind the increasing income diversification of the rural households in sub-Saharan Africa (SSA) in the past 20 years or so (Bryceson, 1999). Implicit in this argument is the view that the income diversification of rural households is an *unintended* negative consequence of a SAP, seen as a vital coping strategy of poor rural households in the face of increased uncertainty in their economic environment. Furthermore, it is argued that income diversification has profound adverse implications for the African countryside in the long term as it leads to an erosion of an agrarian way of life that combines subsistence and commodity agricultural production with an internal social organization based on family labour and village community settlement (Bryceson, 2000).

If the above argument is correct, then it brings up several points of importance in analysing the efficacy of the economic reform programmes in the SSA region. First, an important aim of a SAP is to bring about a change in relative prices that will lead to a reallocation of resources from the non-tradable and the import-competing sectors to the tradable and the exportable sectors. However, the existence of a large number of households who 'straddle' sectors in their diversification strategies will blunt the effects of the changes in relative prices on resource allocation as these changes 'are internalized within households rather than acting as an external stimulus to the free movement of resources, including labour, between sectors' (Ellis, 2000, p. 188). Second, as one avowed objective of the economic reforms is to redress the 'urban bias' of economic policies followed in the pre-reform period, income diversification from agricultural to non-agricultural sectors may be seen both as a sign that economic reforms have had not the desired positive effects on agricultural incomes and may also be a contributing factor behind the stagnation of the agricultural sector if income diversification weakens rather than strengthens rural productivity.

An important weakness in the literature that finds a causal link between SAPs and rural income diversification is that it does not spell out in detail how SAPs may influence income diversification. The determinants of rural livelihood diversification are many and there is a lack of clarity in the literature on the precise mechanisms by which economic reforms can affect rural livelihood diversification. Furthermore, it is not obvious that economic reforms, even when they contribute to income diversification, do so in a manner that is inimical to the welfare of poor rural households. In this chapter, we set up a conceptual framework within which it would be possible to examine the causal links between macroeconomic policies and livelihood diversification. This framework will then be used to assess the validity of the proposition that SAPs have accelerated livelihood diversification in SSA and have done so in a manner that has accentuated inter-household income differentiation in the African country-side. The proposition will be examined in the context of Malawi, Tanzania and Uganda, all three countries having undergone significant economic reforms in the past two decades.

The rest of the chapter is divided into five sections. The next section attempts to trace out the causal links between SAPs and livelihood diversification by examining the factors that have been taken to contribute to livelihood diversification. Section 9.3 provides some evidence on the apparent increase in the diversification of rural livelihoods in SSA, by examining income portfolios of a panel of households over the period 1992–97 in Uganda. Section 9.4 considers more macro-level data and explores patterns of production in the three sample countries for the past two decades. Section 9.5 assesses the causal linkages between SAPs and rural livelihood diversification proposed in Section 9.2 in the light of the evidence presented in Sections 9.3 and 9.4. Section 9.6 concludes.

9.2   SAPs and rural livelihood diversification: what are the linkages?

What makes households diversify their livelihoods? One can identify two types of households where one would observe this phenomenon. The first type of household diversifies livelihoods to smooth income. We can call these households Income Smoothing households (IS households, in short). The second type of household – the wealth accumulating household (WA households, in short) – diversifies livelihoods to accumulate wealth. These are the entrepreneurial households, for whom a new means of obtaining a living is also a means of augmenting total household income. At first approximation, the IS household diversifies to reduce the variance of their income flows and the WA household diversifies to increase expected mean income.

9.2.1   Livelihood diversification as income smoothing

Perhaps the most important characteristic of household income in rural areas of poor developing countries is their extreme variability. This is most apparent for the majority who are dependent on agricultural incomes. Weather variation, the incidence of disease, pests and fire, and random shifts in international crop prices cause farm incomes to fluctuate unpredictably in these countries. In a context where per capita income and consumption are very low, fluctuations of income can pose a serious threat to people's livelihoods, and for poor households, finding ways to smooth out their consumption between good years and bad can mean the difference between life and death (Case, 1995).

There are three ways in which poor rural households may attempt to smooth out their consumption in the face of large shocks to their income. The first of these is the *pooling* of risk by which households within a village, kinship group or social network may share each other's risk through institutional arrangements which lead to the efficient allocation of risk. If such arrangements work well and if shocks or adverse events are idiosyncratic, peculiar to the household, then for any particular household, its consumption would track the aggregate consumption of the village, kinship group or social network and not be affected by the household's income.[1] In this case, there would be little incentive for the household to diversify risks by diversifying the sources of its income. While several empirical studies have documented the existence of risk-pooling mechanisms at the village level (such as Platteau and Abraham, 1987; Townsend, 1994 for southern India; and Udry, 1994 for northern Nigeria), these studies also show that *full* risk-pooling is rarely observed, particularly among the poorer households.[2] Thus, informal insurance mechanisms that exist among members of the village, kinship group or social network will not enable all households to insulate consumption from income fluctuations. This would particularly be true if fluctuations in household income are more due to aggregate village-level factors than due to household-specific factors.

A second way in which rural households may attempt to insulate consumption from large unpredictable movements in their incomes is to smooth consumption *over time* using saving and credit transactions. Households will save in the face of positive shocks to their income, which are expected to be transitory, and dissave (or borrow) in the face of negative shocks to income. By doing so, they will attempt to keep consumption unchanged. If, however, they expect the shock to income to be permanent, they will adjust consumption in the light of the new information on their permanent incomes. In such a case, a negative permanent shock to income will lead to a curtailment of consumption, both now and in the future, and a positive shock to income, perceived to be permanent, will lead to a higher consumption path.[3] While there is a good deal of evidence that households engage in a substantial degree of intertemporal consumption smoothing using saving and credit transactions (see surveys by Deaton, 1992; Besley, 1995), there are strong reasons to believe rural households in developing countries do not have access to credit markets that allow them to insulate consumption completely from income shocks. If credit markets are not perfect, some rural households will be constrained in their ability to borrow when faced with a large transitory fall in their incomes, leaving these households unable to cope with income variability.

Both risk pooling and the use of saving and credit institutions may be seen as *ex post* means of smoothing consumption. However, if these *ex post* mechanisms fail (or more importantly, if households *anticipate* that these *ex post* mechanisms will fail), then the preferred strategy for the household is to smooth consumption *ex ante* by reducing income fluctuations (Morduch, 1995, refers to this as *income smoothing*). While households may smooth income by favouring variability-reducing inputs and production techniques and shifting production into more conservative but less profitable modes (Binswanger and Rozenzweig, 1993),[4] perhaps the most common method of IS that they choose is to diversify the sources of their income. Thus, livelihood diversification may be seen as an outcome of risk-averse households' strategy to minimize the variance of their income by achieving an income portfolio with low covariate risk among its components (Ellis, 2000). Such a risk-minimization strategy may, however, lead to a lower mean level of income for these households.

The conceptualization of livelihood diversification as a phenomenon of IS by rural households in the absence of markets (and non-market institutions) for credit and insurance is a useful starting point in understanding the causal links between structural adjustment policies and livelihood diversification in SSA. Viewed from this perspective, SAPs may increase livelihood diversification of rural households in two important ways. First, macroeconomic policies may greatly increase the risk associated with agricultural activity in the post-reform period. There are three sets of factors that affect the degree of income risk for an agricultural household; these are (a) risk in input prices; (b) production risk and (c) risk in output prices (Walker, 1990). All three sets of factors may be affected by economic reform measures. With respect to the first, a withdrawal of subsidies to fertilizers and other inputs may accentuate the variation in input prices. With respect to production risk, fiscal austerity measures leading to a reduction of public investment in agricultural extension activities and irrigation may increase the level of risk associated with the production of agricultural output. In the case of output prices, the scaling down or complete elimination of commodity price stabilization schemes and the withdrawal of parastatals from the marketing of crops would also result in increased uncertainty about the level of output prices and their variance. In this context, faced with higher income risk, rural households would attempt to minimize the variance of their incomes by diversifying the sources of their income, with increasing recourse to income obtained from non-agricultural activities. Livelihood diversification can be then seen as an outcome of the *higher degree of risk* associated with the household's economic environment brought about by economic reforms. However, it should be noted that if an increase in risk is actually observed in the agricultural regions of SSA in the post-reform period, the higher degree of risk could also be due to exogenous factors (say, a higher frequency of weather shocks) and not necessarily be a consequence of economic reforms.

A second way in which SAPs may contribute to increased livelihood diversification is by weakening the mechanisms of risk-pooling and borrowing and saving that we have argued are available to rural households to smooth consumption in the face of high variance in incomes. Economic reforms can impact on insurance and credit arrangements in a variety of ways. For example, a financial liberalization programme that leads to a scaling down of rural credit programmes or the withdrawal of banks from rural areas may result in households being more constrained in their borrowing and lending decisions than in the pre-reform period. Also, large cutbacks in government spending that result in a reduction of public health services may also weaken insurance/saving mechanisms by increasing the reliance of households on their savings for sudden and unanticipated occurrence of sickness among members of the household.[5]

9.2.2 Livelihood diversification as a means of accumulation

While the IS motive for livelihood diversification may be considered to be the dominant view in the literature, it is by no means the only one. An alternative perspective on livelihood diversification argues that the latter may be seen as a means of accumulation for rural households in order to invest in high-return production methods in the agricultural sector. Underpinning this view is the empirical observation that, for some countries in the SSA region, a higher share of non-cropping income is associated with higher incomes (Collier *et al.*, 1986; Reardon, 1992). If the high-return production methods or activities in the farm sector need a substantial investment outlay initially, then rural households may diversify into non-farm activities to build the initial capital required for investment in these methods and activities.[6] This view suggests that a dynamic agricultural sector provides the motivation for diversification as the potential for rapid agricultural development leads to the development of non-farm activities that are linked 'downstream' or 'upstream' to cropping or the demand for which is spurred by the increases in farm incomes (Reardon *et al.*, 1992).[7]

The manner in which SAPs may contribute to livelihood diversification will be quite different in the above case as compared to the IS motive for livelihood diversification. In this case, SAPs provide an impetus for livelihood diversification by increasing the potential return to agricultural activities. One simple way this may occur is by shifting the terms of trade in favour of agriculture, particularly export crops. By doing so, economic reforms provide further incentives for investment in export agriculture. Figure 9.1 summarizes the mechanisms through which SAPs may lead to livelihood diversification.

The arguments so far suggest that the relationship between SAPs and rural livelihood diversification is more complex than often portrayed in the literature. SAPs may or may not increase livelihood diversification and, when they do, it is not clear that such diversification is necessarily a bad thing. But what is the evidence on increased income diversification in SSA? The answer to this question can only come from surveys of a panel of households, where the surveys trace changes in income portfolios over a sufficiently long period of time. Such data is extremely difficult to obtain for three reasons. First, most household surveys elicit information on consumption and not income (since these surveys are used in poverty assessments). Second, an understanding of livelihood diversification at the household level can only be done with very disaggregated data on income sources – for example, data that distinguishes between income from food crops and income from cash crops. Such disaggregated data is almost impossible

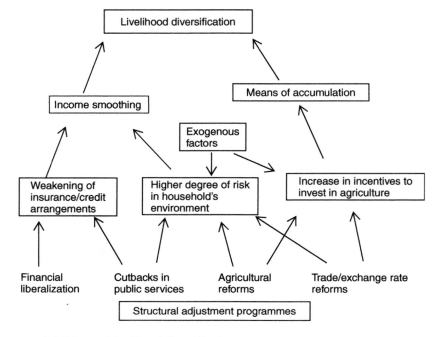

Figure 9.1 SAPs and livelihood diversification.

to find. Finally, the household surveys must obtain data on the *same* set of households – it would be inaccurate to compare income data of one set of households in time *t* with the income data of a different set of households in time *t* + 1.

Perhaps in one of the few instances in SSA case, panel data on households was collected for Uganda in the 1992 and 1999 household surveys of income and consumption. We use this data to make some inferences on the nature of livelihood diversification in Uganda in the 1990s, a period in which the country witnessed major economic reforms.

9.3 Some panel data evidence on rural livelihood diversification in SSA[8]

The household unit record data contained in the Household Income and Expenditure surveys conducted at regular intervals by the Ugandan Bureau of Statistics provide an ideal opportunity to examine whether there is any evidence that rural households in Uganda are diversifying their sources of income, and if so, to what extent. We use the 1992/93 Integrated Household Survey (IHS) and 1999/2000 Uganda National Household Survey (UNHS) for this purpose. There are two advantages in this comparison. First, the 1999 IHS re-surveyed about 800 households who were previously surveyed in the 1992 UNHS. This provides a more accurate picture of income diversification than if the comparison was based on two different samples of households. Second, both the UNHS and the IHS asked detailed questions on the sources of income to these households, which allow for a comparison of income sources in these two years at a fairly disaggregated level. Again, the more disaggregated the sources of income, the more accurate is the information on income diversification.

We compare rural household income shares from different income sources for 836 rural panel households, which are estimated from both the 1992/93 IHS and the 1999/2000 UNHS data. The income source shares are shown in Tables 9.1 and 9.2. The main observations that can be made from the comparisons are that:

- although crop agriculture still remains the major source of income for rural households in Uganda, the share of income from crop agriculture has declined for all regions between 1992 and 1999;

Table 9.1 Major rural income sources, 1992 and 1999

Income source	1992 Share (%)					1999 Share (%)			
	Na	*Ce*	*Ea*	*No*	*We*	*Na*	*Ce*	*Ea*	*No*
Entrepreneurial									
Crops	45.8	44.3	45.7	46.5	47.5	40.4	44.0	35.5	40.3
Miscellaneous	17.0	20.4	17.7	15.0	18.5	31.8	31.5	32.4	17.5
Remittances	9.3	9.6	8.4	8.8	11.2	17.5	15.1	21.7	27.9
Manufacturing	1.5	2.3	1.9	0.7	0.5	1.2	1.7	0.8	2.3
Livestock	0.4	0.4	0.5	0.6	0.2	0.6	1.0	0.6	0.1
Rent	0.6	0.8	0.7	0.4	0.3	0.3	0.1	0.9	0.0
Pension	0.1	0.1	0.0	0.3	0.2	0.5	0.0	0.8	0.0
Construction	0.1	0.3	0.2	0.0	0.0				
Allowances						0.5	0.1	0.5	1.5
Trade	2.0	2.8	1.6	2.9	0.3	0.9	0.0	1.1	2.5
Employment									
Crops	11.5	9.4	12.7	12.3	11.8	3.4	4.0	2.4	5.4
Education	1.8	1.6	2.8	2.3	1.1				
Government						1.4	0.3	2.4	1.5
Construction	0.8	1.2	0.3	1.2	0.6	0.2	0.2	0.3	0.0
Finance						0.1	0.2	0.0	0.0
Trade	0.2	0.5	0.1	0.7	0.0				
Workshops	0.2	0.6	0.1	0.0	0.0				
Livestock	0.2	0.3	0.1	0.1	0.5	0.2	0.0	0.0	0.0
Catering	0.1	0.0	0.0	0.4	0.2				
Manufacturing	0.1	0.0	0.4	0.0	0.2	0.4	0.4	0.4	0.0
Workshops						0.1	0.2	0.0	0.0
Transport						0.1	0.0	0.0	0.0
Sample size	836	250	245	198	143	836	262	230	131

Sources: Integrated Household Survey, 1992–93; Uganda National Household Survey, 1999–2000.

Notes
Na = national; Ce = central; Ea = eastern; No = northern region; We = western region.

Table 9.2 On/off – farm major rural income sources

	Income source share (%)	
	1992	*1999*
On-farm		
Entrepreneurial	47.3	41.0
Employment	11.7	3.6
Off-farm		
Entrepreneurial	30.5	51.8
Employment	3.2	2.3

Sources: Integrated Household Survey, 1992–93; Uganda National Household Survey, 1999–2000.

- the share of income from miscellaneous sources has increased considerably for all regions between 1992 and 1999;
- the share of income from remittances has increased considerably, especially for the Northern Region, between 1992 and 1999;
- the share of employment income from agriculture has generally declined for all regions between 1992 and 1999;
- the share of income from off-farm entrepreneurial activities has increased considerably between 1992 and 1999.

Thus, the results from the IHS 1992/93 and the UNHS 1999/2000 Surveys seem to suggest that indeed rural income diversification may have occurred in Uganda between 1992 and 1999. However, it is not clear from the results whether households have diversified their income sources in order to cope with increasing poverty or to take advantage of the opportunities brought about by increased social and political stability as well as the increased economic liberalization. One piece of evidence in favour of the latter hypothesis is that the average household income in our panel of households has increased. When we apply the Analysis of Variance Duncan's Multiple Range Test to the 1992 and 1999 household incomes of 836 panel households, the results indicate that rural household incomes have significantly increased between 1992 and 1999. This finding seems to be consonant with the finding of overall decreasing poverty in Uganda in the same period (Appleton, 2001).

9.4   Macro-outcomes

While the evidence presented in the previous section is instructive in that it shows a trend of increasing diversification away from on-farm to off-farm sources of income, particularly self-employment in non-agriculture in the Ugandan case, it may well be asked whether the positive aspect of income diversification evident at the micro-level is reflected in the macroeconomic data. Furthermore, the lack of similar panel data on household income portfolios for other countries does not allow for a comparative analysis of the effect of SAPs on rural livelihood diversification in different institutional and socio-economic environments, and with different initial conditions.

In this section, we present macro-level evidence on the impact of SAPs on the agricultural sectors of the three sample countries. The analysis here is subject to several caveats. First, macro-level data may not be representative of the livelihood strategies of many households, given the heterogeneity one observes at the microlevel. Second, much of the macro-level data is heavily biased towards agricultural production data, and there is little information available at the economywide level of the off-farm and non-farm income sources. Third, macro-level data is obtained from country statistical offices, and there are weaknesses in the collection of such data, especially those related to agricultural censuses. Notwithstanding these caveats, the macro-level data may highlight broad trends evident in the rural economy of the country in question, and offer insights on why we seem to see differing outcomes with respect to poverty reduction among the countries considered.

9.4.1 Agricultural production

We present graphs on food crop and export crop production separately for the three countries. In the case of Uganda, prior studies (such as Djikstra and Van Donge, 2001) have found that the economic reforms initiated in the 1980s have led to a significant supply from the agricultural export sector. Figure 9.2 confirms this finding. We observe a significant increase in the procurement of coffee (both robusta and arabica), tea and tobacco from 1987 to 1996. Furthermore, the favourable supply response in the post-reform period is not only confined to the cash crop sector; total food crop production also shows an increase, particularly since the mid-nineties (Figure 9.3). While bananas (*matooka*) remains the staple food crop, cassava and sweet and Irish potatoes are occupying higher weights within total food crop production.

In the case of Tanzania, there seems to be a difference in outcomes with respect to food crops and export crops production in the post-1986 period. There is no evidence of an increase in the production of the major food crops – pulses, wheat, paddy and maize – in this period. Maize still accounts for the bulk of food crops grown by farmers in Tanzania, with a share of 68 per cent in total food crops production over the period 1986–99 (Figure 9.4).

In contrast, there is clear evidence of an increase in export crops production since 1986, with total output from the export crops sector increasing by 50 per cent in the period 1986–99. The increase in export crops production seems to be driven primarily by an increase in the production of cashew nuts, from 29.9 thousand tonnes in 1990/91 to 121.3 thousand tonnes in 1999/2000. There also was an increase in the production of tobacco from 11.8 thousand tonnes in 1990/91 to 24 thousand tonnes in 1999/2000. On the other hand, sisal, which was an important export crop at the beginning of the 1980s, witnessed a fall in its share in total

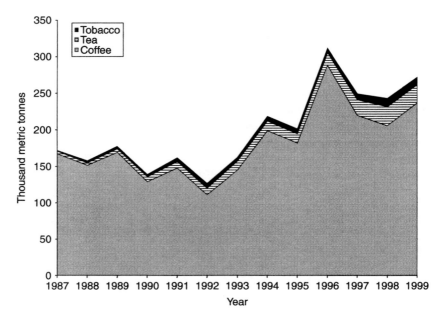

Figure 9.2 Procurement of export crops, Uganda.

Source: Uganda Bureau of Statistics, *Statistical Abstracts*.

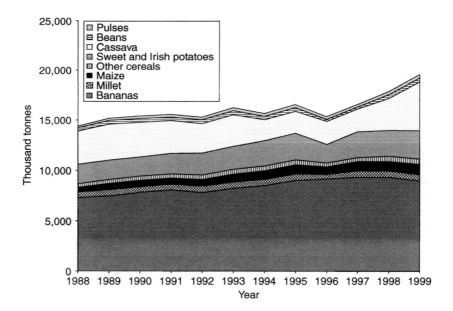

Figure 9.3 Food crops, Uganda.

Source: Uganda Bureau of Statistics, *Statistical Abstracts*.

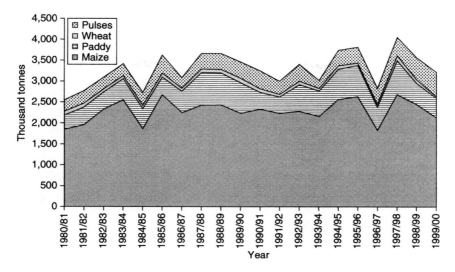

Figure 9.4 Food crops, Tanzania.

Source: Bureau of Statistics, Government of Tanzania, *Statistical Abstracts.*

export crop output from 29 per cent in 1980/81 to 7 per cent in 1999/2000. It is interesting to note that while there has been an increase in total export crop production from 1986, production levels at the end of the 1990s were not very different from what they were at the beginning of the 1980s (Figure 9.5).

In the case of Malawi, there was an initial increase in smallholder food crops production in the period 1994–2000. Total agricultural production in 2000 was five times total production in 1994. The surge in smallholder production since 1994 occurred after a decade of stagnation in production in the smallholder sector since 1984 (Figure 9.6). However, this increase was short-lived as production levels fell dramatically in 2001–02. More importantly, production levels of maize, the staple food crop, were back to its 1980s level by 2002. With the lifting of restrictions on smallholder farmers to grow burley tobacco, there has been an impressive increase in tobacco production in the 1990s, which has continued unabated in 2001–02 (Figure 9.7).

What have been the effects of the trends in agricultural production on poverty? Unfortunately, we do not have longitudinal data on poverty for all three countries. The Ugandan data is the most reliable and it suggests a dramatic fall in the head count ratio from 69.4 per cent in 1992 to 39 per cent in 1999/2000 (Appleton, 2001). Data for Tanzania is more problematic but suggests a minimal decline in the head count ratio from 23.1 per cent in 1991/92 to 19.6 per cent in 2000/01 (National Bureau of Statistics, 2002). Poverty in Malawi is very high at 66.5 per cent in 1997/98 (according to the IHS, held that year) and is mostly concentrated in the smallholder agriculturists.

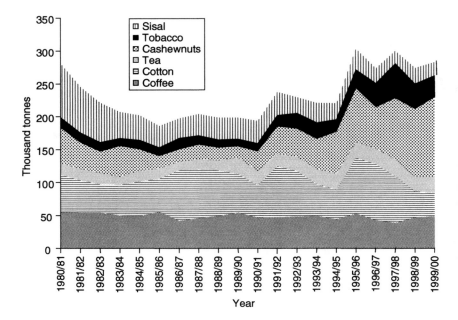

Figure 9.5 Export crops production, Tanzania.

Source: Bureau of Statistics, Government of Tanzania, *Statistical Abstracts*.

9.5   Causal stories

How far does the evidence presented in the previous two sections support the argument that SAPs have been causal in the increasingly diversified livelihood strategies of farmer households in SSA, in a manner that has led to adverse outcomes in the welfare of poorer households? We consider each of our causal mechanisms in turn:

9.5.1   Causal mechanism I: have SAPs led to an increase in the riskiness of the economic environment?

We note a difference in the manner that SAPs have contributed to the riskiness of the economic environment in the three sample countries. In Malawi and Tanzania, the removal of fertilizer subsidies was an important factor in the decline in fertilizer usage in the post-reform period. With output prices more unstable due to the easing out of price stabilization schemes/pan-territorial pricing mechanisms, the removal of fertilizer subsidies could be said to have exacerbated input risk and production risk. In the case of Malawi, there is more direct evidence as, with the 1997 devaluation of the Kwacha and the further scaling back of fertilizer subsidies in the 1990s, prices of fertilizers became exorbitant for many farmers, and by the late 1990s, they may have led to a switch from the quantity rationed

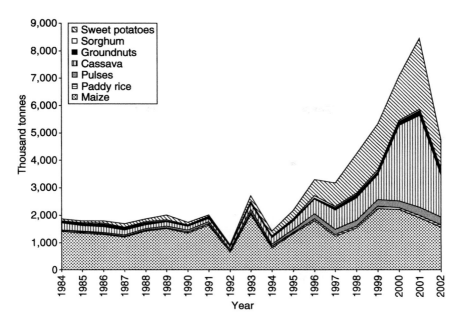

Figure 9.6 Food crops production, Malawi.

Source: *Economic Reports*, Government of Malawi.

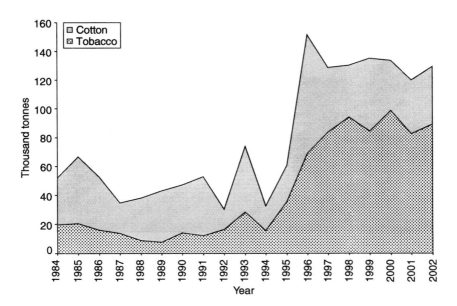

Figure 9.7 Export crops production, Malawi.

Source: *Economic Reports*, Government of Malawi.

regime of the late 1980s and early 1990s to a price rationed regime. Aware of the deleterious effect of the removal of fertilizer subsidies on fertilizer usage among resource-constrained smallholder farmers, the Government of Malawi introduced a Starter Pack scheme distributing free seeds and fertilizers to all smallholder farmers in 1998–99. This was scaled back in 1999–2000 and 2000–01, and the decline in maize production in those years has led many observers to believe that the scaling back of the Starter Pack scheme and the fall in maize output were causally related (Harrigan, 2003). Furthermore, in Malawi, while reforms in input markets have allowed the entry of private agents in the importation and distribution of such inputs, there has been slow progress in the involvement of the private sector in input markets, in contrast to their more active involvement in product markets.

In Tanzania, under the Local Government Reform Programme, all agricultural extension services have been decentralized to the District level. Under the Regional and Local Government Act of 1997, the District Councils are now responsible for the provision of extension services to farmers as well as services such as education, health, roads and water. There is a strong perception that agricultural extension services have declined in the post-reform period (Ministry of Agriculture, 2000). However, it is not clear to what extent the reason for this can be attributed to SAPs and to what extent imperfect local government reform can be held responsible. In the Ugandan case, a different picture emerges – real input prices have fallen in the period 1990–98, and there is evidence of a better provision of inputs to smallholder farmers (Balihuta and Sen, 2001).

A final difference in the riskiness of the economic environment in these three countries is in the behaviour of the inflation rate. This is evident from Figure 9.8, where Uganda's success in reducing inflation to below 5 per cent is quite remarkable. In contrast, Malawi has witnessed high and variable rates of inflation for much of the 1990s. A high and volatile rate of inflation leads to higher variance in relative prices and contributes significantly to increasing the riskiness of economic activities. Here, the slippage in macroeconomic policy evident in Malawi and to some extent, in Tanzania, can be seen as a failure in implementing complementary policies (successful macroeconomic stabilization) that would have supported the longer-term objectives of SAPs.

9.5.2   *Causal mechanism II: have SAPs led to weakening in the provision of agricultural credit?*

There is little doubt that there have been widespread agricultural credit market failures in the three countries in the post-reform period. However, it is difficult to say how much of this can be attributed to SAPs as the weaknesses in the agricultural credit delivery system were apparent even during the pre-reform period. In Uganda, in the wake of the economic reforms, the government guarantee system on crop finance was withdrawn, and producers had to make their own arrangements by either borrowing directly from commercial banks or using their own funds. As the Plan for the Modernization of Agriculture (PMA) notes, the

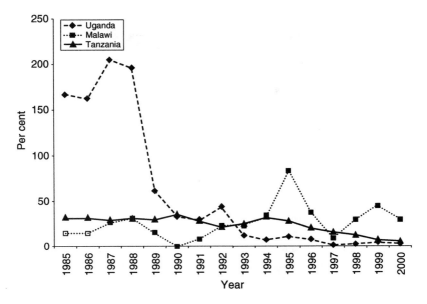

Figure 9.8 The inflation rate, Malawi, Tanzania and Uganda.

Sources: *Economic Reports*, Government of Malawi; Bureau of Statistics, Government of Tanzania, *Statistical Abstracts*, and Uganda Bureau of Statistics, *Statistical Abstracts*.

government's policy on rural finance is that ultimately it should be privately run (Government of Republic of Uganda, p. 114). The PMA places a great deal of emphasis on micro-financial institutions and government initiatives such as the Poverty Alleviation Project and Entandikwa as schemes targeted to the poor. Yet it is not obvious whether such institutions and schemes can effectively play the role of credit providers to the vast majority of rural households. The agricultural sector was receiving a smaller proportion of bank credit over the 1990s, with the share of agriculture in total commercial bank loan to the private sector falling from 34 per cent in 1990 to 20 per cent in 1996. Micro-level evidence obtained from household surveys also highlights the difficulties faced by poor rural households in accessing formal sources of credit, with lack of knowledge about credit providers, tight repayment schedules, high initial capital requirements and the lack of loans for agricultural purposes representing barriers to access (Smith *et al.*, 2001).

A similar picture emerges in Tanzania. Financial sector reforms that resulted in the closure of rural branches of the public sector banks and the withdrawal of directed credit programmes may have led to a significant decrease in the access to credit for smallholder farmers in the rural areas of Tanzania. The lack of access to rural credit has also constrained the entry of new traders in export crop marketing (Kahkonen and Leathers, 1997). Furthermore, the demise of the cooperative unions with the deregulation of export crop marketing meant that the links between inputs, finance and output exchange were broken, and the cooperative system was not replaced by a private sector run system of financing for inputs (Winter-Nelson and Temu, 2002). Prior to liberalization, the cooperative unions operated what in effect was an 'one-stop shop' by providing finance for input purchase, with inputs being distributed to producers and the costs subtracted from the value of output (which the producers were contracted to sell to the cooperatives). In such a system, screening and monitoring costs were low, along with the low possibility of default on the part of the producer. In the liberalized environment, with multiple outlets for a farmer to sell his or her crop, screening, monitoring and enforcement costs have grown too high to allow widespread provision of crop finance (ibid.).

Finally, in Malawi, less than 35 per cent of smallholder farmers have access to formal credit sources (World Bank, 1995). Most farmers rely heavily on informal credit markets as they are timely and easier to access, even though loans from informal credit sources cost more. However, informal financial markets lack the breadth and depth of formal markets and provide little or no medium/long term finance. In 1988, the Smallholder Agricultural Credit Administration (SACA) was established by the government to provide credit to smallholder farmers. There has been a significant deterioration in loan repayment rates in the 1990s, and SACA has been affected by the loan recovery problem for smallholder agriculture. Recently, SACA was privatized and absorbed by Malawi Rural Finance Company (MRFC).

While it is not clear how more effective the rural credit delivery system will be in Malawi under MRFC as compared to SACA, there is little doubt that the lack of access to formal agricultural credit for many smallholder farmers has been a significant constraint on livelihood diversification in rural Malawi. This has happened in two ways. First, with little or no access to formal credit sources, many smallholder farmers have not been able to find the funds necessary to invest in fertilizers and/or hybrid maize seeds. Second, due to lack of available credit, many smallholder farmers have had to work as casual (*Ganyu*) labour during peak periods of agricultural activities for either cash or food (Alwang and Siegel, 1999). The cash obtained from wage employment was then used to purchase fertilizers and seeds often late in the planting season. Thus, this substitution of labour between work on owned and not-owned farms has led to low yields on own farms as crucial farming activities were delayed or were not conducted (ibid.). This has been a clear case of agricultural credit market failures having significant negative effects on agricultural productivity, and thus, on household welfare.

9.5.3   Causal mechanism III: have SAPs led to an increase in the returns to farming?

This question can be answered by examining the terms of trade for agriculture (separately for food crops and export crops).[9] In Uganda, there has also been a long-run upward trend in the terms of trade in favour of food crops (Figure 9.9). However, the terms of trend for cash crops shows a sharp fall from 1994 (driven by the fall in the world price of coffee), after showing a steady increase in previous

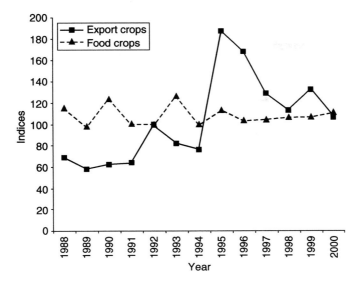

Figure 9.9 Terms of trade, Uganda.

Source: Uganda Bureau of Statistics, *Statistical Abstracts*.

Note
Price deflators for agriculture, cash crops and food crops deflated by the implicit price deflator for manufacturing.

years. Furthermore, with the entry of the private sector in coffee marketing and processing leading to increased competition, there have been significant efficiency gains in these areas (Agricultural Policy Secretariat, 1996). For coffee, the share of producer prices as a ratio of world prices has also steadily increased from 12 per cent in 1987 to 79 per cent in 1998. In the case of cotton, real producer price as a ratio of lint world price increased from 56 per cent in 1990 to 65 per cent in 1998. The increase in the returns to farming could also be explained by the fall in real input prices, following the decontrol of input prices and the greater competition in these markets following government withdrawal from direct procurement and distribution of inputs and the entry of the private sector.

In the case of Tanzania, the terms of trade have improved significantly for export crops in the 1990s, after a period of little or no change in the 1980s (Figure 9.10). The increase in terms of trade for export crops in the post-reform period contrasts sharply with a persistent decline in this variable in the pre-reform period. As Ellis (1982) has shown, the price terms of trade for export crops fell by 42.6 in the period 1970–80. Thus, the evidence from the terms of trade analysis suggests that the deregulation of agricultural pricing and marketing reforms may have led to a reversal of the long-standing bias against export agriculture in the Tanzanian economy that was evident under a policy regime of pan-territorial pricing and highly centralized state procurement systems in the pre-reform period (Ellis, 1983). However, there has been no similar increase in the terms of trade for

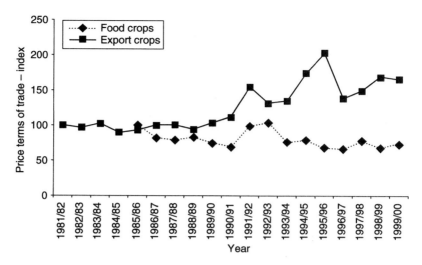

Figure 9.10 Terms of trade, Tanzania.

Source: Author's calculations; from *Ministry of Agriculture* data.

Note
Price terms of trade; Food crops: maize, rice and wheat; Export crops: cashewnut, coffee, cotton, tea and tobacco. Price deflator: Non-food National Consumer Price Index.

food crops in the 1990s. Thus, economic reforms have not led to any significant reversal of the slow but steady long-term rate of decline that has been observed in the case of food crops for Tanzanian agriculture since the 1970s.

For Malawi, similar data on producer prices is not available. We use retail price data to construct pseudo-terms of trade for Malawi. While the graph shows a sustained increase in the 'terms of trade', one should interpret this figure with caution (Figure 9.11). It may well be that the increase is primarily driven by increased profit margins of traders in the period of deregulation. Moreover, such terms of trade rise may not be beneficial to many smallholder farmers who are net buyers of food crops, mostly maize.

It is clear that SAPs seem to have had a differential impact on returns to farming in the two countries where we have reliable data – Tanzania and Uganda. For Uganda, the impact is, on the whole, positive, with the sustained increase in the terms of trade for food crops. In the case of export crops, while the terms of trade are more volatile, farmers are getting an increasingly higher proportion of the world price of the two major export crops – coffee and cotton. This is not the case in Tanzania, where the food crops terms of trade seem to have stagnated.

Perhaps the most important reason for the differences in impact is the more positive response of the private sector to the space left void by the parastatals in the marketing arena in Uganda as compared to Tanzania. This in turn could be linked to the ambivalence of the Tanzanian government, particularly at the local

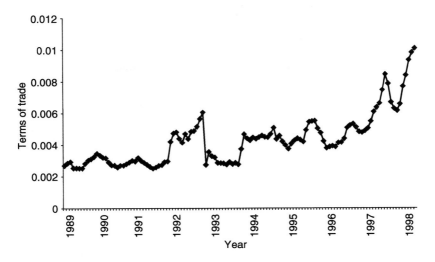

Figure 9.11 'Pseudo-terms of trade', Malawi.

Source: Own tabulation from *Ministry of Agriculture* data, Government of Malawi.

level, towards private traders about their role in agricultural marketing, with the latter often subject to harassment by the local authorities (Amani *et al.*, 1992). This has resulted in a high degree of uncertainty in the minds of traders about their future, and may have led to under-investment in storage capacities (as shown by Kahkonen and Leathers, 1997, 30–40 per cent of maize produced in Tanzania is lost due to poor or non-existent storage every year).

9.6   Conclusions

Returning to the questions asked at the beginning of the chapter, how important have SAPs been in increasing rural livelihood diversification in Malawi, Tanzania and Uganda? And to what extent is this diversification in livelihood strategies been detrimental to the welfare of rural households? In this chapter, we present partial evidence that suggests that rural livelihoods have diversified, at least in the Ugandan case. However, the effects of SAPs on rural livelihood diversification have been complex. Economic reforms have had a positive impact on the livelihoods of small-holder farmers in Uganda, many of whom have moved out of poverty in the 1990s. While coffee and cotton producers have benefited most from the reforms, the response of the Ugandan agricultural sector to the reforms thus far has been broad-based with increasing production evident both in the cash crops and food crops sectors. In the Ugandan case, there seems to be a causal linkage between increasing livelihood diversification evident at the household level and the observed fall in rural poverty in the 1990s. The beneficial effects of diversification could be related to the impact of SAPs which have increased the returns to farming in the country.

In Malawi and Tanzania, SAPs seem to have had a somewhat different impact, one that is not so positive. The removal of fertilizer subsidies and the scaling back of public investment in agricultural extension services has led to an increase in the riskiness of the economic environment and provided little incentive to invest in agricultural activities. This may explain why one observes stagnation in the food sector in these two countries. Furthermore, one observes a significant 'market failure' in agricultural credit with the withdrawal of directed credit programmes to the rural areas, and in the demise of the cooperative unions (in Tanzania), and limited entry of the private sector into rural credit markets. However, it is not obvious that SAPs alone can be held responsible for the adverse outcomes witnessed in Malawi and Tanzania. Certainly, in Tanzania, the weakness of the marketing system – one important reason for the lack of effectiveness of the SAP in this country – can be attributed to 'government failure' in not being able to set up a supportive environment for private sector involvement in marketing. Incomplete macroeconomic stabilization in Malawi may have also contributed to the weak impact of the SAP on the agricultural sector.

The analysis in this chapter suggests a more nuanced understanding of SAPs on rural livelihoods than is often presented in the literature. Neither the pessimistic nor the more sanguine view of how SAPs impact on rural households seem to be supported by the country case-studies. Rural livelihood diversification may or may not be linked to SAPs, and when it is, household welfare may or may not be adversely affected.

Acknowledgements

This chapter is prepared under a research programme entitled LADDER. The programme is funded by Policy Research Program of the UK Department for International Development (DFID); however, the findings and views expressed here are solely the responsibility of the author, and not attributable to DFID.

Notes

1 This is the key empirical prediction of the full insurance model. A simple method for testing the model is to regress household consumption on average group consumption, household income and perhaps shocks like unemployment, sickness and so on. If risk sharing is complete, the coefficient on group consumption will be one and the coefficient on household income and any other variable will be zero (Townsend, 1995).
2 For example, Townsend (1994) finds that the landless are less well insured than their village neighbours in all of his three sample South Indian villages.
3 This is the main implication of the permanent income hypothesis (PIH) as a theory of consumption proposed by Friedman (1957). A simple method of testing for the validity of the hypothesis is to run a regression with household consumption as the dependent variable and the household's transitory income as one of the independent variables. If the PIH is valid, then the coefficient on transitory income will be zero.
4 Examples of this are the planting of low-yielding but rapidly maturing varieties of crops to minimize the probability that rainfall shortages will cause crop failure or planting multiple crops on dispersed fields.

5 In several advanced countries of the North, elaborate insurance arrangements provided both by the market and the state exist that cushion individuals from large and sudden income declines. In poor developing countries, publicly managed or market provided insurance schemes are virtually non-existent and only informal insurance arrangements exist that are often rudimentary. Consequently, the withdrawal of public schemes, particularly for poor households, can greatly increase the need for risk-coping strategies (Morduch, 1999).

6 Some members of the household may also migrate to urban areas for work if these individuals expect to earn income higher than what they may earn in the agricultural sector. A key motive behind rural to urban migration is the possibility that the remittances from the migrant to the migrant's family will initiate technological progress in the family farm (Stark, 1991).

7 It should be noted that similarly to the income-smoothing motive, the existence of imperfect credit markets in the rural areas remains one important causal factor behind households' strategy to diversify as a means to accumulate capital. If credit markets were perfect, households could borrow in anticipation of higher incomes in the future, and would not need to build up their own savings.

8 This section draws from Balihuta and Sen (2001).

9 We consider only price terms of trade here.

Bibliography

Agricultural Policy Secretariat (1996) *The Impact and Consequences of the Liberalization of Coffee and Cotton Processing and Marketing in Uganda*, Report prepared for the FAO.

Alwang, J. and Siegel, P.B. (1999) 'Labor shortages on small landholding in Malawi: implications for policy reforms', *World Development*, 27: 1461–1475.

Amani, H.K.R., Van den Brink, R. and Maro, W.E. (1992) 'Tolerating the Private Sector', Working Paper No. 32, Cornell Food and Nutritional Policy Program.

Appleton, S. (2001) 'Poverty in Uganda, 1999/2000: Preliminary Estimates from the UNHS', mimeo.

Balihuta, A. and Sen, K. (2001) 'Macroeconomic Policies and Rural Livelihood Diversification: An Ugandan Case-study', LADDER Working Paper No. 3.

Besley, T. (1995) 'Savings, credit and insurance', in J. Behrman and T.N. Srinivasan (eds), *Handbook of Development Economics*, Amsterdam: North-Holland.

Binswanger, H. and Rosenzweig, M. (1993) 'Wealth, weather risk and the composition and profitability of agricultural investments', *Economic Journal*, 103: 56–78.

Bryceson, D.F. (1999) 'Sub-Saharan Africa Betwixt and Between: Rural Livelihood Practices and Policies', Working Paper No. 43, De-Agrarianisation and Rural Employment Network, Afrika-Studiecentrum, Leiden.

—— (2000) 'African rural labour, income diversification and livelihood approaches: a long-term development perspective', *Review of African Political Economy*, 80: 171–189.

Case, A. (1995) 'Symposium on consumption smoothing in developing countries', *Journal of Economic Perspectives*, 9: 81–82.

Collier, P., Radwan, S. and Wangwe, S. (1986) *Labour and Poverty in Rural Tanzania: Ujamaa and Rural Development in the United Republic of Tanzania*, Oxford: Clarendon Press.

Deaton, A. (1999) 'Commodity prices and growth in Africa', *Journal of Economic Perspectives*, 13: 23–40.

Dijkstra, A.G. and Van Donge, J.K. (2001) 'What does the "show case" show? Evidence of and lessons from adjustment in Uganda', *World Development*, 29, 5: 841–863.

Ellis, F. (1982) 'Agricultural price policy in Tanzania', *World Development*, 10: 263–283.

Ellis, F. (1983) 'Agricultural marketing and peasant-state transfers in Tanzania', *Journal of Peasant Studies*, 10: 214–242.

—— (2000) *Mixing it: Rural Livelihoods and Diversity in Developing Countries*, Oxford: Oxford University Press.

Friedman, M. (1957) *A Theory of the Consumption Function*, Princeton, NJ: Princeton University Press.

Government of Republic of Uganda (2000) 'Plan for the modernization of agriculture: eradicating poverty in Uganda' available at http://pma.go.ug/pdfs/Plan%20for%20 Modernisation%20of%20 Agriculture.pdf (13 August 2005).

Harrigan, J. (2003) 'U-turns and full circles: two decades of agricultural reform in Malawi, 1981–2000', *World Development*, 31: 847–863.

Kahkonen, S. and Leathers, H. (1997) *Is there Life after Liberalization? Transaction Cost Analysis of Maize and Cotton Marketing in Zambia and Tanzania*, USAID report.

Ministry of Agriculture (2000) *Tanzania; Agriculture: Performance and Strategies for Sustainable Growth*, report.

Morduch, J. (1995) 'Income smoothing and consumption smoothing', *Journal of Economic Perspectives*, 9: 103–114.

—— (1999) 'Between the state and the market: can informal insurance patch the safety net?', *The World Bank Research Observer*, 14: 187–207.

National Bureau of Statistics (2002) 'Results of the Household Budget Survey 2000/2001', mimeo.

Platteau, J.-P. and Abraham, A. (1987) 'An inquiry into quasi-contracts: the role of reciprocal credit and interlinked deals in small-scale fishing communities', *Journal of Development Studies*, 23: 461–490.

Reardon, T. (1992) 'Income diversification of rural households in the Sahel', *Rural Development Studies*, 24: 281–297.

Reardon, T., Delgado, C. and Matlon, P. (1992) 'Determinants and effects of income diversification amongst farm households in Burkina Faso', *Journal of Development Studies*, 32: 899–912.

Smith, D.R., Gordon, A., Meadows, K. and Zwick, K. (2001) 'Livelihood diversification in Uganda: patterns and determinants of change across two rural districts', *Food Policy*, 26: 421–435.

Stark, O. (1991) 'On the role of rural-to-urban migration in rural development', chapter 14 in *The Migration of Labor*, Cambridge, MA: Basil Blackwell.

Townsend, R. (1994) 'Risk and insurance in village India', *Econometrica*, 62: 539–591.

—— (1995) 'Consumption insurance: an evaluation of risk-bearing systems in low-income economies', *Journal of Economic Perspectives*, 9: 83–102.

Udry, C. (1994) 'Risk and insurance in a rural credit market: an empirical investigation in northern Nigeria', *Review of Economic Studies*, 61: 495–526.

Walker, T. (1990) 'Does Knowing More About the Weather Substantially Improve Risk Management in Dryland Semi-Arid Tropics', Paper presented in International Symposium on Climactic Risk in Crop Production Models and Management for the Semi-Arid Tropics, 2–6 July 1990, Brisbane, Australia.

Winter-Nelson, A. and Temu, A. (2002) 'Institutional adjustment and transactions costs: product and input markets in the Tanzanian coffee market', *World Development*, 30: 561–574.

World Bank (1995) *Malawi: Agricultural Sector Memorandum: Strategy Options in the 1990s*, Washington, DC: World Bank.

10 The World Bank and the reconstruction of the 'social safety net' in Russia and Eastern Europe

Paul Mosley

10.1 Introduction

Since its inception the World Bank has been gradually expanding its functions, with a particular kink in the curve during the age of structural adjustment in the 1980s. During that decade, Moises Naim, a Colombian executive director of the Bank, compiled the following list of alternative conceptions of the Bank which were current at the time:

1 'The Bank as a bank': the function in the original Articles of Agreement, of lending at a profit for developmental purposes, usually the provision of infrastructure.
2 'The Bank as a fund': the provision of concessional lending directed at the relief of poverty, which came in with the International Development Association (IDA) in the 1960s and has enjoyed surges of popularity particularly under MacNamara in the 1970s and again in the new poverty strategies from the 1990s until the present time.
3 'The Knowledge Bank': the provision and dissemination of knowledge and skills relevant to development, most particularly policy-making and institution-building skills as an adjunct to lending.
4 'The Bank as instrument of global governance': the provision of global public goods, from environmental protection to agricultural research to the Multilateral Investment Guarantee Authority.[1]

Since that time, there has been intense debate, particularly during the period surrounding the Bank and the International Monetary Fund's (IMF) half-century in 1995, about which of these and other possible functions the Bank should specialize in. The debate, of course, is political rather than simply intellectual: the expansion of the Bank's functions into the provision of 'knowledge' concerning macro-policy, tariff policy and public enterprise reform involved it in a whole series of clashes with the Fund during the era of structural adjustment (Mosley *et al.*, 1995, chapter 2), which calmed down for a time but then reignited during the period of the East Asian crisis (Stiglitz, 2003, *passim* but especially chapters 1, 5 and 7).

In this chapter we consider the implications for the Bank's roles of the Russian and East European crisis of the 1990s. The dimensions of the crisis are familiar but are brought up to date in Table 10.1. During the period from 1989 to 1994, under the impetus of stabilization and severe redundancies across the whole of state-owned industry, all measures of poverty increased, and increased very sharply in every Eastern European country except Hungary and the Czech Republic.

In Russia, headcount poverty increased by a factor of two and a half between these years and the Gini coefficient of inequality increased from one of the lowest levels in the world to a level exceeding that of the United States (Stone, 2002, pp. 64–65). The more long-term indicators also worsened: out of 29 welfare indicators recorded by UNICEF only 2 (maternal mortality and the 1–4 death rate) showed an improvement between 1989 and 1994. The crisis

> entailed a steep rise in overall mortality, which particularly affected adult men but also adolescents, the elderly and in some cases even infants.... As a result, life expectancy at birth, the most comprehensive health indicator, deteriorated in seven countries since the onset of the transition. Health and education conditions also showed a high frequency of deteriorations, as shown by a massive surge in new tuberculosis and low birth weight cases, which clearly confirmed an increase in poverty. Finally, there is evidence that primary and secondary education rates moved downward in a majority of countries and that – with rising youth unemployment, skyrocketing costs of securing a living place and overall uncertainty about the future – marriage, remarriage and birth rates plummeted in all countries.
>
> (Cornia, 1994, pp. 602–603)

This predicament clearly went far beyond everything which had been entailed by the phrase 'social costs of adjustment' in other countries, and offered an enormous challenge to the Bank, particularly in terms of two of its 'new' roles listed above. In terms of the fourth role mentioned by Naim – the geopolitical role – there was obviously the need to try and create a stable post cold war international economic order. In terms of the second – 'the Bank as a fund' – there was the equally transparent and related need to reverse the trend towards increasing poverty. The Bank made it quite clear that it intended to take up the challenge: 'the major thrust of our portfolio (in the transitional countries) consists of social-sector lending. That is where it has to be to offset the terrible increases in poverty of the last few years' (James Wolfensohn, World Bank President, 1997).

In this chapter, we consider the implementation of this commitment, and the implications which it has had for the Bank's role. The next section considers the evolution of the Bank's lending operations in Russia and Eastern Europe, while the following section makes use of these findings in setting up an econometric exercise designed to assess the poverty impact of the financial support provided by the Bank and other donors. The final section examines the policy implications.

Table 10.1 Evolution of poverty in Russia and Eastern Europe 1989–2002

	Russia			Poland			Hungary			Romania			Slovak Republic		
	Headcount (national poverty line)	'Extreme poverty' ($2/day)	Gini coeffi-cient	Headcount (national poverty line)	'Extreme poverty' ($2/day)	Gini coeffi-cient	Headcount (national poverty line)	'Extreme poverty' ($2/day)	Gini coeffi-cient	Headcount (national poverty line)	'Extreme poverty' ($2/day)	Gini coeffi-cient	Headcount (national poverty line)	'Extreme poverty' ($2/day)	Gini coeffi-cient
1980	11.3[1]		27.6[1]												
1989				22.9[3]	5.1[3]		12.3[3]	5.1[3]		29.9[3]	7.7[3]		5.7[3]	0.2[3]	
1990	10.1	14.3	28.4	38.3	11.3					17.6	2.4		6.2	0.2	
1991	11.4		26.5	33.9	8.1		13.9	1.5		25.1	6.8		24.9	2.4	
1992	23.1		28.7	35.7	10.4		14.5			44.3	15.2		30.3	2.9	19.5
1993	24.7		34.6	23.8	10.5								34.5		
1994			40.9												
1995	26.0	13.3	38.1							21.5	27.5	28.2			
1996	21.0		37.5			32.9			30.8					2.4	25.8
1997				17.3			17.3								
1998	25.1		48.7		2.0	31.6		1.7	24.4			28.2			
1999	55.0[2]														
2000	18.8		45.6								5.2	30.3			
2001	33.0[2]														

Sources: Wherever possible from World Bank (2003a), with interpolations from (1) Klugman and Braithwaite (1998), (2) World Bank (2003b) and (3) Cornia (1994).

10.2   The composition and execution of World Bank programmes in Russia and Eastern Europe

10.2.1   The overall picture

The World Bank found itself in the early 1990s with a unique opportunity to entrench its influence across a huge new kingdom in which it had historically been weakly represented, and determined not to squander the build-up of that influence through internecine wrangling with the IMF of a kind which had done damage in Latin America and Africa. Accordingly, it graciously allowed the Fund to lead on macro-economic policy, and as a consequence allowed itself to be sucked into the slipstream of the Fund's large stand-bys to Russia, granting two large structural adjustment loans (SALs) of its own in 1993 and 1996. Following the precedent of previous large SALs in Brazil and Mexico, these loans had minimal conditionality attached (World Bank, 2003b).

But within all of this, as illustrated by Tables 10.2 and 10.3, the status of the social sectors was minor and receded further when, as Stone (2002, p. 158) puts it, 'the Clinton administration completed the transition from treating Russia as a potential superpower to treating Russia as a regional power'.

For as long as it could be reasonably represented to the world that keeping the Russian and Ukrainian nuclear missiles in safe hands depended on something radical being done about poverty in Eastern Europe – broadly from 1992 to 1996 – there was certainly an impetus for extraordinary action within the social sectors, although, as Table 10.3 shows, even that took time to materialize, reaching its peak in 2000. But thereafter, the game was lost: the transitional region ceased to be perceived as a special case, even though its sufferings continued on a scale to

Table 10.2 World Bank commitments to Russia (US$ millions)

	1992–95	1996	1997	1998	1999	2000	2001	Cancelled	Total
Rehabilitation loans	1,200	0	0	0	0	0	0	0	1,200
SALs	0	500	1,400	1,500				1,100	3,900
Oil, gas and energy	1,180	528	40				85	352	981
Social sectors	110	470	137	29	0	0	130	120	755
Private sector development/ financial sector development/ infrastructure	1,519	763	216	0	400	0	182	1,069	2,012
Agriculture/ environment	529	80	0	0	0	60	226	118	777
Public sector management	70	21	58	0	30	30	0	0	195
% to social sectors	15.1	47.9	6.6	13.4	0	0	21.4		9.6
Total	729	981	2,086	2,172	657	606	605		7,836

Source: From table 2.1 in World Bank (2003b).

Table 10.3 Social sector commitments to Russia, Eastern Europe and comparators (% of total portfolio)

	Annual average		2000	2001	2002
	1993–97	1998–99			
Eastern Europe and Central Asia					
Social sector lending[a] $million	290.0	702.5	573.7	446.3	552.7
Other sector lending[b] $million	3,980.0	4,553.0	2,469.0	2,247.0	4,971.0
Total	4,270.2	5,255.1	3,042.2	2,693.1	5,523.6
Social sectors % of total	6.7	13.3	18.8	16.5	10.0
World					
Social sector lending $million	2,262.0	3,974.4	2,695.0	3,120.0	2,469.9
Total	21,510.5	28,794.8	15,276.2	17,250.6	19,519.4
Social sectors % of total	10.5	13.8	17.6	18.1	12.6

Source: From tables 2.2 and 5.4 in World Bank (2002).

Notes
a 'Social protection and risk management' plus 'social development, gender, and inclusion'.
b Economic management, public sector governance, rule of law, financial and private sector development, trade and integration, human development, urban development, rural development, environmental and natural resource management.

warrant its being treated as one. Except in 2000, percentage allocations to social sectors within the Eastern European region have at all times been lower than within the Bank's global budget.

If, therefore, geopolitics were a major factor pushing the Bank away from its pro-claimed poverty focus in Eastern Europe, other factors were also important. A fundamental one, particularly in Russia, was the failure of revenue policy at the macro-economic level. The same botched tax reforms which failed to achieve a stabilization of the Russian budget, and hence of the macro-economy, in 1998 (Stone, 2002, p. 116; World Bank, 2003b) also failed to deliver the revenue needed to finance an expansion of social protection spending. A second factor was the awareness that instruments other than social protection were available to reduce poverty. But maybe the most crucial factor was the fact that not only Russia but nearly the whole of Eastern Europe lacked the kind of politics which in other parts of the world had put vital impetus behind the Bank's poverty reduction programmes.

The model of Figure 10.1 may help explain the process of prioritization within Eastern European governments which has been described. We assume that governments associate reform with a long-term economic gain (measured on the vertical axis) and a short-term risk of political loss (measured on the horizontal axis). Both of them increase with the speed and extent of reform. Collectively, the government has to decide where to position itself on the trade-off between the two, represented by the curved line in the Figure 10.1 In other words, the

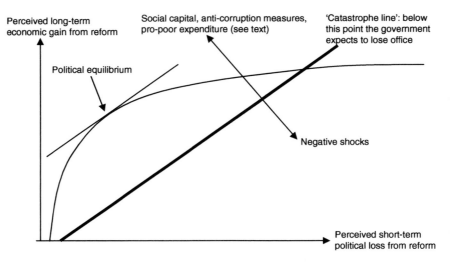

Figure 10.1 Reform decisions as seen by government: a stylized view.

government has to determine what position on the eventual trade-off will optimize its welfare, taking account of the likely future course of negotiations with any international financial institution or group of such institutions.

Above all, it wants to avoid being blown across the 'catastrophe line' – a combination of high risk of political defeat and incomplete reform which it sees as being lethal for its chances of holding on to power. Negative shocks such as natural disasters and market collapse (e.g. for Russia a collapse in the oil price, for Bulgaria a collapse in the wine market, etc.) will push the trade-off south-east, and the question is what will blow it in the opposite direction. We would argue that the following may be treated a priori as assets which will raise the 'productivity' of reform and thus raise the 'production function' by which the risk-taking involved in reform is turned into a political dividend:

1   *A reduction in corruption levels*: as mentioned ubiquitously by small businesses, particularly in Russia and Eastern Europe, as a key determinant of the cost of doing business, and hence of intentions to invest. Its importance in the present context is that it increases the economic, and hence the political, payoff to liberalization measures (World Bank, 1997);

2   *An increase in social capital*: social capital has consistently shown significant impacts on growth, and thence on poverty (Knack and Keefer, 1997; Whiteley, 2000). More specifically, social sector programmes explicitly seek to build linkages within and between communities, and between communities and levels of government. The gravity of the livelihood shocks inflicted by *perestroika* added particular value to whatever networks individuals were able to retain, and the lower strata of transitional societies have been

described by Kennedy *et al.* (1998, p. 2039) as an environment in which 'those who have access to social capital get ahead; those who do not get sick and die'. This does not imply, of course, that social capital can be constructed like a building, and many programmes which have tried to operationalize this kind of metaphor have fallen flat on their face. Nonetheless, to the extent that survey data give evidence of trust having increased, this again will reduce transactions costs, including those of policy makers. Intra-community equality is strongly associated with social capital.

3   *An increase in 'pro-poor' expenditure*: social sector expenditure is a component of 'pro-poor' expenditure. 'Pro-poor' expenditure can be defined as any type of public expenditure which raises the poverty elasticity of growth – either by increasing labour-intensity (World Bank, 1990), or by providing services consumed by poor people, or through any other channel. We believe that the intersectoral mix of government (and other) expenditures has an important influence on poverty through at least three channels:

(a) some expenditures are more intensive in the labour of the poor and hence generate greater labour-market benefits;
(b) some expenditures provide more services for low-income consumers (and in some cases generate externalities for them as well);
(c) some expenditures are better at generating social networks which are economically beneficial ('social capital').

Through all of these channels, 'pro-poor' expenditure reduces inequality, and thereby very possibly acts as a conflict prevention device in the manner described by Collier and Dollar (2002, pp. 10–13).[2] Pro-poor expenditure, in principle, has the ability to deliver the political support of a broad base of low-income people by visibly compensating them, in kind, for the costs of reform. In practice, we have been able to show that the use of this instrument has delivered support for stabilization programmes across a range of developing and transitional countries (Mosley, 2004). We speculate here, and wish to test, that it may also be able to deliver support for programmes of structural reform as well.

The above three assets (i.e. reduction in corruption, increase in social capital and increase in 'pro-poor' expenditure) may be seen as components of a portfolio which is juggled in accordance with a 'survival decision rule', much as resource-constrained households also have to manage such assets as they may contribute to their own survival. But the manner in which this portfolio of assets is juggled in order to move towards 'security' – that is leftwards in Figure 10.1 – and, indeed, the extent to which they are seen as assets at all varies according to states' initial conditions, the personalities of their leadership elite and the strategies which they see as being feasible.[3]

10.2.2   The social protection programmes

By contrast with poorer developing economies, most transitional economies had a range of social benefits in position in 1990, such as old-age pensions, employment-related benefits, and subsidized entitlements to particular services such as housing and utilities. These benefits were embedded in the process of central planning, and few of them were related to levels of individual income or wealth. As the World Bank has become more involved in the process of lending to transitional countries, it has sought to bring about reform in the social protection system through a series of financial and advisory operations, which are listed in Table 10.4 for the sample of countries used in the subsequent empirical analysis.

Table 10.4 World Bank support for social protection in selected transitional countries

	Economic performance: 1995 per capita GDP (1989 = 100)[1]	*Nature of WB intervention[2]*	*Family allowances as % of GDP, 2000 (1989 in brackets)[3]*	*Evolution: selectivity[4]*
Russia	60	1993: Employment Services and Social Protection Loan 1997: Social Protection Adjustment and Implementation Loans	0.7[5] (0.5)	
Poland	98	Poverty assessments only. No financial operations in this sector.	3.0[5] (2.0)	35% of households receiving benefits were nonpoor in 1998
Hungary				87% of households receiving benefits were nonpoor in 1998
Romania	82	1995: Employment Services and Social Protection Loan 1996: Community Social Infrastructure Loan 1998: Child Welfare Reform Loan	0.7 (2.9)	
Slovak Republic	87	1999; Social Benefits Reform Loan	5.0 (2.8)	
Ukraine	42	1997:Social Protection Supplementation Loan 2001: Social Sector Adjustment Loan	(0.1)	
Bulgaria	76	1999: Social Protection Adjustment Operation		

Sources: (1) World Bank (2003a); (2) Andrews and Ringold (1999); (3) Andrews and Ringold (1999) and World Bank (2003a); (4) Braithwaite, Grootaert and Milanovic (1999); (5) Provisional figures.

From the table we may note, first of all, the differentiated way in which social protection schemes evolved after the transition. Although there was a worrying tendency for the real value of benefits, and child benefits in particular, to be seriously eroded by general fiscal weakness – see Andrews and Ringold (1999, p. 31) – this did not occur everywhere, and in the Slovak Republic and Poland there was a significant increase in their real value. In the Eastern European countries, but much less in Russia and central Asia, there was a tendency for subsidies on the consumption of housing and utilities to be converted into cash benefits. In some, but not all, transitional countries specific unemployment benefits were introduced.

The main thrust of the World Bank's approach may be described as:

1   to get rid of the distortions in the price system associated with heavily subsidized housing and utilities;
2   to persuade client countries to move away from universalism towards a means-tested system in which benefits are provided according to need;
3   to complement existing systems of benefit provision for those in need with systems which look forward and provide protection for those who are vulnerable to being in need, as per the approach of the *2000 World Development Report*;
4   in a few cases, to provide supplementary financing for the social security system, in particular by means of *social investment funds* – financial intermediaries which channel resources for the provision of social, health or educational services to private and public organizations and community groups.

As shown by Table 10.4 the Bank did not provide financial assistance everywhere, and in a number of places, such as Poland, functioned purely as a 'Knowledge Bank'. Where financial assistance was provided, as with the Bank's social protection adjustment operations in Russia, it often found itself frustrated by its inability to get the government to accept co-ownership of the objectives it had announced:

> The (1992) Employment Services and Social Protection Loan was a technical assistance loan intended to help deal with the anticipated loss of jobs caused by enterprise restructuring. It also was intended to help develop plans for reforming the pension system and other aspects of the social safety net, but the government was not prepared to address these areas at a time when it had more pressing concerns, such as stabilization and market policy reforms... Insufficient attention was given to social assistance targeting, even as poverty was increasing.
>
> (World Bank, 2003b, p. 23)

Indeed, it was only in Poland and the Czech Republic that the Bank was able to convince the government to implement systems for the effective targeting of welfare benefits, along the lines now widely adopted in industrialized countries. Elsewhere it was frustrated either by lack of government commitment, by lack of government capacity or, as in Hungary, by neither of the above but simply by a serene commitment to whatever could be preserved of a universalistic welfare state in defiance of the Bank's homilies in favour of targeting. In areas of social protection specifically emphasized as priorities by the Bank, such as child allowances and child protection, expenditures nonetheless declined in some countries (see Table 10.4). But within the limits to which it had set itself, some important successes were achieved by the Bank, perhaps especially in the smaller countries – in Romania through a series of social protection operations, in Albania through the Social Investment Fund and in Bulgaria through both.[4] But even in Russia, an experimental spirit has emerged in the design of social protection schemes through the process of decentralization, for which the Bank modestly disclaims any credit in its OED report cited earlier, but which may nonetheless be traceable in however indirect a way to its intellectual influence.[5]

There is one limitation of the Bank's social protection strategies in Russia and Eastern Europe to which specific attention must be drawn. This is the absence of any integration between social protection and policies to develop financial institutions – indeed, the latter are not even mentioned in the Bank's check-list of social protection options for the region (see Appendix 2) even though they have become increasingly fundamental for the relief of poverty in developing countries, in the Bank's strategies for those countries and even for community development in industrialized countries such as the UK and USA (United Kingdom, 1999; Mosley and Steel, 2004). Policy, of course, has increasingly become focussed on the individual coping strategies and informal networks developed by the poor – in Russia, characterized as an 'hourglass society', individuals have a high degree of trust in their immediate social networks of friends, relatives and other face-to-face groups, and a high degree of distrust in the state, even the reformed state. In this climate, far more people rely on informal social capital than in formal institutions of state to deal with their problems, in particular as a source of social protection.[6] It is into these informal networks that microfinance institutions have lent: globally, but maybe with particular success in countries with damaged state banking sectors and a vibrant informal economy, such as Bolivia and Bangladesh, but this applies also to Russia. As they have done so, they have in many cases provided externalities – into the empowerment of women, into the financing of school fees, into the building of social capital and, maybe most relevantly for Eastern Europe, into the reduction of corruption. In other environments, including indeed Bangladesh, the Bank has lent for social protection direct into these institutions by means of NGO sector loans; but not in the transitional region.

What differentiates the transitional region from other parts of the world was that small-scale private economic activity was, until the early 1990s, actually illegal, and in Russia carried severe penalties including imprisonment (Klugman and Braithwaite, 1998, p. 42). Even after 1992, as one of our interviewees put it to us, 'initially, entrepreneurs were hiding from everyone – they didn't want to admit what they were'.[7] In such an environment, small entrepreneurs need special support, going beyond finance into training, legal advice and social capital formation (e.g. through the formation of solidarity groups). Most of this has been forthcoming from NGOs (e.g. Opportunity International in Russia), but there has also been intervention from international financial organizations such as the

EBRD's Russian Small Business Fund. As we have argued above, the form in which social protection is given may determine the externalities it is able to give to the poverty reduction process, in particular by reducing corruption and building social capital. It may be that if these externalities are to be maximized, the Bank needs to complement its 'conventional' social protection support with support for the emergent bottom end of the financial market.

10.2.3 Outcomes for poverty and other variables

Thus the Bank's ability to reduce poverty over the course of the transition was heavily limited by geopolitics and by internal politics as well as by factors internal to the design of social protection. Nonetheless, within these limits, there was on the fragile evidence of Table 10.1 some poverty reduction in the later 1990s in all the Eastern European countries, and even in 2000 in Russia. What was the Bank able, within the limits mentioned, to add to this process and what are the implications for policy? The next section considers these questions in an econometric framework.

10.3 Development assistance and poverty: an explanatory model

As indicated by Table 10.1, it appears as if poverty in the transitional region may at last have begun to fall. To what extent is this due to the influence of aid from the World Bank group and elsewhere? To begin to answer this question, we run a single-equation regression model in Table 10.5 to estimate the impact of aid flows from the World Bank and other donors on poverty levels. We use two kinds of poverty indicator as dependent variable (the headcount index and the level of under-five mortality) and we reproduce, in the right-hand part of the table, results already obtained from a regression of this type for all developing and transitional countries for which data are available. Three of the independent variables are the ones which we have argued, in our discussion of Figure 10.1, to be likely to shift the balance between risk and return 'north-westwards' by increasing the ability of the recipient government to manage crisis: pro-poor expenditure (which diminishes inequality and attracts political support from lower income groups), inequality itself, social capital (assessed by the *World Values Survey* measure of interpersonal trust) which we interpret in terms of the degree of linkage between citizens and government and therefore governability. The fourth, corruption, is simply a measure of the cost of doing business which will impact on levels of enterprise, investment and poverty. All four variables we see as shift parameters which are potentially able to influence the relationship between aid and poverty; in this respect, they play the same role as the 'good policy' variable in the analysis of Burnside and Dollar (2000), without which aid is ineffective, but the components of that measure are mainly macro variables, whereas the ones considered here are more micro in nature. Estimation is by two-stage (or in one case three-stage) least squares, to allow for probable feedbacks from poverty to aid.

The results of Table 10.5 suggest that low levels of corruption, low levels of inequality and high levels of social capital are apparently in Eastern Europe, as well as globally, able to increase the 'poverty-leverage' of aid, and may have contributed

Table 10.5 Estimates of aid impact on poverty, and possible influences on this

Sample estimation method	Dependent variable (poverty indicator)					
	Russia and Eastern Europe			Global comparisons		
	Infant mortality rate	Infant mortality rate	Poverty headcount (at national poverty line)	Infant mortality rate	Infant mortality rate	Poverty headcount (at international poverty line)
	1	2	3	4	5	6
	2SLS	2SLS[a]	2SLS[a]	2SLS[a]	2SLS[a]	3SLS[b]
Constant	7.79**	8.21* (4.61)	4.65** (5.22)	8.92** (21.04)	8.99** (18.63)	5.53** (6.74)
Aid	-0.21* (2.04)	-0.14 (1.34)	-0.09* (1.97)	0.04 (0.03)	-0.11* (1.85)	-0.29 (1.47)
Aid from WB only						
Gini coefficient of inequality	0.065** (3.34)	0.053** (3.61)	0.078** (4.66)		0.034* (2.31)	0.058** (5.51)
PPE (as % GDP)[c]	-0.037 (1.13)	-0.049 (1.77)	-0.145* (2.44)	-0.085** (3.45)	-0.25* (1.90)	-0.198** (3.17)
PPE index squared					0.045 (0.31)	
Social capital indicator	-0.043* (2.15)	-0.007* (1.98)	-0.013* (2.39)			
Social protection spending	-0.037* (1.99)	-0.026 (1.65)	-0.009 (1.34)			
Health spending/GNP						0.234* (2.21)

Transparency international corruption indicator	−0.34** (4.47)	−0.27** (3.98)	−0.38** (6.32)			−0.22* (2.13)
Composite policy indicator[d]						−0.00188 (1.54)
Log (GDP per capita)				−0.635** (10.67)	−0.64** (9.91)	−0.49** (4.15)
Observations	34	36	36	117	117	88
R^2	0.43	0.53	0.37	0.68	0.82	0.49

Sources: Poverty headcount index is calculated at national poverty lines from data in World Bank, *World Development Reports*, successive issues from 1990 onwards – data arrays available from author on request. PPE index is from IMF *Government Expenditure Statistics Yearbook*; for full details see Appendix. *Transparency International* corruption indicator from Transparency International website (http://www.gwdg.de/~uwvw/icr.htm).

Notes

t-statistics in parenthesis; ** and * denote significance at the 1% and 5% level, respectively.

a In regressions 2–5, instruments for aid are:
'*Recipient need*': (i) STAB–inflation in 1990s as a percentage of its average value in the 1980s; and (ii) DEBSER – debt service as % of GNP.
Recipient characteristics and ability to absorb aid: (i) MIL – military expenditure as % GNP, serving as a quasi-war dummy; and (ii) POP – total population.

The instrumenting equation is:

log(aid/GNP) = 0.081 − 0.107*log(STAB) + 0.092(MIL) − 1.34**E-09(POP) + 0.014*(DEBSER)
         (1.85)   (1.24)   (3.16)   (1.89)

$R^2 = 0.087$.

b In addition to poverty, aid, PPE and health expenditure are endogenous variables.

c PPE is a measure of the extent to which public expenditure is intensive in 'priority' sectors likely to have a poverty-reducing effect. It is calculated as detailed in Appendix 1 (without military expenditures).

d The 'Burnside-Dollar' good policy index – a weighted sum of inflation, budget deficit and openness.

to the poverty reduction which at last seems to be occurring. Pro-poor expenditure, in Eastern Europe, has a smaller and less significant coefficient than elsewhere (particularly so when the grant element of World Bank lending is used as the indicator of aid!) although still significant at the 5 per cent level in relation to the headcount measure of poverty; our interpretation of this, and one of the key messages of this chapter, is that overtly redistributive measures appear to enjoy less political leverage in Eastern Europe than elsewhere. Aid itself, holding constant these 'facilitative' variables, is a just-significant influence in relation to headcount poverty only.

A first message which we take from this analysis is that if the 'social sectors' are to have maximum impact on poverty, they need to maximize the level of impact achieved through *indirect* linkages, rather than simply focussing on direct linkages. Examples of such indirect linkages, particularly relevant to the transitional region, are:

1   microfinance and support services to small businesses (as we have seen, somewhat neglected by the Bank in the transitional region), by making possible credit from uncorrupt sources of supply, lower the cost of doing business and raise the rate of investment;
2   aid given to help labour markets operate more flexibly (e.g. by subsidizing child-care services or carers) flattens out the labour-supply curve to *all sectors of the economy* (especially of groups with a high probability of being poor such as lone parents) and thereby increases competitiveness;
3   social investment funds generate both human capital (by the provision of local schools and health centres) but also social capital (by developing democratic community decision-taking procedures in the allocation of funds); and finally
4   aid given direct to the NGO sector reduces the various bureaucratic costs associated with dealing through government.

In addition, these results suggest a possible role for conditionality, applied in particular to the catalytic variables mentioned above. As we have seen, conditionality has been somewhat disowned by the Bank in recent years and has not done well in Russia. But it has done better in smaller countries, witness the case of the Romania Child Protection Loan (see Stone, 2002 for the parallel case of IMF lending to Eastern Europe). Success depends not only on bargaining relationships and country size, but also on pre-existing trust relationships between Bank and recipient country and on the ease with which a target variable can be altered; thus it is easier to increase the level of pro-poor expenditure than to achieve press-button increases in social capital or decreases in corruption. But we have evidence of the success of conditionality applied to pro-poor expenditure in Africa (Mosley et al., 2004) and there is evidence of strong increases in the coefficient of pro-poor expenditure in Hungary, Poland and Romania within our sample. It would not be unreasonable to suggest that the characteristics of pro-poor expenditure within the smaller countries of our sample and the ability of specific social expenditures to increase it might yield a poverty dividend through this route.

10.4   Conclusions and policy messages

In the way we have described it, a great idealistic crusade against the ravages of the transition, which the Bank at one time visualized as offering a distinct extension of its global influence, has turned into something of a damp squib. The Bank has missed an opportunity to consolidate its comparative advantage in the poverty reduction field in relation to the Fund, in part because it deemed that Eastern Europe was not a suitable stage on which to confront the Fund and, unlike the Fund, had come to feel ambivalent about the use of conditionality. Social protection expenditures never attained the salience within the Bank budget which would have made an extension of its influence possible, even during Russia's period of maximum reverse leverage during the mid-nineties; and from that climacteric they have gradually receded. We give various reasons for this in the chapter, including the failure to produce innovative institutional ideas to support the small business sector, lagging tax revenue and maybe most importantly the inability of the Bank to find seriously pro-poor partners within the political structure of transitional countries which had the power to achieve a serious increase in social spending within those countries. In relation to Naim's typology of Bank functions, the idea of 'the Bank as a fund', evening out inequalities on a global scale, has given way to the other functions, in particular the geopolitical one.

Nonetheless, in several transitional countries a modest increase in social spending, and more broadly in 'pro-poor' spending, did occur and, most importantly, a modest decline in poverty did finally happen in a majority of them – but in the case of Russia not until the very end of the 1990s. We have made an attempt to assess the relationship between changes in poverty and a range of variables which the World Bank has tried to influence, including social capital, corruption, inequality and what we call 'pro-poor' expenditures, which is a complex of expenditures of which social spending is a part. All of these turn out to have some bearing on poverty reduction, both globally and within the Eastern European/transitional region, although there are econometric problems still to be resolved and the impact coefficient is often weaker in Eastern Europe than in the global sample. The implication is that the Bank 'missed a trick': had it exercised more leverage, it could well have helped reduce more poverty, although we emphasize that our model is crude, and that there are some 'industrial country-type' linkages increasingly relevant to transitional economies which we have not attempted to model, including the effects of benefit levels on the incentive to work.

For these reasons, any policy messages drawn from this chapter need to be taken as particularly tentative. The one we would offer at this stage, beyond that which the Bank has already drawn about the need for pro-poor policies to be backed by a proper constituency within the recipient country, is that social protection policies need to be assessed not only in terms of their direct impact, but also in terms of their ability to confer 'multipliers' or 'externalities' into the influences on poverty mentioned earlier. We have criticized Bank social protection policies for not linking with policies to stimulate the bottom end of the financial sector, precisely for this reason – because microfinance has a proven ability to generate social capital and reduce the costs of corruption. But more broadly, any social protection policy which is able to increase the level of other pro-poor expenditures, or which increases intra-community trust, or which in any other way represents an investment in social capital, is likely on the evidence here presented to reduce poverty through the back as well as the front door. Work to assess the extent and significance of these multipliers in particular empirical contexts represents, in our judgement, an important research priority.

Appendix 1   The 'pro-poor expenditure index'

The idea of designing a 'poverty sensitive' pattern of public expenditures has been often articulated (notably by Ferroni and Kanbur, 1991), but to our knowledge such a pattern has not been empirically documented. No approach is likely to be perfect because of the range of poverty impacts which are conceivable but the following 'quick and dirty' methods can be visualized. The first two cover only one channel of impact (and we only have data for a few countries), whereas the last two are more general:

- *A labour-intensity approach* – covering effect (a) discussed in the text – the definition of 'pro-poor expenditure' as those expenditure sectors which are most labour-intensive.
- *A benefit incidence approach* – covering effect (b) discussed in the text – the definition of 'pro-poor expenditure' as those sectors whose output, on the evidence of household budget surveys, is consumed by the poor.
- *A regression approach* – the definition of 'pro-poor expenditure' as those sectors where expenditure exhibits correlation with poverty.
- *A CGE approach* – which can hope to trace comprehensively the effects of expenditure on poverty through multiple channels of effect.

Labour-intensity. We know of no statistical exercises which measure the propensity of different public expenditure sectors to take on low-income labour. However, the governments of the two most effective exercises in poverty reduction within low-income countries – Uganda and Ethiopia – prioritized the same expenditure sectors, explicitly on the grounds that they are labour-intensive. These are: primary health and education, agricultural research and extension, rural water and sanitation (Morrissey and Verschoor, 2005; Rock, 2003).

Benefit incidence. Sahn and Younger (2000), drawing on household budget surveys in eight low-income African countries, have assessed the extent to which different public expenditures fall on low-income groups. They conclude that expenditures on primary and secondary education, and all types of healthcare, (but not university education) can be considered progressive and do reduce inequality. Nonetheless, they warn (p. 344) that 'expectations that social sector spending has a substantial redistributive impact are misplaced' and that 'African governments would do well to consider how to better target their expenditures'.

The CGE approach. For Uganda only, Chant *et al.* (2003) have conducted simulations which examine the impact of different expenditures on poverty through *all* market channels, not just the two examined above. For education, health and 'social sector' expenditures only, they find that the impact of increasing the share of public spending dedicated to those expenditure sectors is poverty-reducing.

The regression approach. This attempts to achieve comprehensiveness of coverage while examining tendencies across a wide range of countries. The results from OLS regressions for 34 countries for the years 1980–98 produced the results presented in Mosley *et al.* (2004), which are reported in Table 10A.1.

The set of results obtained by these different procedures is summarized in Table 10A.2 where effects which are ambiguous or insignificant according to a particular methodology are in brackets. From the table it is very clear that educational and 'social' (in the World Bank's classification, 'housing and amenities') expenditure belongs in any pro-poor expenditure index. Health and agricultural expenditure are ambiguous. Health very strongly 'refuses to behave' in both regressions in spite of Sahn and Younger's (2000) weakly positive results on benefit incidence, and agriculture has the right sign but is insignificant in the regressions. Military expenditure is negative and significant for poverty in the regressions but there is a lack of supporting evidence from other methodologies. For the regressions reported in Table 10.5 we omitted health from the calculation of the PPE index given the complete absence of supportive evidence from any comprehensive methodology. The statistical evidence in support of agriculture is weak but we include it in the light of very strong case-study evidence, in particular from Uganda and Ethiopia (Morrissey and Verschoor, 2005; Rock, 2003), that the prioritization of agricultural spending made a very important difference to poverty impact from the early 1990s onward.

Table 10A.1 The regression approach to pro-poor expenditure

	Dependent variable: Log (poverty at international poverty line)	
	Without military expenditure	*With military expenditure*
Constant	12.4	13.8
	(3.46)	(4.31)
Log(GDP per capita)	−1.05	−1.21
	(2.33)	(3.01)
Log(education expenditure/GDP)	−1.86*	−1.69*
	(2.43)	(2.50)
Log(health expenditure/GDP)	1.84**	−1.66**
	(3.17)	(3.24)
Log(housing and amenities[a])	−0.96**	−0.77**
	(3.21)	(2.79)
Log(agriculture/GDP)	−0.43	−0.24
	(1.10)	(0.69)
Log(military expenditure/GDP)		−0.71**
		(2.16)
Observations	34	34
R^2	0.66	0.76

Sources: Public expenditure (PPE) data from IMF *Government Statistics Yearbooks* and UNESCO *Statistical Yearbooks*; poverty data from World Bank *World Development Reports*.

Notes
t-statistics in parenthesis; ** and * denote significance at the 1% and 5% level, respectively.
a Includes water and sanitation and social security.

Table 10A.2 'Poverty elasticity' of components of public expenditure: summary of findings

Components of expenditure	Methodologies			
	'Single-channel' methodologies		'Comprehensive' methodologies	
	Benefit incidence	*CGE (Uganda only)*	*Regression*	*Labour-intensity (Uganda and Ethiopia)*
Educational expenditure	+	+	+	+
Health expenditure	+	+	−	+
Agricultural expenditure			(+)	+
'Social' expenditure		+	+	+
Military expenditure			−	

Sources: For regressions see text; benefit incidence, see Sahn and Younger (2000); CGE, see Chant *et al.* (2003); labour-intensity, see Morrissey and Verschoor (2005) and Rock (2003).

Notes
+ sector indicated has a significant poverty-reducing effect through the methodology stated; (+) sector indicated has a significant negative effect on poverty through the methodology stated; − sector indicated has a significant poverty-increasing effect through the methodology stated.

Appendix 2

Table 10A.3 World Bank taxonomy of social protection options

	Cash benefits	In-kind benefits

Not targeted or targeted
  i. Means-testing
  ii. Indicator-testing
  iii. Self-targeting
	Child allowances (all); Child allowances (age cut off); Single parents; Divorced parents; Families with many children; Disabled children; Student stipends	School lunches; Student transportation; Transportation for aged; Transportation for disabled; Services for aged; Services for disabled; Student scholarships; Services for alcoholism; Services for drug abuse; Homes for the aged; Emergency programmes (war, flood, natural disaster)

Not targeted	Military families; Orphans; Unemployment assistance; Foster-parent allowances; Employer benefits; Union benefits; War veterans' benefits	Employer benefits; Union benefits; Orphanages; Programmes for national/ ethnic groups
Targeted	Assistance for elderly; Assistance for disabled; Emergency aid; One-off benefits	

Source: Adapted from Andrews and Ringold (1999).

Notes

1 The original reference is Naim (1994); there is a summary in Mosley *et al.* (1995), chapter 2.
2 The empirical characteristics of pro-poor expenditure are discussed in Appendix 1.
3 For an attempt to estimate such a model and derive principles of 'optimal conditionality', see Mosley (forthcoming), chapter 9.
4 It is almost axiomatic that the influence of a donor wishing to impose conditionality is greater in small countries. See Mosley *et al.* (1995), chapter 3, or for an extended exposition of the argument in relation to the IMF in Eastern Europe, Stone (2002).
5 Social assistance in Russia is a discretionary benefit paid at the local level and has become increasingly decentralized to the regional and municipal levels. 'With (World) Bank support the Government has been experimenting with three different targeting methodologies in three pilot oblasts including (i) proxy-means-testing; (ii) a 'categorical filter' which pre-screens applicants first on the basis of household characteristics and then applies a means-test; and (iii) a complex means-testing formula which estimates potential household earnings' (Andrews and Ringold, 1999, p. 26).
6 Two-thirds of Russians say that they have a friend who could lend them up to a week's wages if their household was short of money, and more than two-thirds know someone who would help them if they were ill (Rose *et al.*, 1996).
7 Interview, Novgorod State Fund for Support of Entrepreneurship, Veliki Novgorod, 10 September 2002.

Bibliography

Andrews, E. and Ringold, D. (1999) 'Safety nets in transition economies: toward a reform strategy', Washington, DC: World Bank Social Protection Discussion Paper 9914.

Braithwaite, J., Grootaert, C. and Milanovic, B. (1999) *Poverty and Social Assistance in Transition Countries*, New York: St. Martin's Press.

Burnside, C. and Dollar, D. (2000) 'Aid, policies, and growth', *American Economic Review*, 90: 847–868.

Chant, L., McDonald, S. and Morrissey, O. (2003) 'Aid financing of health expenditure: a CGE analysis of the effect on the poor in Uganda', mimeo, DFID Research Programme on Risk, Labour Markets and Pro-Poor Growth.

Collier, P. and Dollar, D. (2002) 'Aid allocation and poverty reduction', *European Economic Review*, 46: 1475–1500.

Cornia, G.A. (1994) 'Income distribution, poverty and welfare in transitional economies: a comparison between Eastern Europe and China', *Journal of International Development*, 6: 569–609.

Ferroni, M. and Kanbur, R. (1991) 'Poverty conscious restructuring of public expenditure' in Chhibber, A. and Fischer, S. (eds), *Economic Reform in Sub-Saharan Africa*, Washington, DC: World Bank.

Kennedy, B., Kawachi, I. and Brainerd, E. (1998) 'The role of social capital in the Russian mortality crisis', *World Development*, 26: 2029–2043.

Klugman, J. and Braithwaite, J. (1998) 'Poverty in Russia during the transition: an overview', *World Bank Research Observer*, 13: 37–58.

Knack, S. and Keefer, P. (1997) 'Does social capital have an economic payoff? A cross-country investigation', *Quarterly Journal of Economics*, 112: 1251–1288.

Morrissey, O. and Verschoor, A. (2005) 'What does ownership mean in practice? Policy learning and the evolution of pro-poor policies in Uganda', in Paloni, A. and Zanardi, M. (eds), *IMF, World Bank and Policy Reforms*, London: Routledge.

Mosley, P. (2004) 'Pro-poor politics and the new political economy of stabilisation', *New Political Economy*, 9: 271–295.

—— (forthcoming) *Risk and Underdevelopment*, Oxford: Oxford University Press.

Mosley, P. and Steel, L. (2004) 'Microfinance, the labour market and social inclusion: a tale of three cities', *Social Policy and Administration*, 38: 721–743.

Mosley, P., Harrigan, J. and Toye, J. (1995) *Aid and Power: The World Bank and Policy-Based Lending* (2nd edition), London: Routledge.

Mosley, P., Hudson, J. and Verschoor, A. (2004) 'Aid, poverty reduction, and the "new conditionality" ', *Economic Journal*, 114: 217–243.

Naim, M. (1994) 'From supplicants to shareholders: developing countries and the World Bank', in United Nations *International Monetary and Financial Issues for the 1990s*, Vol. IV, New York for UNCTAD, Geneva.

Rock, J. (2003) 'Donors, aid, policy learning and the evolution of pro-poor policies in Ethiopia', mimeo, DFID Research Programme on Risk, Labour Markets and Pro-Poor Growth, Sheffield, Nottingham, Cambridge and Open University.

Rose, R., Mischler, W. and Haerfer, C. (1996) 'Getting real: social capital in post-communist societies'. Paper presented to conference on 'The erosion of confidence in advanced democracies', Brussels, 7–9 November.

Sahn, D. and Younger, S. (2000) 'Expenditure incidence in Africa: microeconomic evidence', *Fiscal Studies*, 21: 329–347.

Stigliz, J.E. (2003) *The Roaring Nineties*, New York: W. W. Norton & Company.

Stone, R.W. (2002) *Lending Credibility: The International Monetary Fund and the post-Communist Transition*, Princeton, NJ: Princeton University Press.

United Kingdom (1999) *National Neighbourhood Strategy*, London: Her Majesty's Stationery Office.

Whiteley, P. (2000) 'Economic growth and social capital', *Political Studies*, 48: 443–466.

Wolfensohn, J. (19 April 1997) 'World Bank President: speech at House of Commons', London.

World Bank (1990) *World Development Report: Poverty*, Washington, DC: World Bank.

—— (1997) *World Development Report: States and Markets*, Washington, DC: World Bank.

—— (2002) *Annual Report*, Washington, DC: World Bank.

—— (2003a) *World Development Indicators*, Washington, DC: World Bank.

—— (2003b) *Assisting Russia's transition; An Unprecedented Challenge*, Washington, DC: World Bank Operations Evaluation Department.

Part III

Borrower ownership and the reform of conditionality

11 Conditionality and IMF flexibility

Tony Killick

11.1 Introduction

From the outset of its lending to member countries, the International Monetary Fund (IMF) has made most of its credits conditional upon the implementation by borrowing governments of specified policy measures – known in the jargon as conditionality. As a specific justification, it has pointed to the provision in its constitution – its Articles of Agreement – that Fund resources are to be made 'temporarily available... under adequate safeguards'. Two types of safeguard are sought: (a) that the borrowing member will pursue policies consistent with the Fund's objectives and (b) to bring about sufficient improvements in its balance of payments and other macroeconomic variables to enable the government to repay credits received within their designated maturity term.

But is the Fund's conditionality actually able to exert the influence on policies that was presumed by its architects? There has been only limited controversy about the principle of conditionality but much questioning about whether, in fact, this modality is effective in shaping domestic policy choices. This chapter sets out the reasons for this questioning and how the Fund has responded to it. For long, the institution was in denial; more recently it has been seeking to adapt, raising questions about its flexibility as an organization.

11.2 The growth of doubts about conditionality[1]

There was a veritable explosion in the use of policy conditionality during the 1980s and into the 1990s, as the IMF extended the range of its conditions from a fairly narrow macroeconomic focus to a much wider range of 'structural' matters, as the World Bank became increasingly involved in structural adjustment lending, and as various other multilateral and bilateral donors increased their own use of this instrument. Thus, the number of 'structural' conditions in IMF programmes escalated from an average of 2 per programme in 1987, 4 in 1994 and 14 in 1997–99 (Goldstein, 2000, p. 82). In this period of structural adjustment, it was common for governments also to undertake programmes with the World Bank and this added another thick layer of conditions, with the number of 'binding' conditions in a Bank adjustment programme averaging 33 during the 1990s, to which was added a further 10–20 'desired actions' (Koeberle, 2004, p. 13).

While there was from the beginning much controversy about the appropriateness of the design of the Bretton Woods Institutions' (BWIs') conditionality, it tended to be common ground between them and their critics that these policy stipulations were implemented, whether for good or ill. As the 1990s proceeded and experience accumulated, however, a body of research grew up which cast doubt on conditionality's efficacy.

One reason for the accumulating doubt was long-standing evidence that a high proportion of IMF programmes broke down before the end of their (relatively brief) intended currency. My own work showed even for the early-1980s between 40 and 56 per cent of Fund programmes were 'interrupted' (Killick, 1984, p. 247) and that by the early 1990s this proportion had risen to about 60 per cent (Killick, 1995, p. 61–63). More recent evidence shows little clear sign of improvement since. While a 2002 review of the performance of conditions in 24 operations found that only 10 per cent were not implemented at all, and that 65 per cent were fully implemented (Nestmann and Weder, 2002), results reported in IMF *Working Papers* suggests that programme failure remains a large and growing problem. Mussa and Savastano (1999, table 2) rate as failing programmes where actual disbursements are less than half of agreed amounts and show a rising proportion of programmes failing this test over the last two decades, after an earlier period of apparently improving outcomes. Programmes less than 50 per cent disbursed were 29 per cent during 1983–87, 33 per cent in 1988–92 and 46 per cent in 1993–97.

Ivanova *et al.* (2003, table 1) similarly show that in 1992–98 only a quarter of the programmes of Enhanced Structural Facility (ESAF) and Poverty Reduction and Growth Facility (PRGF) were *not* subject to some interruption and that nearly half (45 per cent) experienced irreversible interruptions.[2] Evidence gathered together by Dreher (2004) provides somewhat more up-to-date statistics suggesting quite the opposite of improving implementation (see Table 11.1).

A 2004 report by the Independent Evaluation Office (IEO) of the IMF evaluating progress with the Fund's Poverty Reduction and Growth Facility (PRGF) similarly suggests that the most recent years have seen little or no improvement, with virtually no change in disbursement and interruption rates, when comparing ESAF and PRGF programmes (IEO, 2004, pp. 101–102).

Another recent IEO report, on fiscal adjustment in Fund programmes, further reinforces the evidence of continuing problems. Of the programmes studied, 60 per cent under-performed and only half of intended improvements in fiscal balances were achieved. Progress in implementing fiscal reforms was limited and

Table 11.1 Programmes with poor implementation

Years	% of programmes irreversibly interrupted	% of programmes less than 75% drawn down
1995–97 (mean)	39	30
1998–2000 (mean)	46	49

in no given reform area was progress satisfactory in more than 40 per cent of cases (IEO, 2003, pp. 9, 19 and *passim*).

Similarly, the first report of the IEO, on the 'prolonged use' of Fund resources, showed that, both absolutely and proportionately, prolonged use had been on a continuously, and rather steeply, rising trend since the late 1970s, at least through to 2000 (IEO, 2002). By 2001 half of all outstanding IMF programmes were with prolonged-user countries. This evidence is again consistent with the view that Fund conditionality remains ineffectual, perhaps increasingly so.

This writer's own work and that of others listed in note 1 began to show the limited impact of BWI programmes and to raise questions about the use of conditionality as a way of achieving policy change. This was reinforced by the perceived failings of 'structural adjustment' in African and other low income countries. Countries which had received a succession of highly conditional credits were still rated by the BWIs as having weak, sometimes deteriorating, policies, with little apparent association between programmes and policy trends (Killick, 1998, pp. 35–38). Programmes were often poorly implemented, so that it was not surprising that they produced weak results, but non-compliance with the BWIs' policy stipulations appeared rarely to be punished in any effective or consistent way. When, as was often the case, a conflict of interest was perceived locally between domestic political imperatives and BWI stipulations, it was usually domestic politics that won out.

Econometric analysis from within the IMF by Ivanova *et al.* (2003) confirmed the dominance of domestic political-economy factors in determining Fund programme success, a result recently paralleled in the case of World Bank programmes by Malesa and Silarszky (2004). Ivanova *et al.* also found that neither heightened 'effort' by Fund staff nor even increased resort to preconditions ('prior actions') could substitute for favourable political-economy conditions and exerted no significant influence on the likelihood of programme implementation (see Thomas, 2002).[3] Given the dominance of local politics, it is not surprising that conditionality relating to governance issues has been found particularly ineffectual (Crawford, 1997, found that in only 2 out of 29 cases examined was donor pressure effective in inducing political change).

The use of conditionality came to be seen as in conflict with a growing consensus about the importance for effective action of local 'ownership' of chosen reforms, and as undermining the credibility, and therefore effectiveness, of the measures undertaken. Governments had learned that probably no more than temporary inconvenience would be visited upon them as a result of failures to implement 'agreed' conditions (amply justified, in the case of the Fund, by research showing little association between past compliance and future credits – Bird, 2002; Dreher, 2003). The BWIs (and other donors) had strong institutional imperatives to 'keep the money moving', not in the least a desire to protect the servicing of past credits, and these were often reinforced by staff incentives within these institutions. There were often strong external pressures on the Fund to pretend that errant governments were on track, because the Fund's 'seal of approval' was formally necessary for aid and/or debt relief to be provided

(IEO, 2002, p. 110). By providing the appearance, but not the reality, of safeguarding against poor policy performance, over-reliance on conditionality was blamed for major misallocations and waste of public monies (Killick, 1998, p. 168). Far better, critics argued, would be greater insistence on local ownership and more selectivity in the choice of governments to be supported.

One important line of defence should be recorded. It is undoubtedly the case that since the early 1990s, if not before, attitudes to macroeconomic and 'structural' policies have changed quite markedly, and in directions reflected in the conditionality of the BWIs. It is unquestionable that most developing-country governments today place greater weight on the maintenance of macro stability – and on the fiscal discipline that entails – than was the case in earlier decades. They are also more likely to pursue policies which rely less on state interventions and more on working through the disciplines of the market. Proponents of conditionality argue that this would not have happened without the influence of the policy stipulations of the Fund and Bank, and the demonstration effect of improved economic results when these stipulations were implemented.

There is clearly some truth in this defence, even though it is impossible to know how much weight should be attached to it. Attitudes to policy in developing countries have responded to a range of influences. The neo-liberal demonstration effects of the Thatcher and Reagan years in the UK and USA, and of the Pinochet regime in Chile, were surely important, and underlying these were major developments in the understanding of economists.[4] Such changes were often reinforced by the passage of time, with new generations of policy analysts, well acquainted with the changing trends in thinking about economic policy, returning to their home countries and beginning to occupy positions of influence. And, quite apart from their conditionality, there was the intellectual influence of the dominant volume of research and advice coming out of the BWIs. The conditionality made a contribution too, although critics would argue that the confrontational nature of conditionality-based negotiations are not an optimal way of winning friends and influencing people.

11.3   Institutional responses

How did the BWIs stand in relation to the emerging critique of conditionality? World Bank staff actually contributed quite strongly to it. Thus, one Bank report (1995, p. 1) stated that, 'adjustment lending has mostly promoted good policies, but got weak program results.' An important Bank study on Africa concluded flatly that 'Conditionality as an instrument to promote reform has been a failure' (Devarajan *et al.*, 2001). Another Bank report (1998) concluded that conditionality had been ineffectual where reform lacked political support and had been counterproductive in some cases. More examples could be cited but the point is that the Bank appeared to acknowledge as valid the critique of conditionality and to share it.

By contrast, the Fund has for the most part remained in denial. However, there have been recent signs of change. A staff paper on conditionality policy issues (IMF, 2001a, p. 55) asserted the position, apparently with approval, that the primary role of BWIs 'is to identify reformers, not to create them' and that 'IFIs should have no illusions that their conditionality will appreciably affect the probability of reform.' Indeed, the Fund's own Executive Board is on record as stating that 'Conditionality cannot compensate for a lack of programme ownership'. More recently, the head of the Fund's powerful Policy Development and Review Department stated in public that the evidence was now 'overwhelming' that conditionality is not an effective means of achieving policy change.[5]

It is reasonable, then, to expect a fairly strong movement away from reliance on conditionality by both BWIs. For the most part, this has not occurred. Some bilateral donors, notably the UK and EU, have been trying to diminish such reliance, moving instead to greater selectivity and to relationships with recipient governments based more on dialogue, ownership and partnership. There are voices within the Bank urging movement in the same directions, particularly in connection with its new Poverty Reduction Support Credit (PRSC) facility. It is also the case that, following a sharp rise in the number of conditions per Bank programme during the later 1980s, there was a decline in the average number of conditions in the latter half of the 1990s (World Bank, 2001, p. 80), although it is unclear what was driving this.

What of the Fund? Perhaps it is quietly getting on with transforming the way it does business? Well, indeed, things are happening, in the form of a substantial 'streamlining' exercise. Introduced in 2000, this aims to reverse the proliferation which occurred in the 1990s and to focus the remaining policy stipulations more on actions regarded as critical to programme success and within the Fund's own core areas of expertise. Revised staff guidelines describe the streamlining programme as based on five interrelated principles (IMF, 2002):

- domestic *ownership* of programmes
- *parsimony* in the application of conditionality
- the *tailoring* of programmes to individual country circumstances
- *coordination* with other multilateral institutions (notably the World Bank)
- *clarity* in the specification of conditions.

To what extent the streamlining exercise should be seen as a response to the weaknesses of conditionality is not clear however. It was initially sold to a somewhat reluctant Executive Board as a rather narrowly conceived *efficiency* measure. This was reflected in the Fund's *Annual Report* for 2001 (IMF, 2001b, p. 45): 'the main goal of streamlining was to make conditionality more efficient, effective and focussed...' The emphasis on using it to strengthen country ownership came later, but by 2003 the *Annual Report* was justifying streamlining because 'Excessively detailed policy conditions can undermine a country's sense that it is in charge of its own reforms' (p. 35).

Whatever the motivation, the evidence indicates that this exercise has indeed resulted in an appreciable decline in the average number of structural conditions in poor (but not in middle-income) countries, although with the extent of this varying greatly from country to country. The IEO (2004, tables 4–6) records a statistically significant reduction in the mean number of 'structural' performance criteria as between ESAF and PRGF programmes – from 4.0 to 2.7 (see also Adam and Bevan, 2001; Killick, 2002; Eurodad, 2003; Thomas and van der Willigen, 2004). However, more up-to-date evidence is awaited and there have been hints from within the Fund that implementation of streamlining has run into problems.

Closely related to the streamlining initiative was the adoption by the Fund in 2002 of new staff guidelines on the application of conditionality (IMF, 2002). These too have been presented as intended to enhance countries' programme ownership, as well as to reinforce the other aspects of streamlining. For example, it seeks to address one of the most strongly negative aspects of the Fund's traditional procedures, that is, of negotiating missions arriving in-country with a ready-completed draft 'Letter of Intent' which a borrowing government must formally write to the IMF requesting assistance and setting out a programme of measures to correct existing balance of payments and other macroeconomic imbalances. The guidelines break new ground by specifying that, 'documents setting out a country's reform agenda will be drafted by the [domestic] authorities with the cooperation and assistance of the Fund staff' (IMF, 2003, p. 36). However, note the immediately following sentence: 'The Board agreed during the course of its review that properly designed conditionality can complement and reinforce national ownership.' How it might achieve this reinforcement is not explained.

The Fund has taken some other measures to reduce the tensions between its traditional ways of doing business and the admitted importance of country ownership (Boughton, 2003, pp. 9–11). It says it wishes to reduce recourse to prior actions (that aspect of conditionality hardest of all to reconcile with the principle of country ownership), although the latest evidence suggests that little reduction has actually been achieved.[6] There have been some moves in staff training to sensitize them more to local political conditions and constraints. There are the first stirrings of a move to increase the presently very limited authority of local IMF resident representatives. And 'the Fund is experimenting with a general injunction to the staff to *encourage* countries to engage in public discussions' before finalizing programmes (italics in original).

The changes just outlined are significant positive moves but whether they represent an adequate institutional response to the now admitted failings of conditionality is questionable. The most recent IEO report (2004, p. 103) emphasizes the need for far-reaching changes in the way the IMF does business in low-income countries and the absence so far of any clear guidance from its Board and management about what the switch to an approach centred around PRSPs should mean for the role of the Fund and its staff. We should remember, too, that the streamlining exercise is confined exclusively to what the Fund classifies as 'structural' conditionality, with no comparable change in its traditional macroeconomic stipulations. It is, in other words, a fairly limited exercise and once we lift our eyes from the purely quantitative aspect, it is by no means clear that it marks any real move away from reliance on conditionality per se.

One reason for doubting whether streamlining is likely to make a large impact is that, rather surprisingly, there is little evidence that the quantity of conditionality has much influence on programme outcomes, raising questions about the likely impact of streamlining on programme effectiveness. Galbis (2001, p. 176) cites Fund evidence showing the rate of programme implementation to be constant with respect to the number of conditions. Ivanova *et al.* (2003) do find outcomes to be inversely and significantly affected by the number of conditions per programme year but, overall, find this and other variables under the Fund's control to be dominated by in-country political-economy variables. Dreher and Vaubel (2004) show that the number of conditions does not affect changes in policy instruments. Evidence from the Bank is similar. Two studies (Dollar and Svensson, 2000, table 3; Malesa and Silarszky, 2004, p. 12) find the number of conditions in Bank adjustment programmes have no significant influence; another investigation (World Bank, 2001, p. 80) finds an *inverse* relationship between the number of conditions and programme outcomes but points out that the causality could run either way, with a tendency for weakly performing countries to receive more intensive conditionality.

Such evidence cautions against expecting streamlining to make any large difference to programme effectiveness. It may still increase national governments' room for policy manoeuvre, but will it? As the Fund acknowledges, implicit in its desire to transfer ownership to borrowing governments is a model, 'in which, beyond the standard that members' policies must meet...there is a "policy space" in which members' choices would not affect the Fund's willingness to support the program' (Thomas and van der Willigen, 2004, p. 4). There is as yet little systematic evidence on whether borrower-governments are being given more policy space, although the IEO evaluation of PRGF programmes does find that 'program design under the PRGF has incorporated greater fiscal flexibility to accommodate aid flows, and there is no evidence of generalized "aid pessimism" or a systematic disinflation bias' (IEO, 2004, p. 9).

In short, while the Fund's tectonic plates have begun to move, these have not yet shifted far. The earthquake has yet to occur. Inevitably, its staff is divided, between reformers and conservatives, with a similar lack of consensus on its Board. Perhaps to a unique extent in the history of the Fund – traditionally a top-down, highly disciplined organization – there has been real resistance to execution of Management policies, leading to uneven execution of intended reforms. Much is likely to depend on the views and leadership qualities of Managing Director Rodrigo Rato, who took office in June 2004.

11.4   The larger picture

A relatively new element in the wider situation, with potential for reduced reliance on conditionality, is the initiation of Poverty Reduction Strategy Papers (PRSPs) as a focus around which the BWIs and bilateral donors are intended to harmonize their assistance (and also their debt relief under the 'enhanced HIPC' scheme). In principle, PRSPs can be viewed as an attempt to get away from old ways of doing business and to substitute these by broad-based, locally owned strategies, in which policy commitments are self-defined by the responsible governments, subject only to 'endorsement' by the BWI Boards.

There is real potential here but it is by no means clear that the move into PRSPs has actually marked a retreat from BWI-defined policy conditions. HIPC governments now have to concern themselves with further conditionality arising from the World Bank's Country Assistance Strategy papers, as well as that specific to the HIPC completion-point arrangements,[7] to say nothing of the stipulations of the Fund and other multilateral and bilateral donors. HIPC conditionality alone is potentially both onerous and wide-ranging, with its content recently summarized as normally centred around macroeconomic issues, structural reforms, social sectors and 'other poverty reduction requirements', especially governance and budget management issues (SPA, 2001, p. 9). Not much is left out there! There are also reports of bilateral donors picking up structural conditions being dropped by the Fund as a result of streamlining (Debt Relief International, n.d., para 13) and of the Fund actually increasing its stipulations for actions in the governance area.

At least for HIPC countries, it seems that governments today are probably confronted by a wider range of policy stipulations than they were two or three years ago. Freedom of action should also be judged according to the importance of the various areas of policy action. Since IMF streamlining is about ensuring that conditionality is focussed on the most critical policy areas, and with both BWIs tending to cut back most heavily in the grey area of second-order benchmarks (non-binding conditionality), here too governments may well be in a more constrained situation, rather than an improved one. It is likely that the E-HIPC/PRSP arrangements have provided a vehicle for further increasing conditionality, despite all the rhetoric of ownership. There is an institutional gap here, for no one agency is responsible for maintaining an overview of the aggregation of conditions being required of a government, not to mention the internal consistency of these. Nor, indeed, is the data generated which would readily permit such an overview.

Two other considerations rather reinforce the view that conditionality continues to abound. One is the prospect that the more important structural conditions dropped as a result of Fund streamlining will be taken up in Bank credits. According to a Fund staff report on initial experiences with streamlining (IMF, 2001c, pp. 17, 34), the Bank is 'strengthening' its conditionality in areas, such as privatization, health system reform and public sector reform, from which the Fund is scaling back. In a number of cases, the report states, 'measures no longer covered by Fund conditionality were incorporated as conditions by the Bank, but in others this was not the case.' The Fund's Board seems clear that such 'strengthening' by the Bank is desirable: 'Effective collaboration with the World Bank is ... needed to ensure that important measures are adequately covered as the IMF applies conditionality more sparingly outside its core areas' (IMF, 2003, p. 37). The Board will therefore be reassured by a finding by Eurodad (2003) that, 'World Bank involvement in the areas where the IMF pulls out is seen as a prerequisite for streamlining and the findings of this paper suggest that indeed the World Bank is taking over conditions left by the IMF in an aggressive manner.' The 2004 IEO report on the PRGF tried to take a view on what had been happening to aggregate Fund–Bank conditionality but was unable to form a firm judgement.

A related consideration concerns the extent of cross-conditionality between the two BWIs. The 2002 IMF conditionality guidelines assert that 'There will be no cross-conditionality' but the reality is more complicated. The formal position has been set out in a joint IMF–World Bank paper in the following rather elaborate statement which is worth reproducing at length:

> Each institution remains separately accountable for its lending decisions, and any conditionality that is critical for the success of one institution's program would continue to be specified in that institution's own arrangement. That said, the Bank would normally regard the presence of an on-track PRGF as adequate evidence that the macroeconomic framework is appropriate, and the Fund would normally regard the presence of an on-track PRSC as adequate evidence that the social and structural program is appropriate. When a PRSC is under consideration or performance under a PRSC is being reviewed without a companion PRGF in place, Bank staff will ascertain, before formulating their own assessment, whether Fund staff have any major outstanding concerns about the adequacy of the country's macroeconomic policies. Fund staff will communicate any such concerns to the Bank in time to be reflected in Bank reporting to its Board. Similarly, when a PRGF is under consideration or performance under a PRGF is under review without a companion PRSC, Fund staff, before formulating their own assessment, will consult with Bank staff to ascertain whether the Bank has major outstanding concerns about the adequacy of the country's poverty reduction strategy, the social impacts of the macroeconomic policies supported by the PRGF, or the country's performance in meeting structural and social conditions in the areas of competence of the Bank. Bank staff will communicate any such concerns to the Fund in time to be reflected in Fund reporting to its Board....
>
> (IMF–World Bank, 2001, p. 26)

The reality is that there has long been a de facto cross-conditionality from Fund to Bank adjustment programmes. Now, under the arrangements between the Bank and Fund concerning their PRGF and PRSC programmes, the extent of this has been increased at the level of broad performance, although the Boards of both institutions state that cross-conditionality should *not* be applied to policy specifics within either programme, with each institution 'separately accountable for its lending decisions...' (ibid.).

In summary, what the above reveals is a major disjuncture between a rather wide perception that conditionality is a flawed instrument and continuing reliance on this instrument by the IMF and its sister BWI.

11.5   Conclusion

The conclusion which suggests itself here, then, is that the politics of Fund (and Bank) governance, as well as internal resistances, have led to a large apparent gap between what the balance of evidence tells us about the efficacy of conditionality as a way of securing desired policies and the continuing policies and practices of these two institutions. Neither organization has proved sufficiently adaptable, and this is particularly true of the Fund. A large part of the problem here is that any major attempt by the Fund's management to move away from the use of conditionality – even supposing it wished to – would be strongly resisted by influential members of its Board. Some representatives of major shareholder countries remain unconvinced by, or unaware of, the evidence, or unpersuaded that any alternative would produce superior results.

It is worth repeating an implication of this: that if indeed conditionality often does not provide an assurance of improved recipient policies – the substitute for borrower collateral – then continuing to use it as if it did is a recipe for a waste of large amounts of scarce public resources. This effect is compounded by the tendency for bilateral donors to piggy-back on the conditionality of the Fund and Bank. Just think of all the 'structural adjustment' credits and grants which they provided during the 1980s and 1990s to governments in Africa and elsewhere which had no serious commitment to policy reform. Lessons have been learned, of course, but we still seem to be stuck with one of the principal instruments which led to this waste.

To be fair, the evidential base on the more recent record with conditionality is too mixed and incomplete to permit a firm judgement on whether the earlier-identified weaknesses have been reduced and whether further action is necessary. Some of the many questions that remain unresolved include:

- Given new developments, such as the HIPC-II initiative, the increased use of PRSPs and the IMF's streamlining exercise, what is the overall trend in the totality of policy conditionality? Do governments today have greater effective room for manoeuvre in the determination of policies?
- Have there been decisive changes in management policies towards the role of Fund representative and other staff members, including the institutional incentives which give priority to new lending over the implementation of past programmes? To what extent have actual in-country negotiation styles and the modalities of the Fund and Bank changed in order to foster improved relationships and greater borrower ownership? To what extent will the Fund management respond to the urgings of the most recent IEO (2004, p. 103 and passim) report for major changes in the role and modalities of the Fund in low-income countries and to what extent will any intended changes be executed by its staff?
- Is there evidence of more effective sanctions against non-compliance with conditionality (other than that which arises from shocks), and of the application of greater selectivity in the choice of governments supported? Has the HIPC initiative made any difference in this respect, by reducing pressures for defensive lending?

In the meantime, we appear fated to continue the present unsatisfactory mismatch between what available evidence tells us and continuing reliance by the IMF and others on a modality of proven impotence.

Notes

1　The following borrows quite heavily from my own work on conditionality (Killick *et al.*, 1998) but see also Collier *et al.*, 1997; Crawford, 1997; Dollar and Svensson, 2000; Mosley *et al.*, 1995.

2　They also show an apparently more satisfactory 73 per cent compliance with programme conditions but this figure is hard to interpret because the authors regard this figure as biased upward. For a useful very brief review of other evidence on programme effects see IMF (2001a, pp. 45–46). See also Bird, 2002, for corroboration of declining IMF programme completion rates.

3 Interestingly, Malesa and Silarszky (2004, p. 11) found (in the case of Bank programmes) that the time devoted by the Bank to programme supervision was negatively associated with programme success, the effort its staff devoted to programme preparation was positively associated with success. This could be interpreted as supporting the dominant influence of ownership factors, with preparation efforts related to the time devoted to policy dialogue and persuasion with the domestic government and with the need for supervision arising from lack of local ownership.

4 I tried to capture these influences in a monograph on changing attitudes to the role of the state in Killick (1989).

5 Statement by Mark Allen at World Bank forum on 'Conditionality Revisited', Paris, 5 July 2004.

6 See IEO (2004, tables 4–6) which shows a non-significant reduction from a mean of 4.8 prior actions in ESAF programmes to 4.5 in PRGFs.

7 For example, at a Commonweath Secretariat–IMF consulatation in July 2001, the Tanzanian delegate reported that his government was confronted with no less than 13 specific HIPC completion point conditions, over and above those of BWIs.

Bibliography

Adam, C.S. and Bevan, D.L. (2001) 'Fiscal policy design in low-income countries', WIDER Discussion Paper 2001/67, Helsinki.

Bird, G. (2002) 'The completion rate of IMF programmes: what we know, don't know and need to know', *World Economy*, 25: 833–847.

Boughton, J.M. (2003) 'Who's in charge? Ownership and conditionality in IMF-supported programs', IMF Working Paper 03/191.

Collier, P., Guillaumont, P., Guillaumont, S. and Gunning, J.W. (1997) 'Redesigning conditionality', *World Development*, 25: 1399–1407.

Crawford, G. (1997) 'Foreign aid and political conditionality: issues of effectiveness and consistency', *Democratization*, 4: 69–108.

Debt Relief International (n.d.) 'Reviewing PRSPs: the views of HIPC ministers and PRSP co-ordinators', London: DRI (processed).

Devarajan, S., Dollar, D. and Holmgren, T. (2001) 'Aid and reform in Africa', Washington, DC: World Bank.

Dollar, D. and Svensson, J. (2000) 'What explains the success or failure of structural adjustment programmes?', *Economic Journal*, 110: 894–917.

Dreher, A. (2003) 'The influence of elections on IMF programme interruptions', *Journal of Development Studies*, 39: 101–120.

—— (2004) 'Does the IMF influence fiscal and monetary policy?', Exeter: University of Exeter, processed.

Dreher, A. and Vaubel, R. (2004) 'The causes and consequences of IMF conditionality', *Emerging Markets Finance and Trade*, 40: 26–54.

European Network on Debt and Development (Eurodad) (2003) 'User guide to the PRGF matrix', May.

Galbis, V. (2001) 'Comment' in IMF 'External comments and contributions on IMF conditionality', Washington, DC: IMF, processed.

Goldstein, M. (2000) 'IMF structural conditionality: how much is too much?', Washington, DC: Institute for International Economics, processed.

IMF–World Bank (joint) (2001) 'Strengthening IMF–World Bank Collaboration on Country Programs and Conditionality', Washington, DC: IMF–World Bank, processed.

Independent Evaluation Office of the IMF (2002) *Evaluation of Prolonged Use of IMF Facilities*, Washington, DC: IMF.
—— (2003) *Fiscal Adjustment in IMF-Supported Programs*, Washington, DC: IMF.
—— (2004) *Report on the Evaluation of Poverty Reduction Strategy Papers and the Poverty Reduction and Growth Facility*, Washington, DC: IMF.
International Monetary Fund (2001a) 'Conditionality in Fund-supported programs: Policy issues', Washington, DC: IMF, processed.
—— (2001b) *Annual Report 2001*, Washington, DC: IMF.
—— (2001c) 'Streamlining structural conditionality – review of initial experience', Washington, DC: IMF, processed.
—— (2002) 'IMF conditionality guidelines', Washington, DC: IMF, processed.
—— (2003) *Annual Report 2003*, Washington, DC: IMF.
Ivanova, A., Mayer, W., Mourmouras, A. and Anayiotos, G. (2003) 'What determines the implementation of Fund-supported programs?', IMF Working Paper 03/08.
Killick, T. (ed.) (1984) *The Quest for Economic Stabilisation: The IMF and the Third World*, London: ODI and Gower Press.
—— (1989) *A Reaction Too Far: Economic Theory and the Role of the State in Developing Countries*, London: ODI.
—— (1995) *IMF Programmes in Developing Countries: Design and Impact*, London: Routledge.
—— (1998) *Aid and the Political Economy of Policy Change*, London: Routledge and ODI.
—— (2002) 'The "streamlining" of IMF conditionality: aspirations, reality and repercussions', Report for Department for International Development, London, processed.
Koeberle, S. (2004) 'Conditionality – under what conditions?', Paper prepared for World Bank forum on 'Conditionality revisited', Paris.
Malesa, T. and Silarszky, P. (2004) 'Does World Bank effort matter for success of adjustment operations?', Paper prepared for World Bank forum on 'Conditionality revisited', Paris.
Mosley, P., Harrigan, J. and Toye, J. (1995) *Aid and Power: The World Bank and Policy-based Lending*, Volume 1, London: Routledge, second edition.
Mussa, M. and Savastano, M. (1999) 'The IMF approach to economic stabilization.' IMF Working Paper, WP/99/104.
Nestmann, T. and Weder, B. (2002) 'The effectiveness of international aid and debt relief: a selective review of the literature', Paper prepared for the 5th Limburg seminar on financing and development, processed.
Special Program of Assistance (SPA) Task team on contractual relationships and selectivity (2001) 'Comparative review of I-PRSP targets and conditionalities for HIPC Completion Point', Brussels: European Commission (DEV/B/2/FCS D), processed.
Thomas, A. (2002) 'Do prior actions achieve their objectives? An evaluation based on active programs over the 1992–99 period', Washington, DC: draft unpublished IMF Working Paper.
Thomas, A. and van der Willigen, T. (2004) 'Fund conditionality – a provisional up-date', Paper prepared for World Bank forum on 'Conditionality revisited', Paris.
World Bank (1995) 'Higher impact adjustment lending', Report of a Working Group to SPA Plenary. Washington, DC: World Bank.
—— (1998) *Assessing Aid: What Works, What Doesn't and Why*, Washington, DC: World Bank.
—— (2001) *Adjustment Lending Retrospective: Final Report*, Washington, DC: World Bank, Operations Policy and Country Services Department.

12 Conditionality, development assistance and poverty

Reforming the PRS process

John Weeks

12.1 Introduction

Until the late 1990s, the policy conditionalities associated with the grants and loans offered by development agencies to recipient governments were treated as technical in nature, and typically associated with the fiction that they were mutually agreed between the funder and the recipient. This approach of treating policy conditionalities as technical issues to be decided between external agencies and governments with little or no consultation or participation by the public took its most extreme form in the so-called Washington Consensus approach to debt repayment.

This top-down and non-participatory character of IMF and World Bank conditionality in the 1980s and 1990s prompted Ravi Kanbur (formerly chief economist for the African region of the World Bank) to conclude, 'in the 1980s, and to a certain extent well into the 1990s, many [Washington institutions] saw the main task as ... storming the citadel of statist development strategies', so that 'the negotiators from Washington always took a more purist stance, a more extreme stance than even their own intellectual framework permitted' (Kanbur, 1999).

From the stand point of the twenty-first century, perhaps the most striking aspect of conditionalities was this uncritical application of the principle of 'donorship', which can be defined as a relationship between funders and recipient governments in which basic development strategy is driven by or heavily influenced by the priorities and ideologies of the former. In the wake of the Copenhagen Social Summit in 1995, bilateral and multilateral agencies providing development assistance committed themselves to a new approach, to 'partnerships' between the governments of developed and developing countries, based on a process of policy formulation that would be 'country-led' and 'nationally-owned', including 'broad participation by civil society' (Malloch Brown, 2002). The partnerships would achieve a set of internationally agreed human development targets, called the Millennium Development Goals (MDGs). The major instrument for implementing this new approach to assistance became the Poverty Reduction Strategy (PRS) process and its associated planning document, the Poverty Reduction Strategy Paper (PRSP), a stated goal of which was to achieve 'national ownership' of development policy (World Bank, 2002).

12.2   National ownership and development strategies

It is one thing to state a radical turn in policy and another to implement it in practice. Immediately the PRS process came under critical attack for a wide range of alleged failings. Foremost among these were that it: (1) lacked meaningful participation by civil society; (2) in practice represented the familiar macro stabilization and adjustment programmes with poverty as an 'add-on'; (3) far from fostering ownership it represented a funder-dictated document written for no reason but to access loans and grants and (4) it in effect represented a 'super-conditionality' upon which all development assistance would be dependent.

Central to all these criticisms is the issue of whether funder conditionality is consistent with the core goal of the new approach to development assistance, national ownership. To put the question bluntly, can a government's development strategy be nationally owned and country driven if it is constrained by conditions laid down by funders? The essence of this question is sharpened by distinguishing between the terms 'nationally owned' and 'country driven', by use of an analogy. A person can purchase a suit of clothes off the rack in a department store, and, having paid for it, is the owner. Alternatively, he or she can engage a tailor and chose the detailed design of the final product. Similarly, a government can be offered funding on conditions, some of which are non-negotiable or only marginally so. After weighting the costs and benefits of the offer, the government may chose to accept the conditionalities, and even consult its population about the need to do so. The resulting development strategy could be said to be nationally owned, but not country driven.

The importance of this distinction can be demonstrated concretely by examples. The Zambian government produced a PRS document written by the government with contributions from civil society, but this was after the World Bank had refused to accept the government's pre-PRS poverty reduction programme (Chisala, 2002). In contrast to this, the government of Vietnam produced a PRS document, called the Comprehensive Poverty Reduction and Growth Strategy Paper, almost entirely based on existing planning documents, and this was accepted enthusiastically by the World Bank (see Pincus and Thang, 2004, chapter 2; Weeks *et al.*, 2004b, chapter 3). In the first case, the 'home-grown' document was judged unsatisfactory by the World Bank, even as a basis for a PRSP (though it had been reviewed by the national parliament), and an entirely new process was initiated. The resulting document was nationally owned in a narrow sense, but certainly not country-driven, and produced purely to access funding. In Vietnam, the World Bank and other funding agencies in effect accepted an amended version of the government's ten year Socio-Economic Development Strategy, which had passed through a consultation process within the ruling party and approved by a national party congress. It is unfortunately the case that the Zambian experience has been the more typical.[1]

The operational effect of initiating a specifically constructed PRS process as opposed to the World Bank accepting an existing national institutional framework is reflected in the resultant documents. In most cases, the latter resulted in comprehensive development strategies, while the former produced orthodox macroeconomic frameworks with a poverty focus incorporating extant World Bank and IMF conditionalities (UNDP-EO, 2003; Weeks *et al.*, 2004a).

The central role of policy conditionalities in PRSP raises the question of whether despite rhetoric the PRS process represented no substantive change in the behaviour of the Bretton Woods institutions, as some have argued (Levinsohn, 2003), or if it is possible to reconcile conditionality and country-driven national ownership of development policies. To answer this question, one must consider the nature of conditionalities themselves.

12.3   Conditionalities, donorship and ownership

The analysis of conditionalities begins with the recognition of two basic facts: (1) to the extent that the funding agency and the recipient government establish a cooperative partnership, it is an unequal one in which the former has a far stronger bargaining position than the latter except in rare circumstances[2] and (2) no grants would be offered or loans extended without conditionalities of some type.

In the era of unabashed donorship, the stronger bargaining position of the assisting agencies gave rise to an omniscient external judgementalism. The combination of conditionalities and judgementalism was particularly pernicious, with the latter justifying the former. The funding agency reserved the right to pass unilateral judgement on the appropriateness of and commitment to recipient government policies. By contrast, in a national ownership regime, assessment of policies should pass to the recipient government, in consultation with the funder.[3]

A central characteristic of donorship was the presumption that if development assistance failed by whatever criteria, the blame lay with the recipient government. This approach can be seen in a recent document from the Overseas Development Institute, which repeats a view commonly found in funder documents: '[recipient] governments need to be convinced of the need for sound policies, rather than coerced' (Foster, 2000, p. 7). This type of comment is often accompanied by invoking the need for the recipient government to show 'political will'. While this statement may seem bland and non-controversial, it is firmly in the donorship tradition. Not withstanding the qualifier, 'rather than coerced', the statement makes a number of presumptions that are the ideological basis of conditional finance:

1   that there exist a set of sound policies which the funders know and recipient governments do not (the recipient is ignorant);
2   that recipient governments must not only be informed of the sound policies of which they are ignorant, but require convincing of the need to implement these (in the absence of funder advocacy, the recipient lacks the judgement to distinguish good policies from bad ones);
3   in the past development failures arose from the mistakes of omission or commission of recipient governments, not in whole nor in part the result of unsound policies of the funders (development failures are recipient government failures).

A variation on the sound policies criticism is that recipient governments may be aware of the policies, and aware of the need for them, but fail to implement them because of special interests within or outside of the government. In such circumstances, the argument goes, funding agencies are justified in their criticism of policy choices, and the criticism may strengthen domestic supporters of sound policies. This justification for conditionalities, that they serve a good political end, implicitly maintains that institutional, political and economic interests do not motivate funders; that is, that policies advocated by funding agencies are never self-serving.

Recognizing that the language of donorship no longer can serve as the explicit justification of conditionalities, the IMF and the World Bank sought in the late 1990s to redefine the purpose and rationale for dictating policy parameters. An attempt to grapple with apparently inconsistent principles can be found in a working paper by Branson and Hanna, 'Ownership and Conditionality'. The authors begin with a statement that follows the language of ownership:

> We propose a broader view of conditionality as an evolving process in support of a policy compact based on mutual commitment. The Bank and its partners would act as enabling agencies to support the country's motivation for reform, leaving significant room for the country to determine the means and timing of reform according to political economy considerations and genuine local learning.
>
> (2000, p. 1)

While vague, this general view of conditionality suggests a substantial change in practice, from the World Bank specifying policy changes, to supporting policies of recipient governments. However, this does not directly address the central question, whether are conditionalities justified. This question is addressed, if not answered, by the following statement of principle:

> Effective conditionality is an instrument of mutual accountability. Rather than imposing a position on the borrower, the Bank and its partners commit themselves to lend under certain jointly determined conditions.
>
> (Ibid., p. 3)

The difficulty with viewing conditionality as involving 'mutual accountability' is that if this accountability is achieved through '*jointly* determined conditions' it is not obvious why one of the 'partners' (the World Bank) should impose conditions while the other (the recipient government) does not. This is not a matter of word play, but quite practical: the conditions imposed by the World Bank provide a basis for a unilateral suspension of the loan programme, and the borrower has no equivalent power over the lender. The authors assert that '[t]his view of conditionality is consistent with the concept of ownership by and partnership with borrowers', because:

> External assistance agencies commit themselves through conditionality, while the borrowing government commits itself through ownership of programs it has designed in consultation with internal and external partners. In this sense, conditionality can be seen as a policy compact or mutual accountability to poverty reduction and policy reform.
>
> (Ibid.)

This statement involves a rather strange use of language. It would seem obvious that the World Bank commits itself through making the loan, not by setting conditions to a loan. And, if the policies in question are nationally owned and country driven, they do not represent a commitment to the World Bank, but to the government's domestic constituencies. Thus, while Branson and Hanna make a number of points that would moderate the donorship approach to lending,[4] they do not resolve the basic issue of the consistency between conditionality and national ownership.

An IMF working paper sought to deal with the same issue and reached the simple conclusion that 'full conditionality' and ownership are incompatible, but varying degrees of ownership can be achieved within a framework of conditionality.[5] As part of the same argument, the authors reversed the common sense view of the balance of bargaining power, to maintain that the IMF faced a disadvantage when extending loans. It is instructive to quote the paper at some length:

> Between every lender and borrower there is always a fundamental asymmetry in information availability. The borrower always knows more about his own abilities, opportunities, and intentions than the lender. This information asymmetry gives rise to two incentive problems: adverse selection and moral hazard. Adverse selection arises before the transaction takes place, and stems from the fact that information deficiencies make it difficult to distinguish good from bad risks. Moral hazard arises after the lender has given the funds to the borrower. Having obtained the funds, it may be in the borrower's interest to take risks that may raise returns but also increase the likelihood of default.
>
> (Khan and Sharma, 2001, pp. 4–5)

This argument, that conditionality results from the borrower having better information than the lender, has four rather serious problems. First, since governments must give IMF mission teams access to whatever macroeconomic information that the teams request, the assertion has at best a weak foundation. It could be argued that if the IMF professionals do a competent job, their knowledge of the country's economic prospects will match that of government officials. Second, it is not clear that the IMF can maintain, on the one hand, that it is a source of great economic expertise, and, on the other, that it is at an asymmetrical information disadvantage. Third, the desire to minimize risks even though they 'may raise returns' seems inappropriate for an organization whose charter calls for fostering growth. One would think that a public, non-profit institution would do exactly this, support more risky programmes that foster the public good than a private bank would. Fourth, and most serious for the public image of the IMF, the asymmetrical information argument implies that the principle purpose of the conditionalities is to ensure loan servicing, not correct economic imbalances. In the event, the authors make this explicit:

> IMF conditionality can be viewed as a complex covenant written into the loan agreement. The policy prescriptions contained in IMF-supported programs *essentially* serve to provide the safeguards that the country will be able to rectify its macroeconomic and structural imbalances, and will be in a position to service and repay the loan.
>
> (Ibid., p. 6, emphasis added)

If this position were officially endorsed by the IMF board, it would confirm the criticism of the institution made by many critics; namely, that it operates *essentially* in its own self-interest. The statement suggests that 'rectifying macro-economic and structural imbalances' is contingent on ensuring repayment. Thus, it is not surprising that this working paper's approach to conditionality was not officially endorsed as IMF policy.

In any case, the view of ownership and conditionality of the paper does not capture some of the important aspects of either conditionality or ownership. We propose an alternative analytical framework that considers conditionality in terms of its motivation, purpose and potential for causing conflict between partners.

The analysis begins with the generalization that conditions on granting assistance cannot be eliminated, but they can be addressed in a transparent manner consistent with a more equal partner dialogue that enhances recipient ownership.

Transparency can be enhanced by organizing conditions into four analytical categories: (1) legally binding requirements on a funder, arising from its relationship to its government or governing body; (2) those derivative from values that should be the basis of assistance, which include the recipient's commitment to a poverty-focused development strategy; (3) those that are technical in nature and (4) those motivated by the funder's desire to modify the behaviour of the recipient government with respect to political, social and economic development (see Table 12.1).

All development assistance agencies, bilateral and multilateral, are legally and politically responsible to constituencies. Category one conditionalities are required in order for funders to conform to the requirements set by those constituencies (see UNCTAD, 2000, p. 198), and represent the 'core conditionality' for its development funding. These are the conditions arising from the legal framework and system of government oversight in which a funding agency operates, which require accounting transparency, demonstration of effectiveness of expenditure, financial risk management and adherence to the statutory mission of the agency. These set the basic legal and operational framework for any development

Table 12.1 Categories of conditionality

Category	Funder motivation	Commentary
1 Legal obligations and shared values (Core conditionality)	These conditions derive from legal requirements set by funding agencies (e.g. financial accounting)	Non-negotiable except in detail. Consistent with national ownership
2 Shared values and commitment (Core conditionality)	Need to conform to values of the funding agency's constituencies (e.g. protection of basic human rights, commitment to poverty reduction)	Negotiable within the bilateral dialogue, but cannot be suspended. Consistent with national ownership. (Can overlap with category 4.)
3 Technically based	Projects and programmes must be consistent with generally accepted scientific and technical knowledge	Non-negotiable. Consistent with national ownership
4 Behavioural modification	Desire to induce the recipient government to: (a) alter its political institutions, (b) change its social policy or (c) adopt a particular development strategy	Usually negotiable, at least at the margin. The essence of donorship

funding. Financial risk management is a complex issue that is not purely technical. The principle that the recipient should be responsible for appropriate use of funds and that conditions will be associated with this responsibility is generally accepted. With rare exceptions, recipient governments accept this category of conditions as inherent in the development assistance partnership.

Category two conditionalities result from shared values. Few funding agencies would allow assistance to countries with governments that engaged in severe human rights violations, though in the past this has not been a strong public concern of the multilateral lenders. The conditions arising from shared values may be negotiated with regard to concrete circumstance, but cannot be suspended. Further, the recipient government must demonstrate a commitment to a poverty-focused development strategy. Following PRSP principles, this commitment involves 'broad based' participation, the creation of a national strategy with clear goals, and the existence of the capability to implement it. These conditions should be distinguished from those in category four, 'behavioural modification', in that they represent the establishing of the initial framework in which the partnership will subsequently develop.

Generally less contentious are category three conditionalities, which have their basis in technical considerations. Such considerations arise most clearly in project funding, which is important to bilateral agencies, though along with the World Bank most bilaterals have shifted towards general or sectoral budget support.

No agency would fund projects if it were public knowledge that the plans did not conform to generally accepted technical requirements. Further, a basic function of development assistance is to transfer knowledge from developed to developing countries. This implies that in a wide variety of development assistance activities, the technical and scientific knowledge of the funder exceeds that of the recipient. One should not naively suggest that technical conditionalities are always unambiguous. But, the basic point is valid: conditionalities that seek to achieve behaviour modification should not be packaged as technical requirements of projects and programmes.

Most contentious are category four conditionalities, whose explicit purpose is to alter the behaviour of governments with regard to political structures, social practice and economic strategy. These conditionalities are most likely to involve unilateral decisions by funders and, as a consequence, carry the greatest potential to compromise ownership of development activities. An extreme case of behaviour modification conditionality arises when, in the funder's view, the recipient government takes an action that violates some fundamental principle of the assistance agreement. An example of this is when the Department for International Development of the United Kingdom suspended the release of funds in response to the decision by the Tanzanian government to purchase a particular air traffic control system.[6] In such a case, a funder makes an explicit choice to drop ownership as a part of the assistance agreement. This example represents a particularly flagrant example of donorship, in that involved an *ex post* conditionality; that is, funds were suspended as the result of an action which had not been specified as unacceptable when the assistance agreement was made. If national ownership of development policy is to mean anything, donors and lenders must refrain from passing *ad hoc* judgements, unless the actions involve clear violations of shared values. Otherwise, funding agencies implicitly reserve the right to pass judgements and take punitive actions at their discretion.

12.4   Conditionality and reforming the PRS process

We have argued that those who view conditionalities as inconsistent with development strategy being nationally owned and country driven are incorrect. There are categories of conditionalities that are accepted as legitimate by both funding agencies and recipient governments. However, the most 'high-profile' conditionalities – involving stabilization, trade policy, privatization and restructuring of the public sector – are, almost without exception, inconsistent with national ownership, since they seek to achieve behaviour modification. If country-driven, nationally owned development strategy means anything, it requires that funding agencies accept recipient government policies with which they disagree.

The legitimacy of behaviour modification conditionalities is called into question by the principles of the PRS process, first because one of its goals is country-driven, nationally owned development strategies and second, because the mandated process of participation provides the legitimacy for those strategies.

Conditionalities set by funding agencies that conflict with the priorities and policies that arise out of the participation process would make a mockery of that process, which the external agencies themselves require. Therefore, several basic reforms of the PRS process are required to render it consistent with national ownership.

The first and most basic reform of the PRS process is that it should be embedded in national planning institutions. In order for the PRS process to produce a document that will represent a government's overall, long-term strategy for poverty reduction, that document must be integrated into the broader policy process. This implies links to medium-term expenditure planning and annual budgets. Establishing *ad hoc* poverty strategy units, even within existing ministries, separates the PRS process from the policy making in general, and may also be in conflict with the established division of labour within the public sector (Weeks *et al.*, 2004a). When governments have existing poverty programmes, the PRS process should involve an elaboration of these, not a separate exercise, which would inevitably be driven by external funders and recognized as such.

The second reform, and derivative from the first, the PRS document should be a development strategy, not a macroeconomic framework with links to poverty reduction. This implies that the macroeconomic policies of a government should be derivative from the government's PRS, not the reverse, which has typically been the case. This requires a review of existing conditionalities for their poverty implications, rather than the automatic incorporation of those conditionalities into the new poverty strategy. In some, if not many cases, review of conditionalities would result in amending on-going World Bank and IMF programmes. The Bretton Woods institutions would show their full commitment to the PRS process and national ownership by accepting such a review and amendments.

The third reform would change the PRS paper from a document written for funders to one written for the national audience. Rather than a 'management tool', as the World Bank tends to view it, it should be a political programme, debated publicly and endorsed by the appropriate representative institutions. In countries with functioning representative institutions, these institutions should be a central part of developing a national poverty strategy. The PRS practice in some countries of substituting an *ad hoc* consultation process for the role of formal representative institutions tends to be driven by external agencies and contradicts ownership. Under present practice, PRSPs must be reviewed by the executive boards of the IMF and the World Bank in what is in practice an approval process. However, there is no requirement that national parliaments must approve these documents. Of all the lingering donorship aspects of the PRS process, this is perhaps the most flagrant.

The PRS process, as the vehicle for the achievement of the MDGs, has the potential to transform the relationship between funding agencies and recipient governments. However, to achieve this goal, a heavy burden of reform is placed on those funding agencies, especially the World Bank and the IMF. If traditional donorship policies are continued under a new rhetoric, PRSPs will be stabilization and structural adjustment programmes under a different name. The result will be disillusionment by recipient governments and their constituencies, and the PRSP, like the Comprehensive Development Framework, will atrophy only to be replaced by the next new 'big' idea of the funding agencies.

Notes

1 See the table in Weeks *et al.* (2004a, pp. 32–34).
2 Most of the exceptions are governments of Asian countries. Obvious cases are: China, because the country stands on the verge of becoming a world power; India, for which development assistance is small compared to other capital flows; and Vietnam, whose extraordinary growth made it much-courted by donors and lenders. In 2003 the government of India reduced to four the number of bilateral agencies that could operate in the country.
3 A document of the Swedish International Development Agency on assistance to Africa reaches the following conclusion:

> Another change [in the partners relationship] relates to attitudes, especially that of the stronger party. Gone are the times when the prescriptions for African success could be written in western capitals. First, these prescriptions have often proved deficient, for the very reason that they are poorly based on African reality; secondly, the new African leaders insist on their right to formulate and impose conditions for programmes focusing on development processes in their own countries.
>
> (SMFA, 1998, p. 8)

4 For example, they call for flexibility on the pace of policy change:

> Allowances would also have to be made for changes in the country's preference for type and pace of reform – for example, to ensure social cohesion and broad-based ownership of the reform process by accommodating particular interest.
>
> (Branson and Hanna, 2000, p. 5)

5   [S]ince only countries in some distress . . . borrow from the IMF . . . there is unlikely to be 'full' ownership, and the problem is really one of trying to maximize ownership within the context of conditionality.

> (Khan and Sharma, 2001, p. 7)

6 The issue was resolved and assistance resumed in July 2002.

Bibliography

Branson, W. and Hanna, N. (2000) 'Ownership and conditionality', OED Working Paper Series No. 8, World Bank.

Chisala, V. (2002) 'Evaluation of UNDP's engagement in the Poverty Reduction Strategy Paper process: The Zambian Case', Centre for Development Policy and Research Working Paper, School of Oriental and African Studies.

Foster, M. (2000) *New Approaches to Development Co-operation: What can be Learnt from Experience with Implementing Sector Wide Approaches?*, London: ODI.

Kanbur, R. (1999) 'The strange case of the Washington Consensus; a brief note on John Williamson's "What should the World Bank think about the Washington Consensus?" ', mimeo, Cornell University. Available online at http://www.people.cornell.edu/pages/sk145/papers/Washington%20Consensus.pdf

Khan, M.S. and Sharma, S. (2001) 'IMF conditionality and country ownership of programs', IMF Working Paper 01/142.

Levinsohn, J. (2003) 'The World Bank's poverty reduction strategy paper approach: good marketing or good policy?', G-24 discussion Paper Series. Geneva: UNCTAD.

Malloch Brown, M. (2002) 'Address by UNDP Administrator Mark Malloch Brown', International Conference on Financing for Development, Monterrey, Mexico, 18 March.

Pincus, J. and Thang, N. (2004) *Poverty Reduction Strategy Process and National Development Strategies in Asia, A Report To DFID: Country Study Vietnam*, London: CDPR.

Sweden, government of, Ministry for Foreign Affairs (SMFA) (1998) 'Government Communication: Africa on the Move: revitalising Swedish Policy towards Africa for the 21st Century', Communication 1997/98:122, Stockholm.

United Nations Conference on Trade and Development (2000) *The Least Developed Countries 2000 Report: Aid, Private Capital Flows and External Debt: The Challenge of Financing Development in the LDCs*, Geneva: UNCTAD.

United Nations Development Programme, Evaluations Office (2003) *Evaluation of the Role of the UNDP in the PRSP Process*, New York: UNDP.

Weeks, J., Lerchem, J. and Pincus, J. (2004a) *Poverty Reduction Strategy Process and National Development Strategies in Asia, A Report To DFID: Synthesis Report*, London: CDPR.

Weeks, J., Thang, N., Roy, R. and Lim, J. (2004b) *Viet Nam: Seeking Equity within Growth*, United Nations Development Programme, Regional Programme for Asia on the Macroeconomics of Poverty Reduction, London: CDPR.

World Bank (2002) *A Sourcebook for Poverty Reduction Strategies – Core Techniques and Cross-cutting Issues*, Volume 1, Washington, DC: World Bank.

13 What does ownership mean in practice?*

Policy learning and the evolution of pro-poor policies in Uganda

Oliver Morrissey and Arjan Verschoor

13.1 Introduction

Is ownership necessary if countries are to implement policy reform? Much of the recent discussion of policy reform in developing countries sees ownership as necessary if policies are to be implemented successfully and sustained (e.g. Killick, 1995; Sandbrook, 1996; Leandro et al., 1999; Dijkstra and Van Donge, 2001). Typically, the concept of ownership is not defined and is used in a loose sense, frequently indistinguishable from the related, and equally rarely defined, notion of commitment. For example, one can find the view that ownership is necessary for commitment, which requires that 'the executive authority must be [cohesive and] firmly convinced of the necessity of [reform]' (Sandbrook, 1996, p. 5). Leandro et al. (1999, p. 288) acknowledge that no clear and unambiguous definition of ownership appears in the literature, and consider it to be some combination of commitment and capacity to 'conceive, negotiate and implement reforms'. The first aim of this chapter is to provide an operational distinction between ownership and commitment in the context of policy reform.

A related issue, on which current understanding is remarkably limited despite the outpouring of papers on the subject, is whether and how donors influence policy reform, especially whether conditionality is effective. World Bank (1998) seems to take the view that conditionality does not work, and it is certainly true that tight conditionality is not an effective instrument to get governments to do something they do not want to do (White and Morrissey, 1997). This may be going too far: governments may only half-heartedly and partially implement the conditions associated with an aid programme, but the conditions nevertheless influence the policy agenda. Policy is learned, in the sense that governments will desire to identify and select those policies that they believe best serve their interests. If current policies are adequate, there is little incentive for reform. If current policies are inadequate and/or alternative policies are believed to be better, then there is an incentive for reform. Influence, in this context, can be exerted at two levels – shaping views on which policies best meet specific objectives, and altering those objectives.

What does ownership mean in this context? Does the observation that a particular policy is selected imply that it is owned? Is conditionality consistent with ownership or are there more effective ways for donors to promote reform by supporting ownership? In other words, at what point can donor influence undermine ownership? These are some of the questions explored in this chapter. We acknowledge that these concepts are inherently difficult to define in an operationally relevant manner, and we doubt that we have discovered complete definitions. However, we try to provide meaningful distinctions to inform discussion of how donors influence policy reform in aid recipient countries.

An example of policy reform and evolution is needed to illustrate how ownership and commitment can be distinguished, and indeed to assess which is really the important factor, whilst identifying inputs by donors (or 'external agents' as a general term). We select the case of pro-poor policies in Uganda, as evidenced by the changing pattern of (donor-supported) public expenditures directed towards the poor, the evolution of a poverty reduction strategy and eligibility for debt relief under HIPC. Williamson and Canagarajah (2003) detail clearly and concisely why Uganda is such a relevant and important case for studying the changing nature of donor–recipient relations, especially in the context of PRSPs (Dijkstra and Van Donge, 2001; see also Adam and Gunning, 2002). Indeed, Uganda is seen as *owning* the reform process: 'the government demonstrably and decisively shapes the policy agenda... [policy] is homegrown and key Ugandan officials are very much in control' (Adam and Gunning, 2002, p. 2056).

Section 13.2 outlines our conceptualization of the policy process, defines and distinguishes the concepts of ownership and commitment and considers the role of external influences in the process. Section 13.3 reviews the poverty reduction policies in Uganda and relates the strategy to the allocation of public spending. Section 13.4 then concentrates on the evolving pattern of public spending in more detail, asking to what extent the pattern has become more 'pro-poor' and assessing some evidence of the impact. Section 13.5 presents some concluding comments, arguing that ownership per se is not the crucial factor, rather it is commitment that is crucial. An incidental benefit of this argument, at least for the analyst, is that it is in practice easier to identify commitment than to attribute ownership.

13.2 Influences on policy learning and policy reform

This section presents a framework for analysing the nature of the policy process that places the emphasis firmly on beliefs and information regarding policy options. Government has objectives, even if these are not publicly known, and selects policies to best meet these objectives. We draw a clear distinction between policy-making – the choice, design and advocacy of policy – and implementation. We recognize the importance of implementation capability, especially insofar as limitations constrain policy choice, and acknowledge that implementation experience should feed back to policy-making, but are not concerned with issues relating to administrative or institutional reform.[1] Policy-making will depend on the way in which government functions, the strength of opposition and the quality of technocrats involved in the process (the same individuals may also be involved in implementation, but that is treated here as a distinct function).

Our approach follows Morrissey and Nelson (2001), who consider three theories of learning to provide a framework of policy-making processes. Policy-makers will have beliefs (priors) about how effective a policy is in meeting their objectives, and these beliefs will be determined by past experience with policies and information on policy options provided by others. If policy-makers engage in pure learning by doing, policy choices are based solely on information relating to the history of the policy they have experienced and policy-makers have no information on alternative policies (as these have not been implemented). In such an environment, unless the current policy is considered unsatisfactory, there is no incentive for change. In this model of learning, policy-makers act largely in isolation – they are either not aware of or not concerned about the policy experiences of others. Change is still possible. The external environment may alter so that a policy that worked in the past becomes unsatisfactory, or a new challenge may emerge that requires policy innovation. The information available on policy options then becomes important. Of course, a new set of policy-makers (regime change) may bring new beliefs and provide impetus for policy change. It is relevant to note that ownership is clear in this model, as the government considers only its own beliefs and experiences.

A second model is social learning, where policy-makers can observe the policies chosen by others (other governments), although they have limited ability to observe the effects of these policies. Social learning provides information on alternatives and therefore enriches the set of policy options. If others are observed to stick to a particular policy, that is different to the one currently chosen, policy-makers will infer that others view the alternative as satisfactory (if not 'good'). Specifically, if the majority of others are seen to be sticking to an alternative policy, policy-makers may alter their beliefs and be induced to choose the alternative. In this way, social learning encourages herding (everybody ends up with the same policy) as policy-makers' beliefs converge on which option is regarded as best.

The concept of ownership is now somewhat ambiguous. One may wish to argue that if a government freely chooses to 'copy' a policy from others, this constitutes ownership, but then it is the free choice that defines ownership rather than the origin and content of the policy. If this is what writers have in mind by ownership, it would be better to simply refer to freely chosen policies (a point we return to in the next section). At the risk of appearing pedantic, ownership should mean something more than free choice: a better definition would be freely chosen because it is believed to be beneficial and adapted to local needs. It is then the process of local adaptation that represents ownership, and in this sense the policy content is changed and tailored. There is then something about the policy that is owned, and this something originated from the policy-makers.

The third model is hierarchical social learning, where there is an agent that declares its belief regarding which policy should be chosen, and has some mechanism to encourage policy-makers to adopt that choice. Such agents are at the top of the hierarchy of policy learning. This is appropriate for describing the role that donors, especially agencies such as the World Bank or IMF, fulfil. If donors have an effective mechanism to ensure that the policy they recommend is chosen, there will again be policy herding. However, this differs from herding under social learning as there need not be convergence of beliefs. It is the mechanism for policy compliance, not convergence of beliefs, that induces convergence on the same policy. If the mechanism (e.g. conditionality) is not effective, the hierarchy does not function and the agents are in effect purveyors of influence and information. An important feature of these agents is that they do not implement policies for themselves, they are not policy-makers in the sense here discussed (of governments who choose a policy and then obtain a signal of whether or not the outcome is satisfactory). External agents are distinct from social learning because policy-makers cannot observe and learn from the agent's policy choices.

The concept of ownership takes on a new light in respect of hierarchical learning, as governments do not own a policy they choose only because it has been 'declared' by an agent. If the hierarchical mechanism is effective, the government will choose the policy and may or may not believe that it is the best policy option. However, if the mechanism is not effective, and most would agree that conditionality has not been an effective mechanism in this respect, the policy will only be chosen by governments that agree with it. This may be what most commentators have in mind when arguing that ownership is necessary if policies are to be implemented successfully and sustained (e.g. Killick, 1995; Leandro *et al.*, 1999). Thus, if a government freely chooses a particular policy and openly expresses its commitment to the policy, then it owns the policy. This may be an acceptable definition of ownership, but is not obviously distinct from commitment (why would a government be committed to a policy it did not freely choose?). Free, or at least willing, choice does not permit one to distinguish between commitment and ownership. For ownership, we will require that the policy *option* (the decision to adopt a new policy) and/or a significant part of the policy *content* originated from the policy-makers. This is a meaningful concept of ownership; it implies commitment, and allows for the fact that policy-makers could be committed to policies they do not own. Thus, we have a distinction between the two concepts.

Commitment, defined as the explicit adoption of a specific policy, can be seen as comprising two elements – preferences and political capacity. Preferences for reform are a sufficient condition to ensure an attempt at implementation (irrespective of ownership), but do not guarantee successful implementation, nor do they guarantee that the government will make its intentions public.[2] Preferences and capacity give rise to commitment to reform, but the ability to implement successfully will then depend on administrative capability and institutional structures. In this sense, we define commitment as revealed preference. If a government favours a particular reform and believes it has the political capacity to advocate and try to implement the reform, it is willing to declare the commitment. If a government has a preference for reform but capacity is weak, it may choose not to declare its commitment (it will be implicitly, but not explicitly, adopted). If there is no preference for the reform, there is no commitment by this definition (irrespective of what the government may declare).[3]

Morrissey (1999, 2001) proposes a framework for analysing the factors influencing governments' choices of which policies to adopt, and the presentation here builds on this. The government has to have a preference for the particular policy or reform. Preferences in this context are policy-specific, and are determined by the policy-makers' priors. A government may wish to retain the status quo or may perceive the need for change. If the latter, there is a preference for reform (with a particular aim), but this does not imply that the government knows what the most appropriate policies to achieve the reform are (this is where external influences come into play).[4] External agents, such as donors, can influence policy choice by contributing to the learning process. For example, donors could provide information on policies that have 'worked' in other countries, or could support analysis of the effects of policies being implemented. Aid, in itself and as a manifestation of donor views on what the appropriate policies are, can play a role in shaping preferences. There is no reason why aid, or donors, should have an immediate effect. It takes time to shift preferences, although this is made easier when there is a policy vacuum to fill (and when governments are receptive).

The political difficulty with pro-poor reforms is that they require redistribution. On the one hand, this implies that there will be opposition to reform (from the rich, who are initially the powerful). On the other, there is the possibility that redistribution 'is conducive to the adoption of growth-retarding policies' (Alesina and Rodrik, 1994, p. 465). This would be of concern to governments as growth is often the most important determinant of the sustainability of policy reform. More can be attempted and support is greater during a period of growth, whereas reforms that are perceived as reducing growth increase opposition. 'Popularly elected governments realize that political survival depends upon good economic performance' (Sandbrook, 1996, p. 6).

This discussion is summarized in Table 13.1, which also indicates the various stages at which external influences can come into play. If policy-making within government is relatively open and based on dialogue there is scope for developing new policies and the government will be receptive to external influences. External influences are often most important in shaping preferences. Donors can encourage governments to give particular issues more priority on the policy agenda, or can try to convince governments that there is 'new' policy knowledge and experience that they should recognize. Disseminating 'good' policy experiences is one of the most effective ways to influence preferences. If a government is presented with evidence of policies that have worked elsewhere, they are more likely to be convinced that the policy is appropriate for them (i.e. external agencies can influence beliefs over the efficacy of policy alternatives).

The willingness of governments to implement reforms (to alter their policy choice) will depend on beliefs regarding the effect of any given policy (described as priors regarding the policy) and the range of policy options. In other words, stages A and B of the process refer to willingness to reform. Donors can influence willingness to reform in a number of ways. They can give information on the probable effects of alternative policies, affecting both priors and options, especially if they provide information on the effects of policy choices in other countries (knowledge transfer). By expressing their own views, preferably supported by analysis of evidence, donors can influence the policy agenda, and thereby influence choice. Note that such actions by donors do not require conditions.

Table 13.1 External influences on the policy reform process

Political dimension	Donor influences
A. Preferences	*The government is in favour of the reform* Placing specific concerns high on the agenda Policy advice and knowledge transfer Evidence of how policy has worked elsewhere
B. Capacity	*Ability to advocate policy and move to implement* Taking responsibility for unpopular policies Providing evidence to build support Assistance for policy advocacy Poverty monitoring and analysis[a]
C. Commitment	*Preference revealed because capacity is adequate* Financial support for adopting policies Building policy-making capability Technical assistance on policy design and analysis
D. Administration	*Process of implementing the policy* Technical support and assistance

Notes
Basic structure taken from Morrissey (1999, table 4.1). The aim is to identify the 'entry routes' of external influences on the politics of policy reform. A definition of the political dimension is provided in italics.
a These contribute to policy-making and therefore enhance capacity, but are also elements in implementing effective policy, therefore contribute to administrative capability.

Donors can also support political capacity – providing evidence to counter opposition and assistance in policy advocacy, for example. The government may support the objectives, but may have limited capacity to advocate an appropriate policy and mobilize support for it. The type of evidence that influences government preferences is essentially the same as that which supports policy advocacy, although dissemination modes differ. The former should be designed to appeal to policy-makers (accentuate the positive) whereas the latter should appeal to the public and interest groups (e.g. deflecting or countering opposition arguments). In these ways, donors can fill the gap where preferences are pro-reform but capacity is weak. This implies working with or even for government.

Once commitment exists, external agencies can help to strengthen it, directly with financial support (to offset costs of implementation) or more generally with advice and help in policy design. Commitment implies the government has advocated the policy and is moving to implementation. External assistance at this stage should be directed on appropriate policy design, such as resolving problems of targeting in pro-poor expenditures. Some see such technical assistance as contributing to ownership (e.g. Leandro *et al.*, 1999). This is true in a dynamic sense, if support for capacity now contributes to enhanced policy-making capacity in the future. However, technical assistance for implementing specific reforms should not be considered as promoting ownership of *that* reform – it is too late. Similarly, such assistance does not establish commitment, rather it assists the process of acting on commitment.

Increasing administrative capability is an essential part of effective policy reform, relevant not only to implementation but also to political capacity itself. 'However difficult and politically risky it is to decide to introduce a reformist initiative, the process of implementing and sustaining that decision is likely to be even more fraught with difficulty and risk' (Grindle and Thomas, 1991, p. 121). A more capable and independent bureaucracy can contribute to effective policy-making as it strengthens capacity (and promotes ownership), whereas weak capabilities undermine implementation and political capacity. Donors can contribute via technical assistance in administration and implementation. Advisors that are based in the country, working with the government, for a relatively long period of time are one example.

13.3   The poverty reduction strategy and pro-poor policy

Our concern is not with the detail of reform areas but with the broad implications for protecting the relatively poor. This requires complementary policies that ensure a pro-poor effect and compensatory policies that minimize or offset adverse effects on the poor (these include pro-poor expenditures). Given the policy environment prevailing in a country, what types of pro-poor policies and expenditures should be promoted?

The essential pro-poor policies in PRSPs can be considered under two headings – those relating to the provision of and access to public services and those relating to the rural sector, as the majority of the poorest in low-income countries are in rural areas. The former are mostly pro-poor expenditures while the latter are mostly pro-poor policies. Consumption of public services is an important element of the well-being (or real income) of the poor, usually omitted from income-based measures of poverty (Kanbur, 2001). The most important services are education, especially at the primary level, health (including nutrition) and water (sanitation and access to safe water). To maximize the consumption of the poor, it is necessary not only that public services are delivered but also that they are available for free (at least for the relatively poor). Charges for access to health or education (including implicit charges, such as for school uniforms, textbooks or drugs) bear disproportionately on the poor. Even if they do make efforts to meet these charges, and thus secure access, this implies a severe reduction in income available for food and other basic needs. Consequently, increased public spending on the provision of social services are central elements of PRSPs. The abolition of charges or the inclusion of specific targeting schemes are means of ensuring that such expenditures are pro-poor.

Policies to address poverty in low-income countries must address the rural dimension, especially the relevance of the agriculture sector that provides the livelihoods for most rural people. '75 per cent of the dollar-poor work and live in rural areas; projections suggest that over 60 per cent will continue to do so in 2005' (IFAD, 2001, p. 15). Policies to address rural poverty must tackle four types of inequalities (IFAD, 2001). First, the rural poor have unequal access to physical and financial assets – distribution of land is highly concentrated and the poor are disadvantaged in access to irrigation, safe water, credit and productive assets. Second, the poor require access to technology and extension services to increase productivity. Third, markets tend to discriminate against the poor (this relates to the issue of market structure mentioned above). Fourth, institutions (political and financial) often fail to serve the poor. PRSPs typically contain a range of policies directed towards subsistence and small-holder farmers, intended to support a pro-poor agriculture policy.

Uganda's PRSP, the Poverty Eradication Action Plan (PEAP) prepared in 1997, reflects these concerns strongly, with a strong emphasis on provision of health and education services and support for the agriculture sector. In fact, Uganda could be considered a leader in devising a strategy to monitor and deliver pro-poor expenditures. The Government of Uganda (GoU) introduced the Poverty Action Fund (PAF) in 1998 to reassure donors that funds for pro-poor spending, especially those released through debt relief, would be monitored and accountable. Indeed, by 2002, the 'agenda of pro-poor public expenditure management goes well beyond the provision of higher levels of efficiency and trust in financial management' (Williamson and Canagarajah, 2003, p. 450). The PAF framework incorporated sector planning and allocations, increasing the effectiveness of spending, and taking a medium-term approach to integrating aid funds into the budget.

The evidence on poverty trends in Uganda is conclusive and downward, in line with impressive growth performance (Table 13.2). Appleton (2001) provides evidence of a decline in poverty: the headcount index fell from 56 per cent nationally (and 60 per cent for the rural population) in 1992 to 49 per cent (54 per cent) in 1995 and 35 per cent (39 per cent) in 1999. Growth in cash crop production was a more important source of poverty reduction than increased food

Table 13.2 Income and poverty indicators, 1985–2000 (selected years)

	1985	1990	1992	1995	1997	2000
GDP (million; constant 1995$)	3,205	4,102	4,478	5,756	6,945	7,728
GDP pc (constant 1995$)	227	251	256	299	322	348
Population (million)	14	16	18	19	20	22
Poverty headcount (%), National	—	—	56	49	44	35
Poverty headcount (%), East Rural	—	—	61	60	57	—
Income Gini, National	—	—	36	37	35	—
Income Gini, Urban	—	—	39	37	35	—
Income Gini, Rural	—	—	33	33	31	—
Infant mortality (per 1,000 live births)	116	104	97	98	99	83
U5 mortality (per 1,000 live births)	—	165	—	—	162	161

Sources: Appleton (2001) for poverty and Gini, World Development Indicators for the other statistics.

crop production over 1992–96, accounting for 48 per cent of the reduction in poverty as compared to 14 per cent for food crops. The proportional contributions were reversed over 1996–2000, with increased food crop production accounting for 43 per cent of the reduction in poverty and cash crops 27 per cent (Appleton, 2001). Uganda implemented significant economic reforms in the 1990s, establishing macroeconomic stability by the middle of the decade with real annual growth rates exceeding 5 per cent per annum for the latter half of the decade (Morrissey and Rudaheranwa, 1998). The main economic gains, supporting growth and poverty reduction, were in agricultural production.

Qualification for debt relief has been very important for Uganda. The ratio of debt interest payments to exports has fallen from 35 per cent in 1997–98 to 10 per cent in 2000–01, while the ratio of debt payments to tax revenue has fallen from 22 to 11 per cent. HIPC savings were equivalent to 13 per cent of tax revenue and 23 per cent of export earnings in 2000–01 (MFPED, 2001). These savings have been channelled to spending on social sectors (especially primary education and health care) through the PAF, which was equivalent to 31 per cent of the budget and 4.8 per cent of GDP in 2000–01. In the late 1990s, expenditure on primary education increased by 307 per cent, on primary health care by 227 per cent, on agriculture by 186 per cent and on roads by 279 per cent (MFPED, 2001). Uganda is a successful example of how debt relief can work when the resources saved are channelled into pro-poor expenditures.

The GoU clearly held a strong commitment to economic liberalization throughout the 1990s, and to implementing pro-poor policies from the mid-1990s. Can one infer ownership from this? The answer depends on which reform areas one considers. The GoU did not design its economic liberalization strategy itself, but largely followed donor, especially World Bank, advice. In many respects the timing was fortuitous. Liberalization of coffee marketing in the early 1990s, for example, coincided with a boom in world coffee prices over 1994–96. The positive effect on growth and sustained inflows of aid added impetus to the reform process that was seen as benefiting the economy and the majority of the population (Dijkstra and Van Donge, 2001). Donors influenced preferences and their continued support reinforced political capacity. While GoU demonstrated commitment to economic liberalization, the reform proposals and much of the policy detail originated from donors. This can be characterized as a case of hierarchical learning where GoU did not own the economic reforms.

The situation regarding pro-poor policies is rather different. It is well known, even if not officially documented, that external consultants made a major contribution to the PEAP, and that external advisors have played a prominent role in improving expenditure monitoring and management, contributing to the success of the PAF. However, the impetus came from GoU and the policy direction was owned. 'A key event was a forum on poverty held in 1995, attended by President Museveni, following which a task force was established and a wide consultative process initiated' (Williamson and Canagarajah, 2003, p. 456). The result was the PEAP and then the PAF; GoU was clearly committed to priorities and detail in both and owned the policy direction, even if it may not have owned all the details (in the sense that not all originated from within GoU). For example, the structure of the PAF was influenced by the existing Multilateral Debt Fund supported by Nordic donors. The evolution of pro-poor expenditure policies could be characterized as pure policy learning, supported (in policy design) by external agents. To the extent that other countries are now looking at the Ugandan experience, it has features of being a leader in social policy learning.

Uganda appears to have revealed a preference for pro-poor policies, influenced by donors but probably not driven by them. Uganda has strong political capacity, given the demonstrated ability to adopt and push the policies preferred by the government. Administrative capability remains weak: the Civil Service is under-staffed and under-resourced, with the few high quality staff under severe pressure. Donors can assist in this by providing more technical support and advice. The presence of expatriates as technical advisors (TAs) in a country facing staff shortages can facilitate the reform process in at least two important ways. First, the TAs can fill capability gaps in the administration, although there has been limited success in transferring skills and training to local counterparts. Second, the willingness to incorporate TAs in the government indicates some credibility towards the reform process. The TAs, by their nature, are closer to the views and beliefs of donors, and can also provide a personal link to donors. It is worth observing that, since the early 1990s, Uganda does not seem to have suffered unduly from the preponderance of expatriate advisors.

13.4   The evolution of pro-poor spending

It is useful to distinguish pro-poor policies from pro-poor expenditures. The requirements to identify and implement pro-poor expenditures are less than to implement complementary policies that make a reform process pro-poor, especially if the reform process is relatively complex and wide ranging. The design and implementation of pro-poor policies is demanding of policy-makers, whose potential is conditioned by the policy environment – the political and administrative constraints to policy. The design and implementation of pro-poor expenditures is somewhat easier. A central argument of this chapter is that, given the policy environment, the objective of poverty reduction can be more effectively promoted through pro-poor expenditures than by requiring pro-poor policies.

We treat Uganda's recent history as paradigmatic for the assertion that conditioning donor influence on the policy environment can help establish and monitor a poverty focus of public spending.[5] At the level of preferences (Table 13.1, stage A), the origin of Uganda's increasing social spending from the late 1980s onwards and its subsequent protection of expenditures on pro-poor sectors under PAF can be traced to a combination of historical factors. The National Resistance Army, harbinger of the National Resistance Movement (NRM), which has been in power since 1986, emerged from the civil war reform-minded. After an initial, short-lived rejection of what was perceived to be an imperialist policy package, the newly installed NRM government accepted an adjustment programme in the late 1980s. This included social spending conditions. Later, in the mid-1990s, when poverty reduction had become a primary objective of most donor agencies, Uganda was willing to accept the advice of donors (and donor-funded consultants) in order to identify sectors for spending that would benefit the poor disproportionately.

Even a government that emerges victorious from a civil war, and with a preference for reform, will be slow to adopt politically risky policies. The willingness to attempt reform will be constrained by political capacity and governments will be wary of trying to push through reforms in the face of strong opposition. For that reason, reform may be slowed down during the process of the transfer of power. Uganda's particular model of 'no-party' democracy, in which an effort is made to convince the media and public that policies are right for the country, but without the risk of losing elections due to unpopular policies, strikes a balance. Opposing factions influence policy-making but not to the extent that they stifle reform.

The government is thus willing and able to declare a commitment to reform (Table 13.1, stage C). Its current commitment to pro-poor spending owes much to donors rewarding previous reform intentions immediately and generously. For example, they responded quickly to the improved circumstances for utilizing aid when Uganda reformed its economy in the late 1980s. Moreover, Uganda was the first country to receive a stock debt rescheduling with the Paris Club (1995). The obvious message that 'good' behaviour reaps large rewards was not lost on the Ugandan government. In the mid-1990s it judged correctly that poverty reduction had become important to donors, and it sensed that an expressed commitment to pro-poor expenditures would probably bring increasing aid inflows. The then Secretary to the Treasury, Emmanuel Tumusiime-Mutibile, with the help of consultants from the UK's Department for International Development, identified a list of pro-poor sectors, spending on which was to be protected from cuts.

Ironically, many donors initially resisted the move because they feared that it would disrupt the consultative process in which donors and government jointly decide on strategic priorities and corresponding expenditure levels. The government persisted and it is by now clear that a ring-fenced set of expenditures works reasonably well in protecting spending levels on pro-poor sectors. Furthermore, the PAF mechanism was considered relatively easy to administer utilizing existing capacity (Williamson and Canagarajah, 2003, p. 459), so the mechanism was tailored to the policy environment.

Table 13.3 provides a 'quantitative' summary of the resulting emphasis in the allocation of expenditure under the PAF (which represented more than a third of budget spending in the 2000s). The PEAP identified five key sectors as priorities for pro-poor spending. Supporting increased linkages between agriculture and other sectors of the economy (such as processing) was viewed as a key to a pro-poor growth strategy. Investment in agriculture and rural roads (to support marketing) accounted for more than 10 per cent of PAF spending. As is evident from Table 13.3, the key sector for pro-poor spending was education, initially to ensure Universal Primary Education (UPE), with health becoming more important as access to education improved. These two sectors accounted for two-thirds or more of PAF spending. The other major sector was water and sanitation, which could be considered as contributing to health status. Uganda has sustained a significant increase in spending on these social sectors, and this is likely to have contributed to poverty alleviation (increasing the welfare of the poor).

Table 13.3 Expenditures on pro-poor policies

Priorities		Share of PAF spending (%)		
		1999/00	*2001/02*	*2003/04*
Agriculture	linkages	3.9	3.3	5.2
Education	UPE	69.9	52.1	44.5
Health	AIDS	7.1	17.7	20.7
Water	access	5.8	7.6	6.8
Roads	rural roads	8.1	6.4	6.3
PAF Budget as % of GoU Budget		26.5	36.0	37.3

Source: Figures derived from GoU *Background to the Budget 2002/03.*

Notes
The aim is to identify patterns of expenditure allocation against priority issues identified in the PRSP (the Priorities columns). Water includes sanitation. Figures for 1999/00 are out turn, 2001/02 provisional and 2003/04 projected. PAF expenditure share on Agriculture includes 'restocking and poverty alleviation', health is primary care, education is mostly primary but includes adult literacy.

Although it can choose the policy direction, Uganda still has limited potential to design and implement policies itself. If donors want to support the pro-poor content of PRSPs, emphasis should be given to the specific concerns in a country, recognizing progress that has been made. For example, Uganda has largely achieved UPE and is now concerned with the implications for secondary education (as larger numbers of students emerge with a primary education), whilst also promoting adult education. Similarly, Uganda has already made progress in AIDS awareness and reducing the incidence of the disease. The essential component of donor support is through ensuring that funds are available for pro-poor expenditures.

However, because of Uganda's weak administrative capability donors must remain aware of a number of pitfalls. First, in a system of decentralized service delivery such as in Uganda, local authorities provide limited transparency and public accountability, and externally imposed monitoring may be required. Examples that have proved successful in Uganda include making public the salaries of public sector workers, and setting output targets (for schools, roads, health clinics) for public service delivery. Reinikka and Svensson (2004) show how monitoring has significantly increased the proportion of education spending allocated for districts that is actually spent on providing education in the districts. Broad cross-sector spending plans, such as the recently agreed Plan for the Modernization of Agriculture (PMA), may face implementation difficulties as they give too much discretion at the local level. As and when a satisfactory comprehensive monitoring and evaluation system is established, donors may relinquish their monitoring role.

Second, during the current period of transition towards a fully transparent budget process, specific as opposed to general budget support still has a place. At present, requests for finance from powerful ministries (e.g. Defence) are granted before those from weak ministries (e.g. Agriculture). Earmarked budget support can help ensure that agreed budgetary priorities are realized. However, ringfencing certain expenditures, as in the PAF, however desirable these expenditures are, can lead to severe pressure on 'unprotected' low priority areas of the budget. For example, the security needs for increased defence spending may displace budget allocations for general administration, leading to a freeze on public sector employment or wages and shortages of basic equipment and consumables. For similar reasons, there is still a place for donor projects that circumvent the government budget in priority and neglected sectors.

A third problem is that the 'PAF has skewed budget allocations towards the direct provision of services to the poor over a very short period, and increasingly away from balanced allocations towards PEAP implementation' (Williamson and Canagarajah, 2003, p. 466). This arose partly because the transparency associated with the PAF encouraged donors to move towards budget, rather than project, support and donors were keen to see aid allocated to social sectors. Furthermore, donors were satisfied to see aid as leveraging an increase in the share of the budget allocated to these sectors. Some important sectors may have lost out, agriculture being perhaps the best example.

There is an alternative view to be found both among donors and government officials that budgetary priorities expressed in official documents are a façade that hide spending inefficiencies and misallocations; that they are, in fact, nothing more than a magnet for aid money. As a crude test of the validity of this alternative reading of Uganda's commitment to poverty reduction, we interviewed 300 farmers in rural Mbale (East Uganda) on their perceptions of recent changes in public service delivery. We focused on primary education, basic health care and agriculture, the three PAF core sectors. Almost nobody reported a deterioration of public services in these sectors, whereas almost 60 per cent found primary schools to have improved, 63 per cent health clinics, and 23 per cent feeder roads and agricultural extension services. The lower figure for agricultural services confirms the relative neglect of this sector remarked on above, but on the whole the commitment to pro-poor spending does seem to have made a difference.

13.5   Conclusions: ownership and influence in policy reform

The potential for implementing poverty reduction policies is conditioned by the policy environment in developing countries. Of central importance are government preferences for pro-poor policies and the political capacity to promote a pro-poor agenda. Taken together these create commitment. Persuasive economic arguments supported by relevant research can shape preferences while technical and financial support can enhance political capacity. Through such interventions donors can help establish commitment to poverty-reduction strategies. Whether this influence is consistent with government ownership depends on the nature of policy learning.

If policy-makers engage in pure learning by doing, policy choices are based solely on information relating to the policy. Ownership is clear in this model, as the government considers only its own beliefs and experiences. External agents can facilitate reform by providing information on alternative policies, especially if the government indicates its preference to introduce new policies. This type of policy learning characterizes Uganda's choice of the PAF mechanism to monitor and allocate pro-poor expenditures. Uganda could be described as having ownership of the pro-poor spending policy, as the government chose the policy direction and actively participated in policy design, while commitment is implied (part and parcel of the policy environment).

Social learning describes a situation where policy-makers acquire information on alternatives and expand the set of policy options by observing the policies chosen by other governments. This may describe Uganda's 'strategic export promotion' policy, as to some extent this was informed by observing the experience of East Asian economies. In this case the policy is not owned, but tailoring and adapting it to local conditions confers ownership of the policy content (the details). While policy experimentation of this type is generally desirable (it increases the information on policies available to all), there is no guarantee that the best policy is chosen. In principle, external agents can assist by increasing the quality of information on alternative policies. In this case, assuming the chosen policy is appropriate, success will depend more on commitment than on any notion of ownership.

Most studies of conditionality and policy reform in developing countries have in mind a model of hierarchical social learning, where an external agent signals which policy should be chosen, and has some mechanism to encourage policy-makers to adopt that choice. If the mechanism is effective, governments will choose the policy even if it is not their preferred option. In this case, the government clearly does not own the policy, if ownership requires that the decision to adopt the policy and a significant part of the policy content originated from the government. However, policy-makers could be committed to policies they do not own, where commitment is revealed preference. By implication, if the 'hierarchical choice' is not the government's preferred option, commitment will be weak or absent, and sustained effective implementation is unlikely. On the other hand, governments can be committed if (they are convinced that) it is their preferred option, irrespective of ownership.

Thus, a sufficient condition for commitment to policy reform is that a government selects a policy that can be implemented and is believed to be superior to the current policy. The chosen policy need not be the optimal policy, although it is obviously desirable that it is if implementation is to be successful and sustained. Morrissey and Nelson (2001) demonstrate that the weakness of hierarchical social learning is that it encourages herding on a policy that is not optimal. The point we wish to emphasize is that it is commitment that matters, not ownership (which may be desirable, but is not necessary). This argument has been illustrated by the case of Uganda. We identified one case, pro-poor spending, where Uganda had ownership of (and thus commitment to) the policy; donors influenced choice and implementation by providing advice and aid. However, in many other cases of reform, most of Uganda's economic liberalization, ownership was limited or absent, but commitment drove adoption of the policies.

Policy advisors and donors, who tend to be the major proponents of poverty-reduction strategies in developing countries, should show greater awareness of the prevailing policy environment, and work with it rather than against it. Donors can assist the policy-making process through providing technical assistance and aid, to support the budgetary costs at the initial stage of moving to poverty-reduction strategies and to support projects and sector programmes directed at helping the poor. Donors can also help to increase administrative capability; support for technical assistance and training is the most obvious mechanism. Technical assistance is equally important in contributing to policy-making capabilities, also enhancing administration but perhaps at a higher level. In both contexts, but especially the latter, it is best if the assistance is in and through, rather than simply to, the government.

Notes

* The research was part of a project on 'Poverty Leverage of Aid' funded by DFID (grant R7617). The views expressed here are those of the authors alone.
1 This is not to deny that implementation is integral to the policy process, but allows the focus to be on policy-making. Grindle and Thomas (1991) provide the seminal discussion of policy-making and implementation in developing countries.
2 As should be clear from the context, preferences here do not mean that the government 'likes' the policy (although it may do). Preferences relate to policy choice, based on information given objectives.
3 It should be admitted that political commitment is difficult to define in an operational way. Ideally, one needs to know the true intentions of the government rather than relying on revealed preferences (which may be opportunistic and politically, rather than policy, motivated). A government may declare an intention to reform simply to receive aid, and then renege on this 'commitment' (the source of aid conditionality ineffectiveness). In practice, stated policy preferences are the best available indicator of commitment.
4 There are two issues here. First, donor and recipient preferences regarding reform may differ; this is the standard case of conditionality failure (White and Morrissey, 1997). Nevertheless, donors can influence preferences (Morrissey and Nelson, 2001, discuss how institutions such as the WTO can influence policy-makers' beliefs and thus shape preferences for reform). Second, having chosen a specific policy, recipients may lack full information on design and implementation. This is where donors can play a directly constructive role, assuming there are shared preferences.
5 The discussion is based on interviews held in the autumn of 2001 with representatives of donor agencies and government officials, both at the level of policy-making and at the level of implementation. Supplementary information was garnered when working with farmers in rural Mbale (East Uganda), a region with a relatively high incidence of poverty (cf. Table 13.2).

Bibliography

Adam, C.S. and Gunning, J.W. (2002) 'Redesigning the aid contract: donors use of performance indicators in Uganda', *World Development*, 30: 2045–2056.

Alesina, A. and Rodrik, D. (1994) 'Distribution politics and income distribution', *Quarterly Journal of Economics*, 109: 465–490.

Appleton, S. (2001) 'Poverty reduction during growth: the case of Uganda, 1992–2000', mimeo, School of Economics, University of Nottingham.

Dijkstra, A. and Van Donge, J. (2001) 'What does the "show case" show? Evidence of and lessons from adjustment in Uganda', *World Development*, 29: 841–864.

Grindle, M. and Thomas, J. (1991) *Public Choices and Policy Change: The Political Economy of Reform in Developing Countries*, Baltimore, MD: Johns Hopkins University Press.

IFAD (2001) *Rural Poverty Report 2001: The Challenge of Ending Rural Poverty*, Rome: International Fund for Agricultural Development.

Kanbur, R. (2001) 'Economic policy, distribution and poverty: the nature of disagreements', *World Development*, 29: 1083–1094.

Killick, T. (1995) *IMF Programmes in Developing Countries: Design and Impact*, London: Routledge.

Leandro, J., Schafer, H. and Frontini, G. (1999) 'Towards a more effective conditionality: an operational framework', *World Development*, 27: 285–300.

MFPED (2001) *Fighting Poverty in Uganda: The Poverty Action Fund*, Kampala: Ministry of Finance, Planning and Economic Development.

Morrissey, O. (1999) 'Political economy dimensions of economic policy reform', in McGillivray, M. and Morrissey, O. (eds), *Evaluating Economic Liberalisation*, London: Macmillan.

—— (2001) 'Pro-poor conditionality for aid and debt relief in East Africa', University of Nottingham, CREDIT Research Paper 01/15.

Morrissey, O. and Nelson, D. (2001) 'The role of the WTO in the transfer of policy knowledge on trade and competition', University of Nottingham, Leverhulme Centre for Research on Globalisation and Economic Policy, GEP Research Paper 2001/32.

Morrissey, O. and Rudaheranwa, N. (1998) 'Ugandan trade policy and export performance in the 1990s', University of Nottingham, CREDIT Research Paper 98/12.

Reinikka, R. and Svensson, J. (2004) 'Efficiency of public spending: new microeconomic tools to assess service delivery' in Addision, T. and Roe, A. (eds), *Fiscal Policy for Development: Poverty, Reconstruction and Growth*, Houndsmills: Palgrave Macmillan.

Sandbrook, R. (1996) 'Democratization and the implementation of economic reforms in Africa', *Journal of International Development*, 8: 1–20.

White, H. and Morrissey, O. (1997) 'Conditionality when donor and recipient preferences vary', *Journal of International Development*, 9: 497–505.

Williamson, T. and Canagarajah, S. (2003) 'Is there a place for virtual poverty funds in pro-poor public spending reform? Lessons from Uganda's PAF', *Development Policy Review*, 21: 449–480.

World Bank (1998) *Assessing Aid: What Works, What Doesn't and Why*, New York: Oxford University Press.

14 Can conditionality improve borrower ownership?

Alberto Paloni and Maurizio Zanardi

14.1 Introduction

The International Financial Institutions (IFIs) have recently conducted a thorough re-examination of their assistance programmes. One aspect that has received particular attention in this context is the use of conditionality (i.e. an agreed set of policies/conditions which recipient countries should implement if they are to receive funding from the IFIs). At the cost of some over-simplification, the position of the IFIs on this matter after such a long process of re-thinking can be summarized as follows.

First, conditionality has generally been ineffective as a mechanism to bring about policy change, particularly if recipient countries lacked commitment to reform or had weak implementation capacity. Second, the crucial element for programme success is ownership by the recipient country, where ownership denotes the extent to which the recipient is interested in undertaking reforms independently of the incentives provided by the IFIs. Third, conditionality remains a central feature of policy-based lending as it is essential for programme success. This requires, however, two important changes in the nature of conditionality. One, conditionality must be streamlined so that the conditions focus on those reforms that are regarded as essential for achieving the programme objectives and are completely owned by the recipient country. Two, conditionality becomes *ex ante*, in the sense that the disbursement of financial assistance takes place after the implementation of reform rather than the promise of implementation.

Thus, the position stated by the IFIs is that conditionality and ownership can be complementary, for conditionality has the role of specifying the crucial elements of a reform programme and helping the government signal its intentions. This manner of reconciling conditionality with ownership is, in our opinion, not very convincing. The main reason is that, despite pronouncements to the contrary, the IFIs remain the judges of what are the key policies to adopt. The IFIs decide whether to provide assistance on the basis of their assessment of the policies in the country, its quality of institutions, and the degree of programme ownership. Programme success is seen to depend exclusively on the recipient country's policies and institutions, rather than the content and design of conditionality. In other words, this reconciliation of conditionality and ownership is rather fictitious because it does not question the quality of the IFIs' policy advice.

In this chapter we put forward a different route for reconciling borrower ownership with conditionality. We do so within the realm of political economy, which in our opinion goes to the heart of the question of country ownership by considering the existence of political constraints facing the government. We follow the insight in Drazen (2002) that conditionality and ownership can be reconciled by focusing on conflicts of interest not between the IFIs and the recipient country but within the recipient country itself. This approach recognizes that the question of ownership is complex and requires the identification of the economic actors whose ownership is crucial to the success of reform. For example, it is possible that, while the country's authorities are in favour of reform and 'own' the programme, their ownership does not coincide with ownership by the country as a whole, since they face some domestic opposition.

We address the issue whether in a policy environment so described conditionality could alter the country's political equilibrium. In particular, we investigate whether the design of conditionality could have an impact on the effectiveness of conditionality by reducing domestic opposition to the reform programme. The results of our chapter show that conditionality can sustain reform and that its design matters, for it affects the domestic political constraint. Thus, an appropriate design of conditionality is an important determinant of the success of the reform programme. For example, our chapter shows that a reform that is too fast (because the IFI conditionality is stricter) could result in a stronger opposition to reform and greater costs in social welfare than a more gradual reform. In other words, it is through the attention to the design of conditionality that conditionality can be made consistent with ownership.

These results derive from the use of a dynamic common agency model where the relationship between a recipient government and an IFI takes explicitly into account the presence of interest groups opposed to reform, which constitutes a domestic political constraint on the government's actions. To our knowledge, the dynamic specification of the common agency model has never been applied to the implementation of policy reforms supported by the IFIs. Yet, such dynamic specification is crucial, since it allows one to incorporate the important insight that the strength of special interest groups opposing welfare-improving reform arises endogenously during the reform process (Olson, 1982, 1993).

The structure of the paper is as follows. In Section 14.2 we discuss the relationship between conditionality and ownership. We present the model setup in Section 14.3 and solve the model in Section 14.4. Some simulations are presented in Section 14.5. Conclusions are in Section 14.6.

14.2   Conditionality and ownership

Should the IFIs continue to associate conditionality to their lending? One view is that conditionality is essential in policy-based lending. Its use in the context of international lending is easily justifiable where the borrower lacks internationally recognized collateral. Conditionality can be seen as a substitute for collateral, in the sense that the set of conditions is meant to ensure that the loan will be repaid.

Conditionality has a long history in sovereign lending. Its early precedents date back to the 'Decree of Mouharrem' in 1881 following the Turkish government's default on its foreign debt or the League of Nations' reconstructions schemes of the 1920s. This justification of conditionality presupposes however a clear, hierarchical power structure between borrower and lender, since the ultimate objective of conditionality is to ensure repayment, rather than 'helping' the recipient country implement policy reforms that would accelerate its development process.

Theoretically at least, conditionality need not imply a conflict between the IFIs on one side and recipients on the other. The political economy literature has put forward a number of arguments why the use of conditionality may be in the recipients' interests. One such argument is that conditionality provides an assurance to the borrowing country that, if previously specified policy measures are implemented, funding will be released.[1] Another argument is that conditionality binds the country to a reform programme, since disbursements depend on reform implementation.[2] Another argument is that conditionality lends credibility to the borrowing government's reform plans by signalling its commitment to reform.

Despite these theoretical arguments, the use of conditionality has in practice conflicted with ownership. In order to salvage the 'Washington Consensus', the disappointing economic performance in programme countries has been attributed to the lack of commitment towards the reform programme by developing countries' governments. Conditionality has thus been an ineffective mechanism to bring about policy change. The problem with conditionality is that it cannot be made 'incentive-compatible'. In the case of a breach of conditions, the threat to suspend funding has low credibility.[3] Knowing that lenders will accept some slippage with conditionality, recipient governments who are not committed to policy reform have incentives to renege on their commitments. Instead of being a device signalling a government's commitment to reform, conditionality undermines the credibility even of the reforms undertaken.

The fact that conditionality has failed to induce reluctant governments to change policies and embrace reforms is not in question. There is now a recognition that ownership of the reform programme by recipient countries plays a key role for the sustainability and the success of reforms. When ownership is present and the government is committed to reform, conditionality is unnecessary. In fact, there may even be an inherent contradiction between conditionality and ownership. The latter is expressed in home-grown policies while the former assigns the IFIs a dominant role in defining country policy agendas and priorities.

More recently, as a result of the comprehensive re-examination of their assistance programmes, the IFIs as well as bilateral donors have articulated the drastic and controversial position that conditionality should be replaced by selectivity, whereby aid and policy lending should be exclusively directed to countries that are likely to be committed reformers. In such good policy environments, conditionality is irrelevant. While a true process of conditionality streamlining can only be welcome,[4] the idea that lending should only be restricted to countries with good policy environments should be less enthusiastically received.

The argument has been made that selectivity is to the benefit of recipients for it would result in more funds being directed towards the more worthy countries.

Yet, the selectivity approach is likely to result in a more covert imposition of conditions, not in unconditional lending. As long as the IFIs continue to define what constitutes good development practice and a good policy environment, national ownership remains more theoretical than real. *Ex post* conditionality, whereby loan disbursements are made following the promise of a policy change, is simply being replaced by *ex ante* conditionality requiring the actual policy change to take place before any disbursement is effected. It is perhaps ironic that, despite the emphasis on the importance of ownership, Poverty Reduction Strategy Papers (PRSPs) present a high degree of similarity with the old structural adjustment programmes. This is not a measure of consensus on the required policies; it rather represents the awareness that PRSPs have to be consistent with the IFIs' preferred policies if they are to receive their endorsement.

Moreover, an obvious consequence of selectivity is that the responsibility for disappointing results of the IFI-supported reform programmes is solely with developing countries' lack of commitment and poor institutions (seen as an exogenous condition). A fundamental re-examination of the programme design and content is essentially precluded.

Both the practical feasibility and the intellectual foundations of the selectivity approach have received criticism. With respect to feasibility, there is the problem that in practice the majority of developing country governments will be neither wholly good nor wholly bad.[5] As will be discussed in Section 14.3, this consideration can be seen as one motivation for the particular setup of our model.

The intellectual foundation of the selectivity approach is the research on aid effectiveness and the factors determining success or failure in the IFI-supported programmes. In particular, Burnside and Dollar (2000) have shown that aid and policy lending have only been effective in 'good' policy environments. Dollar and Svensson (2000) analyse World Bank-supported programmes and conclude that the success of these programmes can be explained by a relatively small number of domestic political economy variables. Variables under control of the World Bank (such as the number of conditions or the resources devoted to monitoring and supervision or to the preparation of the loan) have no effect. Ivanova *et al.* (2003) analyse IMF-supported programmes and reach very similar conclusions.

The reliability of the empirical results that these authors present has been questioned and the ensuing debate has not been settled. Hansen and Tarp (2000, 2001) have subjected the Burnside and Dollar (2000) paper to close scrutiny and, while in their subsequent rebuttal Burnside and Dollar (2004) respond to some criticisms, they leave one of the main accusations unanswered. Hansen and Tarp (2000) contend that the Burnside and Dollar results are dependent on the arbitrary exclusion of five 'outliers' from the sample.[6] Similarly, the work by Dollar and Svensson (2000) and Ivanova *et al.* (2003) has also been criticized for the econometric approach that they follow.[7] Mosley *et al.* (2003) argue that a significant endogeneity bias is likely to be present. The reason is that Dollar and Svensson and Ivanova *et al.* consider variables that turn out to be important in their regressions as exogenous – namely, political stability during the life of the programme and the strength of interest groups respectively – when they are in fact affected by the degree of implementation and the outcomes of the programmes themselves. Consequently, the reliability of econometric regressions that do not correct for the endogeneity of those variables must be in doubt. Interestingly, in their study of World Bank programmes in Africa, Mosley *et al.* (2003) show that the design of the programmes matters for the extent to which recipient governments implement conditionality.

It is in this context that our chapter intends to make a contribution to the literature. It aims to show that an appropriate design of conditionality is a crucial determinant of the reform programme outcomes. In this way it refutes the view underlying the selectivity approach that donors cannot influence the probability of reform implementation, since this is taken to depend on the exogenous characteristics of recipient countries' institutions and political economy. Allowing for the probability of reform implementation to depend to some extent on the design of conditionality is what makes conditionality consistent with ownership.

14.3   The model

Within the recipient country, ownership is unlikely to be universal. It is not inconceivable that the government is genuinely committed to a reform programme but that there are interest groups which are opposed to such reforms and have a greater capacity to form a coalition than the population at large, which might, by contrast, benefit from the reform. This is the form of domestic heterogeneity where, according to Drazen (2002), conditionality may not be in conflict with borrower ownership. This is also the scenario that we assume for our model.

An appropriate framework to model the policy environment so described is that of the common agency, originally developed by Bernheim and Whinston (1986) and later popularized by Grossman and Helpman (1994). In this setup, the government is the agent in charge of using a policy tool and various pressure groups act as its principals. The principals may have different objectives from the agent and attempt to influence the government's policy decision by offering political contributions contingent on the agent's decision.

Mayer and Mourmouras (2002) use a static version of the common agency model to analyse the interactions between a government committed to reform (i.e. a reduction in existing policy distortions), an IFI that is willing to provide financial support to the government and interest groups opposing reform. In this scenario, the interest groups compete with the IFI to push the government to set a favourable policy. Faced with the contributions scheduled offered by the principals (i.e. lending from the IFI and political donations by the interest groups), the government – who also cares about social welfare – chooses whether to reduce the policy distortions and the extent of the reduction and in so doing trades off money for welfare.[8]

In this chapter, we specify a fully dynamic common agency model for the analysis of the implementation of policy reforms supported by the IFI.[9] The dynamic dimension is important because policy reforms affect social welfare as well as the interest groups' incentives and actions over time. Another advantage of our dynamic approach is that it allows for the strength of the special interest groups to be determined endogenously during the reform process, as in Olson (1982, 1993). In this sense, our results suggest that the design of conditionality – in this chapter we consider the speed of reforms – could alter the political opposition to (support for) the reform.

This aspect is extremely important, since a vision of the reform process where opposition is exogenously set – as is the case in the static setting of Mayer and Mourmouras (2002) – would lead one to advocate selectivity in policy-based lending. By contrast, when opposition arises endogenously from the reform process – as in our setting – the design of the reform programme and the quality of the policy advice are at least as important as the country's political economy characteristics in determining the outcome of reform programmes.

The specific setup of our model is as follows. The government is willing to liberalize trade since it cares about social welfare and the IFI is willing to support the government's effort by providing funds, conditional on the extent of reforms. If liberalization takes place, relatively inefficient domestic firms will face stronger foreign competition. Therefore, lobbies of domestic producers exert pressure on the government for continued tariff protection. The government values the support offered by the lobbies and the lending from the IFI besides social welfare. Formally, its objective function in each period t is a weighted average of social welfare (W), political contributions (C) from m interest groups and lending from the IFI (F)

$$G_\tau(\tau) = \sum_{j=1}^{m} C_{jt}(\tau) + F_t(\tau) + aW_t(\tau) \tag{14.1}$$

where τ, the policy variable, is a specific tariff on imports. Welfare W, which is given by the sum of consumer surplus, domestic firms' profits and tariff revenue, is defined gross of contributions and is weighted by the parameter a ($a > 0$). The IFI cares about social welfare in the recipient country and, in this sense, the government and the IFI have a commonality of interests. In other words, the government 'owns' the reform programme. The IFI and the domestic interest groups present the government with contribution schedules. The government chooses its optimal tariff and collects contributions and lending accordingly.

The IFI provides financial assistance to the government conditional on economic policies.[10] On the one hand, lending can improve social welfare in the country, which the IFI cares about, but, on the other, there is an opportunity cost to the institution in providing the funding. Thus, the objective function of the IFI in each period is

$$I_t(\tau) = bW_t(\tau) - F_t(\tau) \tag{14.2}$$

where $b > 0$ measures how much the IFI cares about the recipient country.

For simplicity, we assume that the domestic industry is a duopoly protected from foreign competition by means of a specific tariff τ and where each firm constitutes an interest group that tries to influence the government (i.e. $m = 2$ in equation (14.1) but the results can be generalized to the case of oligopoly). Domestic and foreign firms produce identical goods and y_{1t}, y_{2t} and y_{3t} denote respectively the output of the two domestic firms and of the foreign firm. Total industry output is thus: $Q_t = y_{1t} + y_{2t} + y_{3t}$ with a time-invariant inverse demand function $P(Q_t) = P(y_{1t} + y_{2t} + y_{3t})$ which, for analytical convenience, we assume linear: $P_t = \sigma - (y_{1t} + y_{2t} + y_{3t})$.[11] The firms play a quantity-setting (Cournot) game in each period.

Production takes place with constant marginal costs that depend on the production technology in use. Without loss of generality, we assume that there are only three levels of technology available. The foreign firm has already adopted the newest technology while the two domestic firms initially use less efficient technologies. One domestic firm is less efficient than the other. Faced with a liberalization threat, domestic procedures have the option of investing in cost-reducing technology. However, for producers to be able to do so, liberalization may have to proceed gradually, since investment in technology is costly. Adoption of the new technology entails a fixed cost k for the domestic firms but brings about lower marginal costs of production.

Domestic firms offer the government political contributions C_{jt} to influence its decisions about the setting of the tariff. However, in order to simplify the model, we assume that the two domestic firms are asymmetric in this regard because they start from different technological levels and we assume that only the more efficient of the two firms can upgrade its technology.[12] Thus, in period t, the domestic firms' (gross of contributions) profits are:

$$\Pi_{jt} = P(Q_t)y_{jt} - c_{jt}y_{jt} - k \quad j = 1, 2 \tag{14.3}$$

where k is always zero for the more inefficient domestic firm while, for the other domestic firm, it is zero if it chooses not to upgrade its technology. The foreign firm does not engage in lobbying and does not need upgrading since it is already on the technological frontier. Its profits are:

$$\Pi_{3t} = P(Q_t)y_{3t} - c_3 y_{3t} - \tau_t y_{3t}. \tag{14.4}$$

Social welfare is the sum of consumer surplus, gross-of-contribution profits (of domestic firms), and tariff revenue:

$$W_t = \int_p^\sigma D(u)du + \sum_{j=1}^2 P(Q_t)y_{jt} - \sum_{j=1}^2 c(\theta_{jt})y_{jt} - k + \tau_t y_{3t} \tag{14.5}$$

where consumer surplus simplifies to $\frac{1}{2}(\sigma - P)^2$ with the assumed linear demand function.

In each period, the agent (i.e. the government) and the three principals (i.e. two domestic firms and the IFI) interact in order to set the import tariff. The domestic firms have to decide whether to upgrade their technologies and compete on quantities with the foreign firm in the domestic markets. Since the interaction over time between the domestic lobbies, the government and the IFI are rather complex, the analysis in the chapter is based on a strictly defined sequence of events.

More specifically, we consider a two-period model with three stages in each period, as represented in Figure 14.1. In the first stage, a political equilibrium is reached where the tariff is set as the outcome of the common agency problem

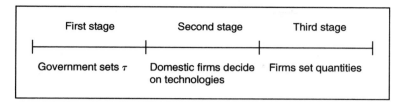

Figure 14.1 Timing in each period.

between the agent and the principals. Then, given the tariff, domestic producers decide their technology investment in the second stage. In the third and final stage of each period, the firms decide their production levels by playing a Cournot game.

In similar models, stages one and two are normally in reverse order and producers typically take some relevant decision before offering their schedule of donations to the government. This is the case, for example, in Brainard and Verder (1994) and Magee (2002) where the focus is on the possible strategic behaviour of the producers to influence the government's decision in a sequential timing. Their sequence, however, may not be appropriate in the presence of an IFI. In fact, despite a recent greater emphasis on country ownership of reform programmes, it is not unrealistic to argue that the IFI retains very significant leverage on the size and terms of the programme. Once the programme is initiated, however, the government decides the extent of conditionality implementation. In these circumstances, the initiation of a programme inevitably leads to some reactions on the part of economic agents in order to benefit from the programme. This suggests that an appropriate sequence of events places the setting of the tariff before the producers' actions, and this is exactly the timing used in this chapter.[13]

14.4 The solution of the model

The solution of the model is found by backward induction, both within each period and from the second to the first period. In the following, we begin by studying the (static) equilibrium in a given period in order to understand the determinants of the firms' decision to upgrade.

14.4.1 The static solution

In the third stage firms compete on quantities taking the import tariff, the contributions and the technologies as given:[14]

$$\begin{cases} \max_{y1} P(Q)y_1 - c_1 y_1 - k - C_1 \\ \max_{y2} P(Q)y_2 - c_2 y_2 - C_2 \\ \max_{y3} P(Q)y_3 - c_3 y_3 - \tau y_3. \end{cases} \quad (14.6)$$

The result of this standard Cournot problem is that the more a firm is efficient, the higher is its level of output. This implies that greater efficiency by the domestic firms will be accompanied by a reduced amount of imports.[15]

In the second stage, the more efficient of the two domestic firms decides whether to upgrade its technology in order to better compete with the foreign firm. This investment will take place if the implied cost savings more than compensate for the cost of the investment, taking into account that a more efficient technology allows the firm to gain a larger market share.

In the first stage of the game, the government decision with regard to trade liberalization is the outcome of the common agency problem. Such problems admit more than one solution depending on the shape of the contribution schedules announced by the principals. However, we follow standard practice and focus on the truthful equilibrium, which can be defined as the equilibrium where the contribution schedules offered by the principals to the agent reflect the principals' true preferences.[16]

In our setup, the chosen tariff level in the first stage has an effect on the investment decision. Indeed, the aim of this chapter is to determine if and when the government finds it optimal to act strategically, that is, to slow down the pace of trade liberalization in order to allow the domestic firm to upgrade. It is of particular interest to see how this strategic effect is affected by the degree of conditionality imposed by the IFI.

The model determines the optimal tariff.[17] In order to understand the intuition behind the result, it is helpful to consider first the extreme case where the investment cost is zero. In this case, the firm will upgrade and the optimal tariff in each period is

$$\tau = \frac{(a + b)(5\sigma + c_1 + c_2 - 7c_3) + 4(\sigma + c_3 - c_1 - c_2)}{19a + 19b - 4}. \tag{14.7}$$

For small investment costs, the firm will still find it optimal to upgrade its technology even if the tariff is unchanged. Thus, the government does not need to act strategically. However, there must be a threshold ($\underline{k}$) above which investment only takes place if the domestic firms are protected by a tariff higher than in (14.7). There is also a level of costs ($\overline{k}$) beyond which the government will not find it optimal to grant the domestic firms the level of protection they require for investment to take place. At this high tariff rate the government would suffer in terms of reduced welfare and reduced lending from the IFI. Hence, above the threshold $\overline{k}$, the government sets a low tariff rate and investment does not occur. The tariff rate is not as low as when investment takes place because the domestic firms are both inefficient compared to the foreign firm and require protection.

Therefore, the government does not act strategically if the investment costs is below $\underline{k}$ and above $\overline{k}$. It can be shown that the optimal tariff rate in (14.7) is decreasing in the weights attached by the government and the IFI to welfare, increasing (decreasing) in the domestic (foreign) marginal costs, and increasing in the size of the market: $\tau = \tau(\overline{a}, \overline{b}, \overset{+}{c}_1, \overset{+}{c}_2, \overline{c}_3, \overset{+}{\sigma})$.

14.4.2 *The dynamic solution of the model*

The dynamic link between the two periods is given by technology since if an upgrade takes place in the first period it will be permanent. In our setup, the firm will never find it optimal to invest in the second period because the investment cost does not change over time and the benefit from lower marginal costs would only accrue in the second period. Nevertheless, the decisions taken by the more efficient firm and by the government are both influenced by a proper consideration of second-period effects. In choosing whether to invest or not, the firm takes into account the cost savings accruing in both periods. In setting the tariff level, the government calculates the resulting levels of welfare in the two periods.

The procedure for solving the dynamic game for intermediate values of the investment cost is rather complex. In this cost range, the more efficient domestic firm invests if and only if the government acts strategically. In order to determine the tariff, it is necessary to ascertain whether the domestic firm invests (in the first period) or not. The investment decision is based on the comparison of net profits with and without technological upgrading. This calculation requires the determination of the principals' contribution levels. They are such that they are the lowest for which the government would still set the policy supported by the principal.[18]

It is not possible to derive closed form analytical solutions of the model and we have to rely on simulations. Yet, the intuition of the forces at work is quite simple. The government may act strategically in the first period and set a high tariff rate in order to induce the firm to invest and reap the benefits over the two periods. Our interest is to see the role that conditionality plays and whether it may affect the probability that the firm upgrades its technology and becomes more competitive.

14.5 Simulations and discussion of the results

Despite the complexity of the model, its results are straightforward. However, attention should only be paid to the qualitative results of these numerical exercises since the values assigned to the various parameters are not calibrated. In order to avoid confusion, the graphs that follow represent the qualitative aspects of the model and do not report any numerical values.[19]

The possible outcomes in terms of optimal tariff rates and investment decisions as a function of the exogenous cost of investment (k) are illustrated in Figure 14.2 for two different cases. In the 'benchmark case' the parameters a and b have the same values (i.e. the IFI and the government put the same weight on social welfare in their objective functions) while in the other scenario the IFI does not offer any lending.[20]

The firm decides to undertake technological upgrading depending on both the cost of investment and the tariff rate. More precisely, the firm invests if, over the two periods, the increased profits resulting from technological upgrading compensate for the cost of making this investment and are greater than the profits that the firm would make without upgrading its technology.

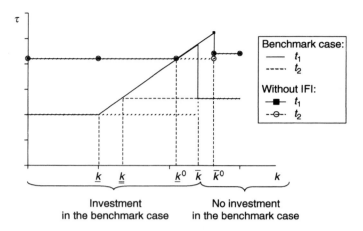

Figure 14.2 Tariff rates with and without the IFI.

As seen in Section 14.4, the government's tariff setting behaviour is crucial. Adopting the modern technology raises profits on two accounts: it reduces the cost of production and allows the firm to gain a larger share of the market. In our setting, these benefits are concentrated over two periods only and are partly off-set by the cost of making the investment. The role of the tariff is that of main-taining the profits of the domestic firm high by protecting its sales in the domestic market. This allows the firm to undertake the investment in technology.

Consistently with our previous discussion, Figure 14.2 shows that the domestic firm finds it profitable to invest when the government does not act strategically if the cost of technological upgrading is below the critical value $\underline{k}$. By contrast, no investment takes place when the cost is above $\bar{k}$. In fact, investment could occur in this case only with such a high tariff that its distorting effects on social welfare would outweigh its benefits in terms of profits. Under these circumstances, a government that cares about social welfare sets a lower tariff which, though result-ing in lower profits for the domestic firms and – accordingly – low political con-tributions, would result in a higher level of social welfare overall. The optimal tariff rate is obviously higher when the investment cost is high, since the high tariff can safeguard a certain level of profits for the domestic inefficient firms.

Figure 14.2 also shows that in the intermediate range of investment costs ($\underline{k} < k < \bar{k}$) the occurrence – or non occurrence – of technological upgrading depends crucially on whether the government raises the tariff sufficiently. From the firm's viewpoint, an inappropriately low tariff rate would increase competi-tion from the more efficient foreign producers and could reduce its profits to a level that would not allow the firm to meet the investment cost. Or, as another possibility, the increase in profits induced by the technological upgrading could fall short of the upgrading cost. A higher tariff rate in period one raises the firm's profits and induces it to undertake the investment. While the tariff rate required by the firm raises with the increase in investment costs, the government is prepared to accommodate the firm's demand for protection since it gains from investment taking place. As discussed earlier, it is only when the cost of technological upgrading is above a critical value $\bar{k}$ that the government is no longer willing to protect the domestic firm to the extent required for investment to take place.

Figure 14.2 shows that the optimal tariff rate in period two is the same as that in period one when investment costs are low ($k < \underline{k}$) or high ($k > \bar{k}$). Since the government does not act strategically in this case, the level of the tariff in period two depends on whether the domestic firm made the investment in period one. If it did not, the government has to maintain a relatively high tariff rate in order to protect the domestic inefficient firms from foreign competition. Thus, as in period one, the optimal tariff rate in period two is higher with $k > \bar{k}$ than $k < \underline{k}$.

In the intermediate range of investment costs ($\underline{k} < k < \bar{k}$) the government prefers to act strategically, setting a high tariff rate in period one in order to induce technological upgrading. Once investment has taken place, the government can reduce protection for the domestic firms and lower the tariff rate in period two. In this second period, the optimal tariff rate is at the same level as when investment occurs without strategic behaviour by the government. Thus, within the intermediate range of investment costs, the optimal reform strategy is a gradual liberalization.

The second case in Figure 14.2 is that of an indigenous reform without financial support from the IFI. For low values of the investment cost as well as for high values the tariff rate set by the government is higher than in the benchmark case.[21] The implication is that, at low investment costs, the relatively high tariff – compared with the benchmark case – makes it unnecessary for the government to behave strategically for investment costs below $\underline{k}^0$, where $\underline{k}^0 > \underline{k}$. At high investment costs, the threshold beyond which the more efficient domestic firm no longer finds it optimal to invest rises to $\bar{k}^0$, where $\bar{k}^0 > \bar{k}$: the range of costs for which investment takes place is wider when the IFI does not offer any (conditional) lending.

In the interval between $\underline{k}^0$ and $\bar{k}$, the tariff rate in period one is identical with or without assistance from the IFI, while in period two it is unambiguously lower when the IFI supports the government's reform effort. The explanation for this result is that, for the parameter values used in the simulations, the amount of financial assistance offered by the IFI is not high enough to persuade the government to set a lower tariff. Doing so would expose the domestic firms to foreign competition and would make it impossible for the more efficient one to upgrade its technology. The small amount of financial assistance from the IFI does not compensate the government for the costs involved in lowering the tariff – arising from the reduction in contributions from the domestic firms and the decrease in social welfare when technological advancement does not occur. Greater financial support from the IFI would lead to a larger reduction in the tariff, but this would be accompanied by a drop in investment and a fall in social welfare.

The government's strategic behaviour allows the more efficient domestic firm to upgrade its technology. Once such investment has been made in period one, the government can reduce the tariff in period two. The tariff reduction is greater when the IFI provides financial assistance than when it does not.[22]

The comparison of the two cases in Figure 14.2 suggests that conditionality can alter the country's political equilibrium and lead to a greater reduction in economic distortions than when the IFI provides no assistance. This is beneficial for the country's welfare but Figure 14.2 also shows that conditionality may be counter-productive. In fact, in the range $\bar{\bar{k}} < \bar{k} < \bar{k}^0$ conditionality leads the government to liberalize too early, effectively eliminating the possibility for the domestic firm to upgrade. Thus, in this case, second-period welfare might well be lower than if the government had not sought assistance from the IFI. In this case, conditionality has been successful in delivering the IFI's objective of fast reforms by forcing the government to do something that it would not choose to do without financial assistance (Collier *et al.*, 1997). In other words, in this range, conditionality 'buys reform'. Conditionality as an inducement is obviously not compatible with borrower ownership.

What is the effect on the economy if the IFI imposes tighter conditionality, in the sense of wishing to see the government setting even lower tariff rates? It is important to remember two characteristics of our setup. One, the benchmark case assumes communality of interests between the government and the IFI; hence it is possible to speak of government's ownership of the reform programme. Two, our model is an optimizing model, in the sense that the adoption of a policy other than the equilibrium policy cannot deliver a better outcome for all parties simultaneously, given the specific form assumed for each party's objective. Therefore, because of these two characteristics, a reduction in tariff rates greater than in the benchmark case can only result either from a change in the hierarchical relationship between the IFI and the government (whereby the IFI can impose the policies they prefer on the government) or from a shift in the parties' objectives. In our chapter we attempt to model both cases.

In the simpler scenario, we assume that the IFI has the power to impose that the government undertakes a faster liberalization by adopting in period one a tariff not higher than the period-two optimal tariff. The effect of this policy, which can be intuited from Figure 14.2, is that the domestic firm upgrades its technology for a narrower range of investment costs. If these are higher than $\underline{\underline{k}}$ (where $\underline{\underline{k}}$ is the cost for which the strategic tariff equals the tariff with no investment and $\bar{\bar{k}}$ is such that $\underline{\underline{k}} < \underline{k}$), the firm chooses not to adopt the modern technology. The government maximizes its utility by keeping the tariff rate high – at the level of the tariff in the range for $k > \bar{k}$ – even for values of $k < \bar{k}$. In other words, the imposition of a faster early liberalization results – in the intermediate range of investment costs $\underline{\underline{k}} < k < \bar{k}$ – in greater backwardness, lower social welfare, and eventually slower liberalization in comparison to the benchmark case.

A more complicated scenario is obtained by changing the slope of the IFI's objective function. A change that gives rise to faster liberalization is to assume that the parameter *b*, which represents the weight that the IFI attaches to the recipient country's social welfare, is larger.[23] In this case, the IFI is willing to provide more financial support for policies that raise social welfare.

Figure 14.3 illustrates this case and compares it with the benchmark.[24] It shows that a larger *b* induces faster liberalization only for certain ranges of investment costs. More precisely, the tariff set by the government is always lower than in the benchmark case when the government does not act strategically (i.e. for $k < \underline{k}$ and $k > \overline{k}$). The government is prepared to reduce the tariff rate because of higher social welfare and, above all, the larger contributions it receives from the IFI (due to a higher b). In equilibrium, the increase in these two components of the government's objective function outweighs the reduction in the domestic firms' contributions. Indeed it was shown earlier that the optimal tariff rate without strategic behaviour by the government is decreasing in b (see 14.7). However, because of the stronger competition from the foreign firm that the low tariff induces, the government needs to behave strategically for a range of investment costs lower than in the benchmark case (in fact, for $k_1 < k < \underline{k}$).

A larger b results in a lower tariff than in the benchmark case also for a range of investment costs lower than $\overline{k}$, that is, for $k_2 < k < \overline{k}$. This result obtains because the domestic firm does not upgrade its technology. The higher value for b makes the IFI less willing to provide lending for high tariff rates. For $k_2 < k < \overline{k}$, the domestic firm invests only if the tariff rate is high but, at this rate, the government would receive a lower amount of financial support from the IFI with the consequence that its utility would be lower. Thus, tighter conditionality and faster liberalization, as produced by a larger b, reduce the range of investment costs for which it is worthwhile for the domestic firm to upgrade its technology, resulting in greater technological backwardness than in the benchmark case. Moreover, since in the second period inefficient firms require higher tariff protection than if they had invested in technological upgrading, the resulting tariff rate may be higher than in the benchmark case. Correspondingly, social welfare may also be lower.

Figure 14.3 shows that for $\underline{k} < k < k_2$ the first-period tariff does not vary with the increase in b. Over this range of costs, the tariff rate that the government sets is at the lowest possible level that ensures that investment takes place. Faster liberalization would make it impossible even for the more efficient domestic firm to upgrade its technology. The increase in b does not affect the government's tariff

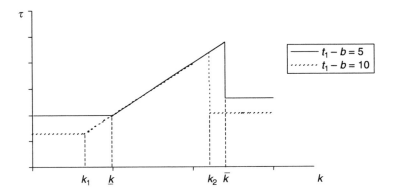

Figure 14.3 Comparison of different conditionality levels.

Note
When $b = 5$ ($b = 10$), investment takes place up to $\overline{k}$ (k_2).

setting behaviour because, for the parameter values used in the simulations, the amount of financial assistance offered by the IFI is not high enough to compensate the government for the costs of faster liberalization – arising from the reduction in contributions from the domestic firms and the decrease in social welfare when technological advancement does not occur. Greater financial support from the IFI – resulting from higher values of b – would lead to a larger reduction in the tariff, but this would be accompanied by a drop in investment and a fall in social welfare.

We now turn our attention to discuss the effects of policy decisions on welfare. Figure 14.4 illustrates welfare in the two periods as a function of the investment cost. The origin in Figure 14.4 represents the case where $k = 0$. Welfare in period one is a decreasing function of the cost of investment. If there is no strategic behaviour, welfare decreases in a one to one ratio with the cost, that is, for $k < \underline{k}$.

However, when the government raises the tariff level in order to induce the upgrade (for $\underline{k} < k < \overline{k}$), welfare declines more than in a one to one ratio because the higher tariff decreases consumer surplus more than it raises profits and tariff revenue, as can be seen more clearly in Figure 14.5. When the investment cost rises to the point that no upgrading takes place (for $k < \overline{k}$), welfare in period one increases but the increase is less than proportional to the saved investment cost. The reason is that the economy is now more inefficient, which leads to lower and more expensive output.

If investment occurs, period-two welfare is constant at the level that would have obtained if the cost of investment had been zero. Obviously, the cost of investment has no effect on period-two welfare. If investment does not occur, period-two welfare is similarly unaffected by the cost of investment but is lower than what it would be after technological upgrading because of the economic distortions caused by the higher tariff.

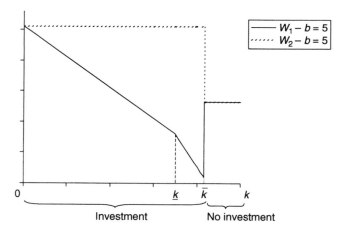

Figure 14.4 Welfare in the two periods.

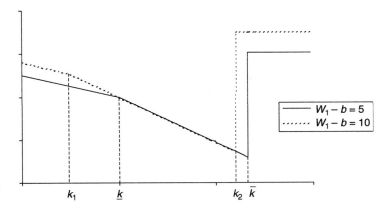

Figure 14.5 Welfare in the first period.

What is the effect on welfare of stricter conditionality? Figure 14.5 compares the benchmark case with one where the parameter b in the IFI's objective function is larger. In the latter, period-one welfare is higher than in the benchmark case if investment takes place without strategic behaviour (for $k < \underline{k}$)[25] or if it does not take place (for $k > \bar{k}$). As we have seen, a larger b leads to lower tariff over those ranges of investment costs. Between $\underline{k}$ and k_2, where the government acts strategically, tighter conditionality does not result in lower tariff rates and, therefore, its effect on welfare is the same as the benchmark case. However, for the range of costs where investment does not take place because of stricter conditionality, period-one welfare is higher than in the benchmark case while period-two welfare may be lower. In this sense, pressure to liberalize may result in an inferior outcome in terms of efficiency and welfare.

More simulations could be presented to investigate the effect of other parameters (e.g. marginal costs, size of the market, etc.) on the relationship between conditionality and tariff outcome (and the implied investment decision) but the qualitative conclusions would not change. In particular, stronger conditionality can achieve lower tariff rates and therefore higher welfare for a range of investment costs. However, stronger conditionality can also eliminate the possibility of efficient investments and therefore be welfare decreasing for other ranges of the investment cost.

14.6 Conclusions

The aim of this chapter was to show that conditionality and ownership need not be in conflict and that the design of the reform process can be the cause of such conflict. The design may be the cause when reform ownership is not universal within a country. In our model, there are powerful domestic interest groups opposing the reform programme to which the government is committed and this heterogeneity may create a wedge between the government's intentions and its actions. We have adopted the common-agent framework to model the interactions between an IFI, the government and the domestic interest groups. The IFI is willing to provide conditional finance to support the government's reform effort and, in this sense, it is in competition with the interest groups in attempting to influence government's policy. In this setup it is clear that the principal-agent framework is not necessarily inconsistent with the notion of ownership, as it is in IMF (2001).

Our specification of the common agency model is dynamic. Notwithstanding the increase in complexity, there are two important advantages over a static specification. One is an obvious increase in realism of the model. When deciding about the implementation of reform, the government can act strategically and take into account that the extent and pace of reform have an impact over time on social welfare and change the interest groups' incentives. The other advantage of our dynamic specification is that it incorporates the important insight that the strength of interest groups arises endogenously from the process of reform. This modelling strategy has a far-reaching implication, namely, that the implementation of reform programmes or the opposition to them depends in an important way on their design and the quality of policy advice. This stands in sharp contrast to the principle of selectivity according to which the responsibility for limited reform implementation rests with the recipient government's lack of commitment and inadequate institutions.

We solve the model and simulate different scenarios. The results show that conditional assistance from the IFI may lead to a lower distortion and higher social welfare than without IFI's involvement, even when the government is committed to the reform programme. This favourable outcome of conditionality is not guaranteed however. In our model, where domestic firms can better compete with foreign firms if they incur a cost for upgrading their production technologies and become more efficient, we show that there is a range of investment costs for which conditionality prevents the domestic firms from improving their technologies. By contrast, had the IFI not been present, technological improvement would have occurred even at those investment costs. Consequently, the future tariff may be higher and social welfare lower when the IFI provides financial assistance than when it does not.

We show that the effects of stricter conditionality also depend on the investment costs facing the domestic industry. When associated with greater financial assistance for a reduction in economic distortions, stricter conditionality will result in an early faster liberalization for some investment costs or in no change in tariff for other investment costs compared with more lax conditionality. Faster liberalization gives rise to one of two outcomes. If investment costs are low, investment occurs and thus second-period tariffs are lower and social welfare higher with stricter conditionality. Alternatively, if investment costs are in a critical intermediate range, faster liberalization will make it impossible for firms to upgrade their technologies and, consequently, second-period tariffs may be higher and social welfare lower than with looser conditionality.

These results indicate that conditionality can alter the country's political equilibrium. This may be beneficial for the recipient country's welfare unless the costs of technological upgrading are in a critical intermediate range, the size of which depends on all the parameters of the model, such as the strength of domestic pressure groups, the country's economic characteristics (e.g. the size of the domestic market, the backwardness of technology and the inefficiency of domestic industry), the impact of economic distortions and their removal on the general public's welfare, the responsiveness of the government to social welfare. The model thus suggests that conditionality must be tailored to each country's special characteristics. There is no single blueprint for reform that will work in all countries. Conditionality, therefore, need not be detrimental to reform ownership but, in order for this to be the case, it is necessary that the design of the reform programme be appropriate to the country's circumstances. In particular, it is important to consider how conditionality directly affects the domestic political constraint.

Various extensions would add further realism to the model. The removal of tariffs could entail significant transaction costs, at least in the short run. The reform programme could be broadened to include macroeconomic policies, which through their impact on aggregate demand might cushion domestic firms' profits and enable them to undertake costly investment. Political elections or other forms of political consensus could be considered. The initial economic situation could be such that the status quo would not be tenable. The relationships between the IFI, the pressure groups and the government could be characterized by the presence of asymmetric information. In short, the model used in this chapter had the minimum degree of complexity required to highlight certain political economy issues and we hope it opens the way for more research effort in this direction.

Notes

1 Drazen (2002) notes that this argument for reconciling conditionality with ownership is not entirely convincing. If there were no conflicts of interest between recipients and IFI – and conditionality were wholly consistent with ownership – it is not clear why conditions should be placed upon the party who needs assurances.

2 One version of this argument is the 'scapegoat' theory, whereby policy makers who are committed to reforms but are politically weak may enter an IFI programme to push through reforms while using the obligations deriving from conditionality as a pretext to soften resistance to the reform programme.

3 One reason is that such measure would lead to an inferior outcome, that is, to default and no improvement in government policy. Another reason is that, once the initial tranche of a loan has been disbursed, the staff of lending institutions have a strong incentive to make the loan 'work'.

4 Killick (2005) shows that the process of streamlining in the IFIs has been accompanied by an increase in the number of the more legally binding conditions as well as by an increase in the conditions imposed by bilateral donors who have often picked up the conditions that the IFIs dropped. As a result, developing countries face in fact more conditions than in the past, not less.

5 There are other problems concerning the feasibility of adopting selectivity as the overriding principle in policy-based lending. An important one is based on the

consideration of political realism that the IFIs may not be able to withstand political pressure to lend to particular countries in certain circumstances.

6 According to Hansen and Tarp (2000), the exclusion of these five observations is arbitrary as none of these is identified as an outlier by any of the standard outlier detection tests.

7 It is also somewhat puzzling that Ivanova *et al.* (2003) find little confirmation for the statistical importance of the political economy variables that work so well in Dollar and Svensson (2000) and have to introduce a different set of variables, representing the strength of interest groups.

8 The political contributions offered by the interest groups need not be bribes. They can take the form of various supporting activities that a government values for its own benefit.

9 Mourmouras and Mayer (2004) use a dynamic version of the common agency model but their model is stationary, since every period is like the initial one, and neither economic nor political conditions are expected to change from period to period.

10 We abstract from the issue of repayment of the loan, essentially treating the loan as a grant.

11 In this formulation, σ can be interpreted as the size of the market.

12 We are implicitly assuming that the cost of upgrading from the most inefficient technology is prohibitively high. This simplifying assumption has the advantage that the model can ignore the strategic interactions that would occur when both forms can upgrade their technologies. This would unnecessarily complicate the model and muddle the analysis of the role of conditionality.

13 In the model, conditionality is neither *ex ante* nor *ex post*, since the amount of lending is strictly and continuously related to the actual extent of the reform. This modelling strategy would be more appropriate to the case of floating tranches (an arrangement quite common in the World Bank) which can be viewed as an attempt to relate disbursement to the actual implementation of conditions.

14 In this section we will not keep track of the time subscript.

15 Given our assumptions, the second order conditions are satisfied as well.

16 Bernheim and Whinston (1986) show that players are not worse off by playing truthful strategies rather than any other strategy and that truthful strategies are also coalition-proof. See Grossman and Helpman (1994) for more details.

17 In our duopoly setting the optimal tariff is higher than zero, as instead would be the case under perfect competition, even for zero investment costs. This is because the government can extract rents from the foreign firm by imposing a tariff.

18 Mathematically, the calculation of these net payoffs is based on what would happen if the principals were not to contribute.

19 The graphs are also drawn with different scales for the horizontal and vertical axes and in different proportions in order to focus on the aspects being evaluated.

20 Specifically, the parameters used in the benchmark case are as follows: $a = b = 5$; $\sigma = 6$; $c_1 = 1$ (before upgrading); $c_2 = 1.5$; $c_3 = 1$; $\beta = 0.7$.

21 It will be shown later that whether conditionality is effective in reducing the tariff rate set by the government depends on the amount of financial assistance provided by the IFI, which is in turn affected by the size of the parameter b in the IFI's objective function. This parameter represents the weight of the recipient country's social welfare in the IFI's utility.

22 In Figure 14.2 the period-two tariff rate is always lower in the benchmark case, even in the interval between $\bar{k}$ and $\bar{k}^0$. However, this is only due to the specific parameter values used in the simulations.

23 Other changes in the objective function of the IFI can also result in faster liberalization.

24 For simplicity, the figure focuses on the first period tariff rates since it is only in the first period that investment can take place and the government may act strategically. The tariff rate in the second period can be easily inferred from this figure since it

equals the lower tariff (for each b) when investment takes place and the higher one when it does not.

25 When b is larger, the welfare line runs parallel to the benchmark case and above it for $k < k_1$. For $k_1 < k < \underline{k}$ welfare decreases faster than in the benchmark case – because the gap between the tariff rates in the two cases is narrowing – until welfare becomes identical in the two cases at $\underline{k}$.

Bibliography

Bernheim, D.B. and Whinston, M.D. (1986) 'Menu auctions, resource allocations, and economic influence', *Quarterly Journal of Economics*, 101: 1–31.

Brainard, L. and Verdier, T. (1994) 'Lobbying and adjustment in declining industries', *European Economic Review*, 38: 586–595.

Burnside, C. and Dollar, D. (2000) 'Aid, policies, and growth', *American Economic Review*, 90: 847–868.

—— (2004) 'Aid, policies, and growth: revisiting the evidence', World Bank Policy Research Working Paper 3251.

Collier, P., Guillaumont, P., Guillaumont, S. and Gunning, J.W. (1997) 'Redesigning conditionality', *World Development*, 25: 1399–1407.

Dollar, D. and Svensson, J. (2000) 'What explains the success or failure of structural adjustment programs?', *Economic Journal*, 110: 894–917.

Drazen, A. (2002) 'Conditionality and ownership in IMF lending: a political economy approach', *IMF Staff Papers*, 49: 36–67.

Grossman, G.M. and Helpman, E. (1994) 'Protection for sale', *American Economic Review*, 84: 833–850.

Hansen, H. and Tarp, F. (2000) 'Aid effectiveness disputed', *Journal of International Development*, 12: 375–398.

—— (2001) 'Aid and growth regressions', *Journal of Development Economics*, 64: 547–570.

International Monetary Fund (IMF) (2001) 'Conditionality in fund-supported programs: policy Issues', Policy Development and Review Department.

Ivanova, A., Mayer, W., Mourmouras, A. and Anayiotos, G. (2003) 'What determines the implementation of IMF-supported programs?', IMF Working Paper 03/8.

Killick, T. (2005) 'Conditionality and IMF flexibility', in Paloni, A. and Zanardi, M. (eds), *IMF, World Bank and Policy Reforms*, London: Routledge.

Magee, C. (2002) 'Declining industries and persistent tariff protection', *Review of International Economics*, 10: 749–762.

Mayer, W. and Mourmouras, A. (2002) 'Vested interests in a positive theory of IFI conditionality', IMF Working Paper 02/73.

Mosley, P., Noorbakhsh, F. and Paloni, A. (2003) 'Compliance with World Bank conditionality: implications for the selectivity approach to policy-based lending and the design of conditionality', CREDIT Research Paper 03/20, University of Nottingham.

Mourmouras, A. and Mayer, W. (2004) 'The political economy of conditional and unconditional foreign assistance: grants versus loan rollovers', IMF Working Paper 04/38.

Olson, M. (1982) *The Rise and Decline of Nations*, New Haven, CT: Yale University Press.

—— (1993) 'Dictatorship, democracy and development', *American Political Science Review*, 87: 567–576.

Index

eBooks – at www.eBookstore.tandf.co.uk

A library at your fingertips!

eBooks are electronic versions of printed books. You can store them on your PC/laptop or browse them online.

They have advantages for anyone needing rapid access to a wide variety of published, copyright information.

eBooks can help your research by enabling you to bookmark chapters, annotate text and use instant searches to find specific words or phrases. Several eBook files would fit on even a small laptop or PDA.

NEW: Save money by eSubscribing: cheap, online access to any eBook for as long as you need it.

Annual subscription packages

We now offer special low-cost bulk subscriptions to packages of eBooks in certain subject areas. These are available to libraries or to individuals.

For more information please contact webmaster.ebooks@tandf.co.uk

We're continually developing the eBook concept, so keep up to date by visiting the website.

www.eBookstore.tandf.co.uk